New Visions of Crime Victims

This innovative collection presents original theoretical analyses and previously unpublished empirical research on criminal victimisation. Following an overview of the development and deficiencies of victimology, subsequent chapters present more detailed challenges to stereotypical conceptions of victimisation through their focus on: male victims of domestic violence; victims of male-on-male rape; corporate victims; and the 'victim-offenders' who are the recipients of IRA punishment beatings. The second half of the book considers criminal justice responses to victimisation, focusing in particular on the potential of, and limits to, restorative justice, the social (and gendered) construction of the victim within contested trials and the exclusionary nature of current 'victim-centred' initiatives. This important book will further the debate on how we conceptualise victims as well as their appropriate role within the criminal justice system.

New Visions of Crime Victims

Edited by

Carolyn Hoyle and Richard Young

Centre for Criminological Research
University of Oxford

·HART·
PUBLISHING

HART PUBLISHING
OXFORD AND PORTLAND, OREGON
2002

Published in North America (US and Canada) by
Hart Publishing
c/o International Specialized Book Services
5804 NE Hassalo Street
Portland, Oregon
97213–3644
USA

Distributed in Netherlands, Belgium and Luxembourg by
Intersentia, Churchillaan 108
B2900 Schoten
Antwerpen
Belgium

Hart Publishing is a specialist legal publisher based in Oxford, England. To order
further copies of this book or to request a list of other publications please write to:

Hart Publishing, Salters Boatyard, Folly Bridge, Abingdon Rd, Oxford, OX1 4LB
Telephone: +44 (0)1865 245533 Fax: +44 (0) 1865 794882
email: mail@hartpub.co.uk
WEBSITE: http//:www.hartpub.co.uk

British Library Cataloguing in Publication Data
Data Available

ISBN 1–84113–280–2 (hardback)

Typeset by J & L Composition, Filey, North Yorkshire
Printed and bound in Great Britain by
Biddles Ltd, www.biddles.co.uk

Preface

The idea for this book stemmed from the development of new insights into the phenomenon of criminal victimisation by postgraduate students at the universities of Oxford (Heather Hamill, Stephanie Allen), Birmingham (Ann Grady) and Bristol (Jo Winter). Whilst the data collected through their doctoral research was fascinating in its own right, this body of work also interrogated standard concepts and theories used in talking about, or analysing, crime victims. We saw the book as providing an outlet for these 'new voices'. In addition, we wanted to include some more explicitly theoretical challenges to stereotypical representations of crime victims. The two most established academics in this volume (Paul Rock and Andrew Sanders) have a long-time interest in critiquing and re-working such representations. We invited them to take their thinking further through contributing new essays to this collection, and count ourselves fortunate that they both responded with such enthusiasm. Our own chapters lie somewhere in the middle of the empirical–theoretical spectrum inasmuch as they both present data not previously published and both pursue the need to rethink images of, and attitudes towards, victims of crime.

In producing this book we have sought to address the main weaknesses of edited collections as identified in countless journal reviews: incoherence; uneven quality; and lack of novelty. The chapters in this collection cohere well, for they all address neglected aspects of crime victimisation. Coherence was also encouraged by circulating to all of the authors early drafts of some of the chapters and summaries of the others. We were the main defaulters in this part of the exercise, as our own chapters were the last to reach final draft stage. The problems of incoherence and uneven quality were also addressed through our own editing of all of the drafts. We have spent many months encouraging our authors, and each other, to strengthen any weak areas in arguments or prose, with some chapters (including our own) going through numerous drafts. In recognition of the likelihood that we would not be sufficiently objective about the merits of the Hoyle and Young chapters we secured Professor Andrew Ashworth's kind agreement to referee these for us.

It might be thought that the above paragraph (apart, perhaps, from the last point) merely describes a process which all editors undertake as a matter of course. But we know this not to be true from our many conversations with the various publishers we have worked with in the past. We have been told, for example, that an 'editor' of one collection remarked with surprise 'Oh, did I edit this?' on seeing his name on the cover. More often, some editors apparently do little to contributors' chapters other than correct typographical errors and insert references to their own work. Small wonder then that chapters in edited collections are often uneven in their quality. It is for others to judge whether this collection is of a reasonably uniform high quality, but any failure on our part to achieve this should not be attributed to want of trying. A related deficiency is that editors sometimes allow too long a period between the first and last contributions arriving on their desks. This can result in some chapters appearing in print in an obviously out-of-date state, or in somewhat unfair requests to the early birds to re-write their chapters (lengthening the production process still further). We tried to keep tightly to our deadlines for submission of first and final drafts and, despite our own failings as contributors on this front, the gap between finalising the first chapter to be submitted and the last was nine months.[1] None of the chapters included here suffer from staleness, although no doubt the reckless speed with which criminal justice policy develops these days will present plenty of new material against which readers can judge the worth of the authors' various arguments.

Another reason for deficiencies in the quality of edited collections is summed up well in a recent book review by Gary LaFree:

> One of the common limitations of edited books is that the academic system that produces them generally puts greater value on refereed publications than book chapters. As a consequence, individual contributors to edited volumes often save their strongest, most original work for journals or monographs and write book chapters that to varying degrees are based on work that they have already published, or work that has less methodological sophistication than is demanded by journals.[2]

The problem of lack of novelty was partially obviated by the inclusion in this collection of chapters by authors at an early stage in their careers. The fruits of doctoral research that appear here represent for most of the younger writers their first substantial piece of writing for publication. The more established writers generally met their brief to submit something distinctively new, although in one case a chapter was withdrawn by mutual agreement after it became clear that the author concerned did not have the time to do this. For our own chapters, Hoyle has taken three short paragraphs from a recently published report which she co-authored[3] and expanded them into a 14,000 word analysis of an issue which has received little attention: how to secure restorative justice for victims who do not wish to meet their offenders. Young has pursued a concern raised in a few throwaway lines in a previous edited collection[4] by exploring in detail the challenges posed by corporate victims of crime to the restorative justice paradigm. Neither of us would claim that our chapters are a model of methodological sophistication, but we

---

[1]   It would have been a narrower, more respectable, gap were it not for Paul Rock's demoralising efficiency in producing his chapter last summer.

[2]   G LaFree, 'Explaining the Crime Bust of the 1990s' (2001) 91 (1) *Journal of Criminal Law and Criminology* 269, 291.

[3]   C Hoyle, R Young and R Hill, *Proceed with Caution: An evaluation of the Thames Valley Police Initiative in Restorative Cautioning* (Joseph Rowntree Foundation, York, 2002) 19–20.

[4]   R Young, 'Integrating a Multi-Victim Perspective into Criminal Justice Through Restorative Justice Conferences' in A Crawford and J Goodey (eds), *Integrating a Victim Perspective within Criminal Justice* (Ashgate, Aldershot, 2000).

consider that they represent an advance on much of what passes for research and analysis in the restorative justice literature. More generally, we hope the academic system is mature enough to assess the contributions to this collection on their merits rather than judging the book by the word 'edited' on the cover.

Further novelty is lent to this collection by the number of chapters that either focus on men as victims of crime or analyse the gendered assumptions that inform thinking and action about victimisation. Allen discusses male on male rape, drawing on her interviews with 50 victims garnered from a variety of sources. The chapter presents a typology of male rapes based on the circumstances of the offence and explores how a key factor in the victim's recovery is the extent to which the rape is interpreted as undermining masculinity. Hamill examines punishment beatings by the IRA for persistent young offenders (mostly male) in Northern Ireland. Based on her qualitative interviews she argues that not only does her work illustrate the overlap between offenders and victims, but that there are some young people who actively seek out victim status in order to enhance their standing within their communities. Whereas these two chapters focus on the nature of victimisation itself, Grady's chapter draws on her doctoral work in exploring how feminist-influenced stereotypes of crime victims have rendered male victims of domestic violence invisible within police processes. While Grady's analysis highlights the blind spots in thinking about crime victims that 'core feminism' has generated, Winter's chapter illustrates and adds to the positive contributions that feminist analysis has made to victimology. Her chapter takes us further into the criminal process by presenting a case-study of the trial of Rosemary West, wife of the serial killer Fred West. She examines the gendered ways in which the defence and the prosecution each sought to construct the victims and survivors of the Wests in order to further their adversarial purposes.

Rock and Sanders, each in their own way, have provided excellent bookends for this collection. We had originally planned to contribute an introductory essay setting out the development, limitations and omissions in criminological thinking about crime victims but Rock far surpassed anything that we could have achieved in this regard so we happily adopted that as a suitable opening to the book proper. Sanders (or Andrew, as he likes to be called) presents a theoretical exploration of victims' rights to participate within the criminal process. His argument, that victims are currently invited to participate in ways that do little to increase their sense of inclusion, provides an overarching backdrop against which more finely grained analyses of related policy issues (such as Hoyle's) may be located. It also provides a suitably provocative essay on which to bring the book to a close.

The inspiration for the brevity of these prefatory remarks was one of Mike Tonry's many delightful introductions to edited collections. In it he wrote:

> This introduction, most readers will be relieved to learn, does not summarize and comment on the contents of each of the essays. I have never understood why introductions

so often do that; the essays are after all but a few pages away, and if they do not stand on their own and say what they mean [they] should not have been published.[5]

That leaves us with little else to do here save to express our sincere thanks to all our contributors. Whilst it should not be assumed that we agree with every argument they advance, we are proud to be associated with their work. We would also like to express our gratitude to our friend and colleague Andrew Ashworth for his helpful comments on this work and for doing so much to make our chaotic and exhausting lives in Oxford not just tolerable but enjoyable. Hart Publishing were supportive throughout, and Hannah (Editorial and Production Manager) did a magnificent job of sub-editing the entire manuscript. Finally, our thanks to our respective families, David and Jacob Rose, and Hannah Young (Mutt and Jeff's only contribution was to increase stress levels by chewing the furniture). This book is dedicated to Jacob, too young to have begun his offending career as yet (we assume New Labour will not have lowered the age of criminal responsibility to three year olds by the time this book appears) and, to the best of our knowledge, not yet a victim of crime. It is also dedicated to Ian Young, who grew out of crime in the normal way, only to become the victim of three armed robberies when a store manager. He now has something much more troubling occupying his mind. Long life, health, and happiness to them both.

Carolyn Hoyle and Richard Young
Oxford
31 May 2002

---

[5]   M Tonry, 'Ethnicity, Crime, and Immigration' in M Tonry (ed), *Crime and Justice: A Review of Research* (University of Chicago Press, Chicago Ill, 1997) Vol 21.

Contents

Notes on Contributors

Stephanie Allen was awarded her DPhil from the University of Oxford in 2001. She is currently a management consultant with Deloitte & Touche working with a variety of Criminal Justice agencies throughout the UK.

Ann Grady was awarded LLB (Hons) in Law at Coventry University in 1993. Since 1995, she has studied for a PhD and taught at the School of Law, University of Birmingham.

Heather Hamill was awarded her DPhil in 2001. She is currently a Research Officer in the Department of Sociology, University of Oxford.

Carolyn Hoyle is a Lecturer in Criminology at the Centre for Criminological Research and a Fellow of Green College at the University of Oxford.

Paul Rock is Professor of Social Institutions at the London School of Economics. He was educated at the London School of Economics and Nuffield College, Oxford. He is the author of a number of books and articles focused on the development of policies for victims of crime in Canada and the United Kingdom.

Andrew Sanders is Professor of Criminal Law and Criminology at the University of Manchester. His research has covered aspects of prosecutions and police powers, as well as the involvement of victims in the criminal justice system.

Richard Young is a Lecturer in Criminal Justice and Assistant Director of the Centre for Criminological Research at the University of Oxford.

Jo Winter is a Lecturer in Law at the University of Manchester, having recently completed a PhD at Bristol University. Her research interests span gender and the law, criminal law and criminal evidence.

1

On Becoming a Victim

PAUL ROCK

T HE STUDY OF VICTIMS of crime is now buoyant, but it contains at its
core a number of problematic gaps, and I shall describe how one in particular came into being and consider how it might filled. What follows will
necessarily be focused and exaggerated so that the analysis of a few traits can
become the starker.

INTRODUCTION

Until the late 1970s, victims were almost wholly neglected in criminology and
criminal justice. Crime and deviance were characteristically treated in the
following ways:

— by the more positivistic, and especially by the more clinical, criminologist as
discrete, material states inhering in individuals who could be examined
independently of social context, relations and history (including any history
of dealings with victims);
— by the more sociological as properties of structure and belief, and particularly of the larger structures of economic inequality and cultural difference,
and victims were there analytically finessed;
— by the Marxist and radical, initially, as a facet of social disorganisation without reference to any victims other than deracinated industrial workers, then
as the figments of a proletarian false consciousness that was turned towards
the wrong objects[1] and, latterly, as the sometimes righteous, sometimes pos-
sessive, individualistic responses of the anomic poor and dispossessed to the
pathologies of capitalism, and victims, by extension, were either
undeserving or descriptively excluded[2]; and

---

[1] See F Pearce, *Crimes of the Powerful* (Pluto Press, London, 1976).
[2] Consider the rank indifference to victims displayed in I Taylor, P Walton and J Young, *The New
Criminology* (Routledge & Kegan Paul, London, 1973); I Taylor, P Walton and J Young (eds), *Critical
Criminology* (Routledge & Kegan Paul, London, 1975); or S Hall *et al*, *Policing the Crisis* (Macmillan,
London, 1978).

—   by the interactionist and phenomenologist as symbolic constructions manufactured in dialectical interchange with significant others, and with the powerful above all—control, not crime, was the problem—and victims did not seem to figure.

'Thoughts of security and public order, of fear of crime and concern for its victims, had little prominence in this literature,'[3] Garland remarked. Where victims *were* invoked by interactionists, it was, chiefly and paradoxically, not as suffering, solid and creditable individuals but in an ironic vein or, more commonly, in their virtual absence. They were barely visible, often not much more than rhetorical artefacts that were of interest because they awaited neutralisation and annihilation in the accounting systems of deviants,[4] or because they were the distorted subjects of *folies à foule*: recall Cohen's original concept of moral panics[5] and Wilkins's notion of deviance amplification[6] which belittled the importance of social problems; Sutherland's and Cressey's *Principles of Criminology*[7] and its catalogue of risible criminal laws; Gusfield's work on temperance as a form of status politics which gratuitously oppressed an immigrant grouping as deviant;[8] and Schur's polemic of a criminology of crimes without victims.[9] Perhaps early non-interactionist exceptions were the work of Wolfgang on homicide[10] and of his student, Amir, on rape,[11] but they were to engender their own difficulties.

Equally unpropitious were the writings of scholars on the boundaries of criminology such as the proto-victimologists, Von Hentig,[12] Mendelsohn,[13] Schafer[14] and others, with their talk of the functional responsibility of the victim, guilty victims and victimicity. The discipline they sired, victimology, was to be another *rendezvous* subject, and it was long occupied with the compiling of empirically-driven lists of items sharing the word 'victim' as a denominator: 'so far', the conclusions of the International Study Institute on Victimology declared in 1975,

[3] D Garland, *The Culture of Control* (Oxford University Press, Oxford, 2001) 66.
[4] See F Davis, 'Deviance Disavowal' in H Becker (ed), *The Other Side* (Free Press, New York NY, 1964); M Scott and S Lyman, 'Accounts, Deviance and Social Order' in J Douglas (ed), *Deviance and Respectability* (Basic Books, New York NY, 1970); and G Sykes and D Matza, 'Techniques of Neutralization' (1957) 22 *American Sociological Review* 664.
[5] S Cohen, *Folk Devils and Moral Panics* (Paladin, London, 1973). Cohen has subsequently talked about 'positive' moral panics prompted by issues of concern and whose consequences are benign.
[6] L Wilkins, *Social Deviance* (Tavistock, London, 1964).
[7] E Sutherland and D Cressey, *Principles of Criminology*, 5th edn (JB Lippincott Co, Chicago Ill, 1955).
[8] J Gusfield, *Symbolic Crusade* (University of Illinois Press, Urbana Ill, 1963).
[9] E Schur, *Crimes Without Victims* (Prentice-Hall, Englewood Cliffs NJ, 1965).
[10] M Wolfgang, *Patterns in Criminal Homicide* (University of Pennsylvania Press, Philadelphia Penn, 1959).
[11] M Amir, *Patterns of Forcible Rape* (University of Chicago Press, Chicago Ill, 1971).
[12] See H Von Hentig, *The Criminal and his Victim* (Yale University Press, New Haven Conn, 1948).
[13] B Mendelsohn, 'The Origins of the Doctrine of Victimology', reprinted in I Drapkin and E Viano (eds), *Victimology* (DC Heath and Company, Lexington Mass, 1974).
[14] S Schafer, *The Victim and His Criminal* (Random House, New York NY, 1968).

it can only be stated that the universe of events that have some probability of being defined as victimizing, conceptually define the parameters of victimology. Beyond this admittedly circular definition, little consensus has emerged.[15]

The early victimologists themselves were often not much more than abstracted empiricists searching for a theory, a language and academic legitimacy. Viano, one of their patrons, wrote in the 1970s:

> any new field . . . initially struggles to develop its terminology, define its boundaries, justify its existence, gain respectability and eventually claim its place among the already established disciplines. . . . Victimology is no exception.[16]

It was all too easy at first to dismiss victimology, in the words of Becker, as 'the lunatic fringe of criminology',[17] and it did not make an appreciable impact on its parent discipline.

Much of the early, victim-free phase of criminology was the creature of what appears in retrospect to have been an innocent time and place, described by Young as the criminological 'Golden Age of the post-war period within the First World'.[18] The volume of recorded crimes in that English and Welsh Golden Age was small and diminishing in the early 1950s, although there were fears about youthful offending,[19] and about offences of violence above all.[20] Criminologists and penal reformers (and the two groups often converged) tended to dismiss those fears as unfounded.[21] Indeed, the most influential British criminologist of his day, Radzinowicz, took it to be part of his task at that time to explain why the United Kingdom had so *little* crime: 'There was even a drop,' he remembered. 'We thought we were coming out of the wood. With prosperity, better education, full employment and the welfare state, the very roots of criminality might be starved.'[22]

Crime was taken to be a minor social problem the management of which could be entrusted to the expert—including the criminologist—who had a civilising mission to educate the public and politicians and reform the machinery of welfare, control and rehabilitation. Morris recalls of that time, there was 'a great optimism that the practical application of the knowledge derived from criminology could produce a more just and more effective criminal justice system.'[23] If victims *were* acknowledged, it was as people seen from afar and imagined to be angry,

---

[15] 'Conclusions and Recommendations. International Study Institute on Victimology. Bellagio, Italy, July 1–12, 1975' in E Viano (ed), *Victims and Society* (Visage Press, Washington DC, 1976) 604.

[16] Viano, 'Introduction' in *Victims and Society*, n 15 above, 3.

[17] C Becker, *Criminal Theories of Causation and Victims* (Unpublished PhD dissertation, University of Cambridge, 1981) 4.

[18] J Young, *The Exclusive Society* (Sage, London, 1999) 1.

[19] See L Wilkins, *Delinquent Generations* (HMSO, London, 1960).

[20] See G Pearson, *Hooligan* (Macmillan, London, 1983) esp 12.

[21] See Howard League for Penal Reform, *Annual Report 1952–1953* (Howard League for Penal Reform, London, 1953); and CH Rolph, 'Wild Justice' *New Statesman*, 18 January 1958.

[22] L Radzinowicz and J King, *The Growth of Crime* (Penguin, Harmondsworth, 1979) 16.

[23] T Morris, 'British Criminology: 1935–1948' (1988) 28 *British Journal of Criminology* 164.

vengeful and therefore hazardous to that process of amelioration, best bought-off by criminal injuries compensation in the short term so that needed reforms could be introduced and take effect in the long term. If they did appear, they were spoken about or spoken for but they were rarely allowed to speak, and they acquired a correspondingly fantastic appearance.

Recorded crimes may have started rising again in the late 1950s, but cultural lag and an engrained scepticism about the State and its counting practices,[24] led influential members of the academic generations who were trained in the 1950s, 1960s and early 1970s to mistrust or ignore both government-generated crime rates and the State's analysis of what they portended.[25] 'Many sociologists', Box asserted in 1971, 'deny that these data really reflect what is going on 'out there' in society.'[26] Habits of thought and training die hard and there were to be several decades in which criminologists and penal reformers persisted in holding to that imagery of crime as an exaggerated problem manufactured largely by bureaucratic processes for political, administrative and populist ends[27] and of the victim, by extrapolation, as a kind of dangerous harpy. During the 1960s, 1970s and beyond, libertarians, such as Douglas, radicals such as Reiman, populists such as Quinney, and phenomenologists such as Kitsuse severally expressed their misgivings about the State-ratified depiction of the social reality of crime. If crime was a problem, they argued, it was not necessarily as politicians and government agencies represented it. It was as if some criminologists had decided that they did not wish to be associated with the discreditable victim, but, if they *were* obliged to be, the victim to be considered would be defined principally by the criminologists' criteria of eligibility as the deviant, offender, prisoner, proletarian or other neglected casualty of capitalism,[28] racism, imperialism and class exploitation.[29]

Becker constructed one version of that argument in his metaphor of the hierarchy of credibility: the task of the sociologist of crime, he claimed, was to restore balance and challenge from below the seemingly authoritative accounts of crime and control supplied by the powerful.[30] Hall and his colleagues constructed another: crime was a mystifying diversion introduced to divide the subaltern and working classes in a capitalist state that was entering what could well be its

---

[24] See J Kitsuse and A Cicourel, 'A Note on the Uses of Official Statistics' (1963) 11 *Social Problems* 131.
[25] Garland observed of the radical criminology of the 1960s and 1970s, '[a]lthough its appearance coincides with some of the fastest rising crime rates recorded in the twentieth century, many of its themes appear quite disconnected from that phenomenon'. Garland, *The Culture of Control*, n 3 above, 66.
[26] S Box, *Deviance, Reality and Society* (Holt, Rinehart and Winston, London, 1971) 16.
[27] See Hall *et al*, *Policing the Crisis*, n 2 above.
[28] See Pearce, *Crimes of the Powerful*, n 1 above.
[29] See A Platt, 'Prospects for a Radical Criminology in the USA' and H Schwendinger and J Schwendinger, 'Defenders of Order or Guardians of Human Rights' both in I Taylor, P Walton and J Young (eds), *Critical Criminology* (Routledge, London, 1975).
[30] H Becker, 'Whose Side Are We On?' (1967) 14 *Social Problems* 239.

terminal phase, and the criminal himself was a scapegoat in a politics of crisis.[31] Cohen constructed a third version:

> The [new] orientation is part of what might be called the sceptical revolution in criminology . . . The older tradition was canonical in the sense that it saw the concepts it worked with as authoritative, accepted, given and unquestionable. The new tradition is sceptical in the sense that when it sees terms like 'deviant', it asks 'deviant to whom?' or 'deviant from what?' . . . when certain conditions or behaviour are described as functional, embarrassing, threatening or dangerous, it asks 'says who?' and 'why?'[32]

The sceptics did not speak with one voice, but for years they rejected the conventional politics of law and order, and, it may be presumed, rejected many of its themes, including talk of victims, in their turn (I write 'presumed' because there was almost *no* discussion of victims). For some, after all, invoking the victim smacked of an ideology that was tainted by false consciousness, the distortions of the moral panic, retributivism, and what Hall called 'authoritarian populism'[33] and Garland 'punitive populism.'[34] Such an allusion, it was argued, could feed repression, hysteria and a culture of malicious blaming.[35] Garland, for instance, has written more recently of how:

> The interests and feelings of victims—actual victims, victims' families, potential victims, the projected figure of 'the victim' are now routinely invoked in support of measures of punitive segregation.[36]

It was only when criminology confronted a piecemeal battery of brute facts and criticisms that it somewhat grudgingly, raggedly and belatedly gave ground. Those facts and criticisms, it should be noted, almost invariably emanated from outside criminology. Let me review some of them in turn.

THE REDISCOVERY OF THE VICTIM

First, there was the question of the sheer volume of crime in the West, the problem it was supposed to represent, and, for a few, whether official talk about the nature and scale of offending was to be identified as part of a hegemonic project to divide and mislead the populace. Recorded crime in England and Wales grew ten-fold between the 1950s and the 1990s to five million a year, from 1.1 offences per 100

---

[31] Hall *et al*, *Policing the Crisis*, n 2 above.

[32] Cohen, *Folk Devils and Moral Panics*, n 5 above, 12.

[33] S Hall, *Drifting into a Law and Order Society* (Cobden Trust, London, 1980).

[34] D Garland, 'The Limits of the Sovereign State: Strategies of Crime Control in Contemporary Society' (1996) 36(4) *British Journal of Criminology* 445.

[35] See R Ofshe and E Watters, *Making Monsters: False Memories, Psychotherapy, and Sexual Hysteria* (André Deutsch, London, 1995) and C Sykes, *A Nation of Victims: The Decay of the American Character* (St Martin's Press, New York NY, 1992).

[36] Garland, *The Culture of Control*, n 3 above, 11.

population in 1950 to 9.5 in 1996.[37] However much quibbling there may have been about changes in reporting tendencies and counting rules, however much the State and its purposes may have been eyed with suspicion, that rise in crime did eventually come to seem incontestable and it did make its mark on criminology. Reiner was moved to write at the end of 1994 (just when rates began to fall):

> So many people are rightly more cautious nowadays about saloon-bar pontifications on rising crime . . . Yet even with appropriate warnings most commentators—and I certainly include myself—feel this time things are really different. We are caught up in a long-term expansion of crime and disorder, which has been with us for nearly forty years, and which has intensified greatly in the last year and a half.[38]

It had become more and more difficult to disparage crime as an over-inflated social problem.

Secondly, America saw lurid displays of violence in the assassination of politicians and the urban rioting of the 1960s especially in New York City, Philadelphia and Rochester, New York, in 1964; in Watts in 1965; Chicago, San Francisco, Dayton and Cleveland in 1966; and in over 150 cities in 1967. Politicians and lay commentators were jolted into suspending their belief in a social world that was safe, predictable and expertly-managed. Lipsky and Olson reflected that the 'summer of 1967 represented to many observers the greatest internal crisis experienced by the United States since the Civil War.'[39] Questions were asked and inquiries were subsequently published—most notably the reports of the President's Crime Commission in 1967,[40] the Kerner Commission in 1968[41] and the Eisenhower Commission in 1970.[42] The third and fourth sentences of the President's Crime Commission report recited that: 'Every American is, in a sense, a victim of crime. Violence and theft have . . . injured, often irreparably, hundreds of thousands of citizens'.[43] It did not then pursue that line of reasoning much further, and neither did criminologists rush to talk about victims. But work for the Commission included some of the very first crime surveys[44] that were intended to

---

[37] Taken from M Maguire, 'Crime Statistics, Patterns, and Trends: Changing Perceptions and their Implications' in M Maguire, R Morgan and R Reiner (eds), *The Oxford Handbook of Criminology*, 2nd edn (Clarendon Press, Oxford, 1997) 135.

[38] R Reiner, 'The Mystery of the Missing Crimes' (1994) 1 (2) *Policing Today* 16.

[39] M Lipsky and D Olson, *Commission Politics: The Processing of Racial Crisis in America* (Transaction, New Brunswick, 1977) x.

[40] *The Challenge of Crime in a Free Society: A Report by the President's Commission on Law Enforcement and Administration of Justice* (US Government Printing Office, Washington DC, 1967).

[41] See *Report of the National Advisory Commission on Civil Disorders* (Bantam, New York NY, 1968).

[42] *The Report of the National Commission on the Causes and Prevention of Violence* (Bantam, New York, 1970). The report declared that: 'Violence in the United States has risen to alarmingly high levels. Whether one considers assassination, group violence, or individual acts of violence, the decade of the 1960s was considerably more violent than the several decades preceding it and ranks among the most violent in our history' (xxv).

[43] *The Challenge of Crime in a Free Society*, n 40 above, 1.

[44] See A Biderman and A Reiss, 'On Explaining the "Dark Figure" of Crime' (1967) 374 *Annals of the American Academy of Politics and Social Science* 1.

enhance the analysis of crime by 'more rational ways . . . [of] measure[ment] than those currently in use',[45] and *they* led in their turn to the permanent establishment of national crime surveys in the United States from 1972 onwards and then, in different policy contexts in 1981, in Canada, the United Kingdom and elsewhere. Canadian surveys were initially presented as a means of preventing crime and violence in the heightened politics of debate about capital punishment.[46] In England and Wales, in the wake of Britain's own riots, and as a means of doing *something* about an abrupt crisis of public order, they were instituted in the name of 'improving the criminal justice database' (and it is revealing that surveys of victims are very generally called *crime* surveys).

Successive surveys in those different countries proceeded to illuminate new facts about the demography, epidemiology and geography of victims, their apprehensions about crime, and their encounters with the criminal justice system. The first British Crime Survey showed, for example, that, contrary to prevailing belief, the elderly are the least likely to be victims of crime; and that, importantly for the reformers' iconography of the vengeful victim, victims were characteristically no more punitive than the courts.[47] Subsequent studies explored such issues as the fear of crime;[48] the losses incurred by victims; victims' lifestyles and assessments of risk,[49] and the decision to report an offence.[50] From the outset, they explored aspects of victimisation in ways that had been impracticable before. They revealed the distribution, scale, depth and injuries of crime and, in particular, its heavy impact on working class and minority ethnic groups, and the findings were not easily ignored. Crime, said Downes, had been shown to be a regressive tax on the poor. Although it was inevitable that diverse inferences were drawn about how they should be read, the surveys disarmed some of the sceptics. For instance, Platt argued of the volume of street crime revealed by the American surveys that they

> supported the conclusion that 'street' crime is not simply a *by-product* of the capitalist mode of production. . . Rather, it is shown to be a phenomenon *endemic* to capitalism at its highest stage of development.[51]

On the other hand, Lea and Young, radical criminologists who had once been prone to dismiss victimisation as an epiphenomenon of false consciousness, acknowledged on the heels of the first British Crime Survey:

---

[45] President's Commission on Law Enforcement and Administration of Justice, *Field Surveys III: Studies in Crime and Law Enforcement in Major Metropolitan Areas* (US Government Printing Office, Washington, DC) Vol 1, 6.

[46] Under the mandate provided by the Peace and Security Program of 1976.

[47] M Hough and P Mayhew, *The British Crime Survey: First Report* (HMSO, London, 1983) 32–33.

[48] See M Maxfield, *Fear of Crime in England and Wales* (HMSO, London, 1984).

[49] See M Hough and P Mayhew, *Taking Account of Crime: Key Findings from the Second British Crime Survey* (HMSO, London, 1985).

[50] W Skogan, *The Police and the Public in England and Wales: A British Crime Survey Report* (HMSO, London, 1990).

[51] A Platt, ' "Street Crime"—A View from the Left' (1978) 9 *Crime and Social Justice* 29.

There was a schizophrenia about crime on the left where crimes against women and immigrant groups were quite rightly an object of concern, but other types of crime were regarded as being of little interest or somehow excusable. Part of this mistake stems . . . from the belief that property offences are directed solely against the bourgeoisie and that violence against the person is carried out by amateur Robin Hoods in the course of their righteous attempts to redistribute wealth. All of this is, alas, untrue.[52]

There was, thirdly, a revelation of the abundant injuries inflicted by crime on vulnerable populations, and on children and women in particular. Clinicians and police discovered child abuse.[53] Feminism[54] and the feminist criminology of the 1970s and early 1980s[55] discovered widespread and ever multiplying incidents of domestic violence, rape and incest, transformed private troubles into public issues through 'speak-outs', marches and demonstrations,[56] and argued that the neglect of violence against women by practitioner and academic was insupportable—and the academics came in time to concur. Children and women were difficult to regard as either politically legitimate or inconsequential victims and they created new dilemmas for the campaigning criminologist and for left-wing criminologists especially. The radical criminologists, Jones, Maclean and Young, admitted that:

> Feminist victimology was to create enormous theoretical problems for the radical paradigm in criminology . . . Radical criminology had tended to focus on crimes of the powerful and on the way in which vulnerable groups in society are criminalized. . . . But the power of the feminist case resulted in a sort of cognitive schizophrenia amongst radicals.[57]

Fourthly, there was the so-called victims movement—very much more of a political and ideological movement in North America than in the United Kingdom—which declared angrily and at length that the victim was, as its members put it, 'the forgotten party of the criminal justice system' who was doubly victimised by the crime and by the State's response to crime. Their cry was 'what about the victim?' and it was to be timeously heard by the politician and practitioner[58] (if not at first by the more wary criminologist[59]). The opening statement

---

[52] J Lea and J Young, *What is to be Done about Law and Order?* (Penguin, London, 1984) 262.

[53] See C Kempe *et al*, 'The Battered Child Syndrome' [1962] 181 *Journal of the American Medical Association* 17 and D Griffiths and F Moynihan, 'Multiple Epiphysical Injuries in Babies ("Battered Baby Syndrome")' (1963) 11 *British Medical Journal* 1558.

[54] See S Griffin, 'Rape: The All-American Crime' (1971) 10 *Ramparts* 26; M Wasserman, 'Rape: Breaking the Silence', *The Progressive*, November 1973.

[55] See C Smart, *Women, Crime and Criminology* (Routledge & Kegan Paul, London, 1977); SM Edwards, *Female Sexuality and the Law* (M Robertson, Oxford, 1981); and Z Adler, *Rape on Trial* (Routledge & Kegan Paul, London, 1987).

[56] See, for instance, L Smith's judgement in *Concerns about Rape* (HMSO, London, 1989) 1.

[57] T Jones, B Maclean and J Young, *The Islington Crime Survey* (Gower, Aldershot, 1986) 2–3.

[58] In England, the former probation officer, Philip Priestley, published a NACRO Regional Paper with that very cry as its title in 1970.

[59] Jan Van Dijk, a criminologist and a policy official in the Dutch Ministry of Justice, called them 'retribution with a human face.'

of the 1982 report of the US President's Task Force on Victims of Crime declared passionately that:

> The innocent victims of crime have been overlooked, their pleas for justice have gone unheeded, and their wounds—personal, emotional, and financial—have gone unattended.[60]

In the populist 1980s, politicians introduced Victims' Rights Acts in America and Australasia and bodies such as the United Nations[61] and the Council of Europe formulated declarations of victims' rights.

Fifthly, there was the work of Reiss,[62] Ericson[63] and others which showed that police work was not, as the academics, practitioner and politicians had tended to portray it, a technically competent, professional and self-reliant exercise in the detection of crime and enforcement of law, but, to the contrary, an activity which leaned heavily on the lay knowledge and observations of victims, witnesses and bystanders on the scene. For example, 81 per cent of police 'mobilizations' in Reiss's 1971 study, *The Police and the Public,* were initiated by calls from citizens rather than by the police themselves. In the context of a rising volume of crime rates and a declining rate of detection, the emphasis grew on helping victims to *cope* with the effects of crime through victim support programmes rather than to expect arrests, punishment and the restoration of property. There was to be a new conception of community and multi-agency co-operation in which victims were enlisted to add informal social control to the armoury of a now less than confident State in the 'fight against crime.'

There was an accompanying administrative fear in North America,[64] but not in the United Kingdom, that the criminal justice system's alienation of lay witnesses and victims could jeopardise their willingness to report crime, give evidence and secure prosecutions, thereby endangering the system's very viability. Remedial victim-witness programmes were subsequently instituted in Canada and the United States to soften the impact of the criminal justice system and reclaim the witness. And in all this, there was a new authority vested in the victim by politicians and the mass media as they constructed narratives about crime and

---

[60] President's Task Force on Victims of Crime, *Final Report* (Government Printing Office, Washington DC, 1982) ii. See also the Canadian Federal–Provincial Task Force on Justice for Victims of Crime, *Report* (Ministry of Supply and Services Canada, Ottawa, 1983). The brief version of the report opened: 'Concern for victims of crime has recently been an important focus of attention for criminal justice agencies, as well as for private sector groups in Canada', 1.

[61] United Nations Declaration of Basic Principles of Justice for Victims of Crime and Abuse of Power (November 1985).

[62] A Reiss, *The Police and the Public* (Yale University Press, New Haven Conn, 1970).

[63] R Ericson, *Making Crime* (Butterworth, Toronto, 1981).

[64] See R Knudten, 'Will Anyone be Left to Testify?' in E Flynn and J Conrad (eds), *New and Old Criminology* (LEAA, US Department of Justice, Washington DC, 1978). See also R Knudten *et al, Victims and Witnesses: Their Experiences with Crime and the Criminal Justice System* (LEAA, US Department of Justice, Washington DC, 1977) and F Cannavale and W Falcon, *Improving Witness Cooperation* (Government Printing Office, Washington DC, 1976).

punishment in a world that seemed to be growing uncertain about the moral legitimacy and technical proficiency of the State and its institutions.[65]

There were, finally, the victim–offender reconciliation projects designed (in the Canada[66] and United States[67] of the 1970s) to deal with the strained capacities and fiscal and administrative crises of overcrowded courts and prisons; replace the estranging polarities of the adversarial trial process; and reinforce Christian themes of peacemaking. They led into the reparative justice movement[68] which foundered on the economics of criminal justice in the mid-1980s, only to be revived in the 1990s as politicians and practitioners embraced John Braithwaite's 'big idea' of reintegrative shaming.[69]

The increasing scale and gravity of crime, and the growing prominence of the victim in many of the regions abutting their discipline, conspired to bring fractured images of victimisation more fully to the criminologist's attention. 'Victims, once on the margins of criminological research, are now a central focus of academic research,'[70] and the consequence has been that we now know more, think differently and ask new questions. The rediscovery of the poor, proletarian, female and black victim galvanised those in and around radical criminology in the mid-1980s and led to left realism. 'Left idealists', it was argued of the realists' ideological opponents, had 'ignored the fact that crime really was a problem for the working class'. In contrast, the realists asserted that it was necessary 'to consider the importance of . . . map[ping] out the patterns of victimization in which the disenfranchised figured more prominently'.[71]

The discovery of repeat victimisation transformed crime prevention policy and led to the idea of 'cocooning' and targeted strategies.[72] The revelation that crime has its spatial concentrations or 'hot spots'[73] led to new forms of intelligence-led or problem-oriented policing. We know that our earlier assumptions about the impact, quantity and spread of crime[74] have had to be replaced not only by an

---

[65] Based on unpublished research on crime and the mass media by Sonia Livingstone and Robert Reiner.

[66] See W MacPherson and M Yantzi, *Victim–Offender Reconciliation Program* (Kitchener, Ontario, 1979).

[67] See J Hudson and B Galaway (eds), *Restitution in Criminal Justice* (Lexington Books, Lexington Mass, 1977).

[68] See J Harding, *Victims and Offenders: Needs and Responsibilities* (Bedford Square Press, London, 1982); and T Marshall and M Walpole, *Bringing People Together: Mediation and Reparation Projects in Great Britain* (Home Office, London, 1985).

[69] J Braithwaite, *Crime, Shame and Reintegration* (Cambridge University Press, Cambridge, 1989).

[70] L Zedner, 'Victims', in M Maguire *et al* (eds), *The Oxford Handbook of Criminology* (Clarendon Press, Oxford, 1997) 577.

[71] J Lowman and B Maclean, 'Introduction' in *Realist Criminology: Crime Control and Policing in the 1990s* (University of Toronto Press, Toronto, 1992) 6.

[72] See, for example, K Pease, 'Repeat Victimisation: Taking Stock' (Briefing note, Police Research Group, Home Office, London, undated) and J Hanmer and S Griffiths, 'Domestic Violence and Repeat Victimisation' (Briefing note, Police Research Group, Home Office, London, undated).

[73] See L Sherman, 'Hot Spots of Predatory Crime' (1989) 27 *Criminology* 27.

[74] Exemplified most powerfully in I Waller and N Okihiro, *Burglary: The Victim and the Public* (University of Toronto Press, Toronto, 1974).

appreciation of its deep, persistent, pervasive and often unexpected[75] effects, but also by an awareness of its capacity to confound typifications of who the victim and offender might actually be. We no longer talk so glibly in the language of Christie's ideal victim,[76] the little old lady, as if she were a good enough ideal-type.[77] We now know that victims are not always simon-pure but recruited in great measure from much the same demographic and geographical populations as offenders, bystanders and witnesses,[78] and that violent people are likely to become the victims of violence.[79] 'Generally', Antilla remarked, 'one can say that the earlier stereotypes of 'black and white' have been exchanged for 'grey versus grey'.[80]

SOME LIMITATIONS OF KNOWLEDGE ABOUT VICTIMS

All those images were prefabricated in sites outside criminology before they were imported.[81] They were not designed for academic criminology.[82] They were infused with strong sentiments of the place and time of their creation, emotionally charged, and subject to proprietorial claims. They meant quite discrepant things to different audiences, having been the motivations and objects of political campaigns, academic study and administrative action; those who brought them into focus had had varying, often ill-matched purposes and interests in mind; and their different methodologies had shaped what could be observed and thought and, by extension, what could not be observed and thought.[83]

---

[75] See M Maguire, 'The Impact of Burglary on Victims' (1980) 20(3) *British Journal of Criminology* 261.

[76] See N Christie, 'The Ideal Victim' in E Fattah (ed), *From Crime Policy to Victim Policy* (Macmillan, Basingstoke, 1986).

[77] See R Clarke *et al*, 'Elderly Victims of Crime and Exposure to Risk' (1985) 24(1) *The Howard Journal of Criminal Justice* 1.

[78] Smith remarked that 'people who tend to be repeatedly victims also have a much higher chance of being arrested'. DJ Smith, *Police and People in London* (Policy Studies Institute, London, 1983) Vol 1, 124.

[79] See W Pedersen, 'Adolescent Victims of Violence in a Welfare State' (2001) 41(1) *British Journal of Criminology* 1.

[80] I Antilla, *Victimology—A New Territory in Criminology*, Scandinavian Studies in Criminology, Vol 5 (M Robertson, Oxford, 1974) 8.

[81] For a more general discussion of the links between criminology, research and policy on victims, see L Sebba, 'On the Relationship between Criminological Research and Policy' (2001) 1(1) *Criminal Justice* 27.

[82] Thus Weed remarked of the United States, 'The victims-rights movement has developed outside of the academic disciplines of criminology and penology. The victim advocates, for the most part, have not been interested in social research.' F Weed, *Certainty of Justice: Reform in the Crime Victim Movement* (Aldine de Gruyter, New York NY, 1995) 138.

[83] For instance, a number of the more positivist scholars who had drifted away from a criminology that concentrated on the objective and measurable attributes of criminals founded a victimology that performed very similar forms of methodological operation on victims. Indeed, at the very outset, recall that some searched for the correlates of a thing called 'victimicity' as they had once looked for the factors associated with criminality.

All frameworks have their opportunity-costs and the outcome of using these imported ones has been the creation of fuzzy areas at the heart of criminology that obscure scholarly understanding of who and what victims are. For some, perhaps, there was a distaste about the prospect of moving nearer to an ideologically-uncongenial figure. For others, identification with the newly-defined victims nonetheless led to its own analytic taboos. And for a third group, methodology prevented any close examination of the nature of the victim at all.

I have already discussed how the more radical and political criminologists had been hesitant to talk about victims. But there have been countervailing hesitations. Take the more campaigning strands of victimology. They stemmed from an activism that sought to accomplish political objectives, and, however interlaced they may have become with academic work, that teleology remains a force, patrolling the moral standing, ontology and claims of the victim, editing what may be done and said, and erecting barriers around critical questions.[84] A number of radical criminologists have been somewhat disinclined to explore the newly-championed proletarian, minority-ethnic or female victim's role in crime. There has been, for instance, a marked nervousness about consideration of the black woman's exposure to domestic violence from what, in the main, could only have been a black partner.

More generally, the female victim has sometimes been represented in feminist analysis as an undeserving and innocent casualty of patriarchal relations who requires support and who is best described not in a language of victimisation at all but in that of survival. Pahl noted, for example, how the residents of a women's refuge were described as 'the women in the house' rather than as 'battered women'.[85] Some rape crisis centres preferred to talk of survivors or of 'raped women' rather than of victims: ' "Victims" cannot fight back,' it was said, but '"raped women" will.'[86]

Descriptions of female victims as people actively participating in evolving social relations have from time to time been dismissed as mere 'victim-blaming'[87]; *blaming* itself being construed as almost any allusion to the victim's role in criminal transactions, from Mendelsohn's odd and freighted notion of a victim's 'guilty contribution to crime',[88] through Wolfgang's more neutral idea of victim-precipitation, to the argument that 'victim' is a social and rhetorical role fashioned collaboratively with others.[89] 'Innocent [female] victims', Kantor argued, 'continue to be blamed for the behavior of their attacker or for contributing to their own

---

[84] See the chapter by Ann Grady in this volume.

[85] J Pahl, 'Refuges for Battered Women: Social Provision or Social Movement?' (1979) 8 *Journal of Voluntary Action Research* 25.

[86] Rape Counselling and Research Project, *First Annual Report* (London, undated) i.

[87] See L Clark and D Lewis, *Rape: The Price of Coercive Sexuality* (The Women's Press, Toronto, 1977).

[88] B Mendelsohn, 'Une nouvelle branche de la science bio-psycho-sociale' (1956) 11(2) *Revue internationale de la police technique* 95.

[89] See J Holstein and G Miller, 'Rethinking Victimization: An Interactional Approach to Victimology' (1990) 13(1) *Symbolic Interaction* 103.

violent victimization.'[90] It was partly for that reason that Amir's *Patterns in Forcible Rape* was to be vilified for its discussion of victim-precipitated rape.

Alleged equivalencies between the plight of female and male victims[91] are held, at least in some texts, to neglect the distinctive and vitally gendered properties of violence under patriarchy. Stanko wrote:

> Creating a category 'victim' is one way of dealing with women's experiences of male violence. The role and status of 'victim' is separate from that of all women. 'Victimism', the practice of objectifying women's experiences of male violence, serves to deny the commonality among sexually and/or physically assaulted women and their oneness with all women.[92]

The third source of difficulty has been methodological. Take crime surveys: they have yielded abundant information that no other method could have produced and they have transformed the criminological landscape, but they were constructed (for precise policy and administrative ends) to count aggregations of somewhat atomised, deracinated and anonymous responses set in a limited context of social statics, rather than with appreciation of some of the more complicated and intertwined social relations that extend beyond the individual and evolve over time. They inevitably mask the existential elements in the development of victimisation.

THE PROBLEM OF IDENTITY

There is an ensuing conceptual void that has yet to be filled by an adequate description of the victim as a situated, reflective self in interaction with others, and it could be a useful description because much that is important in personal and collective conduct and belief in this area turns on what it is to *be* a victim. Any such examination must deal with how people cope with the here-and-now experience of crime; what sense they come to make of it; how they account to themselves and others about what has transpired (and, indeed, when and how accounting needs to be done); what materials are available to construct such accounts; what identities are implicated and how, if at all, they are acquired. The list could be extended but it does outline the kind of programme to be pursued, and what follows is a sketch of a framework in which it might be set.

A victim is one who is defined voluntarily or involuntarily, directly or indirectly, abruptly or gradually, consequentially or inconsequentially, by the proven or

---

[90] G Kantor, 'Victim-Blaming and Victim-Precipitation, Concept of' in N Rafter (ed), *Encyclopedia of Women and Crime* (Oryx Press, Phoenix Ariz, 2000) 266.
[91] There was, for instance, some disquiet about the apparent implications of the 1995 British Crime Survey which showed that men suffered the same rate of domestic violence as women in the last year (although their injuries were less acute and the overall prevalence of violence in their lifetime was smaller).
[92] E Stanko, *Intimate Intrusions* (Routledge & Kegan Paul, London, 1985) 16.

alleged criminal or crime-like actions of another. 'Victim', in other words, is an *identity*, a social artefact dependent, at the outset, on an alleged transgression and transgressor and then, directly or indirectly, on an array of witnesses, police, prosecutors, defence counsel, jurors, the mass media and others who may not always deal with the individual case but who will nevertheless shape the larger interpretative environment in which it is lodged.

Not all those who are transgressed against will evolve into full-blown victims. So abundant and varied is crime, and so contingent is its impact, that the mere fact that one has become or been made a victim lacks immediate predictive power about who one is, how one regards oneself or is regarded by others, or what one might do or become as a result. A *victim* could be little more than an item in an accounting system, a statistical entry with slight existential weight for one who has been so classified, a primary victim or victim *an sich*, as it were, whose experience is confined to a fleeting episode without significant aftermath. Some people might not even notice the transgression. It was certainly the claim of the authors of the first British Crime Survey that many crimes were unreported because they were of such little consequence to the victim.[93] Other people might eschew the designation of victim or refrain from reflecting upon it. There are alternative frames which could enable a potential victim to be defined, say, as a disabled person, a claimant, survivor, patient, invalid or plaintiff instead. Indeed, at the July 2001 Annual Conference of Victim Support, a succession of speakers from the floor and the platform proposed that the organisation be renamed because the very term 'victim' was considered less desirable and apposite than, say, 'survivor.'

'Victim' itself is not then necessarily considered an appealing term. It is contradictory, connoting, in Downes's metaphor, images of pariah and saint, and those conflicting images have already been revealed in the stances of certain criminologists and campaigners. But it tends preponderantly to convey stigmatised meanings of weakness, loss and pain. The *New Shorter Oxford English Dictionary* includes in its definition of the word,

> a person killed or tortured by another; a person subjected to cruelty, oppression, or other harsh, or unfair treatment, or suffering death, injury, ruin, etc., as a result of an event, circumstance, or oppressive or adverse impersonal agency,

and it is to be presumed that most people in everyday life would not willingly court any of those circumstances or eagerly build an identity upon them.

On the other hand, becoming a victim can have its rewards: sympathy; attention; being treated as blameless; the ability to bestow meaning and control on an untoward and disturbing experience; the receiving of exoneration, absolution, validation and credit, exemption from prosecution, mitigation of punishment and financial compensation. Those qualities are continuously refined and reinforced

---

[93] See Hough and Mayhew, *The British Crime Survey*, n 47 above, 11.

in the binary oppositions or 'opposing distortions'[94] that are fabricated in and about the adversarial trial, political speech and press reporting about crime, where innocent victims tend to be depicted as the very antithesis of wicked criminals. Becoming a secondary victim or a victim *für sich* can then supply a privileged moral place, a history, a present and a future, and there has been increasing competition in a more litigious, expressive and reflective[95] world to earn the title, and some policing of applicants by those who would regulate their admission and acceptance. There have been complaints about what is said to be a growing and unattractive culture of victimisation in which more and more people abjure responsibility for their own actions or refuse to accept that events may be beyond human control.[96] There have been disputes about whether the holocaust included Christians, communists and homosexuals. Legal definitions of genocide extend to race but not to the victims of mass killings based on politics and class, and powerful states, such as Turkey, can still withstand the charge. The classes of victims of rape and domestic violence have now been validated, but it is not clear whether they are always and everywhere permitted to include males. After agitation, the relatives of homicide victims have only very recently been classified as victims proper for certain purposes in England and Wales,[97] but other groups are only uncertainly and unevenly acknowledged as casualties of crime: children in households that have been burgled;[98] the relatives of serious offenders who sometimes represent themselves as 'the other victims of crime';[99] those injured in, or related to people who have been injured or killed in, road crashes; offenders injured by their victims; prisoners injured whilst making their escape from prison; suspects and offenders injured or killed in custody; the police and ambulance staff who attend serious crime scenes; ushers and court staff who hear the harrowing testimony of victims every day; defendants who claim that they were the victims of food additives or bullying fathers; teenage prostitutes and 'trafficked' women;[100] defendants who claim the 'battered woman's defence' of 'slow burn

---

[94] M McConville, 'Justice in the Dock' *The Times Higher Education Supplement*, 8 February 1990.

[95] See A Giddens, *Modernity and Self Identity* (Polity Press, Cambridge, 1991).

[96] See Sykes, *A Nation of Victims*, n 35 above.

[97] They were acknowledged as victims in, for instance, the 1985 United Nations Declaration of Basic Principles of Justice for Victims of Crime and Abuse of Power which stated that: 'The term "victim" also includes, where appropriate, the immediate family or dependants of the direct victim and persons who have suffered harm to assist victims in distress or to prevent victimization'. But they were excluded from the 'trialling' of what were to become called victim personal statements on the grounds that the real victims of homicide were the dead who could not speak.

[98] See J Morgan and L Zedner, *Child Victims: Crime, Impact, and Criminal Justice* (Clarendon Press, Oxford, 1992).

[99] See G Howarth and P Rock, 'Aftermath and the Construction of Victimisation: "The Other Victims of Crime" ' (2000) 39(1) *Howard Journal of Criminal Justice* 58.

[100] J Doezema, 'Loose Women or Lost Women? The Re-emergence of the Myth of "White Slavery" in Contemporary Discourses of "Trafficking in Women" ' (Paper presented at the ISA Convention, Washington DC, February 1999).

provocation',[101] and women who plead that they were coerced into offending by dominant male partners.[102] Such a jostling for inclusion and exclusion repeatedly tests, delineates and, indeed, complicates what it is to be a victim.

The issue is complicated because becoming a victim can be a matter of contrasting claims made before disparate audiences with different powers to censure and reward, and the recognition of one victim may be secured only at the perceived cost to another. On 2 March 2001, for instance, the Hillsborough Family Support Group, representing the relatives of those who had died in the Hillsborough football stadium in April 1989, publicly voiced their anger at the award of £300,000 in compensation to a former police officer who had been traumatised by what he had seen and heard on the day of the deaths. The Family Support Group did not take the police to be the principal victims of the event, and the award challenged their very identity and understanding of the event and its impact. Its vice-chairman was reported to have said:

> There are people who lost their sons, daughters and loved ones and received nothing. There is a huge difference between the amount paid to the police and the amount paid to survivors.[103]

Victimisation is critically a process of alter-casting, and the victimisation of one can entail the criminalisation of another. Rape constitutes the rapist just as the rapist constitutes the raped person; witchcraft defines the bewitched, the witchfinder and the witch;[104] and genocide defines a victimised people and a victimising nation. Becoming a victim then has a ramifying significance for troupes of people—for what used to be called role-sets—just as criminalising others can sometimes cast the accuser as a victim.[105] Intentionally or unintentionally, it establishes a frame in which networks of identities may be transformed. So it was that Pitch argued of the politics of the women's movement and ecologists in Italy that their:

> struggles are to be understood in a context of a more generalized attempt at reintroducing on the political and social scene intentional and conscious actors, actors who can be held accountable for the consequences of their actions. Such reintroduction is a condition for the recognition of the criminalizing actors themselves as intentional and conscious actors. Whereas the criminal justice terrain and discourse appear as particularly appealing and

[101] J Nadel, *Sara Thornton: The Story of a Woman who Killed* (Victor Gollancz, London, 1994) and S Westervelt, *Shifting the Blame: How Victimization Became a Criminal Defense* (Rutgers University Press, New Brunswick NJ, 1998).
[102] A Matravers, *Justifying the Unjustifiable: Stories of Women Sex Offenders* (Unpublished PhD thesis, University of Cambridge, 2000).
[103] *BBC News On-Line*, 2 March 2001.
[104] See M Douglas (ed), *Witchcraft Confessions and Accusations* (Tavistock, London, 1970).
[105] I Buruma, 'The Joys and Perils of Victimhood' in A Lightman and R Atwan (eds), *The Best American Essays 2000* (Houghton Mifflin, Boston Mass, 2000).

forceful instruments toward the reconstruction of 'responsible' actors, they entail also that the requesting actors construct themselves as *victims*.[106]

On a yet larger scale, that process of claims-making may be viewed in the contests within and between political regimes undergoing radical transformation. Framing discourses about victimisation and aggression may be reversed, and reversed more than once, as trials, war crimes tribunals, truth commissions and inquiries unfold.[107] Thus, just as the Germans were victims of the 'stab in the back' of the First World War, only to be cast as perpetrators of crimes against humanity at Nuremberg, so the Serbian victims of the 1990s were defined as aggressors in the early 2000s.

Becoming a 'victim', in short, is an emergent process of signification like many others, possibly involving the intervention and collaboration of others whose impact and meaning change from stage to stage, punctuated by benchmarks and transitions, and lacking any fixed end state. At an extreme pole, the existential consequences of being a homicide survivor, for instance, are not at first self-evident, but are built up step by step, over time, prompted by professionals and lay people engaged in the processing of crime and death, and embellished by readings provided by relatives, friends and the occasional fellow survivor. Such a process is an existential or moral career:

> The moral career of a person of a given social category involves a standard sequence of changes in his way of conceiving of selves, including, importantly, his own. These half-buried lines of development can be followed by studying his moral experiences—that is, happenings which mark a turning-point in the way in which the person views the world.[108]

Careers can be contingent, fluctuating in importance for the self and its others, and enlivened by its contrasts. Their development may be so gradual that it will only be the passing of some turning-point that enforces awareness.[109] But they may also be abrupt and traumatic—as in a rape, robbery or assault. Indeed, some forms of victimisation are *designed* by the offender to be disconcerting precisely because it is then that the victim is at his or her most defenceless and malleable.[110] It may only be by rendering a victim confused and helpless that an offence can be efficiently committed.[111]

---

[106] T Pitch, 'From Oppressed to Victims: Collective Actors and the Symbolic Use of the Criminal Justice System' (1990) 10 *Studies in Law, Politics, and Society* 103–04 (emphasis in original).

[107] See S Cohen, *States of Denial* (Polity Press, Cambridge, 2001).

[108] E Goffman, *Asylums* (Anchor Books, New York NY, 1961) 135.

[109] See, for instance, the diaries of Victor Klemperer, who was transformed little by little by the growth of Nazism from being a *bourgeois*, converted German professor into a fugitive Jew seeking to escape the death camps. The second diary was published as *To the Bitter End* (Weidenfeld and Nicolson, London, 1999). Fictional accounts of the same process may be found in A Appelfeld, *The Retreat* (Quartet Books, London, 1984) and M Frisch, *The Fire Raisers* (Methuen, London, 1962).

[110] See R Wright and S Decker, *Armed Robbers in Action* (Northeastern University Press, Boston, 1997).

[111] See W Einstadter, 'The Social Organization of Armed Robbery' (1969) 17(1) *Social Problems* 64.

Critical passages may be eased by pre-existing narratives supplied by 'status-coaches'[112]: by texts, self-help manuals and agony columns; television programmes, films and newspapers; counselling and therapy; 'helplines', survivors' campaigns, 'speak-outs' and support groups, and the guiding procedures of police interrogation and prosecution examination-in-chief.[113] There are abundant scripts which lay out much of how to be a victim—what to do, feel and say, at a difficult juncture. What else do crime series and shows such as *Kilroy* and *Oprah* achieve if not to offer public representations of wounded sentiment?[114] Passages may even be eased by offenders themselves. After all, it is palpably in the interest of the offender to pacify the victim and reconcile him or her to what has happened.[115] So established and conventional have some of those scripts become that questions have been asked about the authenticity of the victim experience, about whether stock accounts of victimisation are not merely being reproduced in routine fashion,[116] and whether, indeed, stories are retrieving a past and a self or imposing them afresh with the help of recovered memories and ready-made templates.[117] And, following WI Thomas's dictum that what people define as real is real enough in its consequences, and if it *is* the case that such 'off-the-peg' selves are thus available to be donned, it could be asked quite what is meant when it is said that they are existentially inauthentic. After all, many of the more stereotyped roles of public life are modelled and adapted in precisely this fashion.[118]

It is perhaps about this point that understanding begins to falter. If becoming a victim depends in part on the borrowing or construction and application of frames to experience, more must be learned about how that process is negotiated. What remains is the progressive elaboration of the kinds of questions that might be asked.

There is, first, a problem of the substantial neglect of victimisation as *interaction*. We know, for instance, that much violence, and especially violence against females and children, is committed by members of the victim's intimate circle.[119] We may also surmise that much property crime is also committed by people known to the victim. Yet, despite work by Straus and his colleagues,[120]

---

[112] See A Strauss, *Mirrors and Masks* (Free Press, Glencoe Ill, 1959) ch IV.

[113] See M McConville, A Sanders and R Leng, *The Case for the Prosecution* (Routledge, London, 1991).

[114] See R Sparks, *Television and the Drama of Crime: Moral Tales and the Place of Crime in Public Life* (Open University Press, Buckingham, 1992).

[115] See, for example, E Goffman, 'On Cooling the Mark Out' (1952) 15(4) *Psychiatry* 451.

[116] See I Hacking, *Rewriting the Soul: Multiple Personality and the Sciences of Memory* (Princeton University Press, Princeton NJ, 1995).

[117] See K Plummer, *Telling Sexual Stories* (Routledge, London, 1995).

[118] See O Klapp, *Heroes, Villains and Fools: The Changing American Character* (Prentice-Hall, Englewood Cliffs NJ, 1962).

[119] Only 12% of rapes recorded by the police in England and Wales in 1996 were committed by strangers, and 54% of male and 79% of female homicide victims in 1997 knew their killers: *Information on the Criminal Justice System in England and Wales: Digest 4* (Home Office, London, 1999).

[120] MA Straus *et al*, *Behind Closed Doors: Violence in the American Family* (Anchor Books, Garden City NY 1981).

Hoyle,[121] Athens,[122] Katz,[123] Wright and Decker[124] and a few others, there has been very little description of crime as an embedded transaction unfolding in space and time. At best, there have been a few academic and lay descriptions of the stages of victimisation,[125] on the one hand, and of the stages of criminal acts,[126] on the other, but we lack any unifying *Rashomon*-like analysis of crime in the round, as a process involving people in interaction, constituting themselves and one another, and deploying situated gestures, emergent meanings and changing identities. We have looked a little at strings of parts but not at larger wholes, and analysis is dismembered as a result, a collection of discrete monologues rather than of conversations.

Secondly, we need to describe the materials with which victimisation is construed in everyday life. When and how do people come to take it that they have been a *victim* of an act identified as a *crime*, and what is meant when they say that that is what has happened? What is victimisation supposed to be when it is invoked, and when is it considered to be a problem; what is the significance of being a victim (as opposed to being the occupant of some other or no well-defined role at all); how are identities distinguished, selected and enacted as, say, angry, campaigning, chastened, fearful, self-reproachful, cynical, nonchalant or resigned victims; how do those selves interplay with the wider biography of the victim and with retrospective and prospective readings of his or her identity; how much are they stereotyped and how much the result of reflective consideration and remodelling by the victim himself or herself; how are they shaped by readings of the offender and his or her motives and, reciprocally, of the offender's readings of the victim's behaviour; how do they sit with beliefs about fate and agency in human affairs; what practical, existential and moral consequences flow from the acquisition of victim selves; what parts do others play in formulating those interpretations; when and how would a victim seek their support, take action or call upon outsiders, amongst them the police; and when, most importantly, is victimisation an enduring signifier? In short, when and with what consequences does a person understand himself or herself to have *become* some existential entity called a victim?

---

[121] C Hoyle, *Negotiating Domestic Violence: Police, Criminal Justice, and Victims* (Clarendon Press, Oxford, 1998).

[122] L Athens, *Violent Criminal Acts and Actors Revisited* (University of Illinois Press, Urbana Ill, 1997).

[123] J Katz, *Seductions of Crime* (Basic Books, New York NY, 1988).

[124] Wright and Decker, *Armed Robbers in Action*, n 110 above.

[125] See, for example, J Shapland, J Willmore and P Duff, *Victims in the Criminal Justice System* (Gower, Aldershot, 1985); P Rock, *After Homicide: Practical and Political Responses to Bereavement* (Clarendon Press, Oxford, 1998).

[126] Rational choice theorists like Cornish and Clarke are beginning to deconstruct ideal-typical crimes—and particularly organised crime—as scripts or patterned performances. See, for example, RV Clarke, 'Situational Crime Prevention' in M Tonry and D Farrington (eds), *Building a Safer Society: Strategic Approaches to Crime Prevention*, Crime and Justice: A Review of Research (University of Chicago Press, Chicago Ill, 1995) Vol 19, 91–150.

Bittner argued that the police are summoned typically not to deal with precisely classified crimes but with loosely defined problems and troubles that are held to be beyond the immediate competence of people on the social scene.[127] Any initial common-sense understanding of victimisation and victim identity may be similarly nebulous, and interpretative work must sometimes be done to fix their character. Such work would presumably be shaped by everyday moralities of troubles, problems, disputes and dispute-resolution that point to how, when and by whom conflicts between people are deemed to be consequential or inconsequential, criminal or non-criminal, fair or unfair, provoked or unprovoked, avoidable or inevitable; soluble or insoluble; entailing proper chastisement or improper aggression?[128] 'Identical' acts of violence may be deemed to be no more than fun or rumbustiousness, but they may also be construed as bullying—a non-actionable but undesirable attack, or as an intolerably disturbing assault on the body and spirit that demands a response by the State. Crime is quite clearly context-dependant: Mike Hough, co-author of the early British Crime Surveys, was wont to talk about what he called the 'education effect', the markedly greater propensity of middle-class than working-class men to report offences against the person. Out of the responses to those questions, it may be assumed, will arise the situated actions and identities of the protagonists embroiled in crime.[129]

Lamb,[130] Lerner[131] and Sasson[132] have made a beginning, but there is still more to learn about how lives are constituted by what might be called vernacular narratives of crime. Wachs explored crime victim stories as one of the themes in the urban folklore of New York City, and she focused on frightening encounters, preventive measures, lucky escapes and dangerous places.[133] Such a folklore may be supposed to condense a common-sense etiquette of prudent behaviour in the metropolis, but she did not probe how, where and by whom those stories were told, and how and to what extent they affected conduct and the presentation of self. What seems to be required, in the words of Girling, Loader and Sparks, is a more sophisticated understanding of the meanings-in-use of crime, of the:

---

[127] E Bittner, *The Functions of the Police in Modern Society* (National Institute of Mental Health, Chevy Chase MD, 1970).

[128] We do know that some victims of violence tend to think that their assaults are purposive, meaningful and planned, whilst the perpetrators tend to dismiss the act as unplanned, spontaneous and lacking in significance. See R Baumeister, A Stillwell and SR Wotman, 'Victim and Perpetrator Accounts of Interpersonal Violence' (1990) 59(5) *Journal of Personality and Social Psychology* 994.

[129] Sally Merry made an interesting beginning in *Urban Danger* (Temple University Press, Philadelphia Penn, 1981).

[130] S Lamb, *The Trouble with Blame: Victims, Perpetrators and Responsibility* (Harvard University Press, Cambridge Mass, 1996).

[131] M Lerner, *The Belief in a Just World* (Plenum Press, New York, 1980).

[132] T Sasson, *Crime Talk: How Citizens Construct a Social Problem* (Aldine de Gruyter, New York NY, 1995).

[133] E Wachs, *Crime-Victim Stories: New York City's Urban Folklore* (Indiana University Press, Bloomington Ind, 1988).

nuance, detail and variety of things *that people may be saying when they speak about crime* and . . . the particularities of the contexts in which they are said.[134]

Girling and her colleagues did not themselves talk about the experience and construction of *victim* identity unless, perhaps, it was obliquely and inferentially. Their principal concern was with the spatially embedded character of the fear of crime, but, appropriately modified, their analysis could lead to an examination of forms of victim talk that are bound by the exigencies of space, time, relations, purposes, risk and, in Sparks's words, 'metaphors and narratives about social change'.[135]

The need for that examination would apply *a fortiori* to heavily-victimised populations. Something is known of their demographics and geography. They tend to be those at the margins of groups and the feet of hierarchies: the young, male, members of minority-ethnic groups,[136] offenders, squatters, single adults,[137] the geographically mobile,[138] the homeless and the residents of inner city and satellite estates. Hazel Genn offered a tantalising glimpse of the chaotic lifestyles and kaleidoscopic identities of one such group who were at once victims and victimisers.[139] There have been ethnographies of high crime areas which map the contingent and local character of permissible and impermissible criminal behaviour with its suitable and unsuitable victims,[140] but they do not dwell overmuch on how victims constitute *themselves* in such places. There is Pat Carlen's[141] and John Hagan's and Bill McCarthy's[142] more diffusely criminological work on young street people, and that does touch lightly on victimisation. But there are few other examples of research in the area. Victims and offenders overlap in such groups, but criminologists know only too little about how patterns, moralities and narratives of offending and victimisation intertwine and co-exist. What, for example, are the vocabularies of motive which permit one to victimise others but never the less condemn (if one does condemn) one's own victimisation or the victimisation of others close to one?[143] Other questions would centre on how and in what

---

[134] E Girling, I Loader and R Sparks, *Crime and Social Change in Middle England* (Routledge, London, 2000) 2 (emphasis in original).

[135] R Sparks, 'Reason and Unreason in Left Realism: Some Problems in the Constitution of the Fear of Crime' in R Matthews and J Young (eds), *Issues in Realist Criminology* (Sage, London, 1992) 131.

[136] See P Mayhew, D Elliot and L Dowds, *The 1988 British Crime Survey* (HMSO, London, 1989).

[137] See R Sampson, 'Personal Violence by Strangers' (1987) 78 *Journal of Criminal Law and Criminology* 327.

[138] See J Short, *Poverty, Ethnicity and Violent Crime* (Westview Press, Boulder Col, 1997).

[139] H Genn, 'Multiple Victimization' in M Maguire and J Pointing (eds), *Victims of Crime: A New Deal?* (Open University Press, Milton Keynes, 1988).

[140] See, for example, E Anderson, *Streetwise* (University of Chicago Press, Chicago Ill, 1990) and J Foster, *Villains* (Routledge, London, 1990).

[141] P Carlen, *Jigsaw* (Open University Press, Buckingham, 1996).

[142] J Hagan and B McCarthy, *Mean Streets* (Cambridge University Press, Cambridge, 1998).

[143] They might well rest on the cynical metaphor of a feral world in which everyone preys on everyone else, in which the only moral imperative is not to be caught and not to be a sucker. See T Parker, *The Courage of His Convictions* (Hutchinson, London, 1962).

manner members of such groups can have become so disproportionately exposed to victimisation; how variegated are their experiences; how they move in and out of vulnerable situations and what their careers as victims might be;[144] whether and how, indeed, they define themselves as victims; what, if any, defensive strategies they adopt; how they mobilise informal controls; and what, if any, recourse they make to formal agencies such as the police.

CONCLUSION

This catalogue of unanswered questions could have been extended but it may now have achieved its object of underscoring how little exploration there has been of some of the principal actors and activities in criminal processes. If appreciating deviants was one of the big criminological projects of the 1960s, and appreciating control agents a project of the 1970s, it is now timely to enhance an appreciation of victims. Just as the constitutive analysis of crime and control led to a more sophisticated grasp of how deviance has emergent properties that fuse the act and actor with the responses they evoke, just as it came to be realised that an analysis of the one cannot be undertaken apart from that of the other, so a bolder phenomenology of the victim would not only revive a somewhat marginal figure but also inject another dialectical strand into the criminology of offences, offenders and control. Only then would we be able more completely to decipher much crime as a conversation of significant gestures in which victims and offenders construct themselves, the offence and one other in the unfolding stages of the act. Only then, too, would we move away from the misleading polar oppositions of the politicians who cast victims as the invariably affronted 'Us' and criminals as the alien 'Other' who are locked into a state of warfare.[145]

Such a shift would open up a space within which more progressive criminal justice policies might flourish. There might be, for example, a greater readiness to move towards restorative justice if the estranging moral contrasts of the adversarial system were diminished.[146] And crime reduction might become more effective if the charge of 'victim-blaming' were no longer so routinely levelled at attempts at what some have infelicitously called 'responsibilisation', the greater involvement of people in their own protection.

---

[144] Racial assault and domestic violence, for instance, are not discrete events but take some of their meaning and effect from their character as an interlocking sequence of acts taking place over time. See B Bowling, *Violent Racism: Victimisation, Policing and Social Context* (Clarendon Press, Oxford, 1998).
[145] See Young, *The Exclusive Society,* n 18 above, and the chapter by Andrew Sanders in this volume.
[146] On these contrasts see further the chapter by Jo Winter in this volume.

2

Male Victims of Rape: Responses to a Perceived Threat to Masculinity

STEPHANIE ALLEN*

INTRODUCTION

R ECENT YEARS HAVE witnessed a revival of interest in victims of
crime. Indeed, the past 30 years have seen a burgeoning of victim studies
and of services for victims.[1] A great deal is now known about the effects
of crime on victims, the needs that may arise from victimisation and the reaction
of various agencies to those needs. Yet, in spite of these developments, virtually no
attention has been paid to male victims, particularly adults experiencing sexual
assault.

This chapter attempts to enrich our understanding of the nature of rape against
men and the consequences it has for victims by presenting a typology based on in-
depth interviews with 50 male victims. In particular, it illuminates how men
define and understand their experiences of sexual victimisation and the pivotal
role of masculinity in this process. The chapter has five main sections:

— section one provides a brief summary of the current research literature on
  male rape and highlights the theoretical and methodological limitations of
  existing studies;
— section two briefly describes the challenges of generating a sample of men
  who have been raped and how these were overcome;
— section three explores how the men in this sample came to view their
  experiences as rape;

* It would have been impossible to undertake research of this kind without the co-operation of the
victims themselves who talked openly about their most intimate and traumatic experiences. Their
courage to tell the truth was not only a source of inspiration, but was fundamental to my understanding of male rape. I hope that I have not let them down. I also owe a particular debt of gratitude to my
DPhil supervisor, Professor Roger Hood. Male rape is not a light subject and our endless conversations
about the subject matter helped me to refine my ideas and strengthen the quality of the analysis.
[1] For a review of the vast literature in this area see L Zedner, 'Victims' in M Maguire, R Morgan and
R Reiner (eds), *The Oxford Handbook of Criminology*, 3rd edn (Clarendon Press, Oxford, forthcoming
2002).

— section four presents a typology of male rape based on the descriptions victims gave of their assaults; and

— section five discusses the theoretical implications of the findings.

THEORETICAL AND METHODOLOGICAL LIMITATIONS OF EXISTING STUDIES

Rape has been a major concern of the feminist movement since its revival in the late 1960s.[2] Feminists refuted the long-held belief that rapists were pathological men helplessly controlled by an overwhelming sexual impulse.[3] They redefined rape from the victim's perspective, arguing that it was primarily an act of violence, rather than merely involving the pursuit of sexual gratification.[4]

Although rape has been interpreted by feminists in a variety of different ways— in terms of patriarchal power and authority,[5] sexual access and conflict,[6] and male ownership of female 'property'[7]—there is a common thread in the various interpretations; that rape is just another aspect of male and female relations and so reflects the conventional pattern of male control and female subordination. This focus on inter-gender relations led to an unprecedented criminological interest in women's experiences of sexual violence,[8] while male victims of rape were ignored.

Research on men's experiences of sexual assault has developed largely outside of the academe and has become the preserve of practitioners such as counsellors, psychiatrists and staff in sexual health clinics. This has resulted in a number of

---

[2] The feminist movement which developed in the 1960s is often referred to as 'second wave feminism' to distinguish it from earlier feminist movements in the Britain and the United States in the late nineteenth and early twentieth century. The earlier feminists did not concern themselves, explicitly at least, with sexual violence and abuse but many of the issues on which they campaigned, notably the status of married women and electoral reform, were closely related to the concerns that would occupy their successors almost a century later. See ML Shanley, *Feminism, Marriage and the Law in Victorian England* (Princeton University Press, Princeton NJ, 1989) and D Rhode, *Justice and Gender: Sex Discrimination and the Law* (Harvard University Press, London, 1989).

[3] During the twentieth century, the writings of Sigmund Freud and other psychologists spurred an interest in understanding the causes of sexual aggression. Many hypotheses were developed, but most theories rested on the belief that rape was a perversion and that rapists were mentally ill (see M Amir, *Patterns in Forcible Rape* (University of Chicago Press, Chicago Ill, 1971)). The focus was on understanding the plight of the rapist and the act of rape was simply a by-product of individual pathology.

[4] See L Kelly, *Surviving Sexual Violence* (Polity Press, Cambridge, 1988) for a review of the literature.

[5] See S Brownmiller, *Against Our Will: Men, Women and Rape* (Penguin, London, 1975). Brownmiller has been criticised for failing to take account of historical and cultural variations in gender relations and male dominance. For a full discussion see PR Sanday, 'The Socio-Cultural Context of Rape: A Cross Cultural Study' (1981) 37 *Journal of Social Issues* 5–27.

[6] GD LaFree, 'The Effect of Sexual Stratification by Race on Official Reactions to Rape' (1980) 45 *American Sociological Review* 842–54.

[7] L Clark and D Lewis, *Rape: The Price of Coercive Sexuality* (Women's Press, Toronto, 1977).

[8] I am not suggesting here that we now know all we need to about female victims, merely that there has been a substantial (and much needed) development of research in this area.

limitations to both the methodological approaches and the theoretical frameworks used to explore the phenomenon.

First, the existing research concentrates on describing the symptomatic response of victims to their experiences of sexual violence. Thus, it focuses on changes observed in the behaviour of victims but does not seek to explain the cause of those changes. Moreover, this information has often been gleaned from either the retrospective examination of clinical case records of men attending medical or support services,[9] or the results of postal questionnaires.[10] The rare exceptions are a study by Mezey and King, who interviewed eight victims to verify and expand information already gained by a questionnaire,[11] and a later study by Hickson *et al*[12] which consisted of face-to-face interviews with 46 men recruited through advertisements placed in local and national newspapers and sexual health clinics.

Clinical case records are of limited value as a basis for understanding the nature of male rape because the information recorded within them is highly selective. Both the purpose of the record and the accuracy of the record-keeper affect the type and quality of information that can be gathered from this source. In addition, men recruited from clinical populations over-represent those severely traumatised by their experiences and there is a danger that the conclusions drawn from such samples will erroneously be assumed to hold true for all cases. More importantly, it is likely that men who managed to cope with their experiences without seeking psychiatric or clinical assistance represent a different type of population; one which could provide valuable information on factors that aid recovery.[13]

There are also potential biases in the findings of postal questionnaires. Most obviously, they are sent only to known victims, which limits the inferences that can be drawn from them. Furthermore, given the paucity of research in this area, it is questionable whether the assumptions used to inform the content of a structured questionnaire can accurately reflect the whole range of experiences of men who have been raped. Moreover, postal questionnaires are unlikely to be

[9] For examples, see RJ Hillman, N O'Mara, D Taylor-Robinson, and JRW Harris, 'Medical and Social Aspects of Sexual Assault of Males: A Survey of 100 Victims' (1990) 40 *British Journal of General Practice* 502–03; HB Lacey and R Roberts, 'Sexual Assault on Men' (1991) 2(4) *International Journal of STD and AIDS* 258–60; and PL Huckle, 'Male Victims of Rape Referred to a Forensic Psychiatric Service' (1995) 35(3) *Medicine, Science and the Law* 187–92.

[10] For examples see S Lees, *Ruling Passions: Sexual Violence, Reputation and the Law* (Oxford University Press, Oxford, 1997) and FCI Hickson, PM Davies, AJ Hunt, P Weatherburn, TJ McManus and APM Coxon, 'Gay Men as Victims of Non-consensual Sex' (1994) 23 *Archives of Sexual Behaviour* 281–94.

[11] GC Mezey and MB King 'The Effects of Sexual Assault on Men: A Survey of 22 Victims' (1989) 19 *Psychological Medicine* 205–09.

[12] FCI Hickson, L Henderson and P Davies, *Patterns of Sexual Violence Among Men* (Unpublished summary research report, 1997).

[13] For studies of men who were receiving treatment see N Groth and W Burgess 'Male Rape: Offenders and Victims' (1980) 137 *American Journal of Psychiatry* 576–79; PF Goyer and HC Eddleman, 'Same Sex Rape of Non-incarcerated Men' (1984) 141(4) *American Journal of Psychiatry* 578–79 and MF Myers, 'Men Sexually Assaulted as Adults and Sexually Abused as Boys' (1989) 18 *Archives of Sexual Behaviour* 203–15.

completed by the less literate and will not reach those who frequently change their address or who are of no fixed abode. It is clear that a substantial number of men are excluded from existing studies and that the techniques which have been used in the past to gather information on this subject are unsuitable for capturing an accurate portrayal of men's diverse experiences of sexual violence and its consequences.

Secondly, the literature is characterised by a wide range of definitions of the act of rape. It is only relatively recently that forced anal penetration has been incorporated into the rape legislation of Britain, enabling the official, legal recognition of an offence of male rape. The Criminal Justice and Public Order Act 1994, which came into force in January 1995, widened the definition of rape to include non-consensual penetration of the anus by a penis.[14] In the absence of a legal definition, prior to that date, researchers used the term 'rape' to describe a variety of different behaviours, including those where no penetration of the anus had taken place. Furthermore, the literature does not always distinguish between men who were raped as boys and those raped as adults, despite the fact that studies on the impact of sexual victimisation suggest that the response of a child is likely to be different from that of an adult.[15]

In addition to these limitations, there is the problem that much of the research in this area has been concerned with the experiences of men in the United States of America. A major difficulty when comparing the findings of studies of rape victims carried out in different jurisdictions is that the definitions of rape used may differ. For example, in the USA, rape is defined in broad terms; as the non-consensual penetration of the vagina or anus, by penis, hand or other object. The existing literature also fails to acknowledge and explore the impact of cultural differences, despite the fact that the social environment of the victim has proven to be an important factor in determining their response to rape.[16]

In spite of these limitations, a number of common themes have emerged from the existing research: notably, that the psychological impact of rape derives from the victim's interpretation of the event, not simply from the specific features of the assault itself,[17] and that the consequences of victimisation may undermine the victim's view of himself as a man.[18]

That men understand their experiences of, and responses to, rape in relation to 'being a man' is not surprising, since much of the feminist literature on female victims of rape has highlighted the importance of understanding the experience of

---

[14] Prior to this change in the law, the forced anal penetration of a man was considered to be non-consensual buggery and carried a lesser penalty than rape.

[15] See, for example, K Etherington, *Adult Male Survivors of Childhood Sexual Abuse* (Pennant, Brighton, 1995)

[16] For a critical discussion see Sanday, 'The Socio-Cultural Context of Rape', n 5 above.

[17] See, for example, FCI Hickson *et al, Patterns of Sexual Violence Among Men*, n 12 above.

[18] For example, Myers noted that all the men in his study sustained damage to their subjective sense of maleness as a consequence of the assault, and that a significant number of them equated tarnished

women in a gendered context.[19] However, whilst this is recognised in the existing studies, a number of important questions remain unanswered. There has been no real attempt to tease out:

(1)   why men feel that sexual victimisation undermines their masculine identity;
(2)   in what circumstances this occurs;
(3)   what implications this has for their reactions to rape; and
(4)   whether all male rape victims react in the same way.

To get to the heart of these questions it was vital to explore the meanings that men attached to their experiences of sexual violence when they tried to make sense of what had happened to them.

GENERATING A SAMPLE

The aim of this research was to explore the circumstances of male rape and to understand the impact of this experience on men's lives. To address these aims, it was necessary to assemble a sample of men who had been raped in different circumstances and had reacted in a variety of ways. However, given that male victims of rape are a largely hidden population, the sample selection was constrained by the impossibility of generating a random or representative group. A different approach was needed.

The sample selection strategy was informed by the literature on female rape victims. Harvey suggests that the biographical characteristics of the individual who has been victimised and the circumstances of the assault influence how women respond.[20] Based on the hypothesis that the same variables would be significant in shaping the reactions of male victims, it was important to find good 'exemplars'—men who could provide detailed testimonies which would allow the experience of male rape to be viewed from a variety of angles.[21]

To achieve this, I sought particularly to find men who were 'biographically diverse'—heterosexual, homosexual and bi-sexual men, men with varying histories of previous sexual assault and men from a variety of social groups. It was also important to interview men who had reacted to their rape in different ways so that the factors that shape such reactions could be explored. Consequently, men who had sought help in the aftermath of rape—such as those who reported the matter to the police, or who attended sexual health services or counselling and psychiatric

---

masculinity with loss of power, control, identity, selfhood, confidence, and independence: Myers, 'Men Sexually Assaulted as Adults', n 13 above.

[19]   See D Morgan, *Discovering Men* (Routledge, London, 1992).

[20]   See M Harvey, *An Ecological View of Psychological Trauma and Recovery from Trauma* (Harvard University Press, Cambridge Mass, 1990).

[21]   See R Hood and K Joyce, 'Three Generations: Oral Testimonies on Crime and Social Change in London's East End' (1999) 39 *British Journal of Criminology* 136–60, 139.

support services[22]—were recruited, as well as those who had not. By targeting men who had not sought professional help the sample generated was considerably wider than those used by the majority of existing studies in this area.

The techniques used to encourage eligible men to participate in the research ranged from advertising the project in magazines to making direct contact by telephone or letter with known victims whose names and addresses were supplied by the police.[23] Recruitment sites also included a sexual health clinic and a variety of support services available to victims in the aftermath of rape. In using multiple methods, I hoped to offset the weaknesses of certain research techniques with the strength of others.

Research on female rape and other forms of victimisation indicates that the way in which a person responds changes over time.[24] It was necessary, therefore, to include in the sample men who had been raped a number of years previously as well as men for whom the experience was a more recent one.

There are problems involved in interpreting and comparing accounts of rape from different time periods. Some of the men were being asked to recall events that happened many years before, while others were recounting experiences from the previous few weeks. People forget things, and their memories play tricks by 'telescoping' events together or changing their order. We also know that the memory is selective—that it is shaped by conscious and unconscious suppression, and by reinterpretation.[25] The accounts given by these men were, necessarily, subjective; reconstructions of an event and only one side of the story. However, even if all of the men had been asked immediately after the rapes to explain what had happened to them, their accounts would still have comprised their own interpretations of those events. As such, accounts of rape given some time after the

---

[22] However, it is important to be alert to the possibility that a number of men who had received therapeutic intervention may view their experiences of rape through a 'therapeutic filter.'

[23] The issue of informed consent was handled by providing men who expressed an interest in this piece of research with information on the aims of the study, the focus and length of the interview, how they might feel after the interview, and what would happen to any information they gave. Victims were asked to telephone me a minimum of 24 hours after the initial enquiry had been made if they were still interested in taking part in the research. Not only did this provide an adequate 'cooling off period', it also ensured that victims were able to reach their decisions without feeling pressurised and it eliminated the risk that I would, by re-contacting them, inadvertently compromise the victims' relationships with members of their household or workplace who had not been told about the rape. In addition an insurance policy arranged by Oxford University enabled victims who were re-traumatised as a result of the interview to claim payment for any necessary counselling and support, though none chose to do so.

[24] There is a plethora of studies concerned with the response phases of female victims of rape. See, for example, AW Burgess and LL Holstrom, 'Rape Trauma Syndrome' (1979) 131 *American Journal of Psychiatry* 981–86, who first coined the phrase 'the rape trauma syndrome', referring to two stages of emotional recovery. More recently PA Reswick, 'The Trauma of Rape and the Criminal Justice System' (1984) 9(1) *The Justice System Journal* 52–61, has suggested a model not based on 'stages of recovery' but rather 'patterns of effects.'

[25] See PB Ainsworth and K Pease, *Police Work* (British Psychological Society, Leicester, 1987) 38–51.

occurrence are as valid a subject of analysis as those recounted immediately.[26] The purpose of the research was not to determine the accuracy of the descriptions that the men gave about their experiences of rape, but to explore the meanings they attached to these events.[27] As such, victim testimonies were the most appropriate source of information.

Interviews with raped men took place over ten months between October 1997 and August 1998. The fieldwork produced a total of 50 transcribed interviews providing 'thick descriptions'[28] of the nature of male rape.[29]

DEFINING RAPE

By the time they were interviewed, all of the men in the sample had defined what had happened to them as 'rape'. However, a number of them had only come to think of their experiences as rape some time after the assault had taken place. Although every case was unique, it was possible, nevertheless, to identify some common themes which emerged from the accounts they gave. The differential impact of male rape on heterosexual and homosexual victims, for example, has not been adequately addressed in any previous work. This study provides evidence that the way men define what has happened to them as rape varies most markedly between men of different sexual orientations. Before proceeding, it is worth noting that the sexuality of the victims reported in this research is self-defined. Sexuality is a fluid and multi-dimensional concept which is shaped by ideology, culture, experience and self-perception.[30] While it is important, therefore, to accept victims' own definitions of their sexuality, it is also necessary to bear in

[26] In just under a half of the cases in this study's sample, it was possible to compare the account given by the victim with information obtained from other sources, such as police records and interviews with members of the victim's family and professional support staff. This methodological approach is known as 'data triangulation'. See N Denzin, *The Research Act* (Aldine de Gruyter, Chicago Ill, 1970). It is important to remember that these accounts are not necessarily any more reliable than those given by the victim, and provided only a different interpretation of the same event.

[27] This is not to say, however, that some of the descriptions that the men gave of their assaults appeared less credible than others. In cases where I had serious doubts and was unable to verify the account through some other source, I placed less reliance on this description than others. On the difficulties of understanding how people evaluate and re-evaluate their experiences, over time and in light of new experiences and changing self-perceptions see K Howarth, *Oral History: A Handbook* (Sutton Publishing, Stroud, 1998).

[28] Thick description is achieved by adopting a restricted focus, piling detail on detail to furnish a minute, densely textured, and many layered analysis between actions, situations, and interpretations (see C Geertz, *The Interpretation of Culture: Selected Essays* (Basic Books, New York NY, 1973). 'Thick description succeeds to the extent that it expands the understanding of a strange and alien world': W Sofsky, *The Order of Terror* (Princeton University Press, Princeton NJ, 1997) 14.

[29] Due to space constraints the discussion here presents a sanitised version of the fieldwork undertaken. For example, five interviews were not included in the sample due to problems in the tape-recording process.

[30] See, for example, D Altman, *Homosexual: Oppression and Liberation* (New York University Press, New York NY, 1993).

mind that their experiences of heterosexuality, homosexuality or bi-sexuality might be very different.

Definitions by Heterosexual Men

There were 17 heterosexual men in the sample who had been anally penetrated with a penis and all had defined this experience as rape at the time of the incident. The evaluative process that most seemed to go through, in order to arrive at this definition, was one where they compared the features of the assault with what they understood by the term 'rape' and then judged their experiences to be sufficiently similar to warrant this definition.

Victims' ideas of what events constitute rape are influenced by the attitudes of those in their immediate social network as well as those evident amongst service providers. These ideas and attitudes are themselves shaped by cultural constructions of crime. Reinholtz *et al*[31] state that the dominant culture in western societies sends out powerful messages about rape, sex and violence. They argue that 'real rape' is a narrowly defined set of events which consists of a perverted stranger with a weapon, using physical violence to force a woman to have penile–vaginal intercourse against her will.[32] Although this widespread image of rape fails to acknowledge the possibility of male sexual victimisation, it was nevertheless viewed by the men interviewed for this study as an important yardstick against which to judge their own experiences.

Not surprisingly, the most important feature of the assault which men used to define their experiences as rape was the non-consensual nature of the attack—the fact that the victim had not wanted intercourse with the offender. This definition was reinforced by the 'abnormal' nature of the violence. Since the physical act of anal penetration was different from their usual sexual experiences, heterosexual men perceived it as 'perverse' and this facilitated their early perception of their experiences as rape.[33]

---

[31] RK Reinholtz, CL Muehlenhard, JL Phelps and AT Satterfield, 'Sexual Discourse and Sexual Intercourse: How the Way we Communicate Affects the Way we Think about Sexual Coercion' in PJ Kalbfleisch and MJ Cody (eds), *Gender, Power and Communication in Human Relationships* (Lawrence Erlbaum Associates, Mahwah NJ, 1995).

[32] This image is reflected in official safety advice which concentrates on women as potential victims of crime and in the debate on the fear of crime which is generated around images of vulnerable women who are predominantly at risk of violence by unknown men. It is also interesting to note that crime prevention advice on violence avoidance is non-existent for men despite the fact that they report more physical assaults to the police, and more often seek emergency medical attention for injury than do women: J Shepherd, 'Violent Crime in Bristol: An Accident and Emergency Department Perspective' (1990) 30(3) *British Journal of Criminology* 289–305.

[33] This finding has also been noted in studies of female victims. For example, Raquel Kennedy-Bergen noted that women who had sustained sexual violence from their partners for many years redefined their experiences as rape when they felt that their partners' demands had become abnormal, such as forcing them to have anal sex or penetrating them vaginally with objects such as 'weapons, feathers,

When someone rams their dick up your arse and you don't want them to, I'd say he needs help—cause he's a serious fucking weirdo-bastard—and you've been raped. (Kevin, case 17)

Other aspects of the assault which influenced victims' perceptions included the number of perpetrators and the severity of violence used. For example, Brett (case 8), a young man with learning difficulties, said that he had been befriended then raped by a man called Jordan. The violent nature of the assault, and the resultant injuries, convinced Brett that he had been raped.

I knew that I'd been raped because he didn't stop when I said 'No'; he made my bottom bleed, and he hurt my head.

There is a substantial body of research which suggests that the degree of force used by the rapist is an important factor in determining how female victims label their experiences of sexual violence as rape. In one study it was found that women were more likely to see themselves as victims of rape if they had been choked, tied up, locked up, or otherwise subjected to a high level of violence.[34] Krulewitz and Payne found that members of the general public also tended to label a situation as rape only when there had been 'direct and obvious' use of force by the assailant.[35] It was common for the men in this sample to highlight the degree of violence used when attempting to convince others that they had been raped.

In cases where the victim had been penetrated with an object rather than a penis, defining the assault as 'rape' was not so straightforward. For instance, Edward (case 3) who had been anally penetrated with a toilet brush, initially felt that the violence used against him had been physical, as oppose to sexual. During the interview he tried to explain what prevented him from initially identifying his experience as rape:

I didn't define it as rape initially because, well, I suppose I tried to convince myself that it was more violent than sexual, but, really, deep down, I knew it was more than that. Because, you know, I've been in plenty of fights and I'd never felt like that before. There was no real getting away from it . . . I think at first I did treat it like a physical fight. I convinced myself that having a toilet brush shoved up your arse was no worse than being kicked in the head. But I felt really shit, depressed and tearful and stuff like that.

---

brushes and various types of food' (R Kennedy-Bergen, *Wife Rape—Understanding the Response of Victims and Service Providers* (Sage, Thousand Oaks Cal, 1996) 45).

[34] C Oros, K Leonard and M Koss, 'Factors Related to a Self-attribution of Rape by Victims' (1980) 6(2) *Personality and Social Psychology Bulletin* 193.

[35] J Krulewitz and E Payne, 'Attributions about Rape: Effects of Rapist Force, Observer, and Sex Role Attitudes' (1978) 8(4) *Journal of Applied Social Psychology* 291–305, 301.

Definitions by Homosexual and Bi-sexual Men

Homosexual and bi-sexual men were also more likely to define their experiences as rape if it corresponded to the 'real rape' scenario—in other words, if the assault consisted of an attack by a stranger, carrying a weapon or using physical violence to force the man to have anal intercourse against his will.

Gerard (case 23), a bi-sexual man, who said that he had been raped while taking an evening stroll, gave the following response to the question 'When did you recognise your experience as rape?':

> I recognised it as rape from the beginning. It was not just an unpleasant thing that happened, like a mugging, or consensual sex that somehow went wrong, or something like that. No, I was in no doubt that this was rape. Being a young, bi-sexual man at the time, I had often had sex with men who I had only just met. But this was different; it was so far removed from anything that had ever happened to me that there was no doubt in my mind. For me it just stood out as completely different to anything that had ever happened to me, so there wasn't any question for me [that] it was anything other than rape. It was a classic case—I didn't really know the man, he cornered me in a back alley, he was very violent and then he penetrated me without my consent—so, I saw it as rape from the very beginning.

However, the aspects of Gerard's experience that made it a clear case of 'real rape' were absent, or at least not as readily apparent, for most of the other homosexual or bi-sexual men in the sample. For the majority of homosexual or bi-sexual men, applying the term rape to their experiences of sexual violence was hindered by the fact that they were familiar with the act of anal penetration. Thus, it was not 'abnormal' in the same way as it was for heterosexual men. Consequently it was more difficult for them to distinguish between whether they had been 'forced' or 'persuaded' to have intercourse.[36] As a result, other aspects of the assault were important in their evaluative processes. The degree of intimacy that existed between the victim and perpetrator and the extent of violence used, all were factors which determined the ability and willingness of victims to define their experiences as rape.

In circumstances where the victim knew the perpetrator, victims tended not to initially define their experiences as rape, particularly if the relationship had included consensual sex in the past or if the victim had agreed to some level of sexual intimacy (but not anal penetration) at the time of the assault. Men raped in these circumstances tended to excuse or normalise the violence. This was because what they understood by the term 'rape' did not 'fit' with their experience and they were forced, therefore, to interpret what had happened to them in some other way.

---

[36] It would be interesting to compare the perceptions of women who have been anally raped and the extent to which prior consensual anal penetration affects their ability to define their experiences as rape. I am unaware of any research undertaken in this area.

This type of response fits with the sociological analysis of women's reactions to sexual violence. Kelly argues that 'in order to define something, a word has to exist with which to name it . . . and the name, once known, must be applicable to one's own experience'.[37] Consequently, a vital part of feminist work in the area of sexual violence has been to provide names to describe women's experiences. Over the past 15 years, the terms 'domestic violence', 'sexual harassment', 'marital rape' and 'date rape' have been defined (and indeed have become part of 'everyday' language) partly with the aim of enabling women's disclosure of abuse.

It is only recently that male victims of rape have been publicly acknowledged. Richard's (case 49) testimony about his confusion in the aftermath of one episode in a series of rapes committed against him by his partner in 1968 shows how the absence of a public definition of male rape at the time inhibited his awareness of what had happened to him. He explained:

> I knew it wasn't right, because I felt so awful afterwards, but I didn't know what it was because nobody had heard of male rape in those days.

A social definition not only helps victims to decide what normal sexual behaviour is, but also, as Kelly explains, 'makes it clear that others may share this experience, thereby undermining the isolation of feeling that you are the only one'.[38]

Having a 'name', however, is not enough. Victims must also see the social definition as corresponding to their own experiences of sexual violence. A number of the men raped by their partners said that they were initially hesitant to define their experiences as rape because what they understood by the term 'rape' did not concur with their experiences. Two men said that at the time of the assault they considered 'forced sex' to be a 'normal' part of sexually-active homosexual relationships. As a result, whether or not victims have actively refused consent becomes a critical factor in recognising and labelling their experiences as rape. For example, Tom, (case 38), recalled that his boyfriend often forced him to have sex, but said:

> I didn't see it as rape. I mean, I knew that men could be raped, but it never occurred to me that was happening to me. When I think of rape I think of a stranger attacking me at night, putting a knife to my throat, something like that. John wasn't like that, he was my partner, you know we had a joint bank account, that sort of thing. I didn't think of it as rape for a long time. John had a much higher sex drive than I did and so when he forced me to have sex I thought that it was my fault for, well, not satisfying him.

Lee (case 29) also described the confusion he felt about defining 'normal' homosexual sex when he explained the relationship he had with his partner, Justin:

> He was my first real boyfriend, I had never been with anyone before and I didn't know that what he was doing wasn't normal. Because no-one ever tells you, that's normal and

---

[37] L Kelly, *Surviving Sexual Violence* (Polity Press, Cambridge, 1988) 114.
[38] *Ibid*, 141.

that's not and you're hardly likely to go in to the pub and say, 'my boyfriend forces me to have sex with him,' are you?

The comments by Tom and Lee suggest that some homosexual men consider sex with their partners obligatory, thus making it more difficult for them to draw a line between consensual intercourse and rape. Similar findings have been reported by female victims raped by a partner. For example, in a study of marital rape,[39] the majority of women initially hesitated to apply the term rape to their experiences because they thought that rape happened only between strangers, not between people who loved and cared for each other. Moreover, because vaginal intercourse was seen as a usual feature of heterosexual relationships, the women were often able to normalise the level of violence they experienced by considering sexual intercourse with their husbands, even when accompanied by force, as their 'duty'.

While stereotypical understandings of 'real rape' initially inhibited some of the homosexual men in the sample from naming their experiences as rape, all had redefined their experiences as rape over the course of time. The process of redefinition involved a number of different catalysts, including increasing levels of violence, decreased intimacy, reactions from service providers, or the influence of family and friends.

Homosexual men who were repeatedly raped by their partners were prompted to redefine their experiences as rape when the circumstances surrounding the assaults came to resemble more closely what they considered to be 'real rape'. For example, Tom, (case 38), redefined his experience as rape when he separated from his partner and the violence continued. He explained that he now knew it was rape because:

I wasn't in a relationship with him at that time and I said 'no' and he did it anyway.

Likewise, Louis (case 50) redefined his experience as rape when the assaults reached a level of brutality that he associated with stranger rape. He said,

He'd been out drinking. He came home about midnight. I was getting ready for bed. He came into the bathroom where I was cleaning my teeth and demanded sex. When I said I was tired and that I'd rather go to sleep he went absolutely wild. He grabbed the mirror from above the sink and smashed it over my head and then raped me. This time I knew it was rape because I really thought he was going to kill me.

Service providers were important in helping homosexual men to conceptualise their experiences of sexual violence as rape. For example, Martin, (case 26), told me that the counsellor at the sexual health clinic had been instrumental in helping him to recognise and come to terms with his experience.

She just sat and listened while I went through it in graphic detail over and over again. Eventually I plucked up the courage and asked her if she thought I had been raped and she said to me 'Do you feel like you've been raped?' When I said that I did, she said, 'Well,

---

[39] Kennedy-Bergen, *Wife Rape*, n 33 above, 42.

you've answered your own question then.' She made me feel like I wasn't going crazy. That all the things I was feeling were perfectly normal. As soon as I was able to call it rape, it really helped. It sort of gave me a structure to understand what I had been going through.

In summary, homosexual men generally had more fluid definitions of their experiences of sexual violence, and the processes by which they came to define their experiences as rape were more complicated than for heterosexual men. For both heterosexual and homosexual men, however, social definitions of events constituting 'real rape', and comments made by others, played a crucial role in this assessment.

DEVELOPING A TYPOLOGY OF MALE RAPE

This research presents a typology of male rape based on the descriptions which *victims* gave of their assaults. It is grounded in their interpretations of the event. Having listened to how the men in this sample described their reactions to sexual victimisation it became apparent that the sociological framework which is often used to describe and explain women's reactions to rape fails to accommodate the experiences of men.

Since the mid–1960s feminist researchers[40] have challenged the popular conception of rape as an act occurring only between two strangers and argued that rapists might also be found amongst acquaintances, neighbours, friends, 'dates', relatives and husbands. Consequently, the typologies of rape developed were often based on the nature of the relationship that existed between the victim and the offender, and the influence of that relationship on the impact of the assault. While this approach has highlighted the pervasive and hidden character of sexual violence, it is less helpful in understanding the impact of rape on male victims. For all of the men in this study the most important factor in determining the meaning of the rape was not the nature of the relationship between themselves and the rapist, but rather the method by which they had been raped. This was pivotal because it determined the extent to which the men felt that they had any control over the situation and, therefore, whether or not they felt some responsibility for the rape occurring. In turn, this affected whether or not they perceived the assault as violating their sense of masculine identity.

The literature on the effects of sexual victimisation indicates that rape makes women feel that they have lost their autonomy. For example, Bonnie Katz has

---

[40] I am aware that the short account given in this chapter runs the serious risk of presenting feminist thought as a monolithic phenomenon, as a set of beliefs and demands on which all feminists agree. To convey such an impression would be to conceal the variety of insights, perspectives and conflicts which have emerged from feminist writings and activities during the past 30 years. For a good account of modern feminist thought see N Lacey, 'Modern Feminist Theory' (1989) 9 *Oxford Journal of Legal Studies* 383.

argued that victims of rape should be seen as a special category, because no other crime offers a similarly personal and intimate violation of the self. Moreover, she describes the rape experience as 'involving a total loss of control over one's life, one's body, and the course of events'.[41] Similarly, Keith Burgess-Jackson wrote that 'short of being killed, there is no greater insult to the self'.[42] The men in this sample also described how the assault undermined their sense of autonomy. However, from the accounts they gave, the threat to their autonomy or sense of self, was manifested most acutely in the challenge to their masculine identity.

It appears that while both men and women describe how sexual victimisation undermines their sense of 'autonomy', for men this acts as a direct challenge to the control they exert in the social and sexual arena, and therefore to their identity as men. I would argue that women, by contrast, tend to perceive themselves as having less autonomy over their lives and bodies in everyday life and so the threat to autonomy does not manifest itself as a direct challenge to their sense of femininity. Rather, a woman's sense of femininity may be challenged in the aftermath of rape by feeling 'tainted' and being perceived as 'soiled goods'. The likelihood of women feeling this way has declined as the influence of feminism has grown. It is, after all, in the interests of women to challenge a construction of femininity which emphasises purity and passivity. But it is not in the interests of men to challenge a construction of masculinity which emphasises power and control. Thus, men are more likely than women to experience rape as a threat to their sense of identity, a threat that must somehow be neutralised. This threat was reflected by the ways in which the men in the sample conceptualised what had happened to them.

Four distinct 'strategy types' emerged from the descriptions that men gave of rape; men articulated their experiences in terms of whether they had been 'overpowered', had their wishes 'overridden', were 'intimidated', or were 'entrapped' by the perpetrator.[43]

'Overpower' was the strategy most closely resembling the popular conception of rape and involved the victim being physically overpowered by his assailant(s). The assaults were sudden and took place in secluded public locations in the late evening or the early hours of the morning, making it difficult for victims to summon help. This category included heterosexual and homosexual men raped by strangers, brief acquaintances,[44] or associates.[45]

---

[41] BL Katz, 'The Psychological Impact of Stranger Versus Non-stranger Rape on Victims' Recovery' in A Parrot and L Bechhofer (eds), *Acquaintance Rape: The Hidden Crime* (Wiley, New York NY, 1991) 251–69, 253.

[42] K Burgess-Jackson, *Rape: A Most Detestable Crime: New Philosophical Essays on Rape* (Oxford University Press, Oxford, 1999).

[43] This was, of course, the victim's interpretation of the strategy used and may not have corresponded with the actual strategy used by the perpetrator.

[44] This refers to incidents where the victim had met the perpetrator within 24 hours of the rape occurring.

[45] This refers to incidents where the victim had an established social and non-sexual relationship with the perpetrator but would not describe the rapist as a 'friend'.

'Override', by contrast, described occasions where the victim had been a willing party in sexual intimacy but whose physical or verbal resistance (and lack of consent) to anal intercourse was ignored or 'overridden' by an assailant who threatened or used physical force. What distinguished these incidents from 'real rape' in the minds of these men was that, although they resisted, they did so only after a certain point.

The third type of rape strategy identified by the men in this study was described in terms of 'intimidation'. This occurred in particular situations where the victim had been in a subordinate or vulnerable position to the rapist. The force used in this type of rape was not a weapon or physical violence, but rather the threat of loss of employment or something else of value controlled by the assailant.[46] At the time of the assault, most of the victims felt the consequences of refusing to participate were worse than the consequences of participating.

Finally, the fourth type of rape strategy identified was 'entrapment'. Perpetrators either plied victims with drugs and then took advantage of their vulnerable physical state, or they targeted victims who were mentally vulnerable and exploited this weakness. In either case the victim was rendered incapable of resisting.

In the remainder of this section I attempt to describe and draw out the main features of these 'strategy types' to show the significance of these for victims' understanding of their experiences of rape.

Overpower

The most common experience reported by the men in this sample [n=18] was that they were 'overpowered' by their assailants. In other words, many victims had been subjected to a violent physical assault often involving multiple assailants or weapons. As such, they conceptualised the assault as an 'unfair contest' of masculine skill, which even the most able male could not have resisted. Thus, men who were raped in this manner felt that their inability to protect themselves from victimisation was justified and that the assault did not contradict their masculine self-image.

Christopher (case 9), a 34-year-old homosexual male, was raped by a gang of men behind a parade of shops.

> As I got off the bus I could see through the corner of my eye this group of lads coming round the corner . . . I heard the sound of raucous laughter . . . I turned around and saw the four males that I had seen from the bus . . . the men were all white and I would guess to be in their late twenties. I had walked a matter of a few yards along the pavement when a right arm came around my neck from behind me . . . causing me to fall. Then I heard someone say 'has the poofter got any money?'

[46] Studies of female victims have noted that women similarly perceive their experience of sexual violence as involving their perpetrators trying to assert power and control over them (Kennedy-Bergen, *Wife Rape*, n 33 above, 22).

I could feel a number of pairs of hands searching all my clothing . . . one of the men then said, 'drag the poofter round behind the shops'. I then experienced the most terrible feeling of dread. Words will never be able to describe it.

I was thrown face down on to the floor. I could feel twigs and vegetation on my face as my face was squashed in to the floor . . . one man stood on my shoulders and punched me twice in the head and said, 'shut up queer —you get what you deserve'.

Then I felt these hands come underneath me and someone un-did the zip on my jeans and the button. Then they pulled my jeans and with them my underpants down to my thighs. One of them then said, 'open his legs', and my legs were forced apart. I knew then what was going to happen. I couldn't struggle because I had someone pressing down on my shoulders, a person holding each of my legs. I was petrified beyond belief. My T-shirt was being pushed up and I heard shuffling and what sounded like a buckle and trousers being un-done.

. . . This man shoved his penis in to my anus. The pain was excruciating and I screamed. I pleaded with him to stop and he just said 'shut your fucking mouth—you get what you deserve' . . . the pain was indescribable and he seemed to be raping me for an eternity. I kept pleading with him to stop, which he didn't. Eventually I felt him pull his penis out and then I heard him shout 'I'm coming' and I felt liquid on my lower back and bottom. I knew it must have been his semen although I never actually saw it.

. . . I wanted to die.

In common with other men who described their experiences of rape in terms of being 'overpowered', Christopher emphasised the severe nature of the violence which enabled him to conceptualise the rape as an 'unfair contest', thereby 'neu-tralising' the threat to his masculine identity. He went on to say:

It was so vicious . . . it was an absolute nightmare . . . they didn't have weapons, they didn't need any. I had cracked ribs—I had a fractured jaw. My eyes were black and all cut—they thought that I would need stitches. And because my head was pushed on to gravel the side of my face was all grazed and my nose was broken. This is what I was say-ing earlier to you—there was nothing that I could do—there was nothing any man could have done . . . so no, I never thought that I was less of a man because of it, because there was no way anyone, even someone really hard, like Mike Tyson, would have stood a chance against four blokes.

Override

The second strategy of rape, 'override rape', was experienced by a total of 13 men in this sample. The descriptions that these men gave of the assault were marked by their belief that they had consented to some form of sexual intimacy with the perpetrator, but they had not agreed to anal penetration. All of the men in this group regarded themselves as homosexual, with one exception who defined him-self as heterosexual but was willing to engage in a level of sexual intimacy with another male. The perpetrators were friends,[47] partners,[48] associates and brief acquaintances of their victims. The men were raped in their own homes or the home of the perpetrator.

Women have often been accused of 'crying' rape when what they have experienced is sex with a partner to whom they reluctantly succumbed, or sex which they later regretted. But, consenting to sex, however reluctantly, is conceptually different from being raped and research has shown that rather than being eager to classify themselves as having been raped, women are reluctant to define their experience in this way.[49] The men in this sample who were assaulted by perpetrators with whom they had been sexually intimate were also initially reluctant to define their experiences as rape.

For instance, Lee (case 29), a 17-year-old student, recruited through the sexual health clinic, was raped by his boyfriend Justin. He explains:

> I was raped four weeks ago. I'm gay. I'd just started seeing Justin. We'd probably been seeing each other for about a month . . . He was my first real boyfriend . . . I was having a great night. After the club we went to get a cab home. While we were waiting in the taxi queue Justin suggested that we go back to his place . . . I said yes knowing that it would probably mean that we would end up in bed together. I'd never had sex before and I was nervous but also dead excited.
>
> . . . Eventually we started having a bit of a grope and so Justin suggested that we go into the bedroom. He took off his clothes and then undressed me. I was really aroused. He kissed me all over my body really gently and I just thought that I was going to explode all over him. I was so horny. Then we lay on the bed and stroked each other for about an hour. Eventually he lifted my legs up and started to penetrate me. I just don't know what happened. I must have panicked but I knew that I definitely didn't want this to happen. All of a sudden what we were about to do completely repulsed me and I was terrified.
>
> I said to Justin 'No, hold on a minute, stop'. He tried to reassure me . . . I kept saying, 'no, stop, please stop', but he didn't he carried on. From being really gentle as he increased his rhythm his strokes became harder and more painful. He seemed completely oblivious to what I was saying. It ended when he had an orgasm. By this stage I was crying. I had tears

[47] That is, where the victim had an established social and non-sexual relationship with the perpetrator and would describe the rapist as a 'friend'.

[48] That is, where the victim was in an existing long-term sexual relationship with the perpetrator.

[49] In Britain there has been very little research on rape in non-stranger relationships. In 1991 Painter undertook a study of marital rape for a television documentary. Among a representative sample of 1,007 women in 11 different cities in the UK, she found that one in seven married women said that they had been coerced into sex by their partner which had had a very detrimental effect on their marriages. Studies such as this have concluded that it is far more common for women not to recognise being coerced into sex as rape than to 'cry rape' when dissatisfied with sex. There was no evidence in these studies that women confused the experience of 'bad' sex with rape. Great care was taken in Painter's study to differentiate when women did not really feel like sex and when they clearly refused consent and were raped with violence threatened or used. Women distinguished quite clearly those times when they had sex when disinclined (when tired, uninterested and unwell) from those situations where they had been coerced. On the basis of this, Painter concluded that women are not prone to 'cry rape': see K Painter, *Wife Rape, Marriage and the Law* (University of Manchester Press, Manchester, 1991).

rolling down my face and my shouts had been reduced to whispers of 'no, no, please stop'.

Men, like Lee, who were in sexually intimate relationships with their perpetrators at the time of the assault were reluctant to call their experiences rape and chose instead to view what happened to them as a 'miscommunication'. They chose to believe their partner had not regarded their protests as intended seriously and/or that they should have offered more physical resistance to convince them that they did not wish to proceed with anal intercourse. Conceptualised in this way, victims were able to reassure themselves that the perpetrator had not intended them any harm and, had they been more assertive in the expression of their wishes, the rape would not have occurred. Similarly, in their study of female victims of rape, Weis and Borges found that in circumstances where the rapist was known to the victim, 'her emotional investment in the person . . . will make any definition, other than rape, more plausible and acceptable to her'.[50]

By perceiving that the rape had occurred as a result of 'miscommunication', victims blamed themselves for failing to express more forcefully their desire not to engage in anal intercourse. In a study of date rape between heterosexual couples, Lois Pineau found that women who were forced to have sex with their 'dates' despite making it emphatically clear that they did not want to participate, also held themselves responsible for failing 'vigorously' to inform the perpetrator of their wishes.[51] Furthermore, when 6,000 students, at 32 colleges across the USA, were asked 'have you ever had sexual intercourse with a man when you didn't want to because he used some degree of force such as twisting your arm or holding you down to make you co-operate?', 49 per cent of those who replied 'yes' explained that this was a result of 'miscommunication'.[52]

As discussed above, over the course of time men who felt that their wishes had been 'overridden' re-interpreted their experiences as rape. Lee (case 29) explained:

> Technically you could say that I was raped but it's not as clean cut as that. I'm sure that Justin would be horrified if I said that he had raped me . . . I don't think that Justin was a hundred per cent responsible for what happened. I think it was far more murky than that . . . Yes, I think that this was rape, because I definitely said '*no!*' time and time again throughout the rape. But it wasn't rape like you read about in the newspapers. It was in the context of a relationship where people have feelings for each other. I'm sure that he didn't purposefully want to hurt me. I think it was a bit of a mistake and that because it was my first time, I didn't recognise it as rape straight away and stop him from continuing, so I have to accept some blame.

---

[50] K Weis and SS Borges, 'Victimology and Rape: The Case of the Legitimate Victim' (1973) 8 *Issues in Criminology* 71–115, 83.
[51] L Pineau, 'Date Rape: A Feminist Analysis' in L Francis (ed), *Date Rape: Feminism, Philosophy and the Law* (Pennsylvania State University Press, University Park Penn, 1996) 1–26.
[52] R Warshaw, *I Never Called it Rape: The Ms Report on Recognising, Fighting and Surviving Date and Acquaintance Rape* (Harper and Row, New York NY, 1988).

This group of men had complex feelings of self-blame. Although they held themselves responsible for 'leading the perpetrator on', or entering what they knew was a 'high risk' situation without taking precautions, this did not diminish how culpable they thought the perpetrator was for the violence. Where the violence used by the perpetrator was excessive, the victim felt that they could not be held responsible for failing to counter the assault (in much the same way as men who described their experiences in terms of being overpowered).

In situations where the victim had an established relationship with the perpetrator, where no additional violence was used, they did not perceive the assault as a 'masculine confrontation' in which they were threatened. Instead, they preferred to describe their experiences as an 'unpleasant miscommunication', which could have been avoided. Consequently, homosexual men raped by brief acquaintances or partners did not feel as though their masculine identities were threatened as a result of the assault. For example, Lee (case 29) went on to say:

> No, it didn't make me feel any less of a man because, at the time, I wasn't sure what was happening to me. I didn't see it as a fight, or something that I had to win to prove myself. It just wasn't like that because it was only later that I recognised that I had been raped and if I found myself in a similar situation today I know I would do something about it.

Intimidation

The third strategy of rape, 'intimidation', was experienced by eleven men in the sample, who were in a subordinate or vulnerable position in relation to the rapist. The force used in this type of rape was not a weapon or physical violence but rather the threat of loss of employment or something else of value controlled by the assailant. This group contained men who were heterosexual, homosexual, bisexual, and those unsure of their sexuality. The perpetrators were colleagues, friends, relatives, associates, authority figures and brief acquaintances to the victim. The assaults took place in both semi-public and private locations.

Men who understood their experiences of rape in terms of 'intimidation', held themselves responsible for the rape occurring and felt that their masculine identities were threatened by the experience. This was due to the lack of physical violence to which the victims were subjected and their lack of resistance to the assault. As a result, they perceived the confrontation as a 'fair' contest with another male, but one in which they made no effort to avoid or resist. In the absence of physical force, men raped by intimidation found it difficult to explain their passive submission and only later came to realise that they had been subjected to a level of psychological coercion which had made it difficult for them to challenge the perpetrator.

In situations of confrontation men in western society are expected to remain in control and fight back. Displaying this behaviour to avoid rape therefore becomes an important yardstick upon which the raped man measures his self worth. The absence of these highly valued behavioural traits poses a direct challenge to the masculine identity of the victim.

This finding is reinforced by the experience of George, (case 5) a married man, who was raped by a lorry driver. He made no attempt to resist the assault and, as a result, felt ashamed and angered by his behaviour. Here he describes his experience:

> If you ask any warehouse manager they will all tell you that you can get little bits and pieces of cheap gear from the lorry drivers . . . it was coming up to Christmas and everyone was asking the drivers what they could get. I decided to get something nice for Sue [his wife]
>
> It happened on 22 December. I was working the night warehouse shift. It was about three in the morning when he arrived. I didn't want the other lads to see what I was doing . . . Ron gave me the nod as he pulled in to the forecourt. I jumped into the cab with him and we drove round the corner to a secluded loading bay. Once we'd parked up we got out and Ron told me that the video was in the back of the truck. He asked me to give him a hand.
>
> Once we were in, he shut the side door and said something like 'we don't want any of the others to see, do we boss?' . . . As I bent back down to pick up the video, Ron grabbed me from behind. He put one arm around my waist and pulled my pants and trousers down with the other. It was no problem for him to pull down my trousers because they have an elasticated waist and are standard issue for the warehouse. I then heard him unzip his jeans. He forced his dick in to my arse. He pumped for about five or six times before spurting. That was it, it was all over in about a minute. He didn't get his dick all the way up because I was clenching my arse and he wasn't pumping that hard. But I did feel his tip inside me.
>
> Ron said nothing. Immediately afterwards he said something like 'Oh, I needed that, thanks boss'. He then did his jeans back up as if nothing had happened at all. During the rape I did nothing whatsoever to protect myself except to clench my arse. It was such a shock when he pulled down my trousers and it was over so quickly that I did absolutely nothing. I didn't even think about whether or not I could fight him off, or escape, or anything like that. When he released his arm from around my waist I pulled my pants and trousers up. We then carried on as if nothing had happened. He moved some of the boxes out of my way so that I could get to the side door and undid the lock. Once we were outside he shook my hand and said something like 'Nice doing business with you boss. I hope she likes it. See you again in the New Year' and got back in to his cab and drove off.

George blamed himself for not resisting the assault and felt his identity as a man had been undermined by his lack of resistance during the assault.

> I think that the biggest thing I've got to cope with is that I cannot forgive myself for letting it happen. I felt so intimidated when it happened that I did nothing. I was scared that everyone would find out that I had ordered a video and that I would lose my job. Looking back, losing my job would have been a small price to pay to have stopped him. I also didn't really know what to do. I know that sounds daft, but I didn't feel that I could say anything because this man had done me a favour. I felt that I owed him something

if you see what I mean. It was like he had a right to rape me. Now, I feel like I was a disgrace. Just letting it happen like that. What sort of man lets that happen to them and does bugger all to stop it?

The experience of rape for this group of men encompassed more than the physical act of forced penetration, it was also a symbolic challenge to their self-identity as a man. As George went on to say:

I like to think that I don't have a prescribed view of how a man should behave. But, during the rape I did have a very strong sense of what a 'man' should do in this situation. I don't know where this comes from. It must start in the family, then I suppose it's reinforced in the workplace and through friends . . . but, I certainly knew what was 'expected' of me.

Entrapment

This strategy involved a perpetrator entrapping a known victim, either by plying him with drugs and then taking advantage of his vulnerable physical state or by targeting victims who were mentally vulnerable. In this sample, three homosexual and five heterosexual men were entrapped by friends, colleagues, brief acquaintances and dates. In cases where the victim was drugged, no weapon or violence was needed to ensure compliance because the victims were unable to defend themselves. All the assaults took place in private locations where the victims were unable to summon help by attracting the attention of others.

These men did not feel that they were responsible for the rape occurring. They recognised that they had been incapacitated by the perpetrator who had drugged them, or that their mental vulnerability had been exploited. Dan, (case 28) a heterosexual fitness instructor who agreed to have a drink with Max, a client, after a training session, clearly articulates the strategy of 'entrapment' in his testimony.

He had finished his workout at the same time that I had finished my shift. We were in the shower having a chat. He asked me what I was doing and I said that I was going to grab something to eat and then go home. He asked me if I had time for a quick drink. It was a lovely summer evening and so it sounded like a good idea.

I was drinking pints of orange juice and lemonade because I don't like drinking alcohol after I've been training. After I'd drunk about half of the second pint I started to feel quite light headed and dizzy. I remember thinking that it must be the heat. By the time I had finished the pint I felt awful. I thought that I'd had an allergic reaction because I felt that rough. Max appeared to be genuinely concerned and offered to drive me home. The only thing that I wanted to do was to get into bed and go to sleep.

By the time we reached my house my head was spinning and my limbs felt really heavy. I could hardly walk. Max helped me in to the house. I just wanted to slump on the bed and be left alone to recover. First of all Max insisted that he undress me and put me to bed. To be honest I didn't have the energy to resist anyway. He took off all my clothes, even my underpants and put me into bed. I remember when he was taking off my underpants thinking 'No, no, get off me' and I felt frustrated that I couldn't even co-ordinate my speech enough to object. He then went downstairs to get me some water but when he reappeared in the bedroom with the water he was also naked. I remember trying to say something and literally nothing came out. I remember trying to manoeuvre my limbs to get myself off the bed but finding that I had no control whatsoever. It was like being trapped inside a floppy rag doll. I wanted to get to the bathroom. If I could get to the bathroom I'd be able to lock myself in until this allergy had worn off, but I couldn't.

The next few minutes were so frightening. It was then that I realised what was going to happen. Max came into the bed beside me and started cuddling me. I felt his hands caress my body and I was completely helpless. I could do nothing. I winced as he ran his nails up and down my spine. I could feel his erection pressing into my bottom and I just knew that I was about to be raped. Then it happened . . . I just wanted to die.

Dan clearly felt that he was not to blame for the rape.

He must have been planning it you know. Must have had the drug, whatever it was on him when he asked me to go for a drink. All premeditated—the scheming fucker. I didn't stand a chance. No, I'm certainly not to blame.

The second method by which victims had been entrapped was by targeting men who were mentally vulnerable, either with a history of mental illness or learning disability. These victims were considerably younger than their perpetrators and all had prior experience of sexual abuse as children or adults. All men included in this category were recruited for the research sample via West Yorkshire Police.

Shaun (case 10), a 27 year old heterosexual man with learning difficulties, was befriended and raped by George, a 50-year-old man. Here he describes what happened:

I knew George because I'd met him a few times before, before this happened. When he asked me I dithered and didn't know whether or not to go and then I decided, 'yeah, I might as well go—it's a nice day', so I did . . . we went down by the canal . . . we were under this bridge and that is where he actually raped me.

When we were under the bridge he took off all my clothes and tried to put his willy inside me. While he was doing this he said things like 'I like you', and all that lot . . . he also tried to make me touch him [masturbate him]. I said 'no, I don't want to do that. I just want to go home'. I thought he was my friend before he took me down to the bridge.

Shaun felt no culpability for the rape, recognising that he had been exploited.

I thought he was my friend. He knows I'm not clever because he kept calling me a 'lost geezer'. I didn't do anything wrong, he tricked me. He made out to be my friend and then tried to hurt me.

THEORETICAL IMPLICATIONS

That the experience of rape threatens a man's masculine identity can be explained by the threat rape poses to the masculine social norm. Different men have different expectations and experiences of 'maleness' or masculinity, shaped by race, class, sexuality and the social situation in which they find themselves. And yet, despite these differences, all men are united in their experience of being a 'man' in a society stratified by gender, where social relations and social structures are constructed to benefit men over women. For example, men continue to control the economic, religious, political and military institutions in society. It comes as no surprise therefore, that in a society still structured around male power the most prominent hegemonic masculine stereotype continues to endorse the idea that 'real men' dominate and control.[53]

All of the men that were interviewed for this research held the view that 'real men' would have been able to prevent themselves from being raped in normal circumstances, yet the majority of them felt that their experiences of rape could not serve as an accurate 'measure of manliness' because of 'miscommunication' or the 'unfair' nature of the assault.

Viewing the assault as either 'unfair' or the result of a 'miscommunication' allowed a number of the men to justify to themselves and to others why they had failed to behave in an appropriate 'masculine' manner, and prevent the assault from occurring.[54] They felt that their 'performance' during the assault was not an accurate reflection of their 'character' or 'manliness' and were therefore able to console themselves that their experience of victimisation was not something that impinged upon their manhood.[55] Gresham Sykes and David Matza have noted a similar process in relation to the reasoning of persons who have committed crimes. They argue that criminals rationalise their deviant conduct whilst still retaining a commitment to social norms which condemn such behaviour. They achieve this apparent paradox by using a range of 'techniques of neutralisation'.[56] These techniques are used by individuals to protect themselves from feelings of guilt and shame that they would otherwise experience as a result of their illegal actions.

As techniques of neutralisation, however, 'miscommunication' and the 'unfair contest' extend much further than protecting these men from experiencing victimisation as a threat to their masculine self-image. They also enabled them to retain their internalised ideas about masculinity—their beliefs that men should

---

[53] RW Connell, *Gender and Power* (Stanford University Press, Stanford Cal, 1987) 184.

[54] A similar finding has been noted by Elizabeth Stanko and Kathy Hobdell in a study of male victims of physical violence: see E Stanko and K Hobdell, 'Assault on Men: Masculinity and Male Victimisation' (1993) 33 *British Journal of Criminology* 400–15.

[55] Although it may, of course, continue to be perceived as a threat to their physical or psychological self.

[56] G Sykes and D Matza, 'Techniques of Neutralization: A Theory of Delinquency' (1957) 22 *American Sociological Review* 664–70.

dominate and control—and thus avert crises of identity. Moreover, by maintaining stereotypical views about masculinity, these men were able readily to accept and therefore continue to benefit from their privileged position in a society which rewards characteristics associated with 'masculinity' over those associated with 'femininity'.

However, the most important form of power that men exercise in society is the control they have over 'meaning'. In other words, the basis of men's power comes from their historical ability to control the ways in which society thinks about men (and, for that matter, women) and to cast themselves as having characteristics that make them worthy of their powerful position.[57] For example, Ortner suggests that over the course of the last 300 years, the symbolic equation of women with nature and men with civilisation has had a tremendous impact in terms of the structure of power relations between the sexes.[58] It is often assumed that men are less emotional, more intellectual and physically stronger than women and are therefore most likely to contribute to the advancement of civilisation. Conceptualising these characteristics as 'innately masculine' enables men to justify the privileged position they occupy in society.[59] Thus, men's collective interests and their disproportionate power and influence are not maintained through active and self-conscious male conspiracies; rather, the processes by which men maintain their dominance are more complex, indirect and subtle.

Patriarchy, like any cultural form, presents itself as 'the way' of seeing the world; as entirely natural, normal and straightforward. Consequently, men's power and privilege is naturalised, especially in the eyes of men themselves. As this research has shown, male rape represents an extreme threat to that power base, providing unequivocal evidence that men do not necessarily have the characteristics (such as physical and psychological strength) which are often used to validate their privileged position in society. All of the men in this study recognised that their experiences of sexual victimisation were contrary to the male stereotype in society which emphasises power and control. The rape was therefore felt not only as a threat to their physical and psychological well-being, but also to their identity as 'men'. This was most starkly revealed in the descriptions the men gave of their assaults—they were 'overpowered, overridden, intimidated or entrapped'. In par-

---

[57] Throughout the eighteenth and nineteenth centuries ideas about the 'natural' inequalities of the sexes were common. In response to Mary Wollstonecraft's book entitled the *Vindication of the Rights of Women* published in 1792, evangelical ministers in many British churches began preaching about women as naturally more delicate, fragile and morally weak. By the mid-nineteenth century, ideas about the 'natural' differences between men and women were also being used to justify the stratification of men and women's work. Middle-class women became increasingly concentrated into less physical trades such as dressmaking, school-teaching and the retail industry, whereas in working-class society similar concerns led to the exclusion of women from working underground. See C Hall, *White, Male and Middle Class: Explorations in Feminism and History* (Polity Press, Cambridge, 1992).

[58] See SB Ortner, 'Is Female to Male as Nature is to Culture?' in MZ Rosaldo and L Lamphere (eds), *Woman, Crime and Society* (Stanford University Press, Stanford Cal, 1974).

[59] See VJ Seidler, *Rediscovering Masculinity: Reason, Language and Sexuality* (Routledge, New York NY, 1989).

ticular, they were concerned to justify why they had been unable to defend themselves, thereby protecting their self-identity as men. In doing so, they also neatly averted the challenge that male sexual victimisation poses to the masculine stereotype.

Foucault's theory of normalisation is particularly helpful in throwing light on the behaviour of male victims to an experience of rape.[60] Foucault describes how something threatening to society's values and power structure is often made abnormal in order to reassert the dominant ideal. He identifies the principal method of social control in modern society as discipline, a form of power which regulates the population to produce a stable and functional social order. He describes how the application of discipline is achieved through a process of normalisation. According to Foucault, normalisation is a complex process in which the ordinary citizen becomes both the agent and subject of power.[61] Thus, for example, individual men are subject to 'constant surveillance' from themselves and others to prove they behave in a masculine fashion. In consequence, raped men are labelled and treated as deviant, unless they can prove otherwise, because their experience contradicts expectations of maleness.

The reactions of the men in this sample—their attempts to justify why they had been raped—serve to protect the dominant masculine stereotype in society, that 'real' men are powerful and thus also protects the 'normality' of masculine privilege. David Buchbinder[62] suggests that masculinity is bestowed by men on men as they compete with each other to gain recognition as a man.[63] Men judge each other and encourage compliance by rewarding those who match the said criteria while censuring those who do not. Differences among individual men such as age, physical size and strength, class, wealth, sexual activity and so on are ranked according to the masculine stereotype and invested with varying degrees of patriarchal power; the characteristics become markers of masculinity or the lack of it. The point here, which is made most lucidly by Edley and Wetherell, is that,

> as paradoxical as it might sound, [raped] men are simultaneously the producers and the products of culture: the masters and the slaves of ideology.[64]

---

[60] M Foucault, *Discipline and Punish*, AM Sheridan-Smith (trans) (Penguin, London, 1979) 177–84.

[61] '[Individuals] are always in the position of simultaneously undergoing and exercising power. They are not only its inert or consenting target; they are always also the elements of its articulation . . . The individual is an effect of power, and at the same time, or precisely to the extent to which it is the effect, it is an element of its articulation': M Foucault, 'Two Lectures', in C Gordon (ed), *Power/Knowledge: Selected Writings 1972–1977* (Harvester Press, Brighton, 1980) 98.

[62] See D Buchbinder, *Performance Anxieties: Re-producing Masculinity* (Allen and Unwin, Sydney, 1988) 44.

[63] This idea, that competitiveness is central to western notions of masculinity is also explored by Carol Lee who interviewed men aged between 15 and 25 about their experiences of manhood and noted that 'competitiveness was central to being a man' and that 'winning is crucial to the concept of manhood': C Lee, *Talking Tough: The Fight for Masculinity* (Arrow, London, 1993) 177–78.

[64] N Edley and M Wetherell, 'Masculinity, Power and Identity', in Mairtin Mac an Ghaill (ed), *Understanding Masculinities: Social Relations and Cultural Arenas* (Open University Press, Buckingham, 1996) 97–113.

In summary, this chapter has helped to explain why male victims find it difficult to accept that 'normal' men can be raped. When confronted with this reality, they seek alternative explanations for what has happened, thereby ensuring that the powerful stereotype of masculinity remains unchallenged. This protects the masculine stereotype that 'real' men are powerful and thus also protects the 'normality' of masculine power that continues to pervade the existing social order. In this sense, the reactions of victims to male rape is an example, in the words of Foucault, of the 'micro-physics of power':

> the point where power reaches into the very grain of individuals, touches their bodies, inserts itself into their actions and attitudes, their discourses, learning processes and everyday lives.[65]

A study of the responses to rape by male victims therefore provides an illuminating example of the nature of masculinity and its uneasy relationship with victimisation.

---

[65] Foucault, *Power/Knowledge*, n 61 above, 39.

3

Victims of Paramilitary Punishment Attacks in Belfast

HEATHER HAMILL[*]

INTRODUCTION

I
N A CELEBRATED text, Nils Christie described the ideal victim of crime as a middle-aged woman on a visit to her ill mother.[1] By this he meant that society is most willing to ascribe the label 'victim' to those people who are not only harmed by others, but who are deemed to be in some way vulnerable, and, most importantly, blame-free. In order to receive the benefits of victimisation (sympathy, assistance, support and sometimes financial reparation), those who are harmed must be recognised as victims. To this end, they first need to identify themselves as victims, then to seek help from the relevant agencies and, most crucially, be accepted by those agencies as deserving of victim status.[2] It is relatively uncomplicated to characterise a person who has been harmed as a 'victim' if he or she is considered to have done nothing to provoke or precipitate the offence and had no prior relationship with the offender.[3] Although few victims are directly

[*] This chapter could not have been written without the help and support of a large number of people. First I would like to thank Dr Diego Gambetta who supervised my DPhil thesis on which this chapter is based and Carolyn Hoyle and Richard Young for their editorial assistance. My thanks also go to Breidge Gadd and Brian McCaughey from the Probation Board for Northern Ireland who facilitated access to a number of statutory and voluntary agencies and introduced me to the West Belfast Youth at Risk Programme. I owe an immense debt to the staff and volunteers of 'West Belfast Youth at Risk' who helped me gain access to many of the young people who participated in this research. Finally, and most importantly, I thank each individual who participated in this research and in particular the young people in West Belfast who agreed to be interviewed. I hope I have produced an account that accurately reflects their views and experiences. Ultimately, however the opinions expressed in this chapter are my own and I accept full responsibility for the content of this chapter.
[1] N Christie, 'The Ideal Victim' in EA Fattah (ed), *From Crime Policy to Victim Policy: Reorienting the Justice System* (Macmillan, London, 1986).
[2] See D Miers, 'Taking the Law into their Own Hands: Victims as Offenders' in A Crawford and J Goodey (eds), *Integrating a Victim Perspective within Criminal Justice* (Ashgate, Aldershot, 2000) 77–95, for a more sophisticated account of this process.
[3] See L Zedner, 'Victims' in M Maguire, R Morgan and R Reiner (eds), *The Oxford Handbook of Criminology*, 3rd edn (Clarendon Press, Oxford, forthcoming 2002) for a discussion of the notions of victim-precipitation and victim-proneness.

blamed for the offences committed against them, the majority of victims of vio- lence, whether in the home, in prisons or on the streets, are known to their offend- ers,[4] and many acts of violence are the result of ongoing conflict or dispute, with victims and offenders frequently exchanging roles.[5] Hence, a high rate of victimi- sation is experienced by people who in similar situations have been (or could have been) labelled offenders. Loeber *et al*, for example, found that juveniles who had been killed or wounded by guns had also been highly delinquent.[6] Clearly, many victims are not recognisable as the ideal types presented by the popular press.[7]

This chapter considers one striking example of 'non-ideal' victims—victims of paramilitary punishment attacks (hereinafter referred to as PPAs) in Belfast, Northern Ireland. By describing the factors which result in their victimisation as well as their own and their community's response to it, it is hoped that this chap- ter will provide a vivid example of the consequences of societal failure to respond effectively to harm when there is a general determination to conform to rigid categories of 'illegitimate offenders' or 'legitimate victims'.

Throughout the past three decades in catholic West Belfast, the local para- military organisations, in particular the IRA, have engaged in forms of crime management. These forms include the administration of a system of informal non-statutory policing and 'punishment'. The punishments include attacks with baseball bats and shooting offenders in the knees (known as knee-capping), ankles and elbow joints. PPAs also include a range of non-violent sanctions such as plac- ing a young person under a curfew or enforcing increasingly extensive forms of exclusion (which range from expulsion from a local neighbourhood though to being exiled from Northern Ireland). Violating a curfew or exclusion results in a more serious physical 'punishment'.[8] Although both Republican and Loyalist paramilitaries carry out PPAs, punishments are never sectarian. Republican para- military groups police and punish local catholics in the areas in which they dom- inate, and Loyalist paramilitary groups do likewise in protestant areas. They do not police each other's communities. This chapter, drawing on ethnographic research conducted in catholic West Belfast, discusses only catholic young people who are victims of PPAs perpetrated by the IRA.

---

[4]   Home Office, *The 2000 British Crime Survey England and Wales*, Home Office Statistical Bulletin No 18 (Home Office, London, 2000) 33.
[5]   See, for example, K Edgar and I O'Donnell, 'Assault in Prison' (1998) 38 *British Journal of Criminology* 635 and A Cretney and G Davis, *Punishing Violence* (Routledge, London, 1995).
[6]   R Loeber, M DeLamatre, G Tita, J Cohen, M Stouthamer-Loeber and DP Farrington, 'Gun Injury and Mortality: The Delinquent Backgrounds of Juvenile Victims' (1999) 14 *Violence and Victims* 339–52.
[7]   See further the discussion by Paul Rock in this volume.
[8]   See C Bell, 'Alternative Justice in Ireland' in N Dawson, D Greer, and P Ingram (eds), *One Hundred and Fifty Years of Irish Law* (SLS Publications, Belfast, 1996) 145–70; P Hillyard, 'Popular Justice in Northern Ireland: Communities and Change' in S Spitzer (ed), *Research in Law, Deviance and Social Control*, Vol 7 (JAI Press, London and Greenwich Conn, 1984) 247–67; and C Knox, 'The "Deserving" Victims of Political Violence: 'Punishment' Attacks in Northern Ireland' (2001) 1 *Criminal Justice* 181–99.

The following excerpt from my fieldwork diary serves as an introduction to the notion of 'non-ideal' PPA victims:

> By chance bumped into Mark and Davy[9] in the probation office collecting a letter from Mark's Probation Officer. They wanted to know what I was doing there and I was in the middle of trying to explain that I wasn't a Probation Officer when Mark suddenly shouted 'Fuck' and pushed Davy away from the window. I asked them what was wrong.
> 'It's the [I]RA', Mark replied, 'they're after me and if they catch me I'm a dead man.'
> 'Where?' I asked.
> 'In that red fucking car', Mark said.
> I looked out of the window and saw two middle-aged men sitting in a parked red car. The driver had his window down and was idly smoking a cigarette and watching passers by. They seemed innocent enough to me and after a few minutes they drove off. Mark was very agitated. 'Let's get the fuck outta here,' he said and he and Davy left the office quickly. I watched them flag down a taxi and jump in. It looked as if they didn't want to be seen on the street.

Mark (aged 17) was afraid that the alleged IRA members in the red car were intent on 'punishing' him for his involvement in joyriding and property offences. A year earlier the IRA had kidnapped Mark and hung him upside down from some railings. His eyes were taped shut and he was beaten repeatedly with baseball bats studded with nails until both of his legs were broken. He was left hanging until a passer-by lifted him down and called an ambulance. Mark claimed that, since then, the IRA had threatened him with another PPA. Davy, also aged 17, had been excluded from West Belfast as punishment for his criminal activities and he believed that, if seen in the area, he too would face a PPA. These young men fall far short of the image of the ideal 'innocent' victim. Mark and Davy had been involved in petty crime since they were aged 13. Now, at 17, they self-reported an impressive criminal resumé. Mark was serving a community sentence and Davy had previously been sentenced to six months in a young offender's institution. They had become known locally as 'hoods', a term used by West Belfast residents to describe delinquent young people.

In this chapter I describe the criminal and antisocial behaviour that can result in hoods receiving PPAs; examine the IRA's system of policing and punishment in West Belfast, and explore the effects of PPAs on victims. Three main themes are developed. First, although the hoods are often subjected to multiple PPAs, they are identified as offenders deserving of punishment, rather than as victims of a violent assault. Second, the perpetrators of PPAs are not perceived to be violent offenders, rather, their actions are seen as a necessary intervention in the local fight against crime. Third, while the hoods fear PPAs, they persistently behave in a manner that increases the likelihood that they will become victims of a violent attack.

---

[9]   These two people were 'hoods' with whom I had many passing encounters during the course of the research.

Almost by definition, non-ideal victims are not easy to study. As such victims are largely hidden from public view, and almost invisible as a subject of social concern, research into their experiences poses distinct challenges to the social scientist. In the following section I will discuss the research methods used to collect the data for this study.

Research Methodology

There are persuasive arguments as to why topics of a sensitive kind are unsuited to study by means of large impersonal surveys.[10] Given the highly sensitive nature of the investigation into the experiences of offenders who are often brutally assaulted by paramilitary organisations, and, in particular, the difficulty of gaining access to this largely hidden and taciturn group of young people, it was decided that qualitative methods were the only appropriate research approach. Hence, the thick data reported below derive from one of only a very few ethnographic studies of hoods in West Belfast. In line with the ethnographic tradition this study involved an extensive period of field work (from October 1997 to October 1998); the generation of multiple and descriptive sources of data; the development of close relationships with respondents, and detailed understandings of the research site.[11]

West Belfast is predominantly catholic (74 per cent) and also has the highest concentration of catholics in Northern Ireland. Furthermore, it is the largest of the designated areas of social need in Northern Ireland, characterised by high levels of unemployment, poverty and ill health.[12] While local, informal responses to crime are in operation in many areas in Northern Ireland, the number of initiatives and the frequency of more violent approaches are by far the greatest in catholic West Belfast. Consequently, the area was chosen as the primary research setting.

This chapter draws on academic literature; interview data; observational data and data drawn from the analysis of documents (primarily newspaper articles from the *Andersonstown News*, the *Irish News* and the *Belfast Telegraph*, as well as from police and government reports dating from 1995 to 2001). I carried out

[10] RM Lee, *Doing Research on Sensitive Topics* (Sage Publications, London, 1993); J Brannen, 'The Study of Sensitive Subjects' (1988) 36 *Sociological Review* 552–63; G McCracken, *The Long Interview* (Sage Publications, Newbury Park CA, 1988); and A Oakley, 'Interviewing Women: A Contradiction in Terms' in H Roberts (ed), *Doing Feminist Research* (Routledge & Kegan Paul, London, 1981). See also Paul Rock, 'On Becoming a Victim' in this volume.

[11] WF Whyte, *Street Corner Society* (Chicago University Press, Chicago Ill 1955); L Humphreys, *Tearoom Trade: A Study of Homosexual Encounters in Public Places* (Gerard Duckworth, London, 1970); MB Miles and AM Huberman, *Qualitative Data Analysis: An Expanded Sourcebook* (Sage Publications, London, 1994); M Hammersley and P Atkinson, *Ethnography: Principles in Practice* (Routledge, London, 1995).

[12] The Northern Ireland Census (1991) see Department of Health and Social Services Registrar General Northern Ireland, *Belfast Urban Area Report* (HMSO, Belfast, 1992).

in-depth semi-structured interviews with 50 local residents, 10 members of Sinn Féin, 72 hoods (comprising 64 males and eight females) and 10 former hoods. The active hoods ranged in age from 14 to 25, with an average age of 18 (17 for the females). These samples were generated with the help of the Probation Board for Northern Ireland (PBNI) and by the technique of snowballing through contacts made while I was volunteering with a local community group (West Belfast Youth at Risk Project). Many of the residents and members of Sinn Féin who partici-pated in the research were active in community and youth projects and were influ-ential opinion formers within West Belfast. All of the respondents remain anonymous and the names assigned to the hoods are fictitious.

The local residents and Sinn Féin members interviewed were asked questions aimed at ascertaining: the types of crime that were most prevalent in the area and those which caused them most concern; whether they themselves had been vic-timised in the previous five years; who they believed to be responsible for most of the crime; how crime was managed locally, and their views of the various formal and informal crime management strategies that were in operation. I asked the hoods about their educational, employment and family backgrounds; when and how they started offending and the types and numbers of offences they commit-ted. I also asked them about their experiences of both the statutory criminal justice system and the informal system of social control through threat of para-military punishment. In particular, I questioned them about the nature of local PPAs and the effects of experiencing this kind of assault.

The bulk of the interview data, however, was collected during spontaneous unstructured conversations that arose after the semi-structured interview had been completed. During the course of the study, hundreds of impromptu, infor-mal conversations took place. These ranged from a short chat with two or three hoods on a street corner at night to more lengthy and involved discussions with respondents over cups of tea, bags of chips, pints of beer or cigarettes. Giving or receiving a lift in a car would often result in a long period of interaction.[13] During these unstructured interviews and conversations I constantly kept the research questions in mind, sometimes initiating the topics of discussion, more often allowing the conversation to flow naturally as issues specific to the research were raised and dropped a number of times in the course of the dialogue.[14]

The world of the delinquent young person on the street is difficult to penetrate. Such people are often guarded, aggressive and uncommunicative. Adults are regarded with suspicion and thought to pose a threat, be it the benign 'interference' of social workers or the 'menace' of the police and paramilitary organisations. Thus in this study, five months of semi-structured interviewing, participant observa-tion and general hanging around passed before the hoods and I came to trust one another sufficiently for interview data of any depth or richness to be gathered.

---

[13] I recorded all observations and conversations in a field work diary.
[14] See J Brannen, 'The study of sensitive subjects' (1988) 36 *Sociological Review* 552–63 and M Agar, *Professional Stranger* (Academic Press, New York NY, 1980).

There are a number of ways to record responses to questions during an interview, with the method of recording data necessarily affecting the data itself.[15] Hammersley and Atkinson consider tape-recording, supplemented with jotted notes recording non-verbal aspects and features of the physical setting, to provide the most 'complete, concrete and detailed' data.[16] However, during initial discussions I discovered that the respondents were very wary of being recorded. I considered that a tape recorder would probably hamper further access to the research groups, impinge on the veracity of the responses, and inhibit the establishment of trust between the interviewees and myself.[17] Therefore, I decided not to tape-record interviews but to take notes whenever possible and rely upon memory at other times, writing up an account of the interview as soon as possible after the event. Whilst this is the method that assures least reliability as memory may easily fail and be selective, and detailed information may be lost, I judged that it was the only method that facilitated trust and flexibility in this particular research setting. To enhance the reliability of the data gathered, I adopted the technique of 'triangulation' (assessing the validity of inferences drawn by examining data relating to the same concept from participant observation, interviewing and analysis of documents).[18]

This chapter makes most use of the data collected on the hoods, the young people who are most often victims of PPAs. The following section discusses how their delinquency causes them to be singled out for PPAs.

THE HOODS: PERPETRATORS AND VICTIMS

The observation that many victims have themselves been offenders[19] is crucial to our understanding of the plight of the hoods in West Belfast. PPAs are justified by the perpetrators as being an appropriate response to the hoods' persistent offending. In this section I will describe the nature of the hoods' delinquency, emphasising their position as 'non-ideal' victims.

It is virtually impossible to drive through West Belfast on a Friday or Saturday night without coming across at least one large group of young people drinking, sniffing glue and waiting for joyriders to race by. Any discussion with local residents of the advantages and disadvantages of living in the area will quickly touch upon the problems of delinquency and include stories of victimisation by hoods.

---

[15] MB Miles and AM Huberman, *Qualitative Data Analysis: An Expanded Sourcebook* (Sage Publications, London, 1994).

[16] M Hammersley and P Atkinson, *Ethnography: Principles in Practice* (Routledge, London, 1995) 186.

[17] Similar problems are reported by F Varese, *The Emergence of the Russian Mafia: Dispute Settlement and Protection in a New Market Economy* (Unpublished DPhil Thesis, Faculty of Social Studies, University of Oxford, 1996) 13.

[18] Hammersley and Atkinson, *Ethnography: Principles in Practice*, n 16 above, 230–31.

[19] See Loeber *et al*, 'Gun Injury and Mortality', n 6 above, and Miers, 'Taking the Law into their Own Hands', n 2 above, 77.

A quick scan of the local paper, the *Andersonstown News,* will reveal further stories of vandalism, theft and intimidation. There can be little doubt of the seriousness of these incidents or the distress that they cause.

West Belfast has a high proportion of young people.[20] Community workers estimate that approximately 2,000 young people congregate and disperse across the area's various estates in the evenings.[21] They tend to cluster together based on age, in groups of young, mid and older youths—10 to 15-year-olds, 15 to 17-year-olds and 17 to 20-year-olds. Amongst the last population there are also some adults who are in their early twenties. These classifications are not rigid and some 'upwardly-mobile' 12 and 13-year-olds are found in the middle group and a number of 15 and 16-year-olds in the older group. Many of these young people are involved in minor, occasional delinquency such as substance misuse and underage drinking.[22] Amongst them, according to the police, are between 50 and 70 young people who are responsible for the majority of crime in the West Belfast area.[23] The overall number of these hoods has remained fairly static over the past five years as new recruits replace those who are put of action through imprisonment or a PPA.

Hoods are predominantly young men, but there are some young women whose antisocial and offending behaviour has also earned them this label. The hoods' backgrounds are similar to those of persistent young offenders in North America and elsewhere in the United Kingdom: a childhood characterised by poverty, family instability and poor school attendance.[24] For most hoods, problem behaviours start at a young age. A quarter had been placed in a social services care home at some point in their childhood, and just over half had been made homeless through a break down in their family relationships.

Street life for the hoods tends to begin with abuse of solvents at the age of eight or nine. Glue was once the main substance for inhalation in West Belfast, but

---

[20] In 1999, the population of the parliamentary constituency of West Belfast stood at 90,000, approximately 20% of the population of Belfast (West Belfast Economic Forum, 2000). In Ballymurphy, a housing estate of 11,500 residents, it is estimated that 51% are less than 25 years of age. See T Poland, *A Report on the Logistics of Crime and Young People in West Belfast* (Unpublished report commissioned by PBNI and presented at a meeting of the West Belfast Partnership Board, January 2000).

[21] Personal communication with community workers and probation officers.

[22] The Self-Reported Delinquency study, carried out in Belfast, showed that delinquency was widespread amongst young people, but much of it was of a minor nature and of low intensity. However, there was a minority who reported offending more than 50 times per year, especially in the drug and violence categories: J McQuoid, 'The Self-Reported Delinquency Study in Belfast, Northern Ireland' in J Junger-Tas, G-T Terlaun and MW Klein (eds), *Delinquent Behavior Among Young People in the Western World: First Results of the International Self-Report Delinquency Study* (Kugler Publications, Amsterdam and New York NY, 1994).

[23] All of the young people I interviewed were identified by the PBNI, local youth and community workers and members of the police car crime teams as being persistent offenders.

[24] See DP Farrington, 'Human Development and Criminal Careers' in M Maguire, R Morgan and R Reiner (eds), *The Oxford Handbook of Criminology*, 2nd edn (Clarendon Press, Oxford, 1997) and J Jankowski, *Islands in the Street : Gangs and American Urban Society* (University of California Press, Berkeley Cal, 1991).

correction fluids and thinners, butane gas in aerosols, gas lighter refills, and gas cylinders are all used extensively. Solvents hold a strong attraction for children; they are cheap, accessible and have powerful effects. Whether stemming from a desire to escape a poor home life or from youthful experimentation, children are often enticed to join their friends in using substances:

> There was definitely peer pressure for drugs and glue . . . It was about half-and-half—50 per cent of my friends got involved with antisocial behaviour. (Liam, aged 21)

Groups of young teenagers gather on street corners, on wasteland or in graveyards drinking, sniffing solvents, and smoking cannabis. One such site, for a time, was a street off the lower part of the Falls Road. This became popular with a group who parodied the various paramilitary groups in the area by calling themselves the 'Divis Hoods Liberation Army.' Local people were so intimidated by this group's aggressive behaviour that they claimed their street was 'under siege'.[25]

For these young people, the lure of sniffing solvents with their friends generally proves to be stronger than going to school. None of the hoods were in full or part-time education: 54 per cent had been excluded from school, mostly when they had been between the ages of 12 and 14, and once debarred they had never returned to education.[26] The remaining 46 per cent had simply dropped out of school. Sean (aged 15) gave up on school when he was 12 years old because, he said, 'no-one would listen to me and they made me do things I didn't want to do.' Mark (aged 17) recounted:

> I was always fighting and getting into trouble and the teachers didn't like me. I didn't like them either and I just stopped going. Anyway I was on the run [from the IRA] and I couldn't just walk out of school in broad daylight.

Poor school attendance and association with other children involved in delinquency precipitates offending that intensifies with age. Thus, once very young people voluntarily embark on one course of action, such as abusing solvents and drinking alcohol, they soon become involved in unanticipated offending (for example, shoplifting) as a means to sustain that action. Their entrance into offending is not the result of a thoughtful, careful, reasoned process, but rather as a result of what Matza referred to as 'drift' facilitated by a subculture of delinquency.[27] Once these young people elect to participate in street-life, further offending 'emerges as part of the natural flow of events.'[28]

Hoods are frequently unemployed. With no formal educational qualifications they have limited opportunities in the employment market. Their offending

---

[25] 'Pensioner's Glue Gang Terror Over', *Irish News*, 22 April 1999. After the situation was highlighted in the local newspaper, this 'army' of hoods moved onto another site.

[26] The three primary reasons why these young people were excluded from school were violence against other pupils or teachers (38%), truancy (28%) and vandalism (15%).

[27] M Matza, *Delinquency and Drift* (Wiley, New York NY, 1964).

[28] RT Wright and SH Decker, *Burglars on the Job: Streetlife and Residential Break-ins* (Northeastern University Press, Boston Mass, 1994) 40.

further reduces their chances of gaining and maintaining a job. As Paul (aged 16) said, 'the trouble is your charge sheet if you get caught: you'll never get a job because of your criminal record.' Of the hoods in the sample, 29 per cent claimed to be in some form of full-time employment, examples of which included washing cars, serving in a kebab shop, working as a decorator and doing manual labour. However, they are often in and out of work within a 24 hour period. Hoods lose jobs because of boredom, feeling debased, and the recognition that there will be little financial benefit for the labour. Sammy (aged 18) remarked: 'I lost my job because of not turnin' up and drinkin' at lunchtimes', while Tony (aged 24) explained:

> I didn't like being subordinate and I had a bad attitude. I didn't like the boss so I grabbed him round the neck and then I was fired.

The sporadic nature of their employment leaves the hoods with a lot of spare time to spend in a variety of ways: 'I just lie in bed all day 'til about 5pm . . . Times I'm ok with it. Times that I'm bored to fuck' (Paddy, aged 19).

Hoods also participate in the same types of 'legitimate' activities common to the average young adult. Often when I visited them in their homes during the day they would be watching television or I would learn that they were playing football (either Gaelic or soccer) or pool or snooker. Their social lives are generally limited to what is available to them in the West Belfast area—most often hanging out with their friends and, when they can afford it, going to pubs, clubbing and the cinema.

In addition to these 'legitimate pursuits', the hoods routinely take part in the antisocial and often criminal activities of street life, caricatured as 'runnin' about the streets and fuckin' about with my mates' (Paddy, aged 19). Street life involves hanging around on street corners drinking alcohol to excess and misusing drugs; selling drugs; fighting; stealing, shoplifting and burglary; taking cars and joyriding, and vandalism. All of these activities are collectively known in West Belfast as 'hooding'. Colin (aged 17) described a typical hood 'session' as follows:

> I would go out and steal somethin', sell it, get drugs, a carry out. Fly about in my mate's [stolen] car, three of us smokin' and drinkin'. Probably sit in a mate's house or go to a party—whatever comes up.

To an outsider, such a lifestyle appears unstructured, spontaneous and aimless. For hoods, however, spending time in this way is not pointless, as they have what Lofland (1969) has called a 'transcending commitment' to 'the demands of life on the street.'[29] Sully (aged 18) summed up the hood's lifestyle as centring on 'drink, cars, women, drugs, money; a big long party and you don't think about reality until you sober up.' Younger hoods are drawn to, and seek out, this lifestyle. A youth worker described how:

---

[29] J Lofland, *Deviance and Identity* (Prentice-Hall, Englewood Cliffs NJ, 1969) 91. See also Wright and Decker, *Burglars on the Job*, n 28 above, 205.

> There is a definite culture of it [offending] and now it's seven to eight-year-olds doing what the older ones are doing and tagging along. They know what they are doing but they don't understand the consequences of what they're doing. It's fun, exciting, the thrill of the chase. (Youth worker, P)

Some younger hoods appeared to emulate their older siblings. Amongst the hoods in the study were brothers and sisters from four different families. Three members of one family were all under threat from the IRA for joyriding, vandalism and general antisocial behaviour. A slogan stating their surname and ordering them to leave the area was daubed in paint on a shop front in Andersonstown in West Belfast and could have referred to any one of the three siblings.

The hoods also have a reputation for being violent. One local resident asserted that:

> They [the hoods] would punch your head in for no reason if they're high or drunk. To an extent I'd be scared to walk past a lot of them. (Liam, aged 21)

While they do perpetrate acts of violence against local people, the hoods are more frequently violent towards each other and within this culture of violence it is often difficult to distinguish between victim and offender.

Fighting is integral to street life in West Belfast. Research has indicated that adolescents who use drugs and alcohol are more likely to commit violent acts than those who do not abuse substances.[30] There is also a positive correlation between the severity and frequency of violent delinquency and the seriousness and frequency of drug taking.[31] Drinking and drug-taking can be indulged in without recourse to violence, but in an environment where fighting is common, substances often act to encourage those inclined to be violent. Alex (aged 19) described how he was set upon by a group of other hoods:

> I got beat up with hurley bats for personal reasons. I'm not saying who it was but . . . I was supposed to have said that I was gonna stab him [one of the attackers]. Him and his mates came up to Turf [Lodge] and hit me with hurley bats and I woke up a day later in hospital.

Although the hoods displayed their bruises and scars with bravado, they often sustained serious injuries from the bricks, snooker cues, baseball bats and knives that are used as weapons. As Tim (aged 17) pointed out: 'It's dangerous. I could get killed or kill somebody else'.

These young people have become alienated from their local community and appear unconcerned about their futures, living only for the present. They seem largely untouched by, and impervious to, the views of their families and appear to be out of control. Whilst they are chiefly identified as being perpetrators of crime,

---

[30] See, for example, N South, 'Drugs: Use, Crime and Control' in M Maguire, R Morgan and R Reiner (eds), *The Oxford Handbook of Criminology*, 2nd edn (Clarendon Press, Oxford, 1997) 925–60.
[31] J Fagan, 'Social Processes of Delinquency and Drug Use Among Urban Gangs' in CR Huff, *Gangs in America* (Sage Publications, London, 1990) 183–222.

they are also the victims of multiple violent assaults by paramilitaries. In the following section I will outline the informal system of policing in West Belfast, of which PPAs form an integral part.

THE INFORMAL SYSTEM OF POLICING AND 'PUNISHMENT' IN WEST BELFAST

A major by-product of the 30 years of political and civil conflict in Northern Ireland has been a lack of consensus amongst the population over who should police ordinary crime and how. This has been clearly evidenced amongst the predominantly nationalist and republican inhabitants of West Belfast, who have consistently sought to 'fight' crime with a variety of informal, localised strategies, rather than rely upon the police and statutory criminal justice agencies. The most notorious of these approaches has been the IRA's system of PPAs.

In West Belfast, the IRA will act against any hood who is known to be persistently committing personal and property offences, terrorising or endangering local people and attracting the attention of the police.[32] They administer a system which involves warnings, curfews, exiles, beatings, shootings and ultimately executions. It is impossible to give precise numbers of PPAs that have been perpetrated in Northern Ireland over the course of the past 30 years and the official criminal statistics underestimate the true number of attacks.[33] Many victims, especially those with more minor injuries, do not report the assault to the police. The recorded figures tend to relate to the more severe attacks that have required hospitalisation. In addition, while the police have recorded 'punishment' shootings since 1973, 'punishment' beatings have only been recorded since 1988. According to police statistics, in the period between 1973 and 2001, a total of 2,564 people were victims of 'punishment' shootings, of which 1,408 were perpetrated by Republican paramilitaries, and 1,156 by Loyalist paramilitaries. A further 1,652 people were casualties of 'punishment' assaults in the period 1988 to April 2001, of which 823 were perpetrated by Republican paramilitaries and 829 by Loyalist paramilitaries. The IRA has been responsible for the majority of the 2,143 attacks by Republican paramilitaries since 1973.[34]

Victims of PPAs are predominantly young men. In 1996, 93 per cent of the 393 referrals to 'Base 2', a Belfast based organisation established to assist those under

---

[32] J Conroy, *War as a Way of Life: A Belfast Diary* (Heinemann, London, 1987) 90; R Munck, 'The Lads and the Hoods: Alternative Justice in an Irish Context' in M Thomlinson, T Varley and C McCullough (eds), *Whose Law and Order? Aspects of Crime and Social Control in Irish Society* (Sociological Association, Dublin, 1988) 41–53; C Bell, 'Alternative Justice in Ireland' in N Dawson, D Greer and P Ingram (eds), *One Hundred and Fifty Years of Irish Law* (SLS Publications, Belfast, 1996) 145–70 and Knox, 'The "Deserving" Victims of Political Violence', n 8 above.

[33] Knox, 'The "Deserving" Victims of Political Violence', n 8 above.

[34] Since 1992–1993 Loyalist paramilitaries have carried out more punishment attacks than Republican paramilitaries <http://www.psni.police.uk/stats/securitysit.shtml>.

threat of 'punishment', were men. The largest number of referrals (42 per cent) were in the 17 to 25 age group with only 20 per cent aged 17 or under.[35]

PPAs vary in nature.[36] Intended as warnings, some of the beatings are not much more than a 'cuff around the ear'. Others are more serious:

> The [I]RA used to torture me. I got slapped by the [I]RA. Trailed about by the head and got a couple of slaps and told to stay away from certain people and joyriding and cars and stuff. (Julie, aged 16)

Some severe PPAs require lengthy periods of hospitalisation:

> I was beaten twice, once with hurley bats and once with golf clubs for antisocial behaviour. I was hospitalised when I got the blame for breakin' a window in Turf Lodge. (Steve, aged 18)

Owen (aged 25) described his experiences:

> I've been baseball batted and sledge hammered, and I've had a few tickin' offs as well from the paramilitaries for burglary and car theft. I was put in hospital after a punishment beating, I was beaten on the legs, the hands and the back with a baseball bat and a sledge hammer.

Hoods know what will happen to them if they get caught: 'I haven't experienced any [PPAs]. It looks sore; you don't see it, you only hear' (Eugene, aged 19). Some expressed the belief that 'it will never happen to me' but others lived in terror of being 'punished' by the IRA. Marty (aged 17) said, 'My life's scary, and I can't sleep at nights 'cause I think I'm gonna get done [punished]', while Tommy (aged 23) was '. . . scared to go out at nights in case the Provos [IRA] are going to shoot me'. A community worker (Q) who lives and works in West Belfast noted that:

> It hasn't happened to me, but I know from friends it has happened to. It's a whole different dynamic when your own people batter you, and nothing is done about it. You are left feeling angry and frustrated, powerless and seeking revenge.

Echoing this theme, Tony (aged 24) spoke bitterly as he showed me his scars from being beaten with hurley bats embedded with nails: 'How can they [the IRA] do that to their own people? They're bastards; I hate them.'

In Republican areas such as West Belfast, the legitimacy of the criminal justice system and the police is fiercely contested. Local people are alienated from the largely protestant Royal Ulster Constabulary (RUC) who they view as being sectarian, uninterested, and ineffective.[37] In the words of a local councillor:

---

[35] P Conway, *Development of a Service-based Response to Those Under Threat from Paramilitaries in Northern Ireland* (Unpublished MSc (Social Work) Dissertation, Faculty of Economics and Social Sciences, Queens University Belfast, 1994) 117.

[36] W Thompson and B Mulholland, 'Paramilitary Punishments and Young People in West Belfast: Psychological Effects and the Implications for Education' in L Kennedy (ed), *Crime and Punishment in West Belfast* (The Summer School, West Belfast, 1995) 55.

[37] On 4 November 2001 the RUC's name was changed to the Police Service for Northern Ireland. However as this research was carried our prior to the name change I refer to the police in Northern Ireland in this chapter as the RUC.

> one of the biggest problems here [in West Belfast] is the issue of policing. We do not have an acceptable police force in this area so I think it is inevitable the community will try to defend itself.[38]

Breidge Gadd, former Chief Probation Officer for Northern Ireland, has argued that the inability to trust the police is one reason why the informal system has continued to operate: 'Until there is resolution between the police and those communities most affected by crime and terrorism, there will continue to be punishment beatings.'[39]

Residents in West Belfast are frequently terrorised and intimidated by hoods and their entourages who congregate in large groups to watch the joyriders and are often rude and aggressive. For example, when one local respondent asked the group of young people who habitually gathered in front of his house not to throw their empty beer cans into his garden they threatened to set his car and his house on fire.

The plethora of articles and letters in the local newspaper the *Andersonstown News* provides further evidence of local concerns. For example:

> The place is like Beirut here . . . from 8pm on a Thursday night when there can be anything up to 100 kids drinking and causing trouble, burning out cars and terrorising local people . . . They stand in massive gangs drinking and throwing stones.[40]

Public meetings, at times attended by up to 500 people, are periodically held to discuss the crime problems in the area.[41] I attended four such meetings during which the dominant moods expressed were anger and frustration at the hoods' persistent offending and the seeming lack of effective interventions. A local resident and participant (B) at one such meeting argued:

> We have fought long and hard for everything in this area, for traffic lights, the health centre, the schools and then the hoods come along and break into them and ruin them. The joyriders ram into pensioners' housing terrifying these old people. As a community what are we supposed to do? We have to draw a line and say something is no longer acceptable and can no longer be tolerated.

At each of the meetings I attended, the demands for harsher interventions against the hoods all came from local residents: 'They can't stab other people and get away with it. They need to be taught a lesson they'll never forget' (Participant L). Such calls are also reiterated in the local press:

> After months of sitting on their hands and biting their lips, the IRA resumed their role of jungle law enforcer, and all across the city ordinary decent people breathed a

[38] Paul Butler, Sinn Féin councillor, in 'Shooting Tactics Resume in City', *Irish News*, 21 June 2000.
[39] Human Rights Watch, *To Serve Without Favour: Policing, Human Rights and Accountability in Northern Ireland* (Human Rights Watch, New York and London, 1997) 104–05.
[40] 'Suffolk Residents Plead for Proper Policing to Combat Weekend Anarchy', *Andersonstown News*, 21 September 2000.
[41] These meetings are often attended by local residents and representatives from youth and community projects, statutory agencies and political parties.

sigh of relief. . . . The middle classes and all the trendy lefty, liberal, bleeding heart journalist hypocrites of the day can beat their breasts and turn their eyes to heaven all they like. The plain fact of the matter is if the North Belfast kneecapping squad stood for election tomorrow they would romp home on the first count. We are not a barbaric lot, we are just tired and frustrated, and disempowered by the joyriding and drug-loving crowd of lowlifes who make working class areas their happy hunting ground.[42]

Although many urban areas in England and Wales may suffer crime rates similar to those in West Belfast, the responses available to deal with offending are different. On the mainland there is rarely any organised group, other than the police, to whom residents can turn for help. Sometimes dissatisfaction with the protection the police are able to offer leads to the formation of neighbourhood watch type schemes, sometimes to low-level forms of vigilantism. By contrast, in West Belfast, there exists in the IRA an organised alternative to the police, into which are channelled vociferous demands for tough deterrent action.

Republicans argue that:

> Petty crime is seen as an attack on the community, which has been left without a police service or a police service which is totally inadequate. (Sinn Féin Youth Worker, H)

They claim that they have assumed their policing and enforcement role in response to such popular pressure. While expressing misgivings over the methods they have to use, and their effectiveness, Republicans present their willingness to carry out this task as a strong sign of their commitment to their communities:

> The pressure comes from the community—the IRA know that the beatings and the kneecappings don't work but most of the community want it to happen and the IRA are damned by a small minority if they do and by a large majority if they don't. (Youth Worker, H)

Republicans thus justify their violence against offenders as a last necessary response to demands from a population victimised by antisocial young people and discriminated against by the RUC. A former Republican prisoner who is now a community worker noted:

> Yes it is a dirty job, somebody has got to do it and that somebody is the people who care most about the community. (Ex-prisoner, L)

Republicans also argue that their violent methods are used because of a lack of viable alternatives:

> they [the IRA] couldn't put people in jail, they couldn't give them community service, they couldn't put them on probation, so they had a very different set of options that they could work with. The two main ones were either exclusion or physical punishment. (Local resident and ex-prisoner, E)

---

[42] ' The IRA: Back on the Beat', *Andersonstown News*, 18 March 2000.

Other commentators have argued that PPAs have instrumental political value for the IRA.[43] In assuming the right to resort to violence, to inflict punishment and to offer reprieves at will the IRA continues to reinforce its position as the legitimate and indisputable authority in West Belfast.

The legitimacy of punishment attacks has, however, been challenged both locally and nationally. Locally, community support for PPAs remains ambiguous. As Munck notes,

> Mrs McBride, who called in 'the lads' [the IRA] to deal with a break-in at her home or a mugging, might object if Mrs McCann's son was beaten up by hooded men with hurley sticks the next night.[44]

Nationally, commentators have drawn attention to the human rights implications of PPAs. For example, Human Rights Watch argued in 1997 that:

> Paramilitary punishment assaults and shootings violate the right to life, freedom from humiliating and degrading treatment, the right to due process and the guarantee of a fair trial as codified in Common Article 3 [Geneva Convention, 1949].[45]

Since then, however, the frequency of PPAs has risen and so too has the number of young people suffering the severe, long-term physical and psychological effects which result.

THE PHYSICAL AND PSYCHOLOGICAL EFFECTS OF PPAS

Following the IRA's 1994 cease-fire, there was a significant change in the nature of both Loyalist and Republican paramilitary 'punishments'. The paramilitaries restricted their use of firearms out of concern that they would be held in violation of the cease-fire.[46] As one former political prisoner pointed out:

---

[43] See L Kennedy, 'Nightmares Within Nightmares: Paramilitary Repression in Working-Class Communities' in L Kennedy (ed), *Crime and Punishment in West Belfast* (The Summer School, West Belfast, 1995) and Knox, 'The "Deserving" Victims of Political Violence', n 8 above.

[44] Munck, 'The Lads and the Hoods', n 32 above, 46.

[45] Human Rights Watch, *To Serve Without Favour*, n 39 above. The PPA phenomenon is also prohibited by customary international humanitarian law. In an important 1986 decision, the International Court of Justice held that the rules defined in Common Article 3: 'also constitute a minimum yardstick, in addition to the more elaborate rules which are also to apply to international conflicts; and that they are rules which . . . reflect what the Court in 1949 called "elementary considerations of humanity." ' International Court of Justice, *Reports of Judgments, Advisory Opinions and Orders: Nicaragua v. United States of America*, Merits, Judgment of 27 June 1986, 114, para 218 (cited in *International Review of the Red Cross* (International Committee of the Red Cross, Geneva, September–October 1990) 386. According to this holding, the rules in Common Article 3 are customary international law and, as such, constitute basic, minimum standards applicable in all situations of armed conflict and binding on all parties to a conflict.

[46] This worry has been proven to be unfounded. When taxi driver Charles Bennett was murdered by the IRA in North Belfast in August 1999 the then Secretary of State for Northern Ireland, Mo Mowlam, ruled that the IRA's cease-fire, whilst breached, was still intact thereby not incurring the exclusion of Sinn Féin from the Northern Ireland peace process or the halting of prisoner releases.

These days there needs to be a really, really strong case for someone to be shot and it is more difficult for the IRA to do it now than ever before because of the political process. Since the 1994 cease-fire, punishment shootings have reduced dramatically but beatings and other serious assaults continue. (Ex-prisoner, F)

Over the last six years, while a substantial number of PPAs have involved shootings, victims have been more commonly subjected to beatings, carried out with a variety of implements, including baseball bats and iron bars. This change in the tools of 'punishment' has resulted in an increase in the level of injuries resulting from PPAs. In separate studies carried out in two hospitals in Belfast, Eames *et al*[47] and Nolan *et al*[48] examined injury patterns sustained by victims of PPAs before and after the 1994 ceasefire. Both teams of researchers found that the damage caused by shootings was often much less extensive than that occurring during a beating, and that, following the ceasefire, the injuries sustained were much more serious. Eames *et al* noted that:

Considerable force is necessary to fracture the tibia, which is a strong weight-bearing bone. In the commoner causes of limb fracture, such as road-traffic injury, the forces applied are great but are applied only once, and from only one direction. If, as during an attack, such force is applied to a limb repeatedly and from many directions then its effects on the soft tissue will be enormous.[49]

Nolan *et al* concluded that the injuries sustained by victims of beatings often required multiple operations, a longer stay in hospital and protracted rehabilitation.[50]

Many of the hoods in my sample were suffering long-term physical effects from injuries inflicted during violent PPAs. Sammy (aged 18) believed that he had incurred a PPA in which his legs were broken because, despite an IRA warning, he did not stop joyriding. When, following the attack, he continued to offend, the IRA broke his legs again, even though they had not yet healed from the first PPA. Sammy told me:

[47] MH Eames, B Kneafsey and D Gordon, 'A Fractured Peace: A Changing Pattern of Violence' (1997) 50 *British Journal of Plastic Surgery* 416–20. This study reviewed all cases of PPAs that had been referred to the Northern Ireland Regional Plastic Surgical Unit at the Ulster Hospital, Dundonald, Belfast between August 1994 and November 1997. The researchers reported the significant changes in injuries received prior and post IRA cease-fire, with many of their patients requiring extensive plastic surgery and orthopaedic treatment after being beaten. The mean patient stay was 22.2 days (range 2–52 days). Each patient had a mean of three theatre attendances and seven hours cumulative operating time (range 2–18 hours).

[48] PC Nolan, J McPhearson and R McKeown, 'The Price of Peace—The Personal and Financial Cost of Paramilitary Punishments in Northern Ireland' (2000) 31(Jan) *Injury* 41–45. This study examined injury patterns sustained by victims of PPAs in the ten months prior to the 1994 cease-fire, and compared them with injury patterns sustained in the same manner in the ten-month period after the cease-fire at Belfast's Royal Victoria Hospital. All of the 31 patients admitted following PPAs in the ten months prior to 31 August 1994, had been shot. By contrast, in the ten months after the cease-fire, only one patient out of the 28 admitted for 'punishment' attacks had been shot.

[49] Eames *et al*, 'A Fractured Peace', n 47 above, 417.

[50] Nolan *et al*, 'The Price of Peace', n 48 above.

My muscles in my legs are all twisted and really painful because my legs didn't heal properly. They beat me black and blue. I thought my jaw was broken.

Mark (aged 17) rolled up the legs of his trousers to reveal the scars on his legs where he was beaten with hurley bats studded with nails whilst being hung upside down from railings. Mick (aged 20) was hit in the throat with a baseball bat. Undoubtedly, the physical effects of IRA beatings and shootings are horrific:

I was held in a house for two hours battered stupid and had to have two lumps of muscle taken out of my leg. (Tommy, aged 23)

These attacks do not just cause long-term physical harm but also result in considerable emotional and psychological scars.

Thompson and Mulholland examined the impact of paramilitary 'punishments' on the lives of young people who have experienced 'punishments', with particular reference to their mental health. They found that those who had been shot 'exhibited very high levels of psychological distress and many symptoms of Post Traumatic Stress Disorder (PTSD)'.[51] These symptoms consisted of: intrusive re-experiencing, including flashbacks and dreams; avoidance or numbing reactions, including efforts to avoid thoughts or feelings associated with the trauma, for example minimising the incident; a sense of a foreshortened future, and increased arousal, including hyper-vigilance and difficulty in concentrating.

The long-term effects of PPAs disclosed to me during my field work were similar to those described in Thompson and Mulholland's work, indicating that the hoods in this study may also have been suffering from PTSD. They reported a mix of symptoms, including difficulty in sleeping. For example, four months after he had been shot in both knees Gerry (aged 22) told me:

I'll hopefully make a full recovery from being shot—it depends on the bullet in my right leg. It causes me a lot of pain and I can't sleep at nights with it. I have a whole lot of nightmares where I relive what happened, and I break out in a cold sweat. I have to have a shower every morning.

Often on the run from both the police and the IRA, hoods also reported feelings of loneliness and isolation. Their seeming disregard for the likely consequences of their defiant and persistent offending has largely deprived them of any local sympathy, as noted by this community worker:

They are an easily recognised group, totally isolated from the rest of the community, unemployed and drinking cider on the street corner. Ninety-six per cent of them are unemployed, the criminal justice system discriminates and isolates them and they are scapegoated by the community. It really isn't fair, as they are such easy targets—I mean who cares about them? (Case Worker, Base 2 Community Project).

---

[51] Thompson and Mulholland, 'Paramilitary Punishments', n 36 above, 57.

From the hoods' perspective, Jackie (aged 17) reflected:

> Everybody's depressed. Nobody wants to listen to young people like us, but we want somewhere to go, somebody to talk to, somebody we can trust, but nobody wants to hear about it anyway. People in the past have always let you down. It all builds up until you say, 'fuck it.' You might try and talk to a friend or they might try and talk to you, but then your friend says she feels exactly the same way, and you don't know what to say to each other. You're scared to say that you're feeling suicidal in case people just tell you it'll be all right and don't listen to what you're sayin'. It's worse to say and not be listened to than not say at all. There's nobody out there for us.

These feelings are associated not just with violent PPAs but also with the lesser 'punishments' such as curfews and exclusions. Anne-Marie (aged 17) was excluded from Belfast by the IRA and living in another town in Northern Ireland when she discussed how she felt about herself and her life:

> I don't talk to any of my family, I have no job and I can't get seein' my family. I don't like it, but it's my own fault. I feel stupid, sad and sorry and it's awful lonely down here.

Having to live in a hostel can be particularly unpleasant, and often had a very negative effect on the hoods behaviour:

> Puttin' me out my own area only made me worse. I was less likely to do stuff in my own area. But, see livin' away and sleepin' in hostels and stuff, it just does your head in and you go mad. (Danny, aged 24)

Fear and feelings of powerlessness often result in hoods becoming increasingly dependent on alcohol and drugs as a means of escapism and bravado. For some, however, the experience can be so traumatic that it can lead to total desperation. Just over one third of the hoods in the study described suffering from long periods of depression and having suicidal thoughts. Twenty-two per cent admitted that they had attempted suicide at least once.[52] Angela (aged 19) described a number of incidents when she self-harmed and tried to kill herself:

> The last time was about seven months ago, and before that about three years ago. Life wasn't fair, and if I feel down or weak then somethin' stupid could happen. The first time was an overdose of Anadin. I took 47, second overdose of 65 Paracodal. Third time, I cut my throat with a glass bottle. The first time the tablets went missin' at the training school, so they asked another girl who told them that I took them. They took me to hospital to get my stomach pumped. The second time I was found unconscious by staff and had my stomach pumped. The third time I'd an argument with my girl. I was drunk and said I'd kill myself.
>
> She said: 'Ahh you won't', dead cocky, so I smashed a Bacardi bottle and slashed it twice across my throat. There was a lot of blood and they were deep cuts. I wouldn't go to hospital. I said I'd bleed to death. I cut myself with razors in the arms, a couple of times on my head and legs. About five years, I've been doing it every day.

---

[52] Of the 22% who admitted to attempting suicide at least once, 19% had attempted to hang themselves, 50% had slit their wrists and 31% had taken a drugs overdose.

There are various factors that can lead to depression severe enough for young people to contemplate and even attempt suicide. Suicide attempts are relatively high amongst young men in deprived socio-economic conditions, and particularly high amongst young men in custody.[53] The extent to which PPAs, or the threat of them, lead to suicide is a question beyond the data collected for this study. However, the data at least suggest that PPAs are a significant factor in contributing towards the feelings of isolation and desperation, which might persuade young people to kill themselves. Furthermore, some secondary victims clearly believe that they are a direct cause. In 1995, in an interview with the *Irish News*, the father of a young man who had committed suicide explained:

> The fact is that my son was viciously beaten by known IRA paramilitaries and continually intimidated right up to his death . . . There was continual intimidation by those so-called heroes or vigilantes who administer justice in their own form.[54]

Thomas Clarke blamed the IRA's actions for his son's death, quoting his son's suicide note as proof: 'Do not feel it is your fault as it is not. It is the dirty stinking piggy rats out on the street.'[55] In a similar case in 1997, 21-year-old Gerard Marley hanged himself from railings near the Westlink motorway that skirts the edge of West Belfast. In the newspaper reports that followed Gerard's death, his father disclosed that his son had been a joyrider and had sustained two 'punishment' beatings from the IRA that had destroyed both his legs.[56] He also had to put up with jeers and taunts from Republicans because he walked with a limp as a result of the assaults. According to Gerard's father 'the mental scars refused to heal—and constant taunts pushed him to end his life'.[57]

All of the evidence indicates that PPAs do have a powerful impact on the physical, psychological and emotional health of the victims of these attacks. Although the instances of suicide following an attack are rare, Thompson and Mulholland conclude that:

> The actions of the paramilitaries seem to be part of a self-maintaining cycle . . . of fear, anger, revenge and a sense of having nothing to lose among the hoods. [58]

The question therefore arises: 'why do PPA's not deter the hoods from offending?' This is addressed in detail in my doctoral thesis which shows how the peculiarities of the hoods' offending can be explained as a signalling game. The aim of persistent and non instrumental offending is to display hard-to-fake signals of 'toughness' to other hoods and thereby gain greater prestige. This game also explains how violent physical punishment fails to achieve a full deterrent effect.

---

[53] A Leibling, *Suicides in Prison* (Routledge, London, 1992).

[54] 'Son Killed Himself Over IRA Beatings Says Dad', *Irish News,* 19 October 1995.

[55] Human Rights Watch, *To Serve Without Favour,* n 39 above, 129.

[56] 'Man's Suicide Must be Last', *Irish News,* 29 July 1997.

[57] 'Punishment Beating "Cripple" Hanged on Motorway Railings: Taunts Drive IRA Victim to Kill Himself', *Irish News,* 29 July 1997.

[58] Thompson and Mulholland, 'Paramilitary Punishments', n 36 above, 60.

While some young offenders refrain from antisocial behaviour for fear of punishment, many others reach an even greater prestige by showing how they can take punishment and remain undeterred.[59] It is not that they actively seek out a PPA, but rather that they cannot countenance the loss of prestige associated with abandoning the lifestyle that leads to this form of victimisation.

Miers points out that in order to be seen as 'deserving', a victim 'should try to avoid, in the future, the circumstances that occasioned' their being harmed.[60] Hoods, by contrast, actively seek out such circumstances. The following comment from a local community worker sums up well how this leads to the hoods losing all claim to a victim status:

> Look, the way I see it, the paramilitaries give people as much of a chance as possible. But at the end of the day if they don't take that chance and stop, then they have to take the consequences. I mean, if I stick my hand in the fire then I'll get burnt—right? (Community Worker, R)

Knox notes that although those who have received PPAs are referred to by some as victims, according to local opinion they have forfeited their victim status and deserve their 'punishment'.[61] The use of the term 'punishment' to describe these assaults implies that such actions are in some way justified.[62] This is based on the notion that all those who live in West Belfast are aware of the conventions that govern life in the area, and if these rules are broken then the consequences are inevitable—a hood's continued offending will result in a PPA.

CONCLUSION

This chapter documents a specific instance of the social construction of the inter-related categories of 'crime', 'offenders' and 'victims'. Given that the evaluation of victim status has a direct impact on the perceived culpability of the perpetrator,[63] one outcome of the hoods lack of victim status is that the perpetrators have successfully avoided being labelled as violent offenders. Instead, the IRA legitimises its actions by claiming to be acting in the interests of the community—an argument that, generally speaking, remains acceptable to local people partly because they see no legitimate alternative.

The hoods' refusal to stop offending despite the threat of PPAs suggests that some groups of people will persist in behaviour that dramatically increases their

---

[59] See H Hamill, *Hoods and Provos: Crime and Punishment in West Belfast* (Unpublished DPhil Thesis, Department of Sociology, University of Oxford, 2002).
[60] Miers, 'Taking the Law into their Own Hands' n 2 above.
[61] Knox, 'The "Deserving" Victims of Political Violence', n 8 above.
[62] See Kennedy 'Nightmares Within Nightmares', n 43 above, and Knox, 'The "Deserving" Victims of Political Violence', n 8 above.
[63] D Richardson and H May, 'Deserving Victims? Sexual Status and the Social Construction of Violence' (1999) 47 *Sociological Review* 308–31.

likelihood of becoming victims. This is a challenging situation for policy makers and practitioners working towards reducing the instances of victimisation in society. One strategy would be to ameliorate the structural conditions of poverty, deprivation and lack of opportunity that precipitate and sustain delinquency amongst children and young people, and which, as mediated through the subculture of the hoods, make a PPA less to be feared than loss of prestige amongst peers.

The chapter has also drawn out the relationship between the macro political context and micro-processes of offending and victimisation. PPAs take place in an environment where the legitimacy of the statutory police is heavily contested. Since this research was completed, the police in Northern Ireland have introduced wide-ranging reforms including a drive to recruit more catholics into the force. It remains to be seen what impact these initiatives will have on the reception of the police in areas such as West Belfast and, if positive, whether a more acceptable police force will result in a reduction in PPAs.

4

Female-on-Male Domestic Abuse: Uncommon or Ignored?

ANN GRADY*

INTRODUCTION

T HE POLICE RESPONSE to domestic violence[1] has been the subject of
consistent criticism since domestic violence itself became a major academic
and social concern in the 1970s. The inadequacy of the response has been
well documented, as have changes in police practice, which have been informed by
the academic debate surrounding the issue.[2] However, the attention given to
domestic violence has concentrated on male-on-female abuse, despite evidence
that indicates men and women are victimised in the home to broadly similar
degrees. This chapter will suggest that the dominance of the female victim in the
domestic violence debate is due in large part to the feminist principles that have
been adopted by many researchers in the field. Consequently, a stereotypical perception of domestic violence has been created that dictates women are the victims
and men are the aggressors.[3] The chapter discusses research carried out by the
author that highlights several aspects of police practice that may contribute towards
the invisibility of the male domestic violence victim within the official statistics. It
is argued that the present police response to domestic violence is shaped by powerful stereotypes of who are the victims and the perpetrators. Awareness of this casts
doubt on the accuracy of police statistics on domestic violence and raises questions
about our current perceptions of, and responses to, family abuse.

---

* I would like to thank Richard Young and Carolyn Hoyle for the support they have shown throughout
the writing of this chapter and beyond.
[1] A note on terminology: This chapter tends to talk of 'abuse' rather than 'violence' in recognition of
the fact that domestic victimisation can occur as a result of physical, psychological or emotional acts.
However, the terms are often used interchangeably. References to 'violence' should not be taken to
mean exclusively physical violence.
[2] See especially SM Edwards, *Policing Domestic Violence: Women the Law and the State* (Sage, London,
1989), J Walker and L McNicol, *Policing Domestic Violence: Protection, Prevention or Prudence?* (Relate
Centre for Family Studies, Newcastle, 1994) and S Grace, *Policing Domestic Violence in the 1990s*
(HMSO, London, 1995).
[3] That is not to say that feminist findings on male-on-female abuse are inaccurate, but rather that they
cannot be said to represent the extent of all forms of family abuse, particularly female-on-male abuse.

THE EVIDENCE OF FEMALE-ON-MALE DOMESTIC VIOLENCE

To argue that the police fail to recognise incidents of female-on-male domestic violence, one must first ascertain, or at least estimate, its prevalence. Since the mid 1970s a steady flow of studies has indicated that men and women are equally likely to be subjected to physical assault in the home.[4] The majority of these studies have approached the issue from a 'family conflict' perspective; their aim being to highlight the nature of conflict resolution within the family unit. In adopting this perspective, Murray Straus developed the Conflict Tactics Scale (CTS). Subjects were asked to identify the methods they employed to resolve conflict within their own families. To establish levels of aggression experienced by, and perpetrated by, respondents, the CTS presented them with a range of acts from being 'pushed or shoved' to 'hit with an object'. The range was divided into two categories of minor and severe violence. This enabled the researchers to calculate the frequency with which individuals used, and experienced, differing forms of violence against, and from, their partners.

Straus's study produced interesting results that he extrapolated to create nationally representative figures. Of all the households studied, 27 per cent reported only male-on-female violence, 24 per cent reported only female-on-male violence, and almost 50 per cent reported mutual violence between the couples. Once extrapolated Straus concluded that male-on-female violence occurred at a rate of 38 per 1000 couples per year, whereas female-on-male violence occurred at the rate of 46 per 1000 couples per year. The data also showed that a small proportion of both men and women committed serious acts of violence.[5] Strauss found that women were victims of domestic violence slightly more than men. However, he established that on the ranges of violence that could be referred to as 'spouse beating', men were more likely to be victims. These findings were repeated in a study conducted ten years later.[6] In short, this research reveals high levels of unilateral abuse by women as well as high incidents of mutual abuse between partners. This counters the often-raised claim of other researchers, particularly feminists, that the only context within which women assault their partners is self-defence.[7]

---

[4] See J Archer, 'Sex Differences in Aggression Between Heterosexual Partners: A Meta-analytic Review' (2000) 126 *Psychological Bulletin* 651–80 for the most comprehensive bibliography.

[5] MA Strauss, 'Measuring Intrafamily Conflict and Violence: The Conflict Tactics (CT) Scale' (1979) 41 *Journal of Marriage and Family* 75–88.

[6] MA Straus and RJ Gelles, *Physical Violence in American Families* (Transaction Publishers, London, 1990).

[7] MD Pagelow, '"The Battered Husband Syndrome" Social Problem or Much Ado about Little?' in N Johnson (ed), *Marital Violence* (Routledge & Kegan Paul, London, 1985); RE Dobash and RP Dobash, *Rethinking Violence Against Women* (Sage, London, 1998). This narrow view by feminists of female offending also ignores the prevalence of abuse between lesbian couples, and the role of women as offenders in incidents of elder abuse. See C Renzetti, 'Violence and Abuse in Lesbian Relationships: Theoretical and Empirical Issues' in RK Bergen (ed), *Issues in Intimate Violence* (Sage, London, 1998), where Renzetti notes that theoretical models of heterosexual abuse are not applicable to same-sex abuse. Also K Browne and M Herbert, *Preventing Family Violence* (John Wiley & Sons, Chichester, 1997), particularly ch 10 where it is noted that women may account for the majority of abusers of the elderly.

Feminists have argued that the CTS fails to take into account the greater likelihood of injury to women in violent relationships.[8] However, the findings of CTS studies are too numerous and consistent to ignore or dismiss. Well over 100 other studies have adopted the CTS method developed by Straus.[9] George notes that a number of these studies have relied on self-reporting data gathered from both men and women. They consistently show that women not only admit to using violence against their partners more frequently than men, they are also more likely to use severe forms of violence.[10] George concludes that the evidence broadly supports the assertion that a significant number of men are the victims of unilateral violence by their female partners. Indeed, he suggests that as many as 25 per cent of domestic violence victims could be men in this situation.[11]

George's view is supported by Table 1. In that table, with the exception of Clarke (1987), studies that have used female only samples report male only violence. Of course this is a methodological artefact. These studies were directly concerned with women as victims in differing contexts and did not ask women to self-report their own violence, clearly not seeing this as part of their remit.[12] All of the other studies in the table, with the exception of Smith (1986) and Lockhart (1987), report (varying) rates of violence for both men and women. It is striking that in five of these eleven studies, women were reported to have used a higher rate of violence than their male counterparts. Overall, it is evident that, particularly in studies of couples, women self-report the use of violence in intimate relationships to much the same degree as men.

Archer reached a similar conclusion based on his meta-analysis of 82 CTS studies to determine the overall effect of available research data.[13] A comparison was drawn between self-report data and partner-report data. The differences were significant and Archer concluded that:

> according to self reports, women are more likely than men to commit acts of physical aggression, whereas according to partner reports, their respective levels are similar.[14]

Archer also compared studies that reported the level of injuries sustained by victims or the need for medical treatment and found that significantly more women

---

[8] See Pagelow 'The Battered Husband Syndrome' and Dobash and Dobash, *Rethinking Violence Against Women*, both n 5 above. Indeed, Straus has noted this point himself, 'Measuring Intrafamily Conflict and Violence', n 4 above.

[9] For a full summary of other studies see Strauss and Gelles, *Physical Violence in American Families*, n 6 above; M George, 'Riding the Donkey Backwards: Men as the Unacceptable Victims of Marital Violence' (1994) 3 *The Journal of Men's Studies* 137-59; M George, *Beyond All Help?* (Dewar Research, London, 1998); Archer, 'Sex Differences in Aggression' n 4 above.

[10] Within the CTS severe forms of violence includes the use of weapons and actions defined as 'beating up' a partner.

[11] M George, 'Riding the Donkey Backwards', n 9 above, 12.

[12] Frieze *et al* were specifically concerned with identifying 'battered women', Russell with rape in marriage, Schulman with spousal violence *against* women, and Smith with 'woman abuse'.

[13] Meta-analysis is a statistical review of the available literature on a subject.

[14] Archer, 'Sex Differences in Aggression', n 4 above, 656.

Table 1: Past-Year Prevalence Rates of Violence Among Intimates (Per 1,000 Population)

Study	Sample		Any Violence By:	
			Husband or Male Partner	Wife or Female Partner
1. National Probability Samples				
Straus & Gelles (1990)	N = 6,002		116	124
Straus et al. (1980)	N = 2,143	Couples	121	116
Straus & Gelles (1986)	N = 3,520	Couples	110	120
2. Local or Statewide Probability Samples				
Schulman (1979)	N = 1,793	Kentucky women	100	—
Russell (1982)	N = 644	San Francisco women[a]	260	—
Nisonoff & Bitman (1979)	N = 297	Household sample	160	120
Smith (1986)[b]	N = 315		206	—
Smith (1987)	N = 604	Toronto women	144	—
3. Nonprobability Local Samples				
Makepeace (1983)[c]	N = 244	Dating couples, college students	137	93
Brutz & Ingoldsby (1984)	N = 288	Quakers	146	152
Makepeace (1981)[b]	N = 2,338	Students, dating couples	206	120
Meredith et al. (1986)	N = 304		220	180
Szinovacz (1983)	N = 103		260	300
Clarke (1987)	N = 318	Women	274	102
Lockhart (1987)	N = 307	Blacks and whites	355	—
Barling et al. (1987)[c]	N = 187		740	730
Frieze et al. (1980)	N = 137	Pennsylvania women, ever-Married and comparison group	340	—
Levinger (1966)	N = 600	Divorce filings	370	—
Mason & Blankenship (1987)	N = 155	Michigan undergraduates	18	22

Note: rates are for acts occurring during the past 12 months.
a. Currently or ever married at time of interview
b. Rates only for lifetime prevalence
c. Study did not report whether rates are for the previous year or lifetime.

Source: Davis, Lurigio and Skogan, *Victims of Crime* (Sage, London, 1997) 58.[15]

than men were injured or required hospital treatment as a result of aggression from their partner. However, removing 'outlying studies' from the calculation considerably reduced the effect size in relation to injuries sustained by women.[16] Furthermore, Archer found that when a comparison was drawn between the injuries sustained by male and female victims and the physical aggression used by men and women, injury measures were higher for men. Hence, Archer's analysis indicates that men were more likely than women to be injured in an assault by a

[15] Reproduced by permission of the publisher. One study has been removed from the original table as typesetting error in the original text meant that its findings were not clear.
[16] Outlying datasets were removed because they presented results that appeared spurious in comparison to the main dataset. This is an accepted feature of meta-analysis method.

partner. Archer concluded that the CTS research showed women to be significantly more likely to use physical aggression against their partners and to use it more frequently.

The degree of victimisation suffered by men is also supported by a number of other (non-CTS) studies. The 1996 British Crime Survey included a computerised self-completion questionnaire designed to give the most reliable findings to date on the extent of domestic violence in England and Wales. Using this technique, 4.2 per cent of men and 4.2 per cent of women reported that they had been physically assaulted by a current or former partner in the last year, although women were twice as likely to have been injured by the assault.[17] When asked about the most recent assault, six per cent of repeatedly victimised women as compared with one per cent of repeatedly victimised men reported the injury taking the form of broken bones.[18] By comparison, United States Bureau of Justice statistics show that women are nearly three times more likely than men to kill an intimate partner.[19] Undoubtedly, feminists would argue that such high figures represent the greater need of women to take extreme action in self-defence. However, other homicide studies indicate that this may not be the case; at least not with reference to standard legal notions of self-defence. For example, Mann found that 60 per cent of women had pre-planned their murders.[20] Even if we adopt a broad moralistic definition of self-defence as an act of violence (whether planned or not) in response to a prior pattern of victimisation, the evidence does not support this self-defence thesis. Rather, studies have found that up to 60 per cent of women who kill intimate partners have never reported being persistently victimised.[21] Furthermore, such studies also cast doubt upon the possible reliance by these women upon defences of provocation or diminished responsibility. Similarly, it is unlikely that any of them could claim to have acted violently because they suffered from 'battered woman syndrome'.[22] Accordingly, the traditional stance of 'core feminists',[23] that such actions are the results of sustained or prolonged abuse, can be questioned.

A small number of qualitative studies (the method favoured by core feminists) present evidence of unilateral abuse by women. For example, Cook interviewed 30 men on the west coast of America and found that many were attacked with weapons, ranging from knives to padlocks to guns, with one man being stabbed

---

[17] C Mirrlees-Black, *Domestic Violence: Findings from a New British Crime Survey Self-completion Questionnaire*, Home Office Research Study 191 (Home Office, London, 1999) 20.

[18] *Ibid*, 38.

[19] US Department of Justice Office of Justice Programs, *Survey of State Prison Inmate—1991: Women in Prison*, Bureau of Justice Statistics Special Report NCJ–145321 (GPO, Washington, DC, March 1994), cited in PW Cook, *Abused Men: The Hidden Side of Domestic Violence* (Praegar, London, 1997) 20.

[20] C Mann, 'Getting Even? Women Who Kill in Domestic Encounters' (1988) 5 *Justice Quarterly* 33–50.

[21] See PW Cook, *Abused Men*, n 19 above, ch 1.

[22] As established by Leonore Walker, see LE Walker, *The Battered Woman Syndrome* (Springer, New York NY, 1984).

[23] This term is defined in the next section of the chapter.

repeatedly, and another shot five times in a single incident.[24] A small targeted study of male victims of domestic violence by Stitt and Macklin in the UK revealed a range of physical abuses by female partners from biting, scratching, poking, prodding, slapping, and punching to the use of weapons such as high-heeled shoes, garden tools and knives.[25]

Even a brief perusal of the empirical evidence of male domestic violence victimisation casts doubt on the methodological validity of studies which indicate that women are overwhelmingly the victims of domestic violence.[26] This is especially true of studies that gather data or identify subjects from police records.[27] While CTS studies report an equal incidence of violence between partners, police record based studies clearly indicate that male-on-female violence predominates.[28] Most recently, Stanko reported that 86 per cent of the people contacting the police were the female victims of male partners.[29]

How then can the discrepancy be explained? A starting point must be that the police statistics represent the 'tip of the iceberg', in that only a small proportion of victims report incidents to the police and these victims do not report all incidents of victimisation.[30] Part of the explanation must be that as women are more likely to be injured by domestic violence, they are more likely to come to the notice of an agency such as the police (see, for example, the 1996 British Crime Survey figures). However, other studies discussed above indicate that men suffer rates of injury much higher than police figures suggest. We must therefore look elsewhere for a plausible explanation of the relative absence of male victims from police records.

---

[24] Cook identified the sample during his time working for a charitable organisation that was concerned with the effects of parental separation upon children. All the men admitted to having experienced domestic victimisation on their intake form.

[25] The sample was obtained from publicity in local papers in the North West of England, and radio/TV interviews with the researchers.

[26] See LJF Smith, *Domestic Violence: An Overview of the Literature* (HMSO, London, 1989) for a summary of the evidence.

[27] Edwards, *Policing Domestic Violence*, n 2 above; A Bourlet, *Police Intervention in Marital Violence* (Open University Press, Milton Keynes, 1990); JWE Sheptycki, *Innovations in Policing Domestic Violence* (Avebury, Aldershot, 1993); Walker and McNicol, *Policing Domestic Violence*, n 2 above; Grace, *Policing Domestic Violence in the 1990s*, n 2 above. This is not to suggest that all of these studies have adopted feminist principles or methods.

[28] For example Grace, *Policing Domestic Violence in the 1990s*, n 2 above, reported that 97 % of victims were female. It is accepted that other studies do not rely on police data and yet still show a predominance of violence against women. However, these studies often use self-reporting samples from refuges, for example, where it is unsurprising that such results are obtained. See J Pahl, *A Refuge for Battered Women: A Study of the Role of a Women's Centre* (HMSO, London, 1978) and V Binney, G Harkell and J Nixon, *Leaving Violent Men: A Study of Refuges and Housing for Battered Women* (Women's Aid Federation, England, 1981).

[29] E Stanko, 'The Day to Count: Reflections on a Methodology to Raise Awareness about the Impact of Domestic Violence in the UK' (2001) 1 *Criminal Justice* 215–26

[30] Walker and McNicol, *Policing Domestic Violence*, n 2 above, 3–4, cite Mooney (1993), who estimates that while nearly a third of women have been injured because of domestic assault only a fifth report violence to the police. The 1996 British Crime Survey found that only 12 % of the domestic assaults uncovered were reported to the police: Mirrlees-Black, *Domestic Violence*, n 17 above, 54.

A large part of the explanation lies in reporting behaviour. The 1996 British Crime Survey found that only seven per cent of 'chronic' male victims (victimised three or more times in the previous year) said that the police were aware of their victimisation as compared to 36 per cent of chronic female victims. This lower reporting rate for men is likely to be directly related to their experiences of not receiving helpful advice and support from the police when victimised in the past: 'overall male victims did not rate the police nearly as highly as female victims'.[31] As my own findings (presented below) will show, a further part of the explanation is that, even when they do report their victimisation, the police are much less likely to record male complainants as victims than female complainants. Why do the police appear to regard male victims of domestic violence less seriously than their female counterparts?

I believe that the influence of feminism upon domestic violence research has been so dominant that it has led to the creation of a domestic violence stereotype: that domestic violence is male-on-female abuse. My empirical research suggests that this stereotype has informed operational policing to the extent that officers are almost blind to the existence of male victims. Failure to recognise, and therefore to label, men as victims leads to their significant under-representation in the official statistics and in studies based on samples drawn from police records. But how could feminism have had this strong an effect upon our understanding of domestic violence? In turn, how can it be argued to have affected the police response so greatly?

FEMINIST PERSPECTIVES ON DOMESTIC ABUSE

General Principles of Feminist Study

Before considering the feminist approach to domestic violence, it is useful to consider the general principles of feminism and feminist research which provide the foundation for domestic violence study. Feminism embraces a diverse and complex set of ideas and standpoints. However, a common core runs through virtually all feminist work; it regards the gendered structure of society as the cause of female oppression. Feminists argue that prior social knowledge and understanding have been rooted in 'maleness'; they represent male knowledge of male experiences within a male led world. Hence, from this perspective, there was never real objectivity within previous inquiry, there was only male objectivity. This prompts feminists to assert that their own analysis 'begins with the principle that objective reality is a myth' and furthermore that the most pernicious aspect of this myth is that 'the domination of women is a natural right'.[32] This common strand within feminism can be defined as 'core' feminism. Certainly, there are feminists who

---

[31] Mirrlees-Black, n 17 above, 53–54.
[32] AC Scales 'The Emergence of Feminist Jurisprudence: An Essay' (1986) 95 *Yale Law Journal* 1373.

would not agree that they personally adhere to this fundamental ideal. However, there is a 'hard core' of feminists that do. Hence, one can conceptualise the notion of 'core' feminism in two ways: first the existence of a 'core' central group who generally adhere to the above fundamental principles and second the fundamental principles themselves, principles that may be adopted to varying degrees by any feminist, but are at the 'core' of feminist theory.

Core feminism dictates that female subordination must be explained. Dalton has said that feminism represents a:

> range of committed inquiry and activity dedicated first, to describing women's subordination—exploring its nature and extent; dedicated second, to asking both *how*—through what mechanisms, and *why*—for what complex and interwoven reasons—women continue to occupy that position; and dedicated third to change.[33]

As a principled approach to research, core feminism's purpose is clear. It is committed to the epistemic and practical emancipation of women.[34] The application of these principles to research methods is vital for core feminists. Stanley and Wise describe it as 'crucial to the feminist enterprise.'[35] If women are to overcome the oppression caused by male power gained from male knowledge, the creation of their own knowledge must be true to the female experience. Accordingly, core feminists hold strong beliefs as to the appropriate methods that should be utilised within feminist study. They have long argued that qualitative, not quantitative, methodology should be applied to the research subject. Inverting the common methodological position, they see quantitative methods as presenting a distorted view of the truth because they are so widely open to the interpretation of the researcher and, perhaps more persuasively, because they originate from a patriarchal perspective of the world.[36] Qualitative methods, they argue, while still open to degrees of interpretation, allow 'individual women's understandings, emotions, and actions in the world [to] be explored in those women's own terms.'[37] Kelly *et al* note that an:

> orthodoxy developed in social science . . . best summarised in the phrase 'research on, with and for women', . . . which asserted or implied that 'feminist method' involved face-to-face interviewing.[38]

---

[33] C Dalton, 'Where We Stand: Observations on the Situation of Feminist Legal Thought' (1987–88) 3 *Berkeley Women's Law Journal* 1, 2.

[34] See M Maynard and J Purvis, *Researching Women's Lives from a Feminist Perspective* (Taylor & Francis, London, 1994) for fuller discussion.

[35] L Stanley and S Wise, *Breaking Out: Feminist Consciousness and Feminist Research* (Routledge & Kegan Paul, London, 1983) 167.

[36] K Yllö 'Political and Methodological Debates in Wife Abuse Research' in K Yllö and M Bograd (eds), *Feminist Perspectives on Wife Abuse* (Sage, London, 1990).

[37] TE Jayaratne and AJ Stewart, 'Quantitative and Qualitative Methods in the Social Sciences: Feminist Issues and Practical Strategies' in J Holland and M Blair (eds), *Debates and Issues in Feminist Research and Pedagogy* (Open University Press, Clevedon, 1995) 217.

[38] L Kelly, S Burton and L Regan, 'Researching Women's Lives or Studying Women's Oppression?' in M Maynard and J Purvis (eds), *Researching Women's Lives from a Feminist Perspective* (Taylor & Francis, London, 1994) 29.

For these reasons, many feminists have dismissed the CTS research outlined above as invalid.[39]

From this position, it is not difficult to assert that there is an obvious bias within the fundamental principles of feminist study. Feminism needs to ask the 'woman question'. It is justified in being specific about its subject group, its methods, and its aims. However, what is starting to emerge is its inapplicability to other subjects, most obviously to men. It follows that men are invisible within feminist theory and research. That this has been beneficial to our understanding of women's place in society is incontrovertible. But, it does raise the question as to whether it has been the most appropriate method to adopt for research on domestic violence.

Feminist Method + Domestic Violence = Stereotype?

Bograd outlines clearly the four major dimensions that are common to all feminist perspectives on 'wife abuse':

(1)   the explanatory utility of the constructs of gender and power;
(2)   the analysis of the family as a historically situated social institution;
(3)   the crucial importance of understanding and validating women's experiences;
(4)   employing scholarship for women.[40]

It is thus evident that core feminist principles are seen to have specific application to domestic violence research. Feminists view the gendered structure of society as an instrumental facilitator of violence against women. Men are the holders of public and private power, which creates a subordinate underclass of women.[41] By holding this power, they exercise 'social control' over women, which at its extreme is expressed using violence, especially within the home. Accordingly, 'domination at the social level is the most crucial factor contributing to and maintaining wife abuse at the personal level.'[42] Bart and Moran reinforce this view when they state:

> abusing and assaulting women is prevalent and rooted in misogyny, signifying that this violence reinforces men as a class controlling women as a class. One can conceptualise it as the linchpin of our subordination.[43]

[39]   E Pleck, JH Pleck, M Grossman and PB Bart, 'The Battered Data Syndrome' (1978) 2 *Victimology* 680-84; Pagelow 'The Battered Husband Syndrome' and Dobash and Dobash, *Rethinking Violence Against Women*, both n 7 above.
[40]   M Bograd, 'Feminist Perspectives on Wife Abuse: An Introduction', in K Yllö and M Bograd (eds) *Feminist Perspectives on Wife Abuse* (Sage, London, 1990) 13–14.
[41]   See CA MacKinnon, *Toward a Feminist Theory of the State* (Harvard University Press, London, 1989).
[42]   Bograd, 'Feminist Perspectives on Wife Abuse' n 40 above, 14.
[43]   P B Bart and E G Moran (eds), *Violence Against Women: The Bloody Footprints* (Sage, Thousand Oaks Cal, 1993) 230.

Feminists therefore analyse domestic violence by 'illuminating the experiences of women from their own frames of reference'.[44] Immediately, the male domestic violence victim is deselected from any sample groups. Core feminism's purpose is clear: its aim is to develop knowledge and understanding of the female domestic violence victim's experience. Accordingly, one can assert that the feminist analysis of domestic violence is gender-biased, and its findings will reflect such a bias. The only conclusion to be reached by a feminist analysis of domestic violence is that men are aggressors. Even when it is accepted that women are violent, this is explained by arguments of self-defence on the woman's part against a previously violent husband. As Saunders argues, 'to label self-defence *husband abuse* serves to direct attention away from the victimisation of women and the function of male dominance.'[45] Hence, labelling female violence as self-defence makes female-on-male violence part of the wider problem of 'wife abuse'.

It can be seen, therefore, that there is a stereotypical image of domestic violence. It is inherent in the language used by feminists and in their theoretical explanation of subordination. It has been reinforced through the adoption of qualitative methods of inquiry which have had an obvious effect on the results produced. If women's experiences are sought through this method, then the conclusion is always likely to be that women are the victims, not men. In simple terms, the stereotype of domestic violence is male violence against female victims.

When first encountered, this stereotype seems to represent the reality as documented by the most oft-cited studies on domestic violence. Gaquin, showed women to be 30 times more likely to be victimised than men.[46] Grace cited West Midlands police figures as showing women to be the victim in just over 90 per cent of cases (with the sex of the victim being non-identifiable in 7 per cent of cases).[47] Smith observed that most studies from as early as the 1950s have found women to be the main victims of domestic assault.[48] Indeed, McLeod found that 94 per cent of the victims studied were female.[49] How then can one assert that feminism is at the root of the problem?

In answering this question two points can be made. First, the majority of the most influential publications, such as those produced by Dobash and Dobash, Pahl, Pagelow (all discussed above), apply feminist principles to their work. Females are the subjects of study. Second, it is evident that other studies, although they may not expressly rely on feminism for their methodological approach, identify women as their research subject because of the findings of feminist-based studies. For example, Walker and McNicol state that 'the evidence of most studies

[44] Bograd, 'Feminist Persepctives on Wife Abuse' n 40 above , 15.
[45] DG Saunders 'Wife Abuse, Husband Abuse or Mutual Combat? A Feminist Perspective on the Empirical Findings' in Yllö and Bograd (eds), *Feminist Perspectives on Wife Abuse*, n 40 above.
[46] DA Gaquin, 'Spouse Abuse: Data from the National Crime Survey' (1978) 2 *Victimology* 632–43.
[47] Grace, Grace, *Policing Domestic Violence in the 1990s*, n 2 above.
[48] LJF Smith, *Domestic Violence*, n 26 above.
[49] M McLeod, 'Women Against Men: An Examination of Domestic Violence Based on an Analysis of Official Data and National Victimisation Data' (1984) *Victimology* 171–93.

confirms that it is women who are almost always the victims'.[50] Often, writers use the evidence of these studies to support their own concentration on the female victim. Thus, Binney *et al* make direct reference to the work of Dobash and Dobash when justifying the need to study the female victim.[51] Bourlet does the same.[52] In some cases, writers do not even bother to justify their subject group, clearly implying that they see domestic violence to be a female issue.[53]

Overwhelmingly, domestic violence studies also adopt methodologies that feminists suggest are the most appropriate; that is, qualitative. Most studies identify their 'victims' from self-reporting sample groups such as women in refuges, accident and emergency departments, or those that have responded to direct requests to be involved in a study. The data presented have been obtained from face-to-face or questionnaire interviewing. Any statistical data have been obtained from these interview responses. The only exception to this point is data gathered directly from police records, which tend to be analysed and presented in a more quantitative fashion. What is clear from the studies conducted on domestic violence is that even if researchers do not consciously apply feminist principles and methods to their work, the foundation of feminist theory laid by earlier research still affects their outcomes. Many studies start from the stereotypical proposition that domestic violence means male-on-female abuse. Consequently, no attempt is made to even identify the male victim, let alone contextualise the abuse he suffers. This perspective is supported by a wider view of the problems of the male victim as presented by Newburn and Stanko, who conclude that:

> accepting that men also suffer as a result of criminal victimisation is not to deny that men continue to occupy an advantaged position in relation to women, or that women are 'unequal' victims of crime.[54]

However, they do not go far enough in their call for acknowledgement of the male victim. Rather, they make clear that they seek to 'confront the social reality in which men not only routinely victimise women, but also victimise each other.'[55] Accordingly, even this call for acknowledgement does little to question the domestic violence stereotype.[56]

This stereotype perpetuates a social perception of domestic violence as an offence committed by men against women. The application of this stereotype is at its greatest within domestic violence response agencies, as they have been most

[50] Walker and McNicol, *Policing Domestic Violence*, n 2 above, ix.

[51] Binney *et al*, n 28 above; Dobash and Dobash, *Rethinking Violence Against Women*, n 7 above, ii-iii.

[52] Bourlet, *Police Intervention in Marital Violence*, n 27 above, 1–3.

[53] See especially D Lockton and R Ward, *Domestic Violence* (Cavendish, London, 1997) and F Pickup, S Williams and C Sweetman, *Ending Violence Against Women: A Challenge for Development and Humanitarian Work* (Oxfam Publications, Oxford, 2001).

[54] T Newburn and E A Stanko 'When Men are Victims: The Failure of Victimology' in T Newburn and EA Stanko (eds), *Just Boys Doing Business?* (Routledge, London, 1994) 165.

[55] *Ibid.*

[56] Indeed, Newburn and Stanko hail male-on-female domestic violence research as one of the few areas of victimology that highlight victim experiences, 'When Men are Victims' n 54 above, 159.

directly informed by the feminist analyses of domestic violence. Indeed, the majority, such as refuges and help lines, have been established as a direct result of the need to support 'battered women' identified within research. They are solely geared towards the female victim and this reinforces the stereotype of domestic violence as a crime against women.[57] Arguably, this problem is at its greatest within the police. This agency was so heavily criticised for its response to domestic incidents involving female victims that it has now amended its practices and become more proactive in its response. Furthermore, as noted earlier, the police produce the statistics that contrast most starkly with those research findings that provide conclusive evidence of the existence of the male domestic violence victim. What this chapter proposes is that this is because the police are guided too much by the stereotype and this affects their ability to identify and respond effectively to the male domestic violence victim. But why should this be the case?

POLICE DISCRETION AND ORGANISATIONAL RULES

The importance of police discretion and the organisational rules and structures that affect the exercise of this discretion has been well documented.[58] The factors that inform the operation of police discretion are crucial to understanding the potential for male victims of domestic violence not to be represented in the statistics. Hoyle is correct to criticise feminist researchers who have elevated the supposedly inadequate, misogynistic and sexist police response to domestic violence to the 'status of "fact"'.[59] Similarly, she is right to argue that the 'cop culture' that once embodied this view is an ever-evolving concept, fed by changing social conditions and attitudes, force policies, and the organisational nature of policing.[60] However, there is a level at which Hoyle's work leads one to believe that gendered stereotypes no longer inform police discretion in cases of domestic violence.[61] This may be (largely) true in relation to female victims but it is false where male victims are concerned. Hoyle's reconceptualisation of 'cop culture' is crucial to advancing this argument.

---

[57] Note for example the organisation Refuge that grew from the founding of the first ever refuge for battered women in Chiswick by Erin Pizzey. Pizzey was eventually dismissed by Refuge for her recognition of the female as an offender.
[58] JH Skolnick, *Justice Without Trial* (John Wiley & Sons, London, 1966); M McConville, A Sanders and R Leng, *The Case for the Prosecution: Police Suspects and the Construction of Criminality* (Routledge, London, 1991); C Hoyle, *Negotiating Domestic Violence: Police, Criminal Justice and Victims* (Clarendon Press, Oxford, 1998): R Reiner, *The Politics of the Police* (Oxford University Press, Oxford, 2000).
[59] Hoyle, *Negotiating Domestic Violence*, n 58 above, 7.
[60] *Ibid*, see ch 4. It is especially important to note that an inherent aspect of this change in all three areas has been the new approach to domestic violence that the police now take, informed by feminist research.
[61] Note in particular her conclusion that police discretion 'was not exercised randomly nor was it greatly influenced by individual officer attitudes towards domestic affairs. Rather, it was structured according to evidential criteria and informal working rules established by police officers "on the ground"', *ibid*, 212.

Consider Figure 1, produced by Hoyle to illustrate her view of the creation of cop culture and the factors that influence it. I have already argued that the core feminist perspective of family abuse has directly informed changes in social conditions, and attitudes towards domestic violence. Such a perspective also informs force policy and the organisation of the force. Inevitably, this means that the force perspective of domestic violence is stereotypical. Domestic Violence Units, for example, were established as a response to the need to help the female victim of domestic abuse (although the majority now cater in theory for all victims of domestic abuse, including men, and elderly victims). In addition, probationary officers receive training, normally from domestic violence officers, that indicates women are the usual victims of 'domestics'. All of this informs cop culture.

Figure 1: 'A reconceptualization of cop culture: its creation and its influences'

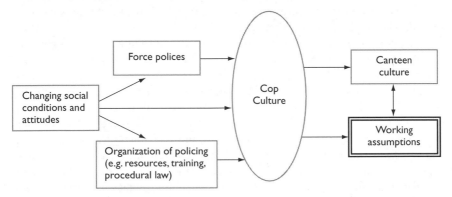

Source: C Hoyle, *Negotiating Domestic Violence: Police, Criminal Justice and Victims* (Clarendon Press, Oxford, 1998) 101.[62]

That this has led to a more sympathetic response from the police towards domestic violence incidents is undeniable. But, I would argue that this has only benefited the female victim; that the cultural stereotype of women as victims of men is firmly entrenched within the psyche of the police officer 'on the ground'. Reiner notes that police suspicion is a key aspect of cop culture and that the reliance of officers upon stereotype is an intrinsic aspect of that suspicion. He concludes that:

> While police suspiciousness and stereotyping are inescapable, the particular categories informing them tend to be ones that reflect the structure of power in society. This serves to reproduce that structure through a pattern of implicit discrimination.[63]

---

[62] Reproduced by permission of the author.
[63] Reiner, *The Politics of the Police*, above n 58, 91.

Police susceptibility to racial stereotyping and prejudice has been much discussed.[64] However, it is evident that stereotypical views of gender and domestic violence are embraced just as readily. Core feminists may argue that this is reflected in the research finding that the police hold a negative view of domestic incidents. I would argue that it also means that officers will readily accept the stereotype of male-on-female abuse because it mirrors their own patriarchal social view.[65] Such views are reinforced within 'canteen culture'.[66]

Accordingly, cop culture intrinsically accepts the stereotype created by core feminists that domestic violence is male-on-female abuse. This will have an obvious effect on the working assumptions that officers develop in relation to domestic violence incidents.[67] Indeed, I believe that the stereotype of domestic violence is so strong that it has of itself become a working assumption. Hoyle suggests that working assumptions are also developed at the scene from the information officers retrieve from those involved.[68] For example, upon attending a scene the officers develop a working assumption that the party who is the most aggressive is the offender. Depending on how that aggression develops or subsides dictates which working rule, if any, they implement. So, a persistently aggressive male may ultimately be arrested for breach of the peace. It could easily be suggested then, that if the information at the scene indicated that the female was the offender, the same working rules would take affect at the appropriate moments. However, it is my belief that the working assumption of male-on-female abuse is so strong that this will only happen in cases where the evidence of female-on-male abuse is overwhelming. Indeed, it is possible that the assumption by the police that the male is the aggressor might itself become somewhat self-fulfilling. It is not difficult to imagine a victimised man becoming angered by the police assumption that he was the aggressor, thus 'confirming' the initial police interpretation of the situation (and increasing the probability of the male victim being arrested, as the literature

---

[64] Reiner, *The Politics of the Police*, above n 58, 98–100, where he discusses various studies, including his own, that highlight the existence of racial prejudice within the police.

[65] Chan argues that 'cop culture' has a socially informed dimension. The example used is racism towards aboriginals that Chan suggests has developed from the historically negative treatment of aborigines in Australia. J Chan, 'Changing Police Culture' (1996) 36 *British Journal of Criminology* 109.

[66] See Hoyle, *Negotiating Domestic Violence*, n 58 above, 74 for a discussion of the concept 'canteen culture'. But note that Waddington suggests we should look beyond 'canteen culture' to the 'circumstances in which they [the police] act' to explain their responses. I would suggest that both the traditional view of 'canteen culture' and Waddington's extended perspective support my argument. If one accepts that 'canteen culture' explains how the police understand the social world then the patriarchal views of the police will direct their actions. Similarly, if one follows Waddington's view, then it can be suggested that police responses to domestic violence are informed by the 'circumstances' of domestic violence as the police understand them, either from experience or as informed by feminist knowledge. PAJ Waddington, 'Police (Canteen) Sub-culture' (1999) 39 *British Journal of Criminology* 287.

[67] Although the relationship between cultural attitudes and behaviour is not a straightforward one, it is widely accepted that the former do influence the latter. See the discussion by A Sanders and R Young, *Criminal Justice*, 2nd edn (Butterworths, London, 2000) 77–78.

[68] Hoyle, *Negotiating Domestic Violence*, n 58 above, see ch 5 for fuller discussion.

also shows that the suspect's demeanour is highly correlated with the decision to arrest[69]).

Consequently, my hypothesis is that the police are very likely to overlook the male victim. They have a working assumption that he does not exist and this assumption is constantly reinforced by cop culture, which is, in turn, informed by the domestic violence stereotype that has emerged as a result of the core feminist approach to domestic violence. My research aimed to identify the extent to which the police operate upon this stereotype.

THE STUDY

During a period of four months between May and September 1997 I conducted an assessment of over 6,000 domestic incidents reported to three divisional domestic violence units in a large metropolitan Police force. I also interviewed both uniformed officers, and officers in the domestic violence units. The uniformed officers were selected from incident report logs that showed they had attended domestic incidents where the victim was identified as male. Twenty officers in total were selected for interview, and 17 were interviewed.[70] Informal, but structured, interviews were conducted with each officer. The decision was taken to avoid asking officers direct closed questions about male victims. Instead, the interview took the officers through the process of dealing with a domestic incident; from how they defined the term 'domestic violence', to the initial incident report and eventually through to the conclusion of the incident and the updating of incident logs. Throughout this part of the interview, non-gendered language was used in the questions when asking about victims or offenders. It was only when the structure of the interview moved to a specific discussion of male victims that any gendered language was used by the interviewer.

The purpose of the interviews was to identify, first, any explicit reliance upon a male-on-female stereotype and, second, any implicit reliance upon the stereotype.[71] In addition, the interviews sought to draw out any working assumptions and working rules that the officers used with a view to addressing the question of whether the police operated within the framework of a male-on-female stereotype. The interviews, combined with information gained from fieldwork observations, highlighted practical problems of police data recording that were also likely to affect the reliability of police statistics on domestic violence. The key findings from the interviews were that:

---

[69] *Ibid*, 114–18.

[70] Six of the officers were from the domestic violence units and eleven were uniformed constables. Three officers were not interviewed because one took long-term sick leave, one failed to attend two appointments and the other arranged three interview times but on each occasion was unable to attend because he'd 'just got a big job to deal with.' Because the study was conducted as part of a PhD thesis, there were time restrictions in place. This meant the author was unable to arrange replacement interviews.

[71] This distinction is important as often officers are aware of the explicit 'policy line' they should follow. Consequently, implicit indicators become more significant.

(i)   data recording methods were likely to lead to the inaccurate identification of men as aggressors;
(ii)   the manner in which working assumptions and working rules were applied was likely to lead to the inaccurate identification of men as aggressors;
(iii)   there was an overt reliance upon, or expression of, the stereotype by officers; and,
(iv)   there was strong evidence that the police subconsciously relied upon a male-on-female domestic stereotype.

Practical Problems of Recording That May Lead to Mis-identification

In the divisions studied, there were slight differences between the three domestic violence units in the method of data recording, but ostensibly all three divisions operated in the same way. The information about a domestic incident was recorded at three different levels:

(i)   by the communications officer who answered the initial telephone call;
(ii)   by the communications officers or the attending police officer updating the incident log during or after the incident; and,
(iii)   by the domestic violence officers who transferred information from the incident logs to their own recording systems, and added additional information after contacting the victim.

Problems were identified at each level of recording. Uniform officers felt that the initial information they received from the communications officers was frequently inadequate.[72] P11 felt that this varied depending on:

> the communicator that's working at that time . . . and unfortunately . . . we've got more civilian staff that haven't had police experience of incidents like this.

P9 stated that:

> we don't get a lot of information, all we're told is basically a violent domestic between two parties.

Similarly, P5 responded that:

> more often than not it's just 'there's a domestic incident', the caller is whoever it is, then the address. That's 90 per cent of the information we get.

Furthermore, P9 noted that it was often the case that important information known to the communications officer was not given over the radio:

> for example, a person that we're going to see might be known to us, he might have a warrant, he could be violent or something, which wasn't mentioned to us before we attended.

---

[72] The study did not include direct analysis of the communications room.

However, most officers rightly recognised that the communications officers were largely reliant upon the information given to them over the phone and it was that information that affected the quality of the information supplied to the officers. This acknowledgment was summed up by P12 'we get as much information as they are given to be honest.'

This highlights an important point. The information received by the officers does not necessarily equip them to act upon a stereotypical perception of the incident they are attending. Indeed one officer (P7) commented that they preferred to have less information as it otherwise gave you a 'preconceived idea of what's going on.' Attitudes were different, however, when it came to the information contained on the incident logs once they had been updated.

Force policy required the attending officer to ensure that the incident logs were accurately updated. Many of the officers stated that they always tried to do this because the communications officers did not enter information correctly. Those who checked the logs found that the updates entered by the communications officer were often inaccurate. P3 admitted that he did not always return to the logs:

> I don't do it as much as I should, but I do check some of the logs. I'll go back to the logs, update it with 'blah, blah, blah.' But, sometimes I will have to type on it, 'I did not say the above, this is what I said' and correct it.

A better gauge of this inaccuracy can be given by the domestic violence officers, as they view all the logs raised for domestic violence incidents: those that have been updated and those that have not. When asked if they felt the information they received on the incident logs was sufficient the answer was firmly negative. Missing information included the details of the parties involved, which meant, as P14 noted, 'I've got nothing whatsoever to go on, and that victim is still out there wanting help.' Obviously, there are likely to be many reasons for this lack of information. The communications officer may not have been given it accurately, or once the officers arrived at the incident those spoken to may have been unwilling to provide further details. What is important about this lack of data is how it is recorded by domestic violence officers. They were asked how they identified the victims from the information on the logs. Consideration of factors such as injuries and direct identification by the attending officers were obviously the most reliable methods. However, when asked how they categorised cases where the information on the log was inadequate, all of the domestic violence officers stated that they would probably record it as a female victim. In some cases, this would be because they had 'intelligence' on the parties. However, this was not always the case as the following extract demonstrates:

> Researcher: Do you think in assessing the logs you have a subconscious idea of who the victim would normally be?

P15:	If it's not obvious on the FWIN and if we can't get any further information and you really don't know who the victim is then I would tend to put the female.[73]
Researcher:	And if you've got a record on your own log then you'll follow the original listing?
P15:	Yeah.
Researcher:	And if it's the first incident you'll assume it's the female?
P15:	Yeah.

Similarly, all of the domestic violence officers stated that if the updated information on the incident logs was poor they would make assumptions from the information originally entered on the logs by the communications officers. Sometimes, quite detailed assumptions were drawn:

P16:	If it [the FWIN] just says something like man and woman fighting in the street, I would think of her as the victim.
Researcher:	So you do operate on preconceived ideas of who the victim is?
P16:	Yeah, and if I had to put them in a category I would put girlfriend/boyfriend, because they're not based at a house.

A similar conversation took place with P17.

P17:	If the opening information has got that she's been assaulted and the officer's gone round and it's got no offences, then I would make contact with her, probably by letter.
Researcher:	But you would go on that initial information?
P17:	Yeah.
Researcher:	Do you think you have a preconceived idea of who the victim is?
P17:	Definitely. No doubt about it. That's going to be the female. I think that is . . . for everyone . . . it's funny isn't it, you read these things but you just automatically think it's the female.

We must conclude that the statistics, which are created by the domestic violence officers, are not as reliable as it is assumed. Certainly, it seems that where the evidence of victimisation is clear, the statistics are more reliable, but if there is lack of clarity at any stage of the information process, the domestic violence officers rely upon the stereotype of male-on-female abuse in categorising incidents. Three of the domestic violence officers (P14, P17, and P18), during their interviews stated

---

[73] FWIN stands for Force Wide Identification Number. This is allocated to the incident by the computer when a call is first made to the communications centre. The term FWIN is used by the police to describe incident logs.

that '97 per cent of all victims are females.' While this is an accurate reference to police compiled statistics, as has been shown, these statistics are partly created as a direct result of reliance upon a particular stereotype.

What is also evident is that domestic violence officers operate a system of working assumptions and working rules. There are several pieces of information that allow them to deduce who the victim is: injuries sustained; evidence of the attending officer; the person who has been asked to leave the premises; the person who has been arrested; and, the person who made the call. But, when some or all of these factors are missing the ultimate working assumption is male-on-female abuse. Once they have identified a victim, their own working rules of proceeding on the basis of that assumption come into play.

It appears that this assumption also comes into play when there is more detailed information available on the incident logs. For example, in determining who the victim was, the officers often relied on who had been asked to leave the premises, or who had been arrested. Obviously, the more information that was available to the domestic violence officers, the more reliable their assessment of who was the victim, and, in turn, the more reliable the police statistics. My own assessment of 6,152 incident logs concluded that either the gender of the victim or the relationship between the parties could not be identified in 25 per cent of the cases. The logs are 'closed' documents and the domestic violence officers would not have further information available to them with which to make a more informed decision about the relationship of the people involved (unless they had prior knowledge about the parties living at a particular address). This means that up to a quarter of the statistics created by the domestic violence officers were created upon the basis of the male-on-female stereotype.

Direct Indications of Stereotype: Comedy Victims?

The above discussion about the recording of information about domestic incidents highlights some very direct applications of the 'female victim stereotype' by domestic violence officers. Next I will look at whether my study revealed any direct indication of this stereotype in the thinking of both domestic violence officers and the attending officers. Such thinking may call into question the validity of the log entries. Overt signs of reliance upon this stereotype were evident in the interviews conducted, although the extent to which this occurred varied from question to question. When the officers were asked to give their own definition of the term 'domestic violence' the majority (12) recognised that it involved a range of relationships, including same sex relationships and abuse between family members other than just spouses or intimate partners. The remaining five clearly indicated that domestic violence only related to intimate partners as opposed to other family relationships. They referred to 'spouses', 'man and wife', 'partners', 'ex-partners', and 'boyfriends and girlfriends'.[74] Only one of these officers indicated an overt reliance upon the female victim stereotype by saying: 'The man is the one who's causing the violence against his wife or girlfriend, where he hits and assaults them.'[75]

Following the question on definition, the officers were asked whether they had a specific concept of who the victim was in domestic incidents. Four officers gave very open answers that indicated they had no specific gendered perspective of the victim.[76] Another six gave qualified answers that indicated a tendency to think of the victim as female. For instance, P16 said: 'No, but it is generally female.' Similarly, P13 answered: 'I think they invariably tend to be females but that's not as it stands, I mean there are men who are victims of it.' The remaining seven officers strongly indicated a belief that the victim was female. P5 stated 'it's between the man and the woman and the man's always at fault,' and P18 described the victim as 'a female, like a girlfriend or wife.' Three of these seven officers were from the domestic violence units and their views undoubtedly reflected their reliance upon the female victim stereotype when analysing the incident logs. Taken overall, from the answers given by police officers analysed so far, it appears that there is a working assumption by the majority of the police officers that domestic violence is inflicted by men upon women.

In the second part of the interview, officers were asked if they had encountered incidents of female-on-male abuse.[77] In particular, they were asked if they thought they had any rigid perception of abuse in this context. Ten of the 17 interviewed appeared to operate upon a stereotype of female-on-male abuse. This stereotype took two distinct forms. At one level it related to the types of abuse suffered by male victims, and at the other level it related to the typical female offender and male victim. For instance, P14 assumed that 'a small stature man, very thin and about seven stone, wet through, is your typical male victim.' Similarly, P2 believed that 'the man is a weak person and the woman is a strong one.' Correspondingly, P5 held the view that 'they're [women] the weaker sex, aren't they, physically?' In terms of the forms of abuse suffered, it was evident that these ten officers believed that men suffered more emotional and psychological abuse than women did. Comments ranged from 'I think the physical side of it doesn't really happen' to 'female-on-male tends to be more mental than physical.' These officers also believed that women were more likely to throw objects than use bodily physical violence.

[74] One also made reference to same-sex relationships.
[75] Although this last quote indicates that some officers regard domestic violence to mean only violence, others gave a broader definition. For instance, P19 stressed 'very strongly that it's not just physical violence.' Indeed, 15 officers thought that emotional, psychological, and verbal abuse came within the definition of domestic violence.
[76] All four had given broad definitions of domestic violence that acknowledged the range of family relationships that might be involved. It is interesting to note that none of them were domestic violence officers.
[77] It was already known that all of them had dealt with female-on-male incidents as they were selected by reference to such cases.

A surprising aspect of this part of the interviews was the humour that some officers attached to the concept of female-on-male abuse. The immediate reaction of two officers to being asked about male victims was to laugh. Another, P13 commented that 'you laugh and joke sometimes and think: "Is he a man or a mouse?"' It appears then that a domestic violence stereotype exists in two forms: the stereotype of male-on-female abuse outlined earlier, and the disbelieving, comedic stereotype of female-on-male abuse. This new stereotype is best summarised by the following answer given by officer P1 when asked what their view of female-on-male violence was.

> To be honest with you, you usually come away and laugh about it, you know, you do because it's like portrayed as a male dominated thing really isn't it? But, you tend to find that the men that are dominated by the woman are usually small men with glasses and things like that—so you're taking the mick out of them anyway, really, when you come away. It's not fair but it's the way things are. They're usually very hard women that they're either married to, or living with them. And some of them tend to get battered by them, you know—they really do. As regards my own view of them—they tend to be small men with glasses. For some reason that's just the way they tend to be.

It is quite clear from the extract that this officer at least operates within a very distinct stereotype, albeit one that may be rooted in his experience, at least as far as he remembers it. In fact, the majority of the officers interviewed appeared to hold such a strong stereotype of male-on-female abuse that they did not even recognise the 'comedy' male victim. Both stereotypes combine to form a pronounced working assumption upon which officers rely when facing a domestic incident. Although not every officer interviewed demonstrated overt signs of reliance upon the female victim stereotype, the majority clearly did.[78] What is more, when one looks to identify subtler, implicit indicators of reliance upon this stereotype it is manifest in all the interviews conducted, as will now be documented.

Implicit Indications of Stereotype

The transcribed interviews were 'content analysed' to determine the degree of subconscious stereotype that existed within the officers' perceptions of domestic violence. Rather than examining the specific meaning and application of a text, content analysis assesses the frequency with which pre-defined categories or themes of text appear in a document. The theme to be identified within the transcribed interviews was very simple. Whenever the officers referred to a victim or offender as 'he', 'she', or 'they' within a portion of the text it was counted.[79] Conclusions were

---

[78] There were only two officers for whom it could be said there was no direct indication that they conformed to a stereotype of male-on-female violence, although both acknowledged that their experience indicated that women were the victims in the majority of cases they had dealt with.

[79] The analysis was not limited to these terms but also to other variations such as 'woman', 'man', and 'people'. Similarly, not every single usage was counted. Rather every section of reference to that person

then drawn from the percentage of the references that identified a particular gender as representing the victim or offender. It must be stressed that this analysis was only conducted upon the initial section of the transcribed interviews where gender-neutral language was used by the interviewer. Any gendered responses could then be seen to represent the officers' own subconscious identification of who the typical victim or offender was.

Table 2: Content Analysis Results by Role and Gender

	Victim N	References %	Offender N	References %
Male	23	11	104	61
Female	144	68	16	9
Neutral	45	21	51	30
Total	212	100	171	100

Table 2 shows that the officers' use of language indicates a subconscious reliance upon the male-on-female stereotype in between 61 and 68 per cent of their responses. The references that indicate officers had an awareness of female-on-male violence account for only 9 to 11 per cent of their comments. Moreover, these comments were often made self-consciously, as an afterthought. For instance, P7 at one point corrected himself when identifying the factors that would help to identify the victim at an incident:

> She is upset. [Pause.] Or he is upset. I mean I keep saying she, we all seem to say she but it's not always the case.

Indeed, similar comments accounted for 23 per cent of those indicating an awareness of female-on-male abuse. This suggests that the concept of female-on-male violence is not at the forefront of officers' minds. The same can be said of the 'neutral' comments that were made during the interviews. On the face of it, using 'them' and 'they' to define the victim or offender implies openness to either gender being the victim or offender. Yet the context within which these comments were made belies this assumption. Of all the neutral comments made, 52 per cent immediately followed answers or sections of text where male-on-female language

was counted. For instance, it may take five sentences to discuss one person, but that will involve several different references to 'her', 'she' 'the woman'. Where such references related to a single person, it would be counted once. Similarly, the reference had to be specific. In other words, if the officer said 'she was black and blue', it would count as one reference to a female victim. It would not be extrapolated to implicitly indicate a male offender, although this could be reasonably assumed. Similarly, where an officer said 'he or she' it would be counted as both a male and female reference rather than a neutral reference.

had been used, thereby suggesting that the neutral language related to a prior gender specific identification of who 'they' were.

It is clear that officers, when talking about domestic violence, have in mind the male-on-female stereotype. This implicit expectation that this is in fact what domestic violence means is likely to affect the manner in which they respond to domestic incidents. The stereotype itself becomes a working assumption of the police. It could still be suggested, however, that the application of other working assumptions and working rules at a domestic incident will overrule any reliance upon stereotype. However, when one considers these assumptions and rules more closely it can be seen that this is not necessarily the case.

The Application of Working Rules and Their Reinforcement of Working Assumptions

Hoyle identified situational and contextual factors that influenced the working assumptions made by officers at domestic incidents.[80] These were information relating to the offence, the victim, and the offender. This, in turn, determined the working rules that were applied by the officers. The officers in my study appeared to rely upon the same factors as those in Hoyle's. For instance, if the victim had visible signs of injury and was willing to complain, the suspect remained aggressive and confrontational, and there was a risk of continuing violence, then the suspect would be arrested. Obviously, the decision to take affirmative action, and the form the affirmative action took, was affected by the strength of any of these factors. So, all of the officers interviewed said that they would not arrest for any assault if the victim was unwilling to proceed. However, they were very likely to arrest for breach of the peace, or to prevent a further breach of the peace. Then again, this was dependant upon the demeanour of the suspect. If the suspect was calm, they might be asked simply to leave the premises and stay with friends or family for the night.

The weaker that any of the factors informing the police are, the less likely they will be to invoke a criminal response, or indeed provoke any action other than calming both parties. My suspicion is that if there is clear indication of female-on-male abuse, taking into account all of these factors, police officers will invoke the same working rules, and the stereotype of male-on-female abuse will be overridden. However, it was clear from the interviews that other working rules to those identified by Hoyle were relevant in domestic violence incidents. What is more it is clear that they would be applied in a gendered way, especially at less serious domestic incidents where there was no direct indication of assault and the officers merely wished to restore calm.

For example, if the officers attended an incident where there was a continuing disturbance between the parties, there would come a point at which they would

---

[80] Hoyle, *Negotiating Domestic Violence*, n 58 above, ch 5.

consider the removal of one party from the premises. This could either be voluntarily or by means of arrest for breach of the peace. Eleven of the 17 officers interviewed indicated that they would remove the male from the premises. The reasons for this included the presumption that women should care for any children present, that is was easier for a man to leave, and that a man was likely to pose a greater future threat. For instance P11 stated that:

> I would say it always tends to be the bloke that gets turfed out only because quite often there's children involved and you tend to leave the woman with the children. A fellow can fend for himself a lot better on the streets than a woman can.

Likewise, P16 said 'if there are kids there . . . I would expect the husband to be asked to go.' There were also indications that officers applied this working rule of removing the male because of stereotypical influences. Accordingly, P4 agreed he would remove the male:

> purely because of his physical make-up . . . The nature of the beast is that men are as a rule—stereotyping—men are stronger than women.

That officers apply stereotypical attitudes about gender to their actions is not surprising. Indeed, some of their justifications for removing the male are not necessarily because of any stereotypical view of domestic violence. Nevertheless, it has a direct impact upon the statistics created. Reconsider the above discussion of the working assumptions and rules used by the domestic violence officers when classifying the logs they received. It is quite clear that if the male is arrested, albeit for breach of the peace, or 'voluntarily' leaves the premises, the domestic violence officers will identify him as the offender and the female as the victim. Given the reasons the attending officers gave in interview for removing the male, this may well not be the case. Consequently, a domestic dispute that involved no obvious violence and had no obvious victim is likely to be defined as male-on-female abuse. Moreover, there is the possibility that the male is in fact a victim, but because it is more practical for him to leave, he is labelled as the offender. If we then consider the influence of this recording on officers' 'intelligence' about persons, it is not hard to see how this inaccurate recording could result in further 'injustices' if the police are called again to the same address.

At the very end of the interviews all of the officers were asked to read a statement and either agree or disagree with it. The statement read as follows:

> It would be fair to say that you hold a view that most of the incidents of domestic violence you attend involve female victims. Consequently, you may have a preconceived idea that domestic violence is committed by men against women. It is therefore possible, especially when it is difficult to determine who the victim is, that male victims will not be correctly identified and slip through the system.

Only one officer disagreed with the statement, on the basis that she always maintained an open mind. A further two accepted that it was possible, but felt they had not made such assumptions, although other officers did. The other 14 officers categorically agreed with the statement. The following are three typical responses:

> P6: Yeah, you do get preconceived ideas. It's only natural because those are the cases that you hear about, so initially when you go into them your subconscious is saying that the man is the aggressor here not the woman.

> P9: I think that is fair to say. I mean, it's like I said, when we get there and we have a woman surrounded by her children in tears, it's so easy to point the finger at the man party saying he's at fault—rather than turn round and upset everyone. . . . It's a lot easier to point the finger at the male party. In fact I have walked away from a situation where I felt, you know, I could have done more for this person, or I felt that he was the victim in this case. I mean most cases have been the male-on-female abuse and so eventually you sort of like—you have that always in your head, and when you go to a situation, you can somehow be biased along those lines. I agree with that statement.

> P16: Yeah definitely, yeah. I've been trained to think that by having . . . having women's groups like Women's Aid coming to talk to us—that's drilled home to you. So, yeah, I took that on board and accepted that.

The impact of the male-on-female stereotype upon the police perspective of domestic violence is clear. It is also evident that this has an impact upon the working assumptions and rules that affect decision-making procedures in relation to domestic incidents.

CONCLUSIONS

This study has shown that there is sufficient evidence of reliance by the police upon a male-on-female stereotype of domestic violence to call into question the validity of police statistics. Moreover, we saw above that male victims are less likely to report domestic violence than are female victims. We know from various research studies that many female domestic violence victims have long found the police unhelpful and are unlikely to call them as a result.[81] Similarly, 'sweeps' of the British Crime Surveys show that amongst the major reasons victims of any crime give for not reporting is that they did not think the matter was 'serious enough', or that it 'would not be taken seriously by the police'.[82] Over the last twenty years feminists have succeeded to a large degree in their campaign to persuade victims, various statutory and voluntary agencies and, in particular, the police to treat domestic violence against women as a serious crime. Reporting

---

[81] See Smith, *Domestic Violence*, n 26 above, 83

[82] The 2001 British Crime Survey shows that 41% of respondents did not report incidents because they believed the incident to be either too trivial, involving no loss, or the police would not do anything. C Kershaw, N Chivite-Matthews, C Thomas and R Aust, *The 2001 British Crime Survey: England and Wales* (Home Office Statistical Bulletin 18 January 2001) 49.

rates by female victims have accordingly risen.[83] What this chapter has shown is that the police do not tend to see domestic violence against men as a serious crime, but rather see male victims (if they see them at all) as rather pathetic figures of fun. In doing so, they are undoubtedly drawing on gendered assumptions that are held throughout much of wider society.[84] Against this background, it is not surprising that men are disinclined to report their experiences of victimisation. If it is the case that the police statistics are unreliable because of under-reporting and under-recording what impact should this have upon our current perceptions of domestic violence? Certainly, it suggests that the CTS data may be more reliable than feminists care to admit.

This raises challenges for policy, for research, and for theory-building. Policy on domestic violence needs to reflect the fact that a significant proportion of violence in the home is committed against males. To ignore a body of victims on the ground that they suffer, on average, less than another body of victims is indefensible. This holds true for researchers as much as for policy-makers. Studies of domestic violence should not start from the position that male victims do not exist, or got what they deserved, or suffer only minimally.

Finally, this chapter has raised serious questions about the application of feminist theory to the topic of violence between partners. The notion that violence in the home is the result of a power struggle between two people is still valid. However, the assertion that gender is the primary cause of the imbalance that causes victimisation may not be. The more research that indicates that men and women *can* equally be victimised within the home, the more that feminist theories of domestic violence become inapplicable. If we are to minimise domestic violence against women, it is vital that its causes are properly understood. To ignore male victimisation is not just indefensible in itself, it is also not in the interests of women. This chapter also raises a separate challenge for feminists: the challenge to offer an identity to the female offender that is not based upon prior victimisation or patriarchy.

---

[83] It is difficult to identify the true increase in reporting rates over this period as the police only started to keep such records in 1995 in line with the requirements of Home Office Circular 60/1990. However, initial findings from the 2001 British Crime Survey show that the number of victims reporting domestic violence to the survey has risen 57% since 1981 (above n 80, 47). It is unlikely that this is solely because of an increase in incidents; rather because of greater social awareness of the phenomenon individuals are happier to report their victimisation. Consider this statistic in light of the reasons given for not reporting incidents to the authorities in the 2000 British Crime Survey. Domestic violence victims did not report incidents at the following rates; 'too trivial' 15%, police couldn't do anything 5%, and police wouldn't be interested 4%. This indicates that domestic violence victims are more comfortable with reporting crimes to the police than they used to be. C Kershaw, T Budd, G Kinshott, J Mattinson, P Mayhew and A Myhill, *The 2000 British Crime Survey: England and Wales*, Home Office Statistical Bulletin No 18 (Home Office, London, 2000) 65.

[84] Masculinities writers have frequently identified the notion of the 'strong man' as a key social perspective of what it means to be male. R Bly, *Iron John: A Book About Men* (Addison-Wesley, New York NY, 1990); VJ Seidler, *Man Enough: Embodying Masculinities* (Sage, London, 1997); IM Harris, *Messages Men Hear: Constructing Masculinities* (Taylor & Francis, London, 1995).

5

Securing Restorative Justice for the 'Non-Participating' Victim

CAROLYN HOYLE[*]

INTRODUCTION

JUST TWENTY YEARS ago there was little focus on the victim's role in the criminal process. Now, after a series of policy initiatives designed to involve victims in the criminal process and to demonstrate greater sensitivity to their needs,[1] it is largely taken for granted that they should have a role to play, and debates are focused on the nature of that role. After countless surveys showing victims' increasing dissatisfaction with being marginalised, they have finally emerged from being mere 'evidential fodder' to become, at least in theory, key participants in the criminal process.[2] Nowhere has this been seen more clearly than in the phenomenal rise of restorative justice. Restorative justice, more than any other initiative since the establishment of the modern justice system, has the potential to reinstate the victim at centre stage with the offender.

This chapter will consider the difficulties in realising that potential, looking in particular at efforts to include victims in restorative cautioning sessions.[3] In so doing, it will take forward critiques of current attempts to integrate victims in the criminal process put forward by the author and colleagues elsewhere[4] and further developed by Sanders in this volume. One key hypothesis to be explored is that victims who do not have a dynamic, participatory role in criminal justice (that is, by being involved in dialogue with the offender and decision makers in the

---

[*] Thanks are due to Andrew Ashworth, David Rose and Richard Young for their helpful comments on a draft of this chapter, and to Roderick Hill for his skill and tenacity in collecting some of the data discussed here.
[1] A Sanders, *Taking Account of Victims in the Criminal Justice System: A Review of the Literature* (Scottish Office, Edinburgh, 1999).
[2] See A Ashworth, 'Victims' Rights, Defendants' Rights and Criminal Procedure' in A Crawford and J Goodey (eds), *Integrating a Victim Perspective within Criminal Justice* (Ashgate, Aldershot, 2000).
[3] It will draw on empirical data gathered in an in-depth study of restorative cautioning in the Thames Valley: C Hoyle, R Young and R Hill, *Proceed with Caution: An Evaluation of the Thames Valley Police Initiative in Restorative Cautioning* (Joseph Rowntree Foundation, York, 2002).
[4] A Sanders, C Hoyle, R Morgan and E Cape, 'Victim Impact Statements: Don't Work, Can't Work' [2001] *Criminal Law Review* 447.

process) will not only be less satisfied with the process than those who do, but will also remain afraid, confused and ignorant about the offender, the decision making of criminal justice agents and the likely recurrence of the offending behaviour. The chapter will reflect on what it means for victims to participate in the restorative cautioning process by considering 'participation' as a continuum, rather than a dichotomous, one-off choice.

The second section will discuss the recent attempts to integrate victims into the criminal justice system. This will include a consideration of the promise of restorative justice and of the challenges posed by victims who choose not to meet their offenders. The following three sections will discuss the potential benefits to victims of involvement in restorative justice in terms of:

1)   the therapeutic benefits derived from being given a role in the process;
2)   the challenges to the stereotypes and justifications of both victims and offenders; and,
3)   reparation for victims.

Each of these sections will be approached by comparing the benefits to victims who participate in restorative sessions with those achievable for victims who choose not to. The sixth section will explore the reasons for the gap in experience between those victims who attend meetings with their offenders and those who do not, and consider the extent to which this gap might be closed. I conclude by reflecting on the rights of victims and the responsibilities of criminal justice agencies, in this case the police, to ensure that these rights are more than just aspirations.

RECENT ATTEMPTS TO INTEGRATE VICTIMS INTO THE CRIMINAL JUSTICE SYSTEM

Government criminal justice policy over the last decade has become dominated by concerns about victims of crime.[5] The stated reasons for increasing victim participation in the criminal process have included: giving victims a voice for therapeutic reasons; enabling their opinions and interests to be taken into account in decision making; ensuring that they are treated with respect by criminal justice agencies; and, partly as a product of the above, increasing their satisfaction with the criminal process.[6] These rationales, perhaps with the exception of the second, led the British government to publish the first Victims' Charter in 1990. This laid down the 'rights' of victims, specifying how they were to be treated and what standards of service they should expect from the criminal justice system. Its message

---

[5]   D Garland and R Sparks, 'Criminology, Social Theory, and the Challenge of our Times' in D Garland and R Sparks (eds), *Criminology and Social Theory* (Clarendon Press, Oxford, 2000).
[6]   A Sanders *et al*, 'Victim Impact Statements', n 4 above.

was reinforced by the publication of several other initiatives and statements of standards of service for victims and by a second Victims' Charter in 1996.

Under this second Charter two different victim-focused initiatives were piloted: the One Stop Shop (OSS) and Victim Statements (VS). These were aimed at improving communication between victims and criminal justice agencies. The OSS was aimed at keeping victims informed about the progress of their case (in selected cases), while VS provided victims with the opportunity to describe the impact of the crime upon them (including psychological, financial, physical and emotional impacts).[7] The author and her colleagues evaluated both schemes and found that they raised expectations of effective communication which neither scheme could meet. Consequently, many victims who participated were left feeling disappointed.[8]

Just under half of all eligible victims opted into OSS, and around 30 per cent opted into VS. A significant minority of victims who opted into the OSS did not recall being told of basic decisions about which OSS schemes undertook to inform them. A third felt that they had received the information too late (either too late to attend court hearings, or after they had received the information from another source, such as a local newspaper in which court verdicts were published). Furthermore, a quarter were unhappy with the manner in which they received the information; they would have preferred the chance to discuss the information provided with the key decision-makers. Not surprisingly, the more victims were told the more they wanted to know, in terms of clarification, explanation for decisions and so forth. Hence, expectations were raised and then dashed by inadequate or insufficient information, with no opportunity for meaningful dialogue with the key decision makers in their cases. We concluded:

> The general message from our research, and experience in other jurisdictions, is that schemes that provide information to victims without interaction and discussion with them do not in themselves increase satisfaction with the criminal justice process.[9]

The VS scheme was equally unsatisfactory as a mechanism for victim participation. While around one third of victims felt better, just under one fifth were upset by the process of making a VS. The rest (about half) were indifferent. As Sanders *et al* make clear, 'a net therapeutic benefit to around fifteen per cent of users of the scheme is not particularly successful.'[10] VS did not adequately fulfil an expressive role (60 per cent of those who chose to make a VS claimed to have done so for 'expressive' or 'therapeutic' reasons). Furthermore, the overwhelming majority had no idea what use had been made of their VS. This lack of knowledge,

---

[7] See the chapter by Andrew Sanders in this volume for a fuller explanation of the two initiatives.

[8] C Hoyle, E Cape, R Morgan and A Sanders, *Evaluation of the 'One Stop Shop' and Victim Statement Pilot Projects* (Home Office, London, 1998).

[9] Sanders *et al*, 'Victim Impact Statements', n 4 above, 452.

[10] *Ibid*, 450. Other studies have found similarly unimpressive results, see, for example, P Tontodonato and E Erez 'Crime, Punishment and Victim Distress' (1994) 3 *International Review of Victimology* 33.

coupled with doubt on the part of many victims that their statements had been used at all, resulted in a great deal of dissatisfaction. While three quarters of the victims who made a VS were initially pleased with the opportunity, only 57 per cent were still satisfied at the close of their case and nearly a fifth felt that they should not have made one.

So, although it could be argued that VS are better than nothing, they do not provide the best opportunity for victims to have their say, with many victims feeling that their voices are not heard by key decision makers. And OSS provides victims with only limited information and no chance of asking the questions they want answered. Neither scheme succeeded in empowering victims by giving them a meaningful role in the state response to their case. Despite our advice to the contrary, the Home Office decided to reintroduce the VS scheme nationally, albeit in a slightly reformed way.[11] In recognition of the dissatisfaction victims felt about receiving no explanation of decisions made, the Glidewell Review of the Crown Prosecution Service proposed that the Service should take responsibility for the OSS, informing victims of their decisions and explaining them in person, when this is requested.[12] This approach is currently being piloted. As Sanders explains (in this volume), with reference to the Glidewell changes and information provision to victims of prisoners serving substantial sentences, communication to victims is clearly improving in the sense that victims are increasingly being informed not only of decisions, but also of the reasons for those decisions. However, following these reforms victims will still largely remain at the periphery of their own cases.

The Victims' Charter is currently under review and revision. The public consultation process was officially launched by the Home Office, the Lord Chancellor's Department and the Attorney-General in February 2001 and, in addition to seeking views on the revised Charter, it sought opinions about a number of significant new measures (including the introduction of statutory rights for victims and the creation of a Victims' Ombudsman).[13] The consultation document also discusses new developments in victims' policy introduced since 1996, making clear that these could be included in the new Charter. One such measure is restorative justice:

> Victims can convey how they've been affected by the offence and receive an explanation, an apology and some practical compensation for the distress and inconvenience caused to them.[14]

---

[11] Home Office 'Home Secretary Announces National Victim Statements', Home Office Press Release 147/2000 (Home Office, London, 2000).

[12] I Glidewell, *The Review of the Crown Prosecution Service: A Report*, Cmnd 3960 (HMSO, London, 1998).

[13] Home Office, Lord Chancellor's Department and The Attorney-General, *A Review of the Victims' Charter* (Home Office, London, 2001). The responses to this consultation exercise, from interested parties such as the police, the courts, the probation service, local authorities and various victim support organisations, have been generally favourable to these suggestions.

[14] *Ibid*, s 18, para xi.

The document clearly reflects national and international interest in the potential of restorative justice.[15]

The Promise of Restorative Justice

Restorative justice holds the promise of restoring victims' material and emotional loss, safety, damaged relationships, dignity and self-respect.[16] Restorative justice initiatives based around cautioning promise to circumvent the problems of 'one-way' victim involvement by allowing victims to engage in dialogue with offenders and criminal justice agents, as well as other significant 'actors' in their cases. In a restorative caution, as distinct from an 'old style' caution,[17] the cautioning police officer (the facilitator) is supposed to invite all those affected by the offence, including any victim, to the cautioning session. The Thames Valley model envisages that a structured dialogue about an offence and its implications, according to a particular sequence of speakers and issues, will have benefits for all concerned. To achieve this structure and sequence, facilitators are provided with a 'script' which provides an ordered set of explanatory statements, questions and prompts.[18] In this sense, it is very similar to conferencing in Canberra, Australia. Both schemes derive from a scripted model of police-led conferencing pioneered in Wagga Wagga, Australia in the early 1990s.[19] That, in turn, was inspired by John Braithwaite's theory of 'reintegrative shaming', which argues that it is best to respond to crime by using processes which shame criminal behaviour, while maintaining respect and concern for the person who committed the offence.[20]

The Thames Valley Police model differs from the Canberra scheme in two main ways. First, reparation agreements reached in Thames Valley conferences are not legally binding and the police can do little if promises are not kept. Conversely, in Canberra the police monitor the agreements and have the power to reconvene the conference or, rarely, send the matter to court if the offender fails to 'pay up'. Secondly, in Thames Valley, conferencing is used mainly for less serious cases which

[15] The use of restorative justice in various jurisdictions, including the United States, Australia, Canada, Europe, New Zealand and South Africa is examined in A Morris and G Maxwell (eds), *Restorative Justice for Juveniles: Conferencing Mediation and Circles* (Hart Publishing, Oxford, 2001).

[16] C Hoyle and R Young, 'Restorative Justice: Assessing the Prospects and Pitfalls' in M McConville and G Wilson (eds), *The Handbook of the Criminal Justice Process* (Oxford University Press, Oxford, forthcoming 2002).

[17] Within the context of criminal justice in England and Wales, a police caution may be defined as a formal disposal of a criminal case determined by the police without the involvement of either prosecutors or the courts.

[18] See Hoyle, Young and Hill, *Proceed with Caution*, n 3 above, for a more detailed description of restorative cautioning in Thames Valley (a police service which covers the English counties of Berkshire, Buckinghamshire and Oxfordshire).

[19] See D Moore, L Forsythe and T O'Connell, *A New Approach to Juvenile Justice: An Evaluation of Family Conferencing in Wagga Wagga* (Charles Stuart University, Wagga Wagga, 1995) for a description of the Canberra programme and its origins.

[20] J Braithwaite, *Crime, Shame and Reintegration* (Cambridge University Press, Cambridge, 1989).

would not have been prosecuted in any event, whereas in Canberra conferencing is offered to offenders and victims whose relatively serious cases would normally not be considered for diversion from court. In this sense, conferencing in Canberra is similar to 'family group conferences' in New Zealand, which, since the introduction of the Children, Young Persons and Their Families Act in 1989, deal with the most serious offending by young people and effectively determine decisions in most of these cases.[21]

Despite these and other differences between restorative cautioning and conferencing schemes around the world,[22] restorative processes generally aim at restoring all of the three groups that are recognised stakeholders in the offence. As the United Nations has put it, these are processes:

> in which the victim, the offender and/or any other individuals or community members affected by a crime participate *actively* together in the resolution of matters arising from the crime.[23] [emphasis added]

The word 'actively' is important in this context. It distinguishes restorative processes from the 'static',[24] largely non-participative transmission of information to assist other 'expert' decision makers which is seen in initiatives like VS and the similarly static transmission of (limited) information from 'experts' to victims introduced by the OSS. In contrast to initiatives such as OSS and VS, restorative justice promotes dialogue between all parties harmed by an offence in pursuit of resolutions which are considered acceptable to all parties. At its best, it can alleviate victims' feelings of anger or fear towards their offender, or crime more generally, and bring about genuine remorse on the part of the offender, encouraging a greater sense of victim empathy. Victims can, and often do, receive explanations and apologies, and occasionally also benefit from compensation.[25] In theory, victims should be able to enjoy the benefits of the restorative process even if they choose not to attend a meeting with their offender. However, the data presented below will show that in practice those who choose not to attend meetings with their offenders, or are not invited, are largely denied these opportunities.[26]

---

[21] See K Daly, 'Conferencing in Australia and New Zealand: Variations, Research Findings and Prospects' in A Morris and G Maxwell (eds), *Restorative Justice for Juveniles: Conferencing, Mediation and Circles* (Hart Publishing, Oxford, 2001).

[22] See n 15 above.

[23] United Nations, *Draft Declaration on Basic Principles on the Use of Restorative Justice Programmes in Criminal Matters* (United Nations, New York NY, 1999).

[24] E Erez, L Roeger and F Morgan 'Victim Harm, Impact Statements and Victim Satisfaction with Justice: An Australian Experience' (1997) 5 *International Review of Victimology* 37.

[25] Hoyle, Young and Hill, *Proceed with Caution*, n 3 above.

[26] In Thames Valley, unlike in some other jurisdictions, restorative sessions can be held without the victim present. Offenders are usually accompanied by supporters but sometimes a 'restorative caution' can involve only the offender and facilitator. In Queensland, Australia, by contrast, a victim's consent is required for the police to refer a case to a restorative conference, and victims can veto the conference outcome (see, for example, Daly, 'Conferencing in Australia and New Zealand', n 21 above, 70).

Over the past few years in the UK, a proliferation of restorative schemes has sprung up around cautioning and, since the Crime and Disorder Act 1998, also around reprimands and warnings.[27] This is partly a product of government enthusiasm for restorative justice, resulting in Home Office and Youth Justice Board resources being given to more or less anyone who wanted to establish a restorative justice initiative. Some of these schemes have paid only lip-service to restorative justice values and, therefore, have not encouraged victims to participate.[28] Recent research on Youth Offender Panels (established under the Youth Justice and Criminal Evidence Act 1999) found that victims chose to attend the panel meetings in less than seven per cent of cases.[29] Judged against this backdrop, Thames Valley Police have been relatively successful in bringing victims face-to-face with their offenders. Of the 13,980 restorative sessions[30] run by the Thames Valley Police during the three years following 1 April 1998 (when the initiative was launched across the Force) 14 per cent were attended by one or more victim.[31] While 14 per cent can be portrayed as a high rate in the UK context (especially when we bear in mind that many offences lack identifiable victims), it still leaves a large number of victims excluded, for various reasons, from the restorative session, and therefore, potentially, from many of the benefits. Data from the Thames Valley Police initiative shed light on the issue of how to involve victims in the criminal justice and restorative justice systems and can be used to explore the concerns raised above.

The data derive from the final phase of a four year, four phase, 'action research' project carried out by the author and Richard Young.[32] Many victims in our three Thames Valley research sites chose not to participate in a restorative session. In 82 per cent of the 334 cases where there had been a victim[33] the victim did not attend the restorative session. In over half of the 56 restorative sessions we observed and researched in depth in phase four of our research there was no victim present.

---

[27] Since the Crime and Disorder Act 1998 juvenile cautions have been replaced by a system of reprimands, (for first time offenders where the offence is not serious) and warnings (for second time offenders or for first time offenders where the offence is fairly serious). Third time offenders are prosecuted save in exceptional circumstances as are first or second time offenders who commit serious offences.

[28] A Wilcox with C Hoyle, *Final Report to the Youth Justice Board on the National Evaluation of Restorative Justice Projects* (Draft Report, April 2002).

[29] T Newburn, A Crawford, R Earle, S Goldie, C Hale, G Masters, A Netten, R Saunders, A Hallam, K Sharpe, and S Uglow, *The Introduction of Referral Orders into the Youth Justice System: Second Interim Report*, RDS Occasional Paper No 73 (Home Office Research, Development and Statistics Directorate, London, 2001).

[30] In the Thames Valley when the victim is present the session is called a 'restorative conference.' When the victim does not attend (including cases where there is no identifiable victim) the session is called a 'restorative caution.' This chapter will refer to both as 'restorative sessions,' as in both cases the facilitator structures the session according to the same 'script.'

[31] Hoyle, Young and Hill, *Proceed with Caution*, n 3 above.

[32] See Hoyle, Young and Hill, *Proceed with Caution*, n 3 above, for a detailed description of the methodology and findings.

[33] Some crimes, such as possession of cannabis, do not have a victim, although restorative sessions can focus on harms done to offenders and their families or friends.

From our observation of sessions, scrutiny of case files and interviews with participants who did attend, we were able to identify 41 'non-participating victims' (NPVs). We sought to interview these absent victims to discover why they did not participate in the session with the offender, how they felt about the offence and how much they understood about the restorative process.[34]

We were unable to locate 11 of the victims[35] identified in the files.[36] Two further victims declined to be interviewed and one of the victims interviewed could not remember the incident and so was not included in the analysis. Hence, we interviewed 27 NPVs (10 females and 17 males).[37] These 27 victims correspond to 19 of our cases as some cases involved more than one victim. Of our NPV interviewees, 14 were personal victims and 13 were 'institutional' victims (11 shopkeepers and shop-managers, one shop security guard and one headmaster of a school).[38] This chapter draws on data from these interviews and, much less, from the interviews we conducted with the 31 victims who attended the restorative sessions.[39]

The Challenge to Restorative Justice: Victims who Choose not to Meet their Offenders

The movement towards greater victim involvement in the criminal justice system is predicated on an often unquestioned assumption that victims want to assume a role in the state response to 'their' offender.[40] However, most restorative justice schemes find that by no means all victims wish to be fully involved. Few studies have examined the reasons why some victims choose not to participate directly in

---

[34] We are grateful to Serena Farrant, an administrator in the Thames Valley Police Restorative Justice Consultancy, who provided valuable help in securing interviews with the 41 NPVs.

[35] A few of these were impossible to contact, despite repeated efforts. Others were shop victims and either the shop was unable to identify who dealt with the matter or that person had since left the job.

[36] It is important to note that our NPV sample comprises easily identifiable victims. In other words, these victims were either clearly recorded in the police case-files or identified as the primary victim in the caution meeting itself. Because roles can blur and victimisation can be multiple and indirect we will have missed out some people harmed by the offences.

[37] Notwithstanding the small sample size the data allow us to identify themes relevant to this group, and they can inform an understanding of the role of victims in the restorative cautioning process.

[38] Only four of the NPVs we interviewed were victims of assault, with the rest being victims of various different property offences.

[39] Interviews were recorded on tape and fully transcribed. Verbatim excerpts from the interviews are used to illustrate points below.

[40] This is partly based on various empirical studies which suggest that a great many victims would like the opportunity to meet 'their' offender. See in particular, J Mattinson and C Mirrlees-Black, *Attitudes to Crime and Criminal Justice: Findings from the 1998 British Crime Survey* (Home Office, London, 2000) and for a review of the international literature see M Umbreit, RB Coates and B Vos, 'Victim Impact of Meeting with Young Offenders' in A Morris and G Maxwell (eds), *Restorative Justice for Juveniles: Conferencing, Mediation and Circles* (Hart Publishing, Oxford, 2001).

the process[41] and fewer still have considered how these NPVs can benefit from a restorative process without meeting their offender.

It is inevitable that some victims will choose not to attend meetings with their offenders, but of more concern is that some will not be given that choice either because they will not be informed of the planned restorative intervention or they will be told about it but not invited to participate. In the Thames Valley study, about four-fifths of our sample of 27 NPVs had been invited, by the trained restorative justice facilitator, to attend the restorative session held to caution their offender. One third (eight) had been willing, but were ultimately unable, to attend, mostly for practical reasons, such as being too busy with work commitments.[42] However, just under two thirds (14) of those invited explained that they had not wanted to attend the session. The majority wanted to leave it to the police ('I'd just rather they'd [the police] go and just, you know, get it over with. . .finished.') or expressed concerns about meeting the offenders and their supporters:

> I was quite happy for the police to deal with it. . . . I don't really want to know who they are . . . do you know what I mean? 'Cos otherwise it would just cause probably more trouble . . . 'Cos I have to live round where they live, so ignorance is bliss sometimes, if you know what I mean.

Others were more specific in mentioning fears of repeat victimisation:

> I wouldn't want to be involved to be honest. I'd rather it be dealt with and then forgotten about, rather than showing my face . . . there, that might re-occur, getting some hassle, some form of hassle.

In this sense, some of our interviewees were similar to victims in various other studies whose reluctance to participate in the criminal process stemmed from fears of retaliation from the offender.[43] However, our NPVs quite specifically rejected the option of a *direct* meeting with their offender. They did not all reject a chance to participate *indirectly*.

While the goal of restorative justice is 'to rebuild ruptured relationships in a process that *allows* all three parties (victims, offenders and the wider community) to participate',[44] 'victims' participation' should not *require* their attendance at a meeting with the offender. Choosing not to participate in the session should not

---

[41] Gwynn Davis's insightful book, *Making Amends: Mediation and Reparation in Criminal Justice* (Routledge, London, 1992) is an exception.

[42] The literature suggests, not surprisingly, that victims are much more likely to attend restorative sessions if they are arranged at a time and place which is convenient for them (see, for example, A Morris and G Maxwell, 'The Practice of Family Group Conferences in New Zealand' in Crawford and Goodey, *Integrating a Victim Perspective Within Criminal Justice* (Ashgate, Aldershot, 2000) 211).

[43] See, for example, J Shapland, J Willmore and P Duff, *Victims in the Criminal Justice System* (Gower Publishing, Aldershot, 1985) 16; A Cretney and G Davis, *Punishing Violence* (Routledge, London, 1995) 15; and C Hoyle, *Negotiating Domestic Violence: Police, Criminal Justice and Victims* (Clarendon Press, Oxford, 1998) 189-91.

[44] L Kurki, 'Restorative and Community Justice' in M Tonry (ed), *Crime and Justice: A Review of Research* (University of Chicago Press, Chicago Ill, 2000) Vol 27, 235.

rule out 'indirect mediation'. As shown below, too often victims' decisions not to participate in restorative cautions are interpreted by the facilitators as a lack of interest in 'their' case; an interpretation which, along with other factors, leads to limited opportunity for indirect participation.

The Thames Valley Police training manual[45] makes clear that facilitators are obliged to explain to victims that a warning is being considered but that the wishes of the victim will be taken into account in the decision. Facilitators also should raise the possibility of the victim attending the session where the warning will be delivered. The manual emphasises that victims should not be coerced into taking part in such a meeting for the good of the offender. Rather, they should be provided with sufficient information about the planned session to make a genuinely informed choice about whether or not to attend.

Where victims want to communicate with the offender, but do not wish to take part in a restorative session, then indirect communication should be facilitated. In such cases victims should be given the opportunity to make a victim statement which the facilitator, with the permission of the victim, should either read out or paraphrase to the participants at the session. It is the responsibility of facilitators, before carrying out a reprimand, warning or adult caution, to contact the victim(s) of all offences to inquire about the impact of the offence and the views of the victim. They should ask sensitively for information about the victim's experience of the offence in order that the victim's perspective can inform any discussion at the session about harm and reparation.

Providing information to facilitators to pass on to the offender, and other participants in the restorative session, is, however, only half of the process. It does not go much further than the VS scheme criticised in the introduction to this chapter. Victim satisfaction is also linked to the amount of information which is *received* on the progress of their case. In particular, the need for information is present *throughout* the case. It is not enough to know that the offender has been arrested; victims want to find out what happens next and how the case is finalised,[46] yet the flow of information between the police and victims tends to diminish substantially after arrest[47] (recognition of this led to the establishment of the OSS). To bring about more than just limited 'one-way' information provision, restorative justice facilitators should re-contact victims after the session and feedback information about the process and outcomes of the meeting.

While the Thames Valley Police training manual does not *require* facilitators to make further contact with NPVs after the session, it states clearly:

---

[45] This is the second training manual that was devised by Thames Valley Police—with the assistance of Guy Masters—in June 1999 and used for the training of UK Youth Offending Teams by Thames Valley Police in Spring and Summer 2000. It was also used for the re-training of the restorative justice coordinators and facilitators immediately prior to the phase of our research on which this chapter is based.

[46] Shapland *et al*, *Victims in the Criminal Justice System*, n 43 above.

[47] Eg, T Newburn and S Merry, *Keeping in Touch: Police-Victim Communication in Two Areas* (HMSO, London, 1990).

It is good practice to inquire if the victim would like to be told of any information or comments made by the offender in the caution.

Furthermore, it argues that if the views of the victim are presented in the session, then it is appropriate that any response from the offender is communicated to the victim. If facilitators in the Thames Valley had communicated effectively with those victims who chose not to attend restorative sessions but wanted indirect participation, in the way their manual intends them to, we would expect all victims involved in the restorative process to have profited (to some extent) regardless of whether or not they met the offender. We did not find this to be the case, as will be shown through consideration of data on three potential benefits of restorative justice: therapeutic benefits, challenges to stereotypes and reparation for victims.

THERAPEUTIC BENEFITS TO VICTIMS FROM THEIR ROLE IN RESTORATIVE JUSTICE

The answers to the questions of who restorative sessions can and should benefit, and in what way, will necessarily be contingent on one's ideological position. For example, victim advocates are wary of victims being used as a tool to prevent re-offending (by providing what some see as the necessary shaming and educative function of restorative justice).[48] Nonetheless, restorative sessions are interactive processes and as such their proponents claim that they offer potential therapeutic benefits to all participants; benefits which tend to be a product of the interaction between the parties.

Do such benefits occur? In our study of the Thames Valley initiative the therapeutic benefits to victims of attending restorative sessions were clear.[49] Of the victims who attended (n=31), the overwhelming majority felt satisfied with the process, and fear of, or anger with, the offender had generally disappeared. Ninety two per cent said that the meeting had been a good idea, with only one victim feeling (marginally) worse for having attended. In most cases where there were short-term positive impacts there were also longer-term positive impacts (borne out by the interviews with victims four months after the session and also by questionnaires returned to us eight months after that), with no long-term significant negative feelings. These findings support previous findings from research in Australia by Daly, in New Zealand by Maxwell and Morris, and in the UK by Newburn *et al.*[50]

---

[48] For an example of such wariness see T Reynolds, 'Restorative Justice—A New Way Forward for Victims of Crime?' (2000) 18(2) *Howard League Magazine* 8.

[49] Hoyle, Young and Hill, *Proceed with Caution*, n 3 above.

[50] Daly, 'Conferencing in Australia and New Zealand', n 21 above; Morris and Maxwell, 'The Practice of Family Group Conferences in New Zealand', n 42 above, and T Newburn, A Crawford, R Earle, S Goldie, C Hale, G Masters, A Netten, R Saunders, A Hallam, K Sharpe, and S Uglow, *The Introduction of Referral Orders into the Youth Justice System: Final Report*, Home Office Research Study 242 (Home Office Research, Development and Statistics Directorate, London, 2002) 47.

Victims who do not meet their offenders may nonetheless achieve these benefits, at least to some extent, by making a victim statement and receiving feedback
at the end of the process. This dynamic involvement in the restorative process
needs to be facilitated effectively. A significant part of effective facilitation is
ensuring that the victim is able fully to explain the impact of the offence both on
them personally and, where relevant, significant others, and accurately delivering
this information to those who participate in the meeting with the facilitator; the
offender and their carers and supporters. Best practice was found where facilitators passed on to the participants at the session *all* of the effects of the offence, not
just those the facilitator thought were important. To illustrate, one victim, the
Head of a school where a theft had taken place, explained to us:

> I gave [the facilitator] a whole series of, of impacts that the theft had had, or could have
> had, because of the action of [the offender]. . . . so I was content that the school's view
> had been put, put across to um, [the facilitator] and I presume that that was then
> conveyed through in the meeting.

We examined the transcript of the session and found that the facilitator had
indeed faithfully reported the effects described by the victim. One outcome of the
conference was that the offender sent a letter of apology to the school. The Head
of the school told us that he had planned to write back to the offender to 'thank
him for the apology and hope that he didn't get into further difficulties'. In the
event, he did not find time to do this but he made clear that he had realised some
therapeutic benefit from having his opinions conveyed to those in the meeting
and hearing from the facilitator that the offender had been contrite. Had the victim
attended the session the offender may well have benefited from his reintegrative
gestures, hinted at by his intention to reply to the offender's letter.

Those NPVs who received adequate feedback on the caution were less angry
with, and less afraid of, the offender and more satisfied with the criminal process.
While they had not benefited from the potentially cathartic experiences of facing
the offender and explaining the impact of the offence, or of witnessing genuine
remorse, they were in a qualitatively different state from those victims who had
not been given the opportunity to make a victim statement or had not been told
what impact their statement had had on the offender or significant others. More
than anything, those who had received feedback had a much better understanding
of what the restorative session had entailed.

Feeding back information to victims after a session is particularly important
where there is a chance that offenders and victims will have further contact. Three
of the NPVs mentioned some form of contact with the offender since the session,
either face-to-face or on the telephone. One young victim at school with the
offender was reassured to be told that the offender had, at the session, expressed
his regret for assaulting the victim. Hence, the victim felt prepared when the
offender apologised to him at school the following week and was able to respond
in a reintegrative way.

Our data provide few such exemplary illustrations. Indeed, we have more cases where a failure accurately to reflect the victim's experiences and wishes, and a failure to feedback to those victims information about the restorative sessions, resulted in victims feeling irate and excluded. In one case a 13-year-old boy who had, together with his friends, been robbed at knife point was too afraid of the offenders to attend the session. His mother told us that she had asked the facilitator to explain to the offender who was being cautioned (his co-offenders were prosecuted) how badly affected both she and her son had been:

> To tell them . . . he hasn't handled this very well at all. . . . I've lost sleep over this—a great deal of sleep—and my son's had terrible trouble at school and been withdrawn from certain lessons because his behaviour has become so erratic and just out of character.

The facilitator did not tell the participants at the session how badly affected this boy was. Indeed, he appeared to underplay the seriousness of the offence and its impact, telling the group:

> The message that came across from all of [the victims] was it wasn't really too much of a problem on the day. It was like lighters and a bit of money and, you know, it wasn't big value stuff. You know, it wasn't things like mobile phones. So it wasn't stuff that they had to really worry about replacing.

The contrast between this statement and the comments made to the facilitator by the victim's mother is stark. The facilitator went on to mention that the boys were nervous about going into town on their own but focused more on the inconvenience that this visited on their parents, who felt obliged to provide transport for them, rather than concentrating on the psychological harm suffered by the victims. Despite a less than faithful representation of the victims' experiences, the offender at the session seemed to have some understanding of the effects of his behaviour on the victims: 'The boys must have been scared of us . . . must be scared to walk the streets and that.' He agreed to write a letter of apology, although the victim claimed not to have received this. The victim's mother told us that neither she nor her son had had any further contact with the facilitator about what had happened at the session: 'we've heard absolutely nothing. . . . I would like to hear something . . . I would like to know what's happened.' Not surprisingly, she remained angry about the incident and her son was still afraid.

Most victims who did get feedback from the facilitator were called on the telephone and given only a brief description of the outcome of the caution: '. . .to say that there would be a letter on the way for [the offender] to apologise.' Those victims who had not attended the session and had received no reliable information from the facilitator were much more likely to feel bitter about the criminal justice response to their victimisation. Most thought that the restorative process was little more than a 'slap on the wrist' or a 'letting off'. As one annoyed victim put it:

> Well basically he gets a slap on the wrist and told [not] to do it again which I don't think is a very acceptable way. This whole restorative justice thing is a piece of nonsense. It's not teaching anybody any lessons at all.

In that particular case the offender had been contrite at the session and, had the victim been told this, it might have reduced his anger.

In the main, NPVs rarely reported any positive impact of their limited involvement in restorative cautioning and were much more likely to have negative feelings over the longer-term. However, those who had fed into the process by making a victim statement and who had then received adequate feedback from the facilitator about the session, including information about any reparation agreements, were much more likely to report moderate therapeutic benefits and were less likely to still feel afraid or angry. It is clear that these benefits are not achieved in all cases because facilitators too often fail to give victims the opportunities to make victim statements, sometimes fail to report accurately these statements, and very often fail to 'close the loop' by reporting back to the victim what happened at the session and what, if anything, the victim can expect by way of reparation. In this sense the NPVs were very much like victims who have never had the chance to attend a restorative caution.[51]

CHALLENGING STEREOTYPES

One of the goals of restorative justice is to challenge stereotypical views held by victims, offenders and their supporters about each other. It is argued that the adversarial court process further entrenches stereotypes about offenders in particular and does little to encourage in offenders understanding of the impact of their offending on others.[52] The dialogic, interactional nature of restorative sessions between victims, offenders and their supporters provides opportunities for the respective parties to help the other participants to better understand them; their behaviours, motivations and feelings.

In a number of the cases we observed, the presence of the victim in the restorative session clearly brought about changes to the perceptions and beliefs of other participants as well as to the feelings of the victims themselves. We found that victim participation made it more likely that offenders were held accountable for their actions, and less likely that they would seek to rationalise their behaviour by

---

[51] They could be compared with those victims in the RISE programme who attended court and were more likely than those who participated in a conference to remain angry and afraid of being revictimised by the same offender: H Strang, G Barnes, J Braithwaite and L Sherman, *Experiments in Restorative Policing: A Progress Report on the Canberra Reintegrative Shaming Experiments (RISE)* (Australian Federal Police and Australian National University, Canberra, 1999) also available at <http://www.aic.gov.au/rjustice/rise/progress>.
[52] See H Zehr, *Changing Lenses: A New Focus for Crime and Justice* (Herald Press, Scottsdale PA, 1990) and, for an overview of the literature, G Johnstone, *Restorative Justice: Ideas, Values and Debates* (Willan Publishing, Cullompton, 2002).

denying that it has caused any harm.[53] The Home Office study by Newburn *et al* similarly found, in relation to referral orders, that the majority (88 per cent) of community panel members felt that having a victim present helps to make the young person recognise the effects of their behaviour.[54] Many sessions in our study facilitated significant shifts in the offenders' perceptions of their behaviour and resulted in genuine apologies and sometimes partial explanations for the unacceptable behaviour. This, in turn, left victims feeling that at least some of the damage caused by the offence had been repaired, somewhat less anxious and less afraid of further victimisation than before they participated in the restorative session.[55]

We found that almost two thirds of the victims (and half of the victim supporters) who attended restorative sessions felt differently about 'their' offender because of the session. Many victims came to the restorative session with preconceived notions of what the offender would be like and why they had committed the crime. Some were surprised by the youth or the apparent vulnerability of the person they met. Others were relieved to find that they had not been targeted by the offender, but were victims of opportunistic crime. For a few, who felt that the restorative process demanded a lot of the offender, anger turned to sympathy:

> I feel sorry for him now to tell you the truth . . . having to go through all tonight [referring to the meeting] . . . because I can put my son in his shoes . . . sitting there trembling.

And sometimes to empathy:

> Before, yeah, I'd love to have met them down a dark alley, sort of thing, but now you've had the meeting with them and you've spoke about it, you feel totally different. You actually find out what they're like as people. You thought they were animals to start off with, but you find out they're actually normal people same as anyone else.

It is important, however, to consider whether those benefits can be achieved when victims do not meet their offenders. As with the more therapeutic benefits, we found that while victims and offenders were most likely to feel differently about each other and about the offence when they had met, a well delivered and accurate victim statement could make a difference to one or more participant, in particular the offender, without the victim having to attend the session.

In one case, for example, a victim statement, informing the participants that the victim had sustained a permanent black eye as a result of an assault, had a clear impact on the offender. When we interviewed him immediately after the session he spoke of his shock at hearing about the extent of the injuries. Before the meeting he had convinced himself that the assault was minor and that he had not really harmed the victim, but then 'because [I] found out he got a permanent injury', he

---

[53] See further G Sykes and D Matza, 'Techniques of Neutralization: A Theory of Delinquency' (1957) 22 *American Sociological Review* 664.

[54] Newburn *et al*, *Final Report*, n 50 above, 32.

[55] See Hoyle, Young and Hill, *Proceed with Caution*, n 3 above.

admitted to us 'I'll regret it for the rest of my life.' A separate interview with his father, who accompanied him to the session, confirmed our impression that the meeting had brought about a significant change in the offender.

Just as information from the victim can only challenge the preconceptions of the offender if relayed accurately by the facilitator, the only hope of changing victims' ideas about offenders is by adequate feedback from the facilitator after the session. Without this, restorative justice is open to some of the same criticisms directed at Victim Statements, discussed above. Some victims consider anyone who offends against them to be a hardened criminal, beyond redemption. Without evidence to the contrary, they may continue to believe this and remain bitter. Many of our NPVs who had not been contacted further by the police, and those who had received only a cursory letter informing them merely that the caution meeting had taken place, made caustic comments to us about the offender such as 'he just doesn't give a damn'. Without feedback from the meeting how could they have thought otherwise? Furthermore, where the meeting had not resulted in a reparation agreement they were even more likely to think this.

SECURING REPARATION FOR VICTIMS

Reparation for harms caused by an offence is one of the many outcomes victims expect from the restorative process and while it is not crucial that a formal written reparation agreement be reached, it is important that where such agreements are made offenders comply with their terms (or that the reasons for non-compliance are accepted as legitimate). If not, other participants may come to feel that the offender misled them at the session and victims may be disappointed or even feel somewhat re-victimised.[56]

Almost a third of the offenders in the 56 restorative sessions we observed in this phase of our research entered into a formal written agreement at the session. When victims were not present, many of these agreements involved symbolic reparation only, for example, a commitment to send a letter of apology to one or more victims. Reparation, unlike purely therapeutic benefits, or challenges to different parties' assumptions about each other, does not seem to be contingent on victim attendance at the session. Our data do not suggest that offenders are more likely to enter into an agreement if the victim is present. However, they appear to be slightly more likely to fulfil the agreement when they have met the victim. One year after the restorative session the majority (59 per cent) of reparation agreements had been completely fulfilled, some (29 per cent) had been only partially fulfilled (for example, some payment, but not all, had been made, or a letter of

---

[56] See D Miers, M Maguire, S Goldie, K Sharpe, C Hale, A Netten, S Uglow, K Doolin, A Hallam, J Enterkin and T Newburn, *An Exploratory Evaluation of Restorative Justice Schemes*, Crime Reduction Research Series Paper 9 (Home Office, London, 2001).

apology was sent but no money) and only three remained completely unfulfilled. These three were all made during a session which the victim did not attend.[57]

Furthermore, we found some qualitative variation in experiences of reparation. Victims who attended sessions were more likely to feel satisfied with the reparation offered. Some of those who attended fully expecting material reparation were satisfied, by the close of the session, with only symbolic reparation when they realised that the offender was genuinely sorry and when they understood the limitations on the offender's resources. This was also found in the Canberra 'RISE' experiments. Strang provides examples of victims who initially wanted material reparation but during the conference decided not to ask for it because they recognised that it was beyond the offender's resources.[58] This was necessarily impossible when victims did not attend. In Thames Valley, NPVs who received a written apology were usually far less impressed by this reparative gesture than those who participated, particularly when they wanted compensation. One victim, who remained angry with the offender for damage to his car after he received only a letter of apology, explained:

> I think the system treated me very unfairly. I've had a letter of apology from him. I was told, after the restorative caution was given, that also I would receive compensation. . . . At no point in time have I ever been offered compensation. . . . I mean, [the letter's] all very well but it still doesn't pay for my car.

In other cases NPVs claimed that the police had told them that compensation would be forthcoming and they were thus naturally disappointed when they received 'only' a letter of apology. Better preparation would undoubtedly result in NPVs holding more realistic expectations.

Victims who watched offenders having to account for their behaviours and answer difficult questions put to them by other participants were more likely to feel that the process was punishment enough without the offenders having to dig deep into their pockets. NPVs, on the other hand, who had not watched their offenders going through the restorative process, and had not received material reparation, were more likely than those who attended sessions to see it as an easy option and sometimes wanted their offenders to compensate them expressly for its punitive effect. As one put it:

> Just get him to realise the extent of the damage caused has to be paid by someone. And it does hurt to have to pay for someone else's damage, and if you have to pay for it yourself, it should hurt you as well. So basically, pain is inflicted through having to compensate for the action.

---

[57] Although not directly comparable, Newburn *et al* found that offenders on referral orders were significantly more likely to complete their contract when the victim had attended the community panel meeting (Newburn *et al*, *Final Report*, n 50 above, 42).

[58] H Strang, 'Justice for Victims of Young Offenders' in A Morris and G Maxwell (eds), *Restorative Justice for Juveniles: Conferencing, Mediation and Circles* (Hart Publishing, Oxford, 2001).

They are therefore more likely to feel that the process has been a waste of time if it does not conclude with a pledge to compensate them.

This is not to argue that victims who meet their offenders are, by the end of the process, no longer interested in compensation. Research suggests that the great majority of victims who suffer material loss would like to be compensated.[59] However, a major difference between those who meet and those who do not seems to be the extent to which victims benefit in other ways. As Zehr points out:

> Victims usually participate in the first place on the understanding that reparation may be possible, even if afterwards they come to value other aspects of the mediation more.[60]

A further difference is that those who meet are more likely to accept that compensation is not practical, due to financial constraints on the offender. As Davis makes clear:

> restitution is not possible in every case; and *complete* restitution may be possible in very few cases; but to the extent that restitution is feasible, but remains undone, it is difficult to see how an apology could be thought sincere, or reconciliation achieved.[61]

When victims attend meetings, especially with young offenders, it is often more than apparent that restitution is not feasible. Hence victims do not feel so disappointed to walk away empty handed. When they do not meet the offender, and therefore learn little or nothing of their circumstances, they are likely to interpret a failure to compensate them as an indication of offender apathy, or failure of the process to hold the offender accountable.[62]

In the Thames Valley, the majority of agreements are for symbolic reparation and there were differences in perceptions of attending and non-attending victims with regards to offenders' apologies. NPVs were more likely to feel confused about, or suspicious of, symbolic reparation, especially where the facilitator had not adequately explained the process or had not made them aware that they were the intended beneficiary of a reparation agreement. Two victims in our sample who had not been contacted by the police after the caution received letters of

---

[59] Davis, *Making Amends*, n 41above, 162.

[60] H Zehr, 'Reparation: Where from Here?' in *Repairing the Damage: Proceedings of the First National Symposium on Mediation and Criminal Justice* (FIRM, Beaconsfield, 1989), cited in *ibid*, 168.

[61] Davis, *Making Amends*, n 41 above, 171.

[62] Ashworth argues that there is a danger of disproportionate reparation agreements if victims attend: 'The principle of proportionality goes against victim involvement in sentencing decisions because the views of victims may vary.' A Ashworth, 'Responsibilities, Rights and Restorative Justice' in M Maguire, R Morgan and R Reiner (eds), *The Oxford Handbook of Criminology*, 3rd edn (Clarendon Press, Oxford, forthcoming 2002) 586. While space constraints preclude a full consideration of this critique, our data suggests that victims who attend are *less* likely to push for material reparation, despite being in a better position than those who did not attend to do so. If facilitators improve the prospects for participation of non-attending victims there is the risk of an increase in slightly more punitive reparation agreements. However, this is not a reason for abandoning victim participation but, rather, for implementing safeguards for offenders such as the upper and lower limits on reparation advocated by M Cavadino and J Dignan, 'Reparation, Retribution and Rights' (1997) 4 *International Review of Victimology* 233.

apology from offenders. Without knowing why the offender had written the letter they questioned their motivation:

> It would have been nice to follow it up with a conversation of why she actually felt she had needed to write, make sure she wasn't doing it for going through the motions, asking her the reason why she had to write to me.

Similarly, it is not enough for facilitators to report such an agreement without explaining to the victim the context within which the agreement is made.

Sometimes facilitators explained that the offender would make reparation to the victim without explaining that any reparation agreement made in the session was not legally binding and could not therefore be fully relied upon. One of our NPVs had been told he would receive a letter of apology and compensation but then only received the letter. He subsequently sought out the offender to demand the promised compensation, which was not forthcoming, leaving him incensed. Full and accurate information from the facilitator might have at least ameliorated his anger and frustration. However, as with the other potential benefits of restorative justice, we did not find such high levels of satisfaction regarding reparation amongst our NPVs because of the generally poor level of communication that characterised their dealings with the police.

EXPLAINING THE GAP

The previous three sections have shown that restorative justice promises many potential benefits to offenders and to victims. These are most likely to be realised when victims attend sessions with their offenders. However, these benefits can be achieved, at least to some extent, even when victims do not meet their offenders by the effective facilitation of indirect communication between victims and offenders—through the construction and delivery of accurate victim statements and through feeding back information about the process and outcome of the restorative session to the victim. Best practice in these two areas leaves NPVs less angry, less afraid, and more willing to make reintegrative gestures towards offenders. Our data show, however, that the benefits of restorative justice are rarely achieved in cases where the victim and offender do not meet. There is, in other words, a gap between sessions attended by victims and those which are not. There are two reasons for this gap. Firstly, as shown above, poor implementation of the restorative model and, secondly, the inevitability of limited gains from a less dynamic process.

Given that the data presented above seem to suggest that benefits to victims are most likely to be achieved when they attend restorative sessions, arguably the most crucial role the facilitator plays is to provide all potential participants with an adequate explanation of the restorative process to enable them to make an informed choice about whether or not to attend the session. Even if this is done, some victims will, for good reasons, decide not to attend and then the facilitator needs to explore with the victim the alternative ways of participating: most obviously by making a statement and by receiving feedback after the session. Decisions about *how* to participate can only be made if the victim has full and accurate information on the restorative cautioning process. It is therefore essential to explore the extent to which invitations to attend a session, opportunities to make a statement, and feedback after the session are managed effectively by facilitators. It is only then that we can really understand whether the less satisfactory outcomes for NPVs are an inevitable result of the non-dynamic nature of their limited participation or, as with so many other criminal justice initiatives, a product of poor implementation of a basically good model.

Poor Implementation

While Thames Valley police do better than most organisations in facilitating restorative sessions with the victim present, it is still the case that the majority of offenders do not meet their victims.[63] Trying to disaggregate the effects of self-selection from poor implementation is not easy, but it is a critical stage in the evaluation of the potential of restorative justice. Our data suggest that, in the majority of cases, poor implementation of the restorative model is the most crucial factor in the widespread failure to bring victims and offenders together.

As discussed above, a minority of victims could not attend a restorative session for practical reasons. Like Morris *et al* we found that facilitators often failed to give victims adequate notice of the meeting or made insufficient effort to hold the meeting at a convenient time.[64] Others chose not to attend for fear of retaliation from the offender. While fear of retaliation may be rational, and for some particularly vulnerable victims a meeting may never seem to be an attractive option, adequate explanations of the restorative cautioning process should go some way towards alleviating victims' fears. However, like Hoyle *et al*'s study of VS, we found that most of the NPVs had, at best, a sketchy understanding of what was on offer and therefore could not make an informed choice about attending.

Explaining the Caution and Inviting the Victim

Adequate explanation of, and information about, the process is crucial if victims are fully to understand what is being offered and make an informed choice

---

[63] Other schemes are examined by Miers *et al*, *Exploratory Evaluation of Restorative Justice Schemes*, n 56 above; T Newburn *et al*, *Second Interim Report*, n 29 above. There are a handful of restorative justice projects across the UK which have a much higher proportion of cases involving victims. However they deal with relatively few cases. No other organisation has such a high victim attendance rate for such a high case load (Wilcox with Hoyle, *Final Report to the Youth Justice Board*, n 28 above).

[64] Morris and Maxwell, 'The Practice of Family Group Conferences in New Zealand', n 42 above.

regarding participation. In various studies of mediation or conferencing involving victims and offenders, preparation is identified as the most important factor leading to the success of the session.[65] As Daly argues, 'The potential for restorativeness is greater when participants . . . have taken the time in advance to think about what they want to say.'[66] However, her data show that most people attending a restorative session have little idea about what is expected of them or what they can expect from the process.

Similarly, most of the NPVs in our study who turned down the chance to meet their offender in a restorative session did so without realising that this is what they were doing. Information about the caution session was received by telephone in the majority of cases, with just four victims reporting a visit at home or work by the restorative justice coordinator, the facilitator, or the officer in charge of the case. Their understanding of what would happen at the caution was, in most cases, poor. There were three common responses to our question of what they had understood would happen at the session after they had been contacted by the facilitator.

'A caution is a caution'
Seven victims responded by saying that *the offender would be cautioned*. This is an interesting finding despite sounding somewhat tautological. It suggests that people have a preconceived idea (however vague or inaccurate) of what a caution is. The responses also suggest a perception that not very much actually *happens* at a caution session; a caution is just something given to the offender. This group knew nothing about the restorative process.

'A slap on the wrist'
Nine victims seemed to have a traditional view of cautioning. They thought that when the offender was cautioned he would get 'a slap on the wrist' or 'a telling off' or, less punitively, 'a warning'. As one put it, 'He would be given a caution. Basically he would be told he'd done wrong, naughty boy, slap him on the wrist, "don't do it again."' Within this group of respondents, just as in the first group, there was no mention of the chance for victims to have their say, to ask the offender questions or to ask for reparation. The language used suggests that these victims did not see the restorative cautioning process as holding offenders accountable.

Allusions to restorative justice principles
The responses of eight victims touched upon practices closer to what might happen in a restorative session. However, three of these had acquired this knowledge

---

[65] See, for example, C Flaten, 'Victim Offender Mediation: Application with Serious Offences Committed by Juveniles' in B Galaway and J Hudson (eds), *Restorative Justice: International Perspectives* (Criminal Justice Press, Monsey NY, 1996).
[66] K Daly, 'Mind the Gap: Restorative Justice in Theory and Practice' in A von Hirsch, J Roberts, AE Bottoms, K Roach and M Schiff (eds), *Restorative Justice and Criminal Justice: Competing or Reconcilable Paradigms?* (Hart Publishing, Oxford, forthcoming 2002) under the heading 'New Justice Scripts and the Legal Consciousness and Moral Development of Participants'.

not through adequate preparation but from prior experience of the restorative approach. The understanding of most victims in this category was limited usually to only one aspect of the process: 'Well they would of let us meet him and ask him questions why he did it and that.' And often they misunderstood the restorative aims, as the following example illustrates:

> All I knew was that she was going to go round there and try and *make him feel guilty*, you know, kind of telling him about me and about how much I was going to have to pay out in damages and that kind of thing.

By alluding to only one aim of a restorative caution, facilitators can mislead victims about the general aims and potential benefits of a restorative approach. Most explanations constructed the victim's role as an essentially passive rather than active participant in the cautioning session.

Such patchy understanding could be the result of facilitators saving the full explanation of restorative cautioning for when victims have decided to attend in principle or express a serious interest. However, as a result of facilitators trying to save time in preparation, some victims will inevitably opt out of a process in which they would have participated had they been better informed. Furthermore, if the victim agrees to attend without very much information, the facilitator often does not discuss the process in detail until just before the session, and sometimes not even then. Consequently, some of the victims who attended the restorative sessions were unprepared.

Of the 31 victims who attended the restorative sessions, 13 per cent had met with the facilitator to discuss the opportunity to attend the session, but the majority (71 per cent) had only had telephone contact, with the rest being informed about the session by letter or being told by someone else (another participant). In line with other studies of restorative processes, we found that many participants (not just the victims) arrived at a restorative session with no idea of what they were walking into.[67]

Inadequate preparation means that victims have no chance to think about what they might want to get out of the session, what they want to say or what they want to ask of the other participants. Nor do they have the opportunity to identify and ask appropriate 'supporters' to attend with them. Furthermore, if victims do not know what to expect from a restorative cautioning session, then what have they agreed to? A restorative caution is not necessarily an easy thing to explain or comprehend, but simply telling the victim that they can go to the caution without explaining what their role and other participants' roles could be—'Well they said that I've got the right to be there while they caution him, would I like to attend'— does not go very far in illuminating the process.

In addition, the knowledge that they can bring friends or family with them to support them in the session could influence the victim's decision to attend. Only

---

[67] See *ibid* and Miers *et al*, *Exploratory Evaluation of Restorative Justice Schemes*, n 56 above.

half of the NPVs who were invited to participate in the restorative session were told that they could take someone with them. Similarly, just over half (17) of the 31 victims who attended restorative sessions had not been asked who they would like to accompany them.

Thames Valley Police makes it clear to restorative justice facilitators that they must not coerce victims into attending caution sessions. However, from the discussion above it seems that the organisation should perhaps be more concerned about facilitators inadvertently dissuading victims from attending by failing adequately to describe the cautioning process.[68] We asked all of the NPVs whether or not they felt that the police had wanted them to participate in the process. Only one victim's response suggested that the police were keen for them to attend, although not keen enough to arrange the meeting at a time when the victim could attend:

> They said they wanted me to be there, and they said that [the offender] wanted me to be there. I wanted to be there, it was just an inconvenient time.

By contrast, two victims in our sample had the impression that the police did not really want them to participate. As one put it: 'It's the way they phrased it: "Would you like to turn up? Most people don't, but it's up to you".' The overriding feeling was that NPVs felt neither pressure to attend nor to keep away from the session: 'They left it basically up to me and that's the impression I got; I could or I couldn't, you know.' By not fully explaining the process and its potential benefits, the facilitators may, perhaps unwittingly, have put victims off participating. This hypothesis is partly supported by our finding that, after we had explained to them what a restorative session should involve, over half of the victims who had not originally wanted to attend the session said that if invited in future they would agree to attend. This still leaves some victims who, even when fully informed about the process, do not wish to meet their offender. It should be explained to these victims that participation is not an 'either/or' option. Even if they choose not to attend a meeting with the offender they should be given the opportunity for indirect mediation; in particular, by being invited to make a victim statement.

The Communication of Victims' Views

Of the 26 twenty-six NPVs who were informed about the session, 16 had been asked by the police facilitator if they wished their views to be communicated to the offender, only two of whom declined. Yet with the remaining ten, it was clearly assumed that a decision not to attend the session ruled out any victim participation in the process.

---

[68] Newburn *et al*'s study of referral orders also found that most community panel members felt that more should be done to encourage victims to attend (*Final Report*, n 50 above, 31).

In relation to those who were invited to make a statement, as with all areas of communication with victims, there was some variance in the approach of facilitators, ranging from cursory requests: 'any messages?' to more comprehensive offers to inform those at the meeting about the impact on the victim of the offence. Getting accurate information on victims' views of their suffering, and on what they would like to see come out of the session, is a crucial part of preparing for a session where the victim does not wish to attend. This is the only chance for NPVs to contribute to the restorative process and the only opportunity for offenders to learn formally about the effects of their offence on their specific victim.

Victims' statements tended to focus on the harm caused by the offence and suggested that they hoped to encourage empathy in the offender:

> I just wanted to get the message across to him that if it happened to him how would he feel, basically. I mean, for him to put himself in my shoes.

A few made clear that they expected or hoped for compensation from the offender, and some put across views which were clearly punitive or deterrent-based. In most of the interviews we conducted it was clear that the victims knew what they wanted the offenders to be told; they did not need much in the way of prompts from the facilitator. Despite this, there was some evidence that facilitators attempted to shape the victim input, by the way they invited the victim to put forward their views, to fulfil their own ideas of an ideal victim statement:

> Well [the facilitator] just wanted me to say what damages I'd had to pay out and the inconvenience and all that kind of stuff. Just to make it seem more of a kind of personal thing rather than just taking a car.

It appears that this victim's statement was being directed rather than facilitated. The process then runs the risk, as Newburn and Merry warn, of criminal justice agents using victims 'as a resource' for their own deterrent or rehabilitative ends.[69] Such a risk was identified by Young in the 1980s, when he observed that in victim–offender mediation schemes, 'a mediator may have a significant degree of control over both the process of mediation and its outcome.'[70] The data here provides proof that this is still a danger with restorative justice schemes.

It is obviously important that if facilitators ask victims for their views, they also accurately communicate them to the participants at the session, having first ensured that the victim is happy for all or part of her 'statement' to be used in this way.[71] We examined caution transcripts in those cases where the NPV had given the facilitator information to feed into the session to compare what victims had told us that they had wanted to communicate with facilitators' reports in the

---

[69] Newburn and Merry, *Keeping in Touch*, n 47 above, 38.
[70] R Young, *Research Report on the Wolverhampton Reparation Scheme* (Institute of Judicial Administration, University of Birmingham, Birmingham, 1987) (cited in Davis, *Making Amends*, n 41 above,168).
[71] As Erez *et al* make clear, some victims do not want their offender to be fully aware of the harm they have suffered: 'Victim Harm, Impact Statements and Victim Satisfaction' n 24 above.

sessions. In almost half of the cases the facilitator accurately represented the victims' views; in five of these the communication was exceptionally good, showing that the facilitator had paid close attention to what the victim wanted. However, in just under half of the cases there were discrepancies between the NPVs statement and the facilitator's version delivered to the session. It is inevitable that there will be minor omissions in relaying views in this way. However, facilitators too often gave undue focus to what *they* thought was important. For example, in a few cases the victims expressed complex feelings about the multiple impacts of the offence, which included distress, inconvenience and loss of trust as well as the financial cost of the damage. In the sessions, however, facilitators often reduced the victim input merely to requests for financial compensation and letters of apology without mentioning how the victims had been affected. In a few other cases we observed facilitators going beyond the statement made by the absent victim and exaggerating the harm suffered, in order to satisfy their own deterrent aim.

Feedback after the Caution

It is not enough for most victims to know that their experiences have been passed on to the offender and others. It is also important for them to know how the offender responded to this information; whether or not they seemed to be contrite and whether or not they intend to do something to repair the harm. Usually, only the facilitator is in a position to tell them this.

Research by Miers *et al* and Newburn *et al*, found that victims typically want more information and feedback on their cases, in particular about the offender and any reparation agreements made.[72] While less than half of our sample of NPVs reported that the police had contacted them after the caution, most of those who had been given the opportunity to have their views fed into the process had been re-contacted after the session. Half reported being contacted by letter, with the others being telephoned by the facilitator. However, the quality of feedback was often deficient.

Victims who received letters fared worse in terms of valuable feedback. They received standard letters simply informing them that the caution had taken place. Not surprisingly, one of these victims did not see this as the police 'getting in touch'. The differing experiences of these victims highlight the significance of the *quality* of contact. In some ways these NPVs were in a similar position to those victims who opted into OSS and received brief letters informing them of the 'result' at various stages of the criminal process but not providing any detailed information on what this meant, either for the offender or for them. OSS victims told us that they usually wanted much more information than was in the letter

---

[72] Miers *et al*, *Exploratory Evaluation of Restorative Justice Schemes*, n 56 above; Newburn *et al*, *Final Report*, n 50 above.

and a better explanation of what the various 'disposals' or stages in the criminal process meant. They wanted to ask questions of the criminal justice agents who had made decisions in their case to help them better understand those decisions and their implications. Many of our NPVs felt the same way. Neither group felt able to find out more. In both studies, some victims asked us, the researchers, to explain to them what had happened.

Narrowing the Gap in Terms of Benefits to Victims

Much has been written and spoken about the importance, indeed the centrality, of victim involvement in restorative justice. Most advocates of restorative justice, both academics and practitioners, have argued that victims must be engaged in the process wherever practicable.[73] Even those, such as Bazemore and Walgrave, who argue for the inclusion of judicially imposed community service under the banner 'restorative justice' (as long as the intent is to bring 'healing' to victims and the 'offended community'), concede that the best outcomes are achieved when victims and offenders are brought together in a face-to-face meeting.[74] While it is true that the best outcomes are reached when victims meet offenders, the differences in outcomes are exaggerated greatly by the poor implementation of restorative justice when no meeting takes place.

Much of the difference in experiences between victims who attend the restorative session and those who do not can be eradicated by improved facilitation. Most of the failings reported above have at their root poor communication. Better communication at all stages of the process would help to realise the promise of restorative justice for NPVs. Achieving a dynamic flow of information throughout would not only serve to allow victims to make informed decisions to attend the session, but would also allow those who do not wish to attend to nonetheless participate in a meaningful way in the process and to better judge the appropriateness of the criminal justice response. Better communication can challenge the assumptions of those with preconceived ideas about 'cautions'. This is crucial if restorative cautioning is to be seen as something other than 'a slap on the wrist', an old-style 'bollocking' or a ritualised telling-off.[75]

Daly explains that:

> Until the argot of restorative justice and the expected script between victim and offender in a mediation-like setting is known to a broader audience, offenders, victims, and their supporters are feeling their way though an unfamiliar justice terrain.[76]

---

[73] See, for example, NACRO, *Victim Policy: Guidance for Piloting YOTs* (NACRO, London, 2000).

[74] G Bazemore and L Walgrave, 'Restorative Juvenile Justice: In Search of Fundamentals and an Outline for Systemic Reform' in G Bazemore and L Walgrave (eds), *Restorative Juvenile Justice* (Criminal Justice Press, Monsey NY, 1999).

[75] The nature of 'old-style' cautions is discussed by Hoyle, Young and Hill, *Proceed with Caution*, n 3 above, 7.

[76] Daly, 'Mind the Gap', n 66 above, under heading 'New Justice Scripts and the Legal Consciousness and Moral Development of Participants'.

It is the job of a facilitator to equip all participants (not only those who attend a meeting) with the necessary information to find their way through, and benefit from, the restorative process. Victims who choose not to participate should be considered before, during and after the process and receive adequate explanation and information about any meetings that take place.

There is clearly tension between the ideals of restorative justice and the practicalities of organising restorative sessions. Umbreit *et al* argue that with some victims preparation may take months, if not years.[77] But as Daly rightly contends, with reference only to the much less ambitious aim of speaking individually to all relevant people about what the session is, what participants' roles are, and what might be achieved: 'It is unrealistic to reach that ideal in a high-volume jurisdiction that uses conferences as a matter of routine. Organisational shortcuts are inevitable.'[78] Some shortcuts are more defensible than others. For example, it is not necessary for facilitators to make home visits to each potential participant in order adequately to explain the process and answer queries. It is often enough to speak with participants on the telephone and arrange a preparatory meeting only in those cases where telephone communication is not possible or has not succeeded in adequately preparing the participant.[79] However, the facilitator should speak to all participants before they arrive for the session.

A balance between pragmatism and good practice should be sought in recognition of both organisational constraints and the unacceptability of managing only a handful of sessions a year because of heavy preparation at the front end. It is also necessary for facilitators to make clear to all victims that they can feed into the process by making a victim statement. Regardless of whether a statement is made or not, facilitators should offer to contact victims again after the meeting to tell them about the process and the outcome, particularly if a reparation agreement has been made. Most importantly, if victims agree to further contact with the offender the facilitator should make sure this is done so that victims are not left 'high and dry'.

Clearly improved facilitation of the restorative model could go a long way towards closing the gap in satisfaction levels between victims who attend restorative sessions and those who do not, and it is crucial when we consider that around half of victims do not wish to meet their offenders (but are interested in reparation).[80] However, I doubt it could ever be fully closed because ultimately indirect mediation can never be truly dynamic if all statements are mediated by a facilitator.

---

[77] Umbreit *et al*, 'Victim Impact of Meeting with Offenders', n 40 above, 129.
[78] Daly, 'Mind the Gap', n 66 above, under heading 'Containment of Justice Ideals by Organisational Routines'.
[79] R Young and C Hoyle, *Restorative Cautioning: Strengthening Communities in the Thames Valley* (confidential interim study) (Centre for Criminological Research, University of Oxford, Oxford, 1999).
[80] Mattinson and Mirrlees-Black, *Attitudes to Crime and Criminal Justice*, n 40 above.

The Inevitability of Limited Benefits

NPVs, with the help of effective facilitators, can have a more dynamic role in the criminal justice response to their victimisation than victims who opted into the OSS or VS schemes. They are also in a better position than victims who will benefit from post-Glidewell reforms to information provision in the sense that they can both give *and* receive information about their case and can have an influence on reparation. However, they are not in the same position as those victims who attend meetings with their offenders.

Comparison of our cases where victims attended restorative sessions with those well facilitated cases where they did not suggests that even where facilitators make great efforts to be a conduit for information between victims and offenders, there is a limit to the changes that can be brought about by indirect communication. Some people seem to remain unconvinced by second hand information and unmoved by messages conveyed through another person.

In one case, which in many ways was an example of 'textbook facilitation', the victim had decided not to attend the session because he felt too angry with the offender: 'If I see him, I'm going to rip his head off.' Had he attended the session, as we did, he would have witnessed a seemingly genuinely remorseful young man talking openly with his friends about his regret at the damage he had caused to the victim's car. The facilitator was impressed by the contrition expressed by the offender and telephoned the victim at the end of the session to explain the promises made by the offender. He made an ethically problematic decision to allow the offender to overhear the responses of the victim (who was himself unaware that the offender was listening in). In interview, the facilitator explained to us this unusual decision:

> I rung the victim up and we were talking about the costs and so forth, and, and I let [the offender] hear the victim saying 'that's a positive move' and 'that's a really positive move' about writing to the neighbours. So he heard all that. . . . I wanted [the offender] to hear me say that the lads [the offender and his friends] were scared to come and approach [the victim] because of his demeanour, and he thought that they might get beaten up. And [the victim] categorically said that that is not his intention; if he wanted to do that he could have done it straightaway afterwards and he just didn't want to do that. I said because the lads do not feel safe walking around [their home town]. He said 'well, reassure them that they are safe, I'm not going to touch them, I'm quite happy with what's happened now' and gave some reassurance which is what I wanted to do, I didn't want [the offender] to go away from here feeling scared.

This highly unusual tactic succeeded in reducing the offender's fear of retaliation from the victim, but it did not change the victim's feelings about the offender, despite his reassurances on the telephone. Having not had the opportunity to confront the offender directly in a safe controlled environment, this victim was still feeling angry when we interviewed him. He told us that he had lost confidence in the criminal justice process, and in the police in particular:

I have to say if I was the victim of a similar crime again . . . I hesitate to say it but I've got a feeling I would administer my own justice and not involve the police . . . okay, it's a bit Neolithic, but, at the same time, if he thinks that, he'll think bloody twice about doing anything else.

His feelings about the offender had not been challenged: 'he has no respect for the law or for other people's property'. It is very hard to know how the session would have proceeded had he attended, but it is unlikely that he would have left without any of his preconceptions challenged.

While it seems obvious that it is difficult to challenge victims' prejudices about offenders without direct communication between the two, it is not so obvious that reparation agreements should suffer under indirect communication. Certainly, the 'quality' of material reparation is unlikely to differ according to the route it takes to the victim. However, it is possible to argue that the same is not true for symbolic reparation. As Strang observes: 'apology (and forgiveness), when it occurs, is most often the end result of a series of interactions between victims and offenders signalling various stages of emotional restoration that the parties experience.'[81] Strang describes a process which cannot easily be reproduced through indirect mediation even according to best practice. It is the 'series of interactions', the dialogue, which is missing in indirect mediation.

The literature on restorative justice and victim offender mediation supports these points. Victims often make clear that the most satisfying part of the experience is meeting the offender so that they could tell the offender about their experience, hear from the offender why he or she committed the crime and 'simply put a human face on the offender'.[82] Research, by Umbreit and Bradshaw, which attempted to disaggregate the various factors leading to victim satisfaction, found that three factors were highly explanatory: victims' attitudes towards the mediator; victims' perceived fairness of the restitution agreement; and the importance of meeting with the offender.[83] To some extent, improved facilitation can go a long way towards achieving the first two for NPVs. However, the third is, by definition, never possible.

CLOSING THE GAP IN APPROACH: THE QUESTION OF RIGHTS AND RESPONSIBILITIES

Considering the main rationales for restorative justice, Edwards concludes that their realisation is seriously impeded if victims are not involved in the process.[84] As Garton has argued, and as we have found in Thames Valley, 'what is clear . . .

---

[81] Strang, 'Justice for Victims of Young Offenders', n 58 above, 187.
[82] Umbreit *et al*, 'Victim Impact of Meeting with Young Offenders', n 40 above, 131.
[83] Cited in Umbreit *et al*, *ibid*, 131.
[84] I Edwards, 'Victim Participation in Sentencing: The Problems of Incoherence' (2001) 40 *The Howard Journal of Criminal Justice* 39.

is the fact that victims rarely spontaneously agree to mediation'. She found that 'persuasion is an integral part of mediator training' despite the stress on the voluntary nature of the process.[85]

Davis recognised, with respect to VOM schemes in the 1980s, that if schemes measure success, even in part, on achieving direct mediation between victims and offenders, victims are likely to feel pressured to attend meetings. More recently, both critics and advocates of restorative justice have expressed fears about victims being coerced into meetings with their offenders. For example, Reeves and Mulley, from the Victim Support National Office, are concerned that restorative schemes place an unacceptable burden on victims:

> Approaching victims to participate in restorative justice initiatives can be very liberating in that it allows victims of crime to confront the offender and to have their say. However, it could also be experienced as an additional burden in the form of unwanted contact with, or even responsibility for, the offender. Although participation in such schemes is voluntary . . . giving them the choice to become involved . . . can place the victim in a difficult position. They may feel guilty if they choose not to participate and yet anxious if they do.[86]

This is a risk and is the reason why some schemes (for example the Canadian Corrections department working with prisoners) wait for victims to contact them before considering attempts at restorative justice.[87] However, the difficulty with this position is that it ignores the interests of victims who would like to meet but do not want to initiate the idea (for fear, perhaps, of sending out the wrong signal to offenders) or do not have any notion that there could be any benefits. Furthermore, our Thames Valley data provide no empirical evidence that victims do feel anxious when given a choice to participate. Victims in this scheme are less likely to feel guilty about a decision not to attend a caution as they know that the caution will still go ahead, with or without their support. Unlike in other jurisdictions, the decision to caution is made irrespective of the victim's willingness to meet with the offender. Victims are more likely to feel pressurised to attend meetings under schemes which aim to use the restorative process to influence decisions made in the criminal justice system (for example, concerning plans about how and when to release prisoners, or how to sentence them).

There is a balance to be struck in restorative justice between the desire to provide victims, and others, with a service which seems to be beneficial, and the concern not to coerce victims into attending, with the risk of re-victimisation. As

---

[85] A Garton, *Preliminary Report on the Leeds Reparation Scheme* (Unpublished research paper, 1986) cited in Davis, *Making Amends*, n 41 above, 172.

[86] H Reeves and K Mulley, 'The New Status of Victims in the UK: Opportunities and Threats' in A Crawford and J Goodey, *Integrating a Victim Perspective within Criminal Justice* (Ashgate, Aldershot, 2000) 139. See also C Griffiths 'The Victims of Crime and Restorative Justice: The Canadian Experience' (1999) 6 *International Review of Victimology* 279.

[87] Presentation by Jane Miller-Ashton at a meeting of the Restorative Justice Development Group hosted by the Thames Valley Partnership on 19 March 2002.

Wright has argued, while coercion should be avoided, it is important conversely that those who might want to take part should be made fully aware of the opportunity, with all its likely benefits and disadvantages so that they can make an informed choice.[88]

The Thames Valley Police training manual makes clear that: 'a service that is truly sensitive to victims will offer them *real choices* and be flexible enough to meet their needs.' (p. 3–8). It emphasises that victims should not be coerced into taking part. Furthermore, the training reinforces this message by warning facilitators that they should be wary of telling victims of the benefits to be gained from participation in cautions for fear that if benefits are not fully realised during the process this could reduce the legitimacy of the process. Herein lies a fundamental tension; can facilitators offer 'real choices', that is, informed choices, if they do not explain the potential benefits? Indeed, is it possible adequately to describe the process without discussing these benefits? The data above suggest not. They indicate that facilitators have erred too far on the side of circumspection and consequently denied many victims a potentially profitable experience.

None of the victims we interviewed felt that the facilitator had tried to coerce them into attending the session, but we did find that they had not been given the means to make informed choices. On the whole, the victims in both of our samples (those who attended the sessions and those who did not) were found to have a limited understanding of the process they had been asked to participate in and what their role could be in that process. Their imperfect understanding was responsible for some 'choosing' not to attend the meeting, but it was also partly responsible for the limited participation in the restorative process of those who did not wish to meet their offender.

Facilitators did not, in most cases, make the distinction between meeting the offender at the caution and the opportunities available to all victims without them needing to attend the meeting; for example, for victims to vent their feelings and address the issue of reparation. This chapter shows that there needs to be a clearer distinction between non-attending victims (victims who do not wish to attend the meeting but still want some form of indirect participation in the process) and non participating victims, victims who do not wish to participate *in any way* in the process. At the start of our research we, as researchers, also failed adequately to conceptualise participation and so fell into the same trap as facilitators. Our acronym 'NPV' was used to refer to all of those who did not attend the restorative meeting because we originally conceived of 'non-attending victims' as 'non-participating'. Analysis of the data and consideration of the potential of restorative justice showed clearly that participation is best conceived as a continuum. Failure fully to appreciate this continuum will inevitably influence facilitation and could result in some victims' deciding not to meet their offender and in inadequate opportunities for indirect mediation for these victims.

---

[88] M Wright, personal communication, April 2002.

Facilitators' 'failures' in implementing fully the restorative model are partly a product of training, which emphasises avoidance of coercion, and limited resources. Neither of these is insurmountable: training can be changed to ensure that facilitators adopt a more 'victim focused' approach towards information provision and flexibility in arranging meetings and, to some extent, adequate resources can always be freed up by changing organisational priorities. However, neither of these can happen without an organisational shift in perceptions about victims' rights and organisational responsibilities.

As discussed in the introduction, there has been much interest over the past decade in victims' rights; both their rights to improved services, such as information about their case, and the more contentious procedural rights to participate in the criminal justice response to their case and, sometimes, to influence the sentence. The restorative justice model clearly assumes victims' *right to* participate in the restorative process. They should be provided with all the necessary information to enable them to play some role in the restorative process, and they should have the opportunity to inform the offender, and others, of their experience of victimisation and find out how the offender responds to that information.

There has, however, been little attention paid by government or service providers to the *duties* of the different criminal justice agencies to provide those rights or meet those expectations,[89] and there are no means of redress for victims denied what they should reasonably expect. This was the main criticism of the Victims' Charters; they made clear what victims should expect of the criminal justice system (they referred to 'standards of service', shying away from the concept of rights) but did not make clear whose duty it was to provide these services and what, if any, the remedies for victims would be if agencies failed to provide them. There were, in other words, no mechanisms for accountability. As Fenwick points out: '. . . the scheme seems to lie within the field of executive as opposed to judicial action and within that field the redress available for breaches of it is left obscure.'[90] She argues that 'the phrase 'victims rights' is misleading and will continue to be so until the rights are afforded greater content and are backed up by forms of redress.'[91] As a recent JUSTICE Report argues, the criminal justice system will have no integrity if it does not take seriously the delivery of services to victims.[92]

The JUSTICE report produced a list of the legitimate expectations of victims. Those most clearly relevant to restorative cautioning are:

> [the] means to ensure timely and accurate provision of information to relevant criminal justice institutions and agencies about the offence and its effects on victims;

---

[89] Not even the European Convention on Human Rights takes a clear position on victims' rights: see A Ashworth, 'Victims' Rights, Defendants' Rights', n 2 above, 189.

[90] H Fenwick, 'Rights of Victims in the Criminal Justice System: Rhetoric or Reality?' [1995] *Criminal Law Review* 845.

[91] *Ibid*, 851.

[92] JUSTICE, *Victims in Criminal Justice* (JUSTICE, London,1998).

compensation and alleviation of the effects of the offence, as well as minimisation of cost to victims in assisting criminal justice;

being made aware of what is expected of them at each stage (when they will be needed, where they go, what will happen.);

minimisation of further damage or harm to victims through criminal justice procedures.[93]

As Shapland asserts, it is the duty of the 'responsible agency', in this case the police, to meet the legitimate expectations of the victims.[94] It is clear that in many cases in the Thames Valley this was not done. Victims did not all receive accurate information in a timely fashion; they did not all receive compensation and for many the 'costs' of attending a restorative session were considered prohibitive, in terms of time or other resources; they were not made aware what would happen to them at each stage, and were certainly not made fully aware what the process might entail when invited to participate; and, a few were further harmed by the process when their expectations of compensation were raised only to be dashed, without explanation. But what is also evident is that the organisation failed to impose on the facilitators this duty. The training manual for facilitators makes clear what it considers to be 'good practice' but imposes no duty on facilitators to do those things which are recommended; for example, it does not *require* facilitators to make further contact with NPVs after the session—it leaves it to the discretion of the facilitator. Leaving 'good practice' recommendations regarding responsibilities to victims to the discretion of busy facilitators denies many victims the very things that the Thames Valley Police publicity material promises them they can expect from the restorative justice process.

CONCLUSION: TOWARDS VICTIM EMPOWERMENT

In the Thames Valley restorative cautioning scheme, ideals of a 'balanced approach' involving victims, offenders and the community, come up against some obstructive realities. One is the reluctance of key parties to meet. Others are seen in the organisational routines which work against the adequate preparation necessary for satisfactory restorative processes and outcomes.[95] The conflict between good preparation and organisational constraints, and the difficulty of explaining the potential of restorative justice without coercing victims, are fairly clear. They can, I think, be relatively easily managed by facilitators if they are given improved

---

[93] *Ibid*, 29.

[94] J Shapland, 'Creating Responsible Criminal Justice Agencies' in A Crawford and J Goodey, *Integrating a Victim Perspective within Criminal Justice* (Ashgate, Aldershot, 2000).

[95] For a very convincing discussion of the 'organisational routines' which push 'justice ideals' into second place, see Daly, 'Mind the Gap', n 66 above, especially under heading 'Containment of Justice Ideals by Organisational Routines'.

training in effective communication. Thames Valley police are committed to a restorative approach to justice. They have demonstrated that they are both willing and able to respond quickly and positively to constructive academic criticism.[96] I have no doubt that they can greatly improve facilitation. This would have the result of closing the gap in the approach taken by facilitators towards victims who meet their offenders and those who are unwilling or unable to meet, thereby narrowing the gap between these groups' experiences of restorative justice. However, there is also a tension within the field of restorative justice between doing what the facilitator or others feel is right for the offender, victim and their supporters, and giving the victim the right to make an informed choice. This tension can only be resolved through changes in organisational culture to bring about the empowerment of victims more generally; changes which would see a move away from ignoring victims' choices towards providing victims with enough information to enable them to make wise choices.

Thames Valley Police, as with most other agencies offering restorative sessions in the UK, lean more towards a 'victim benefits', rather than a 'victim rights' rationale for victim inclusion. The former leads to victims being invited to participate in the criminal process only when some third party considers that they, or others, will benefit.[97] By contrast, a wider victims' rights rationale is less likely to lead to any restrictions on participation: victims have a right to participate and so are told about this in a meaningful way in all cases. Should this right of participation extend to a right to meet the offender? In the Thames Valley scheme an offender can refuse to meet with his or her victim, resulting in a restorative caution, rather than a restorative conference. If meeting the victim was a necessary condition of a caution, failure to accept such a condition could be interpreted as opting out of restorative justice, and, more importantly, as a rejection of the caution. That in turn could result in the case being passed on to the Crown Prosecution Service to consider whether or not it is in the public interest to prosecute. Within this model, the possibility of offenders vetoing a meeting with the victim would be removed in favour of allowing victims' rights to trump offenders' rights. The criminal justice system does many things with offenders without giving them an opt-out right, such as sending them to prison, so there is no reason in principle to insist on an offender's veto. On the other hand, it is arguably not in anyone's interests to compel offenders to meet with victims. The psychological benefits sought through restorative processes are unlikely to be achieved where an offender is *forced* to account to a victim; bitter exchanges and re-victimisation seem more likely to flow from such compulsion than an active acceptance of responsibility and expressions of regret and understanding.

However, under the present system, victims can be excluded by offenders *and* facilitators, the latter possibly in anticipation of the former. Thames Valley Police

---

[96] Hoyle, Young and Hill, *Proceed with Caution*, n 3 above.
[97] Edwards, 'Victim Participation in Sentencing' n 84 above.

do not offer restorative sessions for victims alone. If the offender chooses not to accept a caution there is no role for the victim. If the offender chooses not to meet the victim, the caution is still structured according to the restorative script. It is arguable that this creates the conditions whereby facilitators may see victim participation as a bonus, rather than a critical feature of a successful session. In this sense, the system potentially makes facilitators offender-focused, rather than balanced in their approach. This will only change when facilitators take responsibility for empowering victims.

Restorative sessions are meant to provide safe, empowering forums for all participants to explore their own and others behaviour. Those organising sessions, however, have not been adept at ensuring that participants are empowered to decide on the extent to which they wish to contribute to the restorative process. Giving victims a less than fully informed opportunity to participate can result in their choices being attenuated or coerced. As I have argued elsewhere in the context of victims of domestic violence, the only way to empower victims in the restorative process is to ensure that they can make informed choices.[98] This means providing them with all of the information necessary to see the potential benefits and pitfalls in meeting with the offender and others.

This requires more than just new training and new practice manuals. It can only succeed if the police, or other 'facilitating agencies', have a duty to ensure that victims legitimate expectations are met. Victim empowerment will almost certainly lead to many more victims choosing to meet their offenders. Perhaps more importantly, it will lead to better services for those who do not wish to meet but would like to pass on and receive information and messages indirectly. This would result in a more inclusive, a more effective, and a more restorative response to victimisation. Failure to do this could lead to the bifurcation of victims along the lines of willingness to come face-to-face with 'their' offender, with 'the NPVs' becoming the forgotten actors in restorative justice.

---

[98] C Hoyle and A Sanders, 'Police Response to Domestic Violence: From Victim Choice to Victim Empowerment?' (2000) 40 *British Journal of Criminology* 14.

6

Testing the Limits of Restorative Justice: The Case of Corporate Victims

RICHARD YOUNG*

INTRODUCTION

R ESTORATIVE JUSTICE IS a term encompassing a diverse set of values, principles and practices which, within the context of criminal justice, share in common an orientation towards repairing the harm caused by crime. There are many different definitions of the concept in the literature but most stress the importance of facilitating communication between victims and offenders, whether face-to-face or indirect. This is reflected in the widely cited definition formulated by Marshall:

> Restorative justice is a process whereby all the parties with a stake in a particular offence come together to resolve collectively how to deal with the aftermath of the offence and its implications for the future.[1]

This process is intended to show equal concern to the interests of offenders and victims. As far as the latter are concerned, the interests usually identified as at stake are primarily psychological or emotional in nature.[2] Strang notes that various studies have found that what most victims are seeking from offenders is not material compensation *per se* but symbolic reparation; that is, an acknowledgement

* I am indebted to Harry Blagg, Carolyn Hoyle and Andrew Ashworth for their helpful comments on a draft of this chapter, to Joanna Shapland for pointing me in the direction of relevant literature, and to Andrew Sanders for his help in re-floating this chapter when it became temporarily beached.

[1] T Marshall, 'The Evolution of Restorative Justice in Britain' (1996) 4 *European Journal on Criminal Policy and Research* 21 at 37. For an account of the failure amongst restorativists to achieve a consensually agreed definition of restorative justice see P McCold, 'Restorative Justice—Variations on a Theme' in L Walgrave (ed), *Restorative Justice for Juveniles: Potentialities, Risks and Problems* (Leuven University Press, Leuven, 1998) 19.

[2] See, for example, H Zehr, *Changing Lenses: A New Focus for Crime and Justice* (Herald Press, Scottsdale Penn, 1990) 32 and R Immarigeon, 'Restorative Justice, Juvenile Offenders and Crime Victims: A Review of the Literature' in G Bazemore and L Walgrave (eds), *Restorative Juvenile Justice: Repairing the Harm of Youth Crime* (Criminal Justice Press, Monsey NY, 1999) 306–08.

that they have been wronged, combined with steps taken to put that wrong right.[3] These steps might include offers of financial or practical reparation but more usually what is sought is an apology coupled with reassurance that the offence will not be repeated. The downplaying of the material losses of victims that one finds in large tracts of the restorative justice literature is arguably as much a reflection of the preferences of practitioners and theorists for promoting the non-material aspects of reparation as it is of the actual wishes of victims.[4] Nonetheless, it is undoubtedly the case that victims often value the chance to hear the offender's explanation of the offence, to express their own point of view about the offence, and to be listened to with respect. Moreover, a restorative process helps some victims 'come to terms' with their victimisation, alleviating any lingering feelings of disempowerment, anger or fear.[5] Where offenders are not caught, restorative justice schemes may still aim to serve many of these interests by offering victims the chance to meet with offenders convicted of similar offences.[6]

As far as offenders are concerned, restorativists argue that they should be offered the chance to take active responsibility for the harm caused to victims and the opportunity to achieve a sense of reintegration and self-worth through the process of making amends. It is also assumed that the process will induce victim-empathy and counteract any techniques that offenders might use for neutralising feelings of guilt or shame, such as a belief that the victim was not bothered by the offence or that losses were covered by insurance. By offering offenders active involvement in an even-handed process oriented towards acknowledging harm to victims, repair of that harm, and reintegration, the expectation is that future

[3] H Strang, 'Justice for Victims of Young Offenders: The Centrality of Emotional Harm and Restoration' in A Morris and G Maxwell (eds), *Restorative Justice for Juveniles* (Hart Publishing, Oxford, 2001) 184–85.

[4] In support of this emphasis on the importance of symbolic repair, Strang cites the review of British victim–offender mediation programmes by T Marshall and S Merry, *Crime and Accountability: Victim/Offender Mediation in Practice* (HMSO, London, 1990). However, Davis argues that this review's argument that material restitution is relatively unimportant to victims, and that a focus on it can 'sully' empathetic exchanges between offenders and victims, is 'markedly at odds with the evidence presented by all the more rigorous studies which have been exposed to public view': G Davis, *Making Amends: Mediation and Reparation in Criminal Justice* (Routledge, London, 1992) 171. As he notes, mediators shape the expectations of victims as to what they can legitimately seek from offenders and 'the staff of UK reparation schemes are either not interested in or are positively uncomfortable at the thought of helping to negotiate restitution' (169).

[5] C Hoyle, R Young and R Hill, *Proceed with Caution: An Evaluation of the Thames Valley Police Initiative in Restorative Cautioning* (York Publishing Services, York, 2002) 35–46.

[6] See G Launay, 'Bringing Offenders and Victims Together: A Comparison of Two Models' (1985) 24 *Howard Journal of Criminal Justice* 200. Where either a victim or an offender vetoes the idea of mediation it is arguably still possible to achieve a restorative outcome, so long as restorative justice is defined broadly enough to encompass coerced measures aimed at repairing harm, such as reparation orders or community service orders: L Walgrave, 'Extending the Victim Perspective Towards A Systemic Restorative Justice Alternative' in A Crawford and J Goodey (eds), *Integrating a Victim Perspective within Criminal Justice* (Ashgate, Aldershot, 2000).

offending will be reduced.[7] In some models of restorative justice, importance is attached to involving the 'community of care' of both offender and victim, so that each is supported through the process, and in order that the wider ramifications of the offence, and how to respond to it, can be explored.[8] In models based on Braithwaite's theory of reintegrative shaming, the 'supporters' are seen as having a role in shaming the criminal behaviour while showing continuing respect for the person who committed the offence.[9]

The question addressed in this chapter is whether the emphasis on psychological benefits within restorative justice limits its applicability to stereotypical victimising incidents such as assaults and domestic burglaries. I have written elsewhere[10] that restorativists who believe that 'crime is primarily a violation of one individual by another'[11] considerably underplay the complexity of victim–offender identities and relationships. In particular, much crime is committed against, as well as by, through, or on behalf of, organised groups, corporate entities and organs of the state. Indeed, as we will see below, crimes against institutions make up a large proportion of police and court caseloads. It follows that if corporate victims are not interested in entering into dialogue with offenders, or if offenders are not prepared to acknowledge that they have wronged corporations, then the reach of restorative justice schemes may be somewhat limited.

Following this introduction, the chapter is structured as follows. First, the impact of crime against institutions will be explored, both quantitatively and qualitatively. Secondly, the restorative justice literature will be examined and, on the issue of the applicability of restorative justice practices to corporate victims, found largely wanting. Thirdly, some data from the evaluation of the Thames Valley Police restorative cautioning initiative which bears on this issue will be discussed. In concluding it will be argued that the various facets of corporate victimisation, and of corporate responses to such victimisation, must be properly understood and managed if restorative justice schemes are to operate on a reintegrative rather than an exclusionary basis. Throughout the chapter the term 'corporations' will be taken to include businesses, local and central government agencies, churches, schools, hospitals and any other non-individual victim.

---

[7] For an account of restorative justice along these lines see A Morris and L Gelsthorpe, 'Something Old, Something Borrowed, Something Blue, but Something New? A Comment on the Prospects for Restorative Justice under the Crime and Disorder Act 1998' (2000) *Criminal Law Review* 18 at 19–20.

[8] A good overview of different models of restorative justice is provided by P McCold, 'Primary Restorative Justice Practices' in A Morris and G Maxwell (eds), *Restorative Justice for Juveniles* (Hart Publishing, Oxford, 2001).

[9] See J Braithwaite and S Mugford, 'Conditions of Successful Reintegration Ceremonies: Dealing with Juvenile Offenders' (1994) 34 *British Journal of Criminology* 139.

[10] R Young, 'Integrating a Multi-Victim Perspective into Criminal Justice Through Restorative Justice Conferences' in A Crawford and J Goodey (eds), *Integrating a Victim Perspective within Criminal Justice* (Ashgate, Aldershot, 2000).

[11] J Wundersitz and S Hetzel, 'Family Conferencing for Young Offenders: The South Australian Experience' in J Hudson, A Morris, G Maxwell and B Galaway (eds), *Family Group Conferences* (The Federation Press, Annandale NSW, 1996) 113.

CRIME AGAINST CORPORATIONS

The Still Largely Forgotten Victims?

As a number of the other contributions to this collection make clear, the notion of the 'ideal victim' looms large in the criminal justice system.[12] The victims that most easily attract attention and sympathetic treatment are those who are socially constructed as vulnerable, worthy, individuals who did not contribute to their own victimisation. Corporations are not ideal victims. They lack human vulnerability, having no bloodied faces to display, no feelings to be injured, no fears to be allayed, no lifestyles to be undermined. The social worth of commercial corporations may be placed in doubt by their pursuit of profit. They can even be constructed as knowingly precipitating their own victimisation as is evident in the following observations by Segrave:

> Retailers generally feel that they get no sympathy on the issue [of shop-theft], that people rarely feel any outrage in favour of the retailer when a person pilfers a $5 item from a giant faceless company. They prefer to believe they play no part in the event, except as blameless victims. Yet for decades now those retailers, and their advertising allies, have waged a never-ending campaign to get people to buy more whether needed or not, whether wanted or not. More than a few retailers subscribe to an idea regarding the display of merchandise that goes something like this: if it isn't tempting enough to steal, it isn't tempting enough to buy.[13]

While some forms of corporate victimisation are part of the 'traditional crime scene' (such as shop theft, and burglary or vandalism of commercial premises) it is often assumed that the losses involved are covered by insurance or can easily be absorbed by cutting costs, putting up prices or reducing profit margins.[14] Other forms of corporate victimisation (such as theft or fraud by employees) are largely hidden from public view. Not surprisingly, when British criminologists and policy-makers began to turn their attention to the 'plight of the forgotten victim' in the 1970s and 1980s, little attention was paid to corporate victims.

The primary source of knowledge about victims in this country is the British Crime Survey (BCS). The first survey, in 1982, drew on a representative sample of over 10,000 people aged 16 or above.[15] It has been replicated many times and, since 2001, has become an annual undertaking. The survey has uncovered a wealth of information about, for example, the nature of victimisation; the differential frequency and impact of victimisation amongst individuals; the offender-

---

[12] See, in particular, the chapters by Jo Winter, Heather Hamill, Paul Rock and Andrew Sanders.

[13] K Segrave, *Shoplifting: A Social History* (McFarland & Company, London, 2001) 152.

[14] 'Perhaps one reason why crime against business has attracted less concern in the past than it deserves is the belief that commercial premises can afford to insure themselves against risk': C Mirrlees-Black and A Ross, *Crime Against Retail and Manufacturing Premises: Findings from the 1994 Commercial Victimisation Survey*, Home Office Research Study 146 (Home Office, London, 1995) 49.

[15] M Hough and P Mayhew, *The British Crime Survey: First Report* (HMSO, London, 1983).

victim relationship, and decisions regarding whether or not to report crimes to the police. Of particular interest to early advocates of restorative justice was the finding in the 1984 BCS that 51 per cent of victims were willing to meet their offenders out of court, in the presence of an officially appointed person, to agree a way in which reparation could be made to them. A differently worded question in the 1998 BCS found that 41 per cent of victims would have accepted an opportunity to meet their offender in the presence of a third party in order to ask them why they had committed the offence and tell them how it made them feel.[16]

Local surveys have complemented the BCS by highlighting the concentrated nature of victimisation experienced by some people or some areas, while studies of victims of particular crimes have enriched an understanding of the feelings and expressed needs of victims. For example, the influential study by Maguire found that, when asked about the worst aspect of household burglary, only 32 per cent of victims spoke of loss or damage, while 41 per cent cited feelings of intrusion, and 19 per cent of emotional upset.[17] The even more cited study, by Shapland, Willmore and Duff, of 300 assault, robbery and rape victims found that the generally high levels of satisfaction with the police handling of 'their' cases declined over time, with victims coming increasingly to feel that they 'did not care and were not doing anything.'[18]

It is difficult to overstate the extent to which this body of knowledge has influenced notions of victimisation and appropriate policy responses.[19] Yet this knowledge is heavily slanted towards a particular kind of victimisation.[20] All of the most influential victim studies and surveys, including the British Crime Survey itself, have focussed on individuals as victims and have simply ignored corporate victims. The studies discussed have nothing to tell us, for example, about whether victims of commercial burglaries or shop theft are more concerned by the material losses caused by the crime than by feelings of intrusion and emotional upset, or whether they have an interest in meeting 'their' offender in order to tell them how the crime made them feel. It has become almost trite to observe that the once 'forgotten victim' has now been brought (back) to the 'centre stage' of criminal justice.[21] The victims receiving renewed attention are, however, almost

---

[16] J Mattinson and C Mirrlees-Black, *Attitudes to Crime and Criminal Justice: Findings from the 1998 British Crime Survey*, Home Office Research Study 200 (Home Office, London, 2000) 40–43.

[17] M Maguire, *Burglary in a Dwelling* (Heinemann, London, 1982) 126-31.

[18] J Shapland, J Willmore and P Duff, *Victims in the Criminal Justice System* (Gower, Aldershot, 1985) 85.

[19] M Levi, 'White-Collar Crime Victimization' in N Shover and and JP Wright (eds), *Crimes Of Privilege: Readings in White-Collar Crime* (Oxford University Press, Oxford, 2001) observes that standard victim surveys 'reinforce traditional ideologies of what crime is and who offenders are' (68).

[20] See also J Shapland, 'Preventing Retail-Sector Crime' in M Tonry and D Farrington (eds), *Building a Safer Society: Strategic Approaches to Crime Prevention* (University of Chicago Press, Chicago Ill, 1995) 263 at 264: 'It is as though we are only interested in people while they are in their homes or out in bars, restaurants, and places of entertainment-but lose interest immediately when they go to work, or go shopping.'

[21] For an example, see Immarigeon, 'Restorative Justice, Juvenile Offenders and Crime Victims' n 2 above.

exclusively ideal, individualised victims of traditional street-crime. Corporate victims, along with victims of 'non-traditional' crime such as white-collar fraud,[22] remain in the shadows, backstage, glimpsed only out of the corner of the eye.[23]

Bringing Corporate Victimisation out of the Shadows

The process of finding data on corporate victimisation is rather like trying to locate data on crime handled by specialist 'regulatory' agencies such as the Health and Safety Executive and the Inland Revenue. It is not that the data do not exist, but rather that they exist in somewhat obscure places. Another difficulty is that data on corporate victimisation are typically produced in ways which makes comparison with data on individual victimisation problematic. Furthermore, much of the available data is presented from the fairly narrow perspective of situational crime prevention.[24] The turn in criminal justice policy in the 1980s away from programmes that sought to address the motivations and needs of offenders and towards the reduction of criminal opportunities[25] resulted in a number of studies of different types of corporate victims.[26] Their focus was not so much on uncovering the subjective experience of this type of victimisation, still less on exploring the scope for restorative justice measures, but rather on identifying patterns of risk with a view to developing effective crime prevention measures. These sources, nonetheless, can be mined in order to illuminate aspects of corporate victimisation of relevance to restorative justice.

A major gap in our understanding of corporate victimisation was addressed by the first British Commercial Victimisation Survey (BCVS) of retail and manufacturing premises, conducted in 1993 by the Home Office.[27] Crime was cited as a fairly or very serious problem by 44 per cent of retailers and 36 per cent of manufacturers. It is interesting to compare the findings of this survey on the risks of crime with those presented in the British Crime Survey for the same period. Comparisons are possible only for certain kinds of 'traditional street crime'.

---

[22] E Moore and M Mills, 'The Neglected Victims and Unexamined Costs of White-Collar Crime' (1990) 36(3) *Crime & Delinquency* 408.

[23] It is telling that a recent review of the literature on victim-related issues scarcely mentions corporate victims: L Zedner, 'Victims' in M Maguire, R Morgan and R Reiner (eds), *Oxford Handbook of Criminology*, 3rd edn (Clarendon Press, Oxford, forthcoming 2002).

[24] For a recent list of policy-oriented studies of commercial victimisation, organised by type of business sector, see the website created by the Government: < http:www.crimereduction.gov.uk/toolkits > (23 March 2002).

[25] D Garland, *The Culture of Control* (Oxford University Press, Oxford, 2001) 127–30.

[26] For example, C Austin, *The Prevention of Robbery at Building Society Branches*, Crime Prevention Unit Paper 14 (Home Office, London, 1988); P Ekblom and F Simon with S Birdi, *Crime and Racial Harassment in Asian-run Small Shops: The Scope for Prevention*, Crime Prevention Unit Paper 15 (Home Office, London, 1988); and, J Burrows and D Cooper, *Theft and Loss from UK libraries: A National Survey*, Crime Prevention Unit Paper 37 (Home Office, London, 1992).

[27] Mirrlees-Black and Ross, *Crime against Retail and Manufacturing Premises*, n 14 above.

Table 1 presents two sets of figures, broken down by type of victim. The first focuses on the prevalence of victimisation, that is, the proportion of victims who experienced a particular kind of crime in 1993. The second focuses on the incidence of victimisation, that is, the number of victimising incidents per 100 'targets'. The second set of figures is always greater than the first set due to the phenomenon of multiple victimisation of some households and corporate premises.

Table 1: Comparison of Corporate and Domestic Risks of Crime in 1993

	Prevalence: Percentage Victimised			Incidence: Incidents per 100 targets		
	Retail	Manufacturing	Domestic	Retail	Manufacturing	Domestic
Burglary with entry	24	24	4	43	45	5
Attempted burglary	22	18	3	50	33	4
Vandalism	22	16	9	87	48	16
Theft of vehicles	10	12	3	14	18	4
Theft from vehicles	23	25	12	68	63	17

Source: C Mirrlees-Black and A Ross, *Crime Against Retail and Manufacturing Premises: Findings from the 1994 Commercial Victimisation Survey*, Home Office Research Study 146 (Home Office, London, 1995) 52, Table 6.1

From the first row of data in Table 1 it can be seen that the chance of a retail or a manufacturing premises being burgled was six times higher than for a domestic premises, and that there were nine times as many incidents per 100 targets, this latter point indicating that multiple victimisation was much higher for corporate premises. For all of the five crimes on which data are presented, the pattern is essentially the same: corporate premises have higher risks and suffer greater levels of repeat victimisation than do domestic premises.[28] The average cost of property loss caused by a burglary or act of vandalism is also greater for corporate than individual victims.[29] Similar findings have been generated in other European countries, as well as in Australia.[30]

That these facts are little commented upon in the literature on victims is partly explained by the fact that corporate victimisation is numerically a relatively small

---

[28] See, to like effect, V Johnston, M Leitner, J Shapland and P Wiles, *Crime on Industrial Estates*, Police Research Group Crime Prevention Unit Series Paper No 54 (Home Office Police Department, London, 1994) 9–10.

[29] S Brand and R Price, *The Economic and Social Costs of Crime*, Home Office Research Study 217 (Home Office, London, 2000) vii, Table 2.

[30] J van Dijk and G Terlouw, 'An International Perspective of the Business Community as Victims of Fraud and Crime' (1996) 7 *Security Journal* 157.

part of the 'traditional' crime problem, due to the fact that there are so many more households than business premises.[31] An additional reason for the relative lack of interest in corporate victimisation, however, is undoubtedly the widely-shared assumption that corporate victims experience crime as less damaging than do individual victims (or are simply less deserving of our concern). This is an assumption that may be used by offenders to neutralise their guilt and thus make offences against corporations more likely.[32] The size of the corporation also makes a difference, with some research finding greater disapproval of theft against small businesses than against larger concerns.[33] But it is wrong to assume that all corporate victimisation is easily shrugged off. As Johnston *et al* point out: 'The problem with this stereotype is that it treats businesses as things and forgets that in reality they consist of people.'[34] Their study of industrial estates included an in-depth study of five sites and thus produced much richer data than is the norm within the crime prevention literature. They found that for units employing less than ten people, burglaries:

> ... produced effects very similar to those reported from studies of domestic burglary victims. There was the same sense of invasion of private space and worry about whether the victimisation would be repeated. In some instances a burglary of a small industrial unit may have more serious consequences than household burglary. A burglary can interrupt a business quite severely, may lead to workers being laid off, or in the most severe cases may lead to a business collapsing.[35]

Turning to larger businesses, Levi examined the subjective experience of fraud amongst a sample of victims of prosecuted frauds, the great majority of whom were commercial organisations. Over a third of those interviewed thought the frauds involved serious or very serious losses to themselves or their organisations.[36] Similarly, Johnston *et al* argue that the larger business units they studied could be severely affected by a burglary.

> In larger units, there can be the added stress to some victims (particularly middle management and those in charge of premises) not only of the usual police investigations, but also of investigations carried out by the parent company, or senior managers. Internal auditing checks, to guard against fraud or insider collusion, for example, may be a rational or even necessary response by companies to crime, but they

---

[31] Taking burglary with entry as an example, in 1993 there were just over one million such crimes involving domestic premises compared with 148,000 for retail and manufacturing premises: Mirrlees-Black and Ross, *Crime Against Retail and Manufacturing Premises*, n 14 above, 52, Table 6.1.

[32] J Landsheer, HT Hart and W Kox, 'Delinquent Values and Victim Damage: Exploring the Limits of Neutralization Theory' (1994) 34 *British Journal of Criminology* 44, 51. For a study that found that burglars preferred commercial to domestic targets, in part because offenders were more able to justify the crime to themselves where no individual victim was involved, see E Wiersma, 'Commercial Burglars in the Netherlands: Reasoning Decision-makers?' (1996) 1 *International Journal of Risk, Security and Crime Prevention* 217.

[33] E Smigel, 'Public Attitudes Towards Stealing as Related to the Size of the Victim Organization' (1955) 21 *American Sociological Review* 320.

[34] Johnston *et al*, *Crime on Industrial Estates*, n 28 above, 8.

[35] *Ibid*, 10.

[36] Levi, 'White-Collar Crime Victimization', n 19 above, 71.

can add to the sense of victimisation felt by employees, if the company does not also provide support for victims.[37]

In a study by Redshaw and Mawby of commercial burglary in Devon and Cornwall, a quarter of victims reported an emotional effect on themselves or their staff.[38] Examples of comments made about this included: 'My staff were very distressed and I was scared to sleep over the premises for some time', and 'The cleaner who comes in during the evenings is so nervous her husband accompanies her.'[39] Johnston *et al*'s overall conclusion is that:

> it is wrong to think of the victims of non-residential burglary simply as abstract 'businesses', and instead consideration must be given to the victimisation effects on the individuals who make up the business.[40]

Their emphasis on the multiple ramifications of non-residential burglary is also to be found in some analyses of major frauds against corporations, where legions of largely unseen individuals (both employees and customers) have suffered victimisation through lost pensions, investments and so forth.[41] In a similar vein, the British Retail Consortium has estimated that retail crime costs every household in the United Kingdom an extra £90 each year on their shopping bills, while the Government's Social Exclusion Unit has highlighted the impact that crime against small shops has had in reducing shopping access in disadvantaged neighbourhoods.[42] The BCVS indicates that it is also wrong to assume that companies are always fully insured against their losses. For example, just over a quarter of the retail and manufacturing premises surveyed did not have full insurance against burglary with over 1 in 20 having no cover at all. A third of premises did not have full insurance against theft of or from a vehicle with 1 in 10 having no cover at all.[43] The usual reason given for lack of full insurance was the prohibitive cost involved.

So far we have only considered commercial corporate victimisation. Brand and Price have calculated the estimated total costs of crime against individuals and households (excluding violent crime) in the year 1999–2000 as £8.6 billion. This compares with a figure for commercial *and* public sector victimisation taken together of £9.1 billion (or £8.7 billion if 'robbery or till snatch' is excluded).[44] There were an estimated 1,400,000 burglaries of dwellings, costing a total of £2.7

---

[37] Johnston *et al*, *Crime on Industrial Estates*, n 28 above, 10.
[38] J Redshaw and R Mawby, 'Commercial Burglary: Victims' Views of the Crime and the Police Response' (1996) 1 *International Journal of Risk, Security and Crime Prevention* 185.
[39] These comments are reproduced by R Mawby, *Burglary* (Willan Publishing, Cullompton, 2001) 158.
[40] Johnston *et al*, *Crime on Industrial Estates*, n 28 above, 11.
[41] For example, see B Spalek, 'Regulation, White Collar Crime, and the Bank of Credit and Commerce International' (2001) 40 *Howard Journal of Criminal Justice* 166.
[42] Source: < http:www.crimereduction.gov.uk/toolkits > (23 March 2002).
[43] Mirrlees-Black and Ross, *Crime against Retail and Manufacturing Premises*, n 14 above, 49.
[44] Brand and Price, *The Economic and Social Costs of Crime*, n 29 above, Table 2, viii-ix. Both figures exclude fraud and forgery, estimated to cost a further 13.8 billion. It is important to note the authors' caveat that they were unable to estimate all costs of all crimes (for example, fear of crime and quality of life impacts were not included).

billion, compared with 960,000 burglaries of commercial and public sector non-dwellings, costing a total of £2.6 billion (the narrowness of this gap in total cost reflecting the higher average cost of corporate burglary). Most strikingly, by far the most numerous property or violent crime included in the analysis was theft from a shop. There were 31 million such offences (out of 35 million offences suffered by corporate victims in total); this is nearly double the figure for *all* property and violent crime committed against individuals and households.

Just as with crimes against individuals, some corporate victims suffer particularly high levels of multiple victimisation. For example, the BCVS found that three per cent of retailers accounted for 69 per cent of all thefts by customers, experiencing 300 or more such incidents a year.[45] Criminologists have argued that certain types of individual victim, such as those of domestic violence or racial harassment, experience crime so frequently that the effect of each individual offence becomes both compounded and difficult to distinguish from the generally impoverished quality of their life.[46] Those working in institutions that are victimised on a daily basis may similarly see crime less as a series of discrete incidents than as an ongoing attritional process.

There is clearly an immense amount of corporate victimisation, with many of the effects of these crimes bearing comparison with those which result from crimes committed against households. Most formal restorative justice programmes targeted at offending, however, currently operate only in respect of matters brought within the criminal justice system. The question of what proportion of these matters concern corporate victims is discussed in the next section.

Corporate Victims and the Criminal Justice System

The 'dark figure' of unreported or unrecorded corporate victimisation is unknowable but is certainly immense. That much is evident from the BCVS finding that the corporations surveyed reported only one-fifth of the thefts by customers and staff that had come to their attention.[47] Nonetheless, crimes against corporations make up a significant proportion of the police-recorded statistics of notifiable crime. Quite what proportion is difficult to say given that these statistics only rarely differentiate between offences committed against individuals or households and those committed against corporate bodies. A clear-cut exception is shop-theft. There were 293,000 such offences recorded for the year to March 2001. In the same year some 433,000 out of a total of 836,000 recorded burglaries and 167,000 out of 239,000 offences of criminal damage offences were directed at

---

[45] Mirrlees-Black and Ross, *Crime against Retail and Manufacturing Premises*, n 14 above, 22.
[46] H Genn, 'Multiple Victimization' in M Maguire and J Pointing (eds), *Victims of Crime: A New Deal?* (Open University Press, Milton Keynes, 1988); B Bowling *Violent Racism Victimization, Policing and Social Context* (Clarendon Press, Oxford, 1998) 223.
[47] Mirrlees-Black and Ross, *Crime against Retail and Manufacturing Premises*, n 14 above, 81.

non-dwellings.[48] The difficulty here, however, is that this category has been found to include offences against individuals' sheds, garages and outbuildings, accounting for perhaps a third of 'non-dwelling' burglary and criminal damage.[49] Nonetheless, whereas less than a sixth of the total of 5,171,000 recorded offences can be identified as involving corporate victims, the true proportion is certain to be substantially higher given that many of the close-to one million recorded offences of theft of or from vehicles, and the third of a million recorded offences of fraud, will have involved corporate property.

The official statistics on cautions and court proceedings are even more unhelpful in identifying of corporate victimisation. The only category broken down by type of victim is burglary, and even then this is done only for cautions. In 2000, 6,600 cautions were given for burglary of which 4,400 (two-thirds) were in respect of non-dwellings.[50] However, as noted above, a substantial minority of cautions given for non-dwelling burglary will not have involved corporate victimisation. A better estimate of the presence of corporate victims in cases ending in a caution can be provided by drawing on a database of all cautioning activity taking place in the Thames Valley Police.[51] The details recorded included the identity of the primary victim. For the purpose of this chapter, data were extracted from this database for three police areas (Aylesbury, Banbury and Reading) for the first four months of 2000. The results are presented in Table 2.

Table 2: Identity of Victim as Recorded in Cautioning Records for Three Police Areas (January–April 2000)

Offence	n/a (no victim)	Individual Victim	Corporate Victim	Total
Assault	0	86	0	86
Burglary	0	10	9	19
Criminal damage	1	33	33	67
Drugs	55	0	0	55
Public Order	43	15	1	59
Theft: shoplifting	0	0	104	104
Theft: other	2	28	37	67
Traffic	16	3	0	19
Miscellaneous	10	8	0	18
Totals	127 (25.7%)	183 (37.0%)	184 (37.2%)	494

---

[48] D Povey and colleagues, *Recorded Crime: England and Wales, 12 Months to March 2001*, Home Office Statistical Bulletin 12/01 (Home Office, London, 2001) Table 8, 28–30. Note that there were also 17,468 recorded thefts by an employee in this year.

[49] Redshaw and Mawby, 'Commercial Burglary' n 38 above.

[50] K Johnson and colleagues, *Cautions, Court Proceedings and Sentencing: England and Wales, 2000*, Home Office Statistical Bulletin 20/01 (Home Office, London, 2000) Table 6, 21.

[51] This database was kept from April 1998 for a period of three years, as part of this police service's initiative in restorative cautioning (see the chapter by Hoyle in this volume). One drawback of this source of data is that the structure of the database discourages those entering the data to include details on

The data in Table 2 indicate that offences responded to by way of police caution are as likely to involve a corporate victim as an individual victim. Within this dataset, most offences against corporations involve customers stealing from shops, but corporations also account for about half of all criminal damage and burglary offences, and more than half of other types of theft (often thefts by employees). Other data confirm that, at least for some common offence types, corporate victims feature heavily in police and court workloads. For example, Levi examined court records at the London Central Criminal Court and Cardiff Crown Court in the mid 1980s and found that most victims of fraud whose cases were prosecuted were organisations: only 15 per cent were private individuals.[52]

Brand and Price estimate that the total cost incurred by the criminal justice system, including the police, in responding to crime in 1999 was £11.6 billion, of which £1.4 billion was specifically identified as the cost of responding to commercial and public sector victimisation. Most of the further £0.6 billion cost of responding to fraud, as Levi's survey indicates, will have related to non-individual victims. Crimes against individuals and households accounted for a further £5.7 billion, and traffic, drugs and miscellaneous less serious ('summary') offences £3.9 billion.[53] It is worth bearing in mind, however, that corporations sometimes bear secondary or indirect costs when individuals are victimised, such as where employees require training to deal with violent situations at work or need time off following an assault.[54]

Restorative justice is 'sold' partly on the basis that it provides better satisfaction to victims than conventional criminal justice processes and outcomes. Research cited earlier established that individual victims were increasingly dissatisfied with the criminal justice system over time, feeling that that police did not care about their interests.[55] One might hypothesise that corporate victims, typically occupying more powerful positions in society than individual victims, would receive better treatment from the police and so have less cause to be dissatisfied. This being so, the scope for restorative justice to address any dissatisfaction would be reduced. There is some evidence to support this hypothesis. Kemp, Norris and Fielding found that when business victims demanded prosecution they generally got their way, even when the police had reservations. The same could not be said of individual victims.[56]

---

more than one victim per case. As some cases will have involved both individual and corporate victims (see further Table 3 below) the figures presented here understate the proportion of cases that involved corporate victimisation.

[52] Levi, 'White-Collar Crime Victimization', n 19 above, 68–69.

[53] Brand and Price, *The Economic and Social Costs of Crime*, n 29 above, 56.

[54] Almost 1 in 5 workers have received formal training in their current job about how to deal with violent or threatening behaviour: T Budd, *Violence at Work: New Findings from the 2000 British Crime Survey*, Occasional Paper (Home Office, London, 2001) 11.

[55] J Shapland *et al*, *Victims in the Criminal Justice System*, n 18 above, 85.

[56] C Kemp, C Norris and N Fielding, 'Legal Manoeuvres in Police Handling of Disputes' in D Farrington and S Walklate (eds), *Offenders and Victims: Theory and Policy* (British Society of Criminology, London, 1992).

Most offenders are not caught, however. In such cases it seems that the police may be providing a better service to individual than commercial victims. Redshaw and Mawby, for example, found that only 45 per cent of victims of commercial burglary thought that the police had kept them well enough informed about the progress, if any, of the investigation, compared with 63 per cent of domestic burglary victims.[57] This apparent difference in service is even more marked in the case of Victim Support schemes. In a study by Bunt and Mawby only three per cent of commercial burglary victims stated that they had been contacted either personally or on the telephone by a Victim Support worker, compared with 62 per cent of domestic burglary victims.[58] The larger-scale BCVS found that around one-quarter of the retailers and manufacturers surveyed were dissatisfied with the police. The major reasons for this dissatisfaction were that the police were perceived as uninterested in reported crimes; around 15 per cent of the dissatisfied specifically mentioned that they received little subsequent information from the police about the crimes reported to them.[59]

The BCVS provides no data on whether those surveyed might have been interested in receiving reparation or engaging in a restorative justice process. This omission probably stems from the crime prevention angle taken by the report. The authors top and tail their report with the following passages:

> Given that there are limits to what the police can do to protect businesses against crime, it is important for businesses themselves to understand the patterns of risk against them. This should help them to take the action necessary to minimise risks . . . Although the police undoubtedly have a role to play in preventing business crime, the business sector itself must accept the major responsibility.[60]

The thrust of this message is consistent with Garland's notion of a 'responsibilisation strategy', whereby central government seeks to devolve responsibility for crime prevention onto bodies and individuals quite outside of the state.[61] We can see from this section, however, that crime prevention measures taken by corporate victims have failed sufficiently often to ensure that they remain a major presence in the caseloads of the traditional criminal justice system. We have also seen from the material presented above that there are many aspects of corporate victimisation that bear comparison with the impact of crime on individual victims. Thus it would seem that those running restorative justice schemes should consider the applicability of the services they offer to corporate victims. Indeed, to the extent

---

[57] Redshaw and Mawby, 'Commercial Burglary' n 38 above. It is worth adding that both groups had similar expectations of the need to be kept informed by the police.

[58] P Bunt and R Mawby, 'Quality of Policing' (1994) 2(3) *Public Policy Review* 58. Presumably this difference in service can be attributed in large part to the general lack of awareness of the impact of crime against corporations on the individuals working within them.

[59] Mirrlees-Black and Ross, *Crime against Retail and Manufacturing Premises*, n 14 above, 68–69.

[60] *Ibid*, 1, 69.

[61] D Garland, 'The Limits of the Sovereign State: Strategies of Crime Control in Contemporary Society' (1996) 36 *BJ Crim* 445 at 452–55.

that restorative justice schemes seek to challenge the neutralisation techniques used by offenders, it is arguable that the largely unappreciated aspects of corporate victimisation discussed above provide ideal material for those schemes to work with. Furthermore, as Davis points out, where the representatives of corporate victims have not suffered emotional harm of a kind likely to provoke offender contrition they may nonetheless be quite capable of negotiating restitution.[62] As we shall see, however, corporate victimisation has received only marginal attention in the restorative justice literature.

RESTORATIVE JUSTICE LITERATURE: KEEPING QUIET ABOUT BIG BAD CORPORATIONS?

The Ideologically Uncongenial Victim

In much of the restorative justice literature, victims appear as ageless, colourless, genderless, classless individuals. In other words, they are presented as an undifferentiated homogenised mass.[63] As Kurki notes, even when researchers describe their sample of victims by providing a breakdown of their gender, age and ethnic origin, the results of the research tend not to be broken down in this way.[64] This is partly due to the problem that the size of the sample is often not large enough to allow such a breakdown.[65] When victims are differentiated, however, this is usually by reference not to their own characteristics but to the characteristics of the offence they suffered (studies comparing victims of violence with victims of property offences)[66] or the characteristics of the offender (for example, studies comparing victims of juvenile offenders with victims of adult offenders).[67] It is rare indeed for restorativists to carry out comparative analyses based on victim-centred characteristics[68] and almost unheard of for individual victims to be

---

[62] Davis, *Making Amends*, n 4 above, 29.

[63] See, for example, R Young, 'Reparation as Mitigation' [1989] *Criminal Law Review* 463, Immarigeon, 'Restorative Justice, Juvenile Offenders and Crime Victims', n 2 above, and Strang, 'Justice for Victims of Young Offenders' n 3 above.

[64] L Kurki, 'Restorative and Community Justice in the United States' in M Tonry (ed), *Crime and Justice: A Review of Research* (University of Chicago Press, Chicago, 2000) Vol 27, 273 and 280.

[65] For example, see E McGarrell, K Olivares, K Crawford and N Kroovand, *Returning Justice to the Community: The Indianapolis Juvenile Restorative Justice Experiment* (Hudson Institute Crime Control Policy Center, Indianapolis Ind, 2000) 49–50.

[66] See L Sherman, H Strang and D Woods, 'Recidivism Patterns in the Canberra Reintegrative Shaming Experiments (RISE)' (Center for Restorative Justice, Research School of Social Sciences, Institute of Advanced Studies, Australian National University, Canberra, 2000). A break-down by type of offence, where one of those offences is shop-theft (as in the RISE study), ensures that at least part of the analysis will involve corporate victims only.

[67] For example, M Umbreit and W Bradshaw, 'Victim Experience of Mediating Adult vs. Juvenile Offenders: A Cross-National Comparison' (1997) 61(4) *Federal Probation* 33.

[68] For one exception see the South Australia Juvenile Justice Research (SAJJ): K Daly, 'Restorative Justice in Diverse and Unequal Societies' (2000) 17 *Law in Context* 167.

compared with corporate victims.[69] Indeed, in some research such comparisons are difficult or impossible to make because of the deliberate exclusion from the study of property offences involving commercial victims.[70] In addition, some restorative justice schemes exclude corporate victims as a matter of policy.[71] Not surprisingly, then, three recent overviews of the findings of research on victims within restorative justice processes barely mention corporate victims.[72] What is surprising is the fact that none of these reviews, when discussing the need for further research, identifies corporate victimisation as a phenomenon which presents unexplored or distinctive challenges for restorative justice. Nor do the overviews refer to the article by Blagg, published in the highest profile criminology journal in the UK, in which a distinction is drawn between an 'institutional reparative model' and a 'personal reparative model'.[73]

Blagg bases his distinction on the meaning attributed to the process of reparation by youths who had met their victim. These meetings took place as part of a scheme aimed at diverting offenders from prosecution. The institutional reparative model arose when a youth was 'required' to apologise or make amends to a representative of an organisation such as a shop or business. This process appeared to have little meaning for the youths other than as a coercive encounter with an impersonal and disliked authority figure. Blagg argued that this model offered restricted scope for reconciliation and understanding, observing that:

> The interaction can be understood not as an alternative to the legal model but quite frequently its reproduction in a less formal setting. The shopkeeper now takes on the role of the law, demanding apologies rather than a sentence. This is more the case because the manager will himself be acting as a *representative* of an institution and not a victim with a range of confused personal feelings and hurt emotions to sort out. It turns out that the offender and the manager find it difficult to escape the structural imperatives of their relative positions.[74]

In the personal reparative model, by contrast, offenders met victims who had suffered personal harm or loss. Here the young people found the meeting hard to go through and wanted to put matters right. A youth who had stolen another's

---

[69] The most striking exception is Marshall and Merry, *Crime and Accountability*, n 4 above.

[70] As is the case with the SAJJ research: K Daly, 'Restorative Justice: The Real Story' (paper presented at the Scottish Criminology Conference, Edinburgh, 21–22 September 2000).

[71] Davis, *Making Amends*, n 4 above, 29 and 69.

[72] Corporate victims are mentioned once (105) in E Weitekamp, 'Research on Victim–Offender Mediation: Findings and Needs for the Future' in European Forum for Victim–Offender Mediation and Restorative Justice (ed), *Victim–Offender Mediation in Europe* (Leuven University Press, Leuven, 2000); three times (126–27) in M Umbreit, R Coates and B Vos, 'Victim Impact of Meeting with Young Offenders: Two Decades of Offender Mediation Practice and Research' in A Morris and G Maxwell (eds), *Restorative Justice for Juveniles* (Hart Publishing, Oxford, 2001) and not at all in Immarigeon, 'Restorative Justice, Juvenile Offenders and Crime Victims', n 2 above.

[73] H Blagg, 'Reparation and Justice for Juveniles: The Corby Experience' (1985) 25 *British Journal of Criminology* 267.

[74] *Ibid*, 272 (emphasis in original).

bicycle made an explicit distinction between the impact of personal and corporate loss when explaining how meeting the victim had affected him:

> You feel sick 'cos you've just ripped him off and now there he is speaking to you. If you go to a supermarket when you've nicked something from there, there isn't one single person you have to go back to . . . you don't see the person. But when you nick someone's bike, it's out of somebody's house . . . I didn't know what to do . . . so I just said sorry and gave my racer to him . . . I found it difficult to talk.[75]

Blagg does not dismiss the institutional reparative model as worthless, but rather concludes that: 'Cases involving interaction with authority figures can be particularly problematic and may require sensitive handling.'[76] In practice, however, the article seems to have contributed to what Dignan identifies as 'a widespread view that dialogue involving [corporate victims] would not be 'meaningful' for offenders.'[77]

Quite why Blagg's article has been overlooked so often in recent reviews of the literature[78] is difficult to explain. One possibility is that the results have been treated as unreliable due to its small empirical base (the article is based on interviews with seven offenders who had met their victims in person to apologise). This seems an implausible explanation given that overviews of research typically do discuss small-scale qualitative studies, such as Flaten's study of seven juvenile cases of serious or violent crime.[79] An alternative explanation is that Blagg's study is regarded as pre-dating the rise of 'restorative justice' and dismissed as an example of the controversial schemes in the 1980s that, in prioritising diversion over other aims, paid little attention to the need for a sensitive process that balanced the interests of offenders and victims.[80] Although there is some truth in this, the issues Blagg raised are of general application yet do not seem to have been satisfactorily addressed by the subsequent contributions to the literature. My own speculative opinion is that many of those working within the restorative justice

---

[75] H Blagg, 'Reparation and Justice for Juveniles: The Corby Experience' (1985) 25 *British Journal of Criminology*, 274–75.

[76] *Ibid*, 278.

[77] J Dignan, 'Reintegration Through Reparation: A Way Forward for Restorative Justice?' in A Duff, S Marshall and R E Dobash (eds), *Penal Theory and Practice: Tradition and Innovation in Criminal Justice* (Manchester University Press, Manchester, 1994). Davis, *Making Amends*, n 4 above, 29 and 137, reports that a number of UK reparation schemes cited Blagg's work when explaining their decision not to work with large corporate victims.

[78] It is overlooked not just by the three overviews previously cited, but also in J Braithwaite, *Restorative Justice and Responsive Regulation* (Oxford University Press, Oxford, 2002); Kurki, 'Restorative and Community Justice in the United States' n 64 above, and P McCold, *Restorative Justice: An Annotated Bibliography* (Criminal Justice Press, Monsey NY, 1997).

[79] C Flaten, 'Victim Offender Mediation: Application with Serious Offences Committed by Juveniles' in B Galaway and J Hudson (eds), *Restorative Justice: International Perspectives* (Criminal Justice Press, Monsey NY, 1996), discussed in Umbreit *et al*, 'Victim Impact of Meeting with Young Offenders', n 72 above, 128.

[80] See, especially, G Davis, J Boucherat and D Watson, 'Reparation in the Service of Diversion: The Subordination of a Good Idea' (1988) 27 *Howard Journal of Penal Reform* 127 and R Young, 'Reparation as Mitigation' n 63 above.

paradigm are somewhat reluctant to discuss the role of corporate victims within restorative justice processes. As noted in the introduction to this chapter, the non-ideal status of corporate victims has led to them being ignored in much of mainstream criminology, and that status may also make some restorativists uncomfortable. It is easy to support the furthering of victims' interests when what one has in mind is the stereotypical individual victim assumed to have been 'done down' by an unfeeling offender, but less appealing to do so when the offender is poor and the victim a profitable supermarket chain. The latter may seem to many of those working in this field as, to use Rock's phrase, an 'ideologically uncongenial figure'.[81] This may help explain why some schemes and some research studies have turned a blind eye to corporate victims.

Corporate Victims in the Spotlight

Whether the studied blindness to corporate victims can be sustained in the longer term is highly doubtful. A number of the more recent high-profile, high-volume restorative justice schemes are spending much of their time working with corporate victims. In the Indianapolis experiment, for example, which focuses on offences committed by young 'first-time' offenders, the victim was a shop in at least 36 per cent of all cases.[82] To take another example, in roughly two-fifths of the 13,980 restorative processes conducted in the Thames Valley Police restorative cautioning initiative between 1998 and 2001 the primary victim was a corporation (compared with a similar proportion where the primary victim was an individual, and one-fifth where there was no identifiable victim).[83] The best known study is that which took place in Canberra, Australia, where offenders were randomly assigned to either court or conference. There were four separate experiments, each of which focused on a distinct type of offending: violent offences committed by those under 30, personal property offences by those under 18 (including shop-theft where ordinary shop staff or managers apprehended the offender), drink-driving (any age) and shop-theft by those under 18 where the offender was apprehended by security personnel. The latter experiment, by definition, focuses on corporate victimisation. About a quarter of the conferences held as part of the personal property experiment were for shop-theft, but how many other

---

[81] See further the chapter by Paul Rock in this collection.
[82] McGarrell *et al*, *Returning Justice to the Community*, n 65 above, 34–35. How many other cases also involved corporate victimisation cannot be discerned from the published results.
[83] These proportions are calculated using the same 4-month sample which formed the basis for Table 2 (above). Of the 494 cautions in that sample, 86 did not result in a restorative process, with cases not involving an identifiable victim by far the likeliest to be disposed of in a non-restorative manner (known as an 'instant caution'). For further details about the number and types of restorative processes taking place as part of this initiative, see Hoyle, Young and Hill, *Proceed with Caution*, n 5 above, 8–9.

conferences in this experiment involved corporate victimisation cannot be discerned from the published results.[84]

All of these high-profile schemes are police-led and use the 'scripted model' of restorative justice, inspired, in part, by Braithwaite's theory of reintegrative shaming. The original formulation of this theory was not tied to particular criminal justice initiatives but rather consisted of the general hypothesis that crime would be better controlled if criminal behaviour was shamed while avoiding open-ended stigmatisation of the offender.[85] The theory applies in principle to all crime, not just those involving 'ideal' offenders and victims, as illustrated by Braithwaite's long-standing concern with how best to respond to crime committed *by* corporations.[86] For those running schemes informed by this theory, there would be no reason to rule out handling cases of corporate victimisation. As Dignan notes, the involvement of corporate victims might be helpful in achieving the reintegrative shaming of offenders following an offence even if the victims do not want anything out of the experience for themselves.[87]

It is important to be clear about the mechanism by which the effect of reintegrative shaming on crime might be achieved through a restorative process. We have seen above that offenders may be prone to stereotyping such victims in order to help neutralise their guilt. Meeting representatives of such victims may be an effective way for such stereotypes to be challenged. Any victim empathy and/or shame thus produced may be an important factor in reducing the risk of further offending. The research reviewed above shows (contrary to the assumptions underlying Blagg's institutional reparative model) that representatives of corporate victims often do have personal anxieties of a kind that might make an impact on young offenders. Moreover, studies on a larger scale than Blagg's have confirmed that at least some of these emotionally affected representatives are willing to participate in restorative processes. Dignan, for example, notes that, of those who took part in a reparation scheme he studied, 'many corporate victims were shop-keepers or small business proprietors who felt just as aggrieved as some individual victims.'[88] And while victim-empathy may be unlikely to be provoked or pronounced where the representatives of corporate victims are emotionally unaffected by an offence, there remains the possibility that meeting a representative will give the offender a clearer understanding of the ramifications of an offence. That cognitive gain may itself counter a neutralising technique, such as a belief

---

[84] H Strang, G Barnes, J Braithwaite and L Sherman, *A Progress Report on the Canberra Reintegrative Shaming Experiments (RISE)* (July 1999) Table 3–5. This report can be downloaded from: < http://www.aic.gov.au/rjustice/rise/progress/1999.html > (6 May 2002).

[85] J Braithwaite, *Crime, Shame and Reintegration* (Cambridge University Press, Cambridge, 1989).

[86] A chapter was devoted to this in *Crime, Shame and Reintegration* (*ibid*) and the regulation of businesses forms a major theme throughout Braithwaite, *Restorative Justice and Responsive Regulation*, n 78 above.

[87] Dignan, 'Reintegration through Reparation' n 77 above, 236.

[88] *Ibid*, 243 endnote 5.

that no harm was done by an offence.[89] The hypothesis that a restorative encounter with a corporate victim will impact on re-offending rates is clearly worth testing rather than dismissing a priori.

The research carried out on the four high-profile schemes which are based on reintegrative shaming theory has produced mixed results as far as impact on re-offending is concerned. In Canberra, an analysis of offending rates in the year before and after the disposal of the case found that restorative justice, relative to court, appeared to have brought about a large drop in offending in the violence experiment, a small increase in the drink-driving experiment, and no differences for young offenders in either of the two property experiments.[90] In Indianapolis, another experiment involving random assignment to conferences or some other measure (in this case chosen from the normal range of diversion from court schemes), re-arrest was 40 per cent lower in the conference group than in the control group after six months, and 25 per cent lower after twelve months.[91] Unfortunately, however, the results were not broken down by type of victim so it is impossible to know whether this effect was confined to cases of personal victims (although this seems unlikely given the high proportion of corporate victims handled by this experiment). The Bethlehem experiment proved inconclusive due to problems with the randomisation procedure used there.[92] The Thames Valley researchers adopted a different approach to investigating re-offending, using intensive qualitative methods (including observation, tape-recording of restorative processes, self-report instruments and multiple follow-up interviews with offenders and their supporters) rather than relying on drawing statistical inferences from a matched control group. They concluded that 14 out of the 51 youth and adult offenders on whom in-depth data were collected were helped towards desistance by restorative justice and that one youth's offending pattern worsened as a result of a restorative caution (although this was a case in which the facilitation was so poor as not to merit the label 'restorative'). Thus there was a net shift towards desistance of 25 per cent. Eight out of the 12 cases in which the restorative process appeared to have a causal relationship with reduced offending involved shop-theft.[93]

It is not surprising that the research into these different schemes has produced such mixed results on the link between meeting a corporate victim and subsequent offending patterns, nor would it be surprising if other types of scheme produced a different pattern of outcomes. Criminologists are now well aware that

[89] For an example and further discussion of this point see Young, 'Integrating a Multi-Victim Perspective', n 10 above, 242.
[90] Sherman *et al*, n 66 above.
[91] McGarrell *et al*, *Returning Justice to the Community*, n 65 above.
[92] See the discussion Braithwaite, *Restorative Justice and Responsive Regulation*, n 78 above, 56.
[93] The reductions in offending were mirrored by the smaller proportion of offenders re-sanctioned for an offence committed in the year following the restorative process when compared with those who received a non-restorative caution. See further Hoyle, Young and Hill, *Proceed with Caution*, n 5 above, 46–57.

establishing causal relationships is an enormously complex business and that 'outcomes follow from mechanisms acting in contexts'.[94] It would be naive to think that a model of restorative justice will produce the same results when operating in such different socio-economic, cultural and political contexts as the United States, Australia and England.[95] Moreover, police-led schemes may be more or less effective than schemes based in other agencies, as the mechanisms within conferences are likely to be different depending on who facilitates the process and within which organisational setting. Erring on the side of caution, the conclusion that can be drawn from the available data is that schemes based on reintegrative shaming principles have not been shown to be generally ineffective in reducing offending in cases of corporate victimisation. Even if such ineffectiveness could be demonstrated it would be appropriate to exclude corporate victims from such schemes only if their sole legitimate concern was the future criminal behaviour of offenders. As most of these schemes also claim to be based on the principles of restorative justice, such a stance is untenable.

First, there is more to successful reintegration than achieving a reduction in re-offending. For example, if reintegration resulted in an offender escaping from poor health and inadequate housing, and enjoying warmer relations with victim, family and friends, that would be a positive achievement even if offending patterns were unchanged. Secondly, as Dignan notes, under an even-handed model of restorative justice, in which victim concerns are given as much weight as offender concerns,

> cases should be selected for referral whenever it appears likely that victims might benefit from such an approach and not just when they happen to fit a pre-determined schedule of 'appropriate offences'.[96]

The evidence, although fragmentary in nature, suggests that corporate victims *are* likely to benefit from involvement in restorative justice and that they are willing to meet with offenders. Dignan's own study of a reparation scheme that aimed to be even-handed as between offenders and victims found that proportionally more corporate victims (71 per cent) than individual victims (61 per cent) reported themselves as satisfied with their experience.[97] Where victims were willing to participate, the precise form of their involvement was found to be a matter for genuine negotiation between themselves and the offender, with the scheme acting as an intermediary. Of these cases, those involving corporate victims were slightly more likely to result in a face-to-face meeting with the offender than those

---

[94] R Pawson and N Tilley, *Realistic Evaluation* (Sage, London, 1997) 58.
[95] For a more optimistic assessment of the 'external validity' of the Canberra findings see L Sherman, H Strang, G Barnes, J Braithwaite, N Inkpen and M Teh, *A Progress Report on the Canberra Reintegrative Shaming Experiments (RISE)* (June 1998) 51–52. This report can be downloaded from: < http://www.aic.gov.au/rjustice/rise/progress/1998.html > (6 May 2002).
[96] Dignan, 'Reintegration through Reparation' n 77 above, 235.
[97] J Dignan, 'Repairing the Damage: Can Reparative Work in the Service of Diversion?' (1992) 32 *British Journal of Criminology* 453, 461.

involving individual victims.[98] Similarly, an overview by Marshall and Merry of studies of mediation and reparation schemes operating in the 1980s found that corporate victims were more willing than individual victims to participate. Moreover, cases involving corporate victims were found to be more likely to result in a face-to-face meeting with the offender. Non-commercial corporations, such as local authorities, were particularly likely to engage fully with these schemes.[99] Corporate victims were just as likely as individual victims to find the experience of meeting the offender helpful, and corporate victims were more likely than individual victims to have agreed to participate in the hope of furthering the general public good by helping to reform or deter the offender.[100] In two American studies it was likewise found that victims representing corporations were more likely to agree to enter into restorative justice processes than were individual victims.[101] In the Thames Valley Police research, members of staff in shops where shop-lifting had taken place often proved willing to attend restorative conferences, and this was so whether or not they had personally apprehended the offender.[102] Finally, a German scheme is reported by Messmer to have achieved a 'successfully concluded mediation' in 78 per cent of cases involving individual victims and 92 per cent of cases of corporate victimisation, although corporate cases were much less likely to involve direct contact between offender and victim.[103]

All of these findings taken together suggest that corporate victims are supportive of, and can derive benefits from, their involvement in restorative justice. We have yet to consider, however, the nature of that support and those benefits. It could be, for example, that corporate victims have a sense of getting more out of some restorative justice schemes than individual victims because they have different expectations, expectations that perhaps are more easily fulfilled. It could also be that the benefits they seek are in tension with the principles of restorative

---

[98] 35% compared with 30%: *Ibid*, 459.

[99] Marshall and Merry, *Crime and Accountability*, n 4 above, 108–15.

[100] *Ibid*, 158–62. More recently, the researchers who studied the UK pilot referral order schemes suggest that it proved particularly difficult to encourage corporate victims to attend youth offender panel meetings and that corporate representatives appeared more likely to be dissatisfied with panel outcomes, although poor practice by those organising the panels seems the most likely cause here: T Newburn, A Crawford, R Earle, S Goldie, C Hale, G Masters, A Netten, R Saunders, A Hallam, K Sharpe and S Uglow, *The Introduction of Referral Orders into the Youth Justice System: Final Report*, Home Office Research Study 242 (Home Office, London, 2002) 41–48.

[101] J Gehm, 'Mediated Victim–Offender Restitution Agreements: An Exploratory Analysis of Factors Related to Victim Participation' in B Galaway and J Hudson (eds) *Criminal Justice, Restitution, and Reconciliation* (Criminal Justice Press, Monsey NY, 1990) and A Wyrick and M Costanzo, 'Predictors of Client Participation in Victim–Offender Mediation' (1999) 16 *Mediation Quarterly* 243.

[102] In the only Canberra RISE experiment to involve exclusively corporate victimisation (shop-theft where the offender was apprehended by security personnel), no interviews with victims were conducted on the basis that the role of the security personnel 'was really that of private police rather than public victims' and that they therefore had no sense of victimisation: L Sherman *et al*, n 95 above, 27. It is unclear why this viewpoint was assumed rather than tested, and equally unclear why shop staff were not treated as victims in these cases (as they were in the personal property experiment).

[103] H Messmer, 'Victim–Offender Mediation in Germany' in Davis, *Making Amends*, n 4 above, 180–81.

justice as, for example, where they use the process in the manner of a small claims court to recover compensation they consider due. Alternatively, they might seek to use the process to communicate to offenders that they are banned from their property in future—hardly a reintegrative outcome. And while we noted above the pronounced commitment to 'reform or deter' the offender found amongst UK corporate victims, the precise way in which this goal is sought could range from welfarism, through reintegrative shaming, to stigmatic shaming. As we shall see, there are special features of corporate victimisation that pose more than just hypothetical challenges for restorative justice.

WHEN HARRY MET SAINSBURY'S: CRITICAL REFLECTIONS ON CORPORATIONS IN RESTORATIVE JUSTICE PROCESSES

The literature surveyed above offers us tantalising glimpses of corporate victims in restorative processes but very little by way of illuminating 'thick description'.[104] In research on the Thames Valley initiative in restorative cautioning that I conducted with colleagues between 1997 and 2001, tape-recordings of the restorative process were made in 90 of the 94 cases studied.[105] These recordings allow one to go beyond aggregate data by looking in detail at the tone and content of the exchanges which take place in restorative sessions. The 94 cases studied fell into three groups: a pilot sample of 15 cases processed in the Aylesbury police area in 1997, an interim study sample of 23 cases from Aylesbury, Banbury and Reading police areas in 1999, and a final evaluation sample of 56 cases from the same three areas in 2000. The tape-recordings were fully transcribed and then double-checked against the original tape by a member of the research team. The transcripts enable in-depth analyses of the interactions taking place within restorative processes.

Facilitation practice was found to have improved over time.[106] For this reason, the year in which any given case was collected will be provided after each quote from a transcript. It should not be assumed that the examples used reflect current practice in the Thames Valley Police or, indeed, that they are representative of all practice observed in the research study. Rather, the case-studies presented should be treated as exemplars—good illustrations of the kinds of issues that may arise when corporate victims take part in restorative processes.

---

[104] The most honourable exception is Davis, *Making Amends*, n 4 above, still the finest book on the subject of mediation and reparation. On thick description see C Geertz, *The Interpretation of Culture: Selected Essays* (Basic Books, New York NY, 1973).
[105] For a discussion of the pilot study see R Young and B Goold, 'Restorative Police Cautioning in Aylesbury—From Degrading to Reintegrative Shaming Ceremonies?' [1999] *Criminal Law Review* 126. The main body of the research was co-directed with Dr Carolyn Hoyle and is reported in Hoyle, Young and Hill, *Proceed with Caution*, n 5 above. Details of the Thames Valley initiative are also provided in the chapter by Hoyle in this collection.
[106] Hoyle, Young and Hill, *Proceed with Caution*, n 5 above, 13–15.

First, some details should be given of the proportion of cases that involved corporate victimisation. This is not as straightforward as it might seem. Earlier in this chapter I drew on a database kept by Thames Valley Police of its cautioning activity. One drawback of this source of data is that the structure of the database discourages those entering the data to include details on more than one victim per case. As some cases are likely to have involved both individual and corporate victims a question arises as to the true proportion of cautions in the research sample which involved corporate victimisation. To investigate this I re-analysed the dataset containing information on the three research samples. Table 3 presents the findings of this analysis.

Table 3: Type of Victim in a Sample of 94 Cases Cautioned by Thames Valley Police (January–April 2000)

Type of victim	Number	Percentage
Corporate only: shop	23	24.5
Corporate only: non-shop	8	8.5
Mixed: Corporate and Personal	8	8.5
Personal only	39	41.5
No identifiable victim	16	17.0
Totals	94	100.0

From the first three rows of data in Table 3 it can be seen that 41.5 per cent of cases involved corporate victimisation. Three of the 'mixed' cases involved shops, which means that 27.7 per cent of the 94 cases involved the victimisation of this type of business, most commonly large stores such as Sainsbury's, Debenhams and Tesco's. The corporate victims other than shops in these 94 cases comprised four churches, two local authorities, two schools, a social services department, a restaurant, a utilities provider, the Post Office and a dairy. In what follows I use case-studies of Thames Valley restorative sessions, as well as material taken from evaluations of other schemes, to illustrate some of the challenges posed to the restorative justice paradigm by corporate victims.

Corporate Governance of Private Space: The Practice of Exclusion

The premises of commercial corporations are often left empty at night and at weekends. Their location in non-residential areas where the possibility of (free) natural surveillance is limited, has resulted in an emphasis on physical aspects of crime prevention and the use of private security staff.[107] The implications of the increasing use of crime prevention measures by corporations (such as the use of CCTV and private security personnel) and the privatisation of public space

---

[107] R Mawby, *Burglary* (Willan Publishing, Cullompton, 2001) 160–61.

through the creation of shopping malls, technology parks, and the like, have been explored by various commentators.[108] Crawford notes how the 'private governments' responsible for regulating private spaces

> are often more interested in plugging breaches of security and excluding those that pose a threat to order, rather than relying on the deterrent value of the formal criminal justice process and prosecution.[109]

'Known offenders' are particularly likely to attract an exclusionary response.[110] Bamfield, in considering the management of UK shop-theft in the late 1990s, observes that: 'Most retailers now adopt a practice of banning shop thieves from their stores.'[111] Private sector strategies have also influenced the agenda of those responsible for the public provision of security. Crawford gives the example of local authority town centre managers, who 'are increasingly looking towards modes of regulation and control deployed in privately owned out-of-town shopping centres'.[112] To similar effect, Ericson and Haggerty argue that the public police are increasingly being deployed to provide services (especially the provision of information) to institutions which prioritise the management of risk over law enforcement.[113] In risk management, actuarial techniques are employed so that individuals come to be seen not so much as moral agents but as, 'members of particular subpopulations and the intersection of various categorical indicators',[114] that is, indicators of the threat those in such categories are calculated to pose to 'community safety'. As Crawford argues:

> there are important exclusionary logics within 'community safety'. These can take an explicit form through defensive strategies such as neighbourhood watch, fortress-like security technology, 'defensible space' designs, CCTV, the use of evictions of disorderly tenants by housing authorities supported by court orders or the growing use of school exclusions.[115]

The exclusionary dynamic at work here is fundamentally opposed to such central goals of restorative justice as treating offenders with respect, reducing the social distance between offenders and victims, promoting more law-abiding

---

[108] See, especially, C Shearing and P Stenning, 'Modern Private Security: Its Growth and Implications' in *Crime and Justice: An Annual Review of Research* (Chicago University Press, Chicago Ill, 1983) Vol 3; A Crawford, *The Local Governance of Crime* (Clarendon Press, Oxford, 1997) ch 3, and A von Hirsch, D Garland and A Wakefield (eds), *Ethical and Social Perspectives on Situational Crime Prevention* (Hart Publishing, Oxford, 2000).

[109] A Crawford, *Crime Prevention and Community Safety* (Longman, London, 1998) 250.

[110] A Wakefield, 'Situational Crime Prevention in Mass Private Property' in A von Hirsch, D Garland and A Wakefield (eds), *Ethical and Social Perspectives on Situational Crime Prevention* (Hart Publishing, Oxford, 2000) 125, 131–36.

[111] J Bamfield, *Making Shoplifters Pay: Retail Civil Recovery* (Social Market Foundation, London, 1997) 18.

[112] Crawford, *Crime Prevention and Community Safety*, n 109 above, 251.

[113] R Ericson and K Haggerty, *Policing the Risk Society* (Clarendon Press, Oxford, 1997) chs 1–3.

[114] M Feeley and J Simon, 'Actuarial Justice: the Emerging New Criminal Law' in D Nelken (ed), *The Futures of Criminology* (Sage, London, 1994).

[115] Crawford, *Crime Prevention and Community Safety*, n 109 above, 263.

attitudes in offenders, and securing their reintegration. It follows that tensions may be created when corporate victims enter a restorative justice process in an exclusionary frame of mind.

The 'exclusionary logic' of the crime prevention strategies adopted by commercial corporations was evident in some of the restorative sessions observed. An example is case 510 (1999) in which a youth had been caught stealing items worth about £20 from a large store. Once apprehended, the youth was photographed on the street by security staff and banned from the store. A store detective represented the victim at the subsequent restorative conference. On arriving, he realised that the offender had in fact been back into the store since the ban and gave the offender a long, hard, angry stare. This appeared to make the offender somewhat defiant in manner. The conference did not conform to the principles of restorative justice inasmuch as both the police facilitator and the store detective seemed intent on giving the offender a 'dressing down' and adopted a deterrent strategy throughout the exchanges. It emerged during the early part of the conference that the offender had found that being photographed by the security staff had been the most humiliating part of the experience of arrest. The facilitator's comments made it clear that he completely aligned himself with the practices of the private security staff at the local shopping centre:

> Ok, so you're aware now obviously that, that you are known to the security officers in [the shopping centre] cause that, that is standard procedure that they'll take the picture of people who steal, because obviously, their job is to protect the property that's in there. And, you know, to make the centre, um, a pleasant place to shop, which it isn't if the staff have got to spend half their time, on the till, looking round all the time to make sure that people aren't walking out with their stuff.

The store detective was then asked by the facilitator to say how the offence had affected the store. The following exchange took place between the detective (V) and offender (O).

V   Hmm. Firstly, I mean you were banned from our shop, weren't you, so can I ask why were you at my shop on Saturday?

O   . . . [5 second silence] I went to buy a drink.

V   You're banned. I don't want you in the shop. You're a thief. Yes?

O   No, I *was* a thief . . .

V   You *are* a thief, yes?

O   . . . I *was* . . . I'm not no more . . .

V   I'm not gonna argue the point with you, you were banned from the store.

O   Yeah.

V   Ok? Unfortunately I didn't recognise you, but if I did recognise you, then, how embarrassing do you think it would have been to be removed from the premises with security guards that time, and been on camera, again? You were trespassing, it's private property. You obviously don't take this very seriously, not because of, just today, your attitude of being at this caution, but by going back in, to my shop, you obviously don't really care. Because we don't issue banning notices in writing for no reason, just cause it's the thing to do on the day. You're banned for life from that shop, and every other shop. And when I walked in here and recognised you, I think your mum was wondering why I was looking at you a bit strangely . . . that's why, it's cause you were in there on Saturday. And if I ever see you in there again, then you will be, removed, from the centre, because you'd be banned from the whole centre as well. It's just so cheeky . . . I mean, if I went into, if I went into one of your bedrooms, and stole something from one of your rooms, and left your house with it, and you found out or you saw me . . . how would you feel? [3 second silence] You'd be wanting to get stuff back wouldn't you, I, I would have no right to do that. Just the same as you've got no right to come into our shop and steal.

O   I weren't stealing anything, I was getting a drink.

V   I'm talking about the [day of the offence] . . . you've got no right to come into our shop and steal. If we didn't have a security presence in that store that day, and . . . there's a member of staff on the till, maybe a Saturday girl, say maybe, maybe the same age as yourself, on the till, she's got a queue of ten people in front of her . . . and she turns round, and she sees you, selecting and concealing goods in your bag, or pockets or whatever. How do you think that's gonna make her feel, how'd it make you feel if you were working in Woolworths on that day and you saw someone come in and steal [2 second pause]. It's gonna put you under a bit a pressure isn't it? [2–3 second pause] And it also excludes the fact that you, you obviously if you were offered Saturday jobs anywhere, or, wanted a job in retail sales, where most people start off these days, then, you know, you'd have no hope with that with us anyway. [7–8 second silence]. But the worst thing about it I mean normally, you know, we will, we'll go into detail the fact of the cost of the security for . . . um . . . the managers have to pay five hundred pound a week for people like myself (or guards) to be in there. But I don't think there's any point telling you, because your attitude is just, it stinks. And especially with you being in there on Saturday as well . . . I just, don't know if I wanna waste my breath telling you about the cost of it all, and, everything. And lastly the embarrassment for your parents as well . . . I mean I wasn't given a lot of money when I was a kid, I mean, your mom said that you're given money, so, why, why go out and steal? I mean what sort of example is that, for your for your mum, and your family. If I, if I had a daughter that, that went out and shoplifted, I would be incredibly embarrassed and ashamed. They'd want to do anything to help, . . . you know, stop the reputation of my child becoming sordid, but . . . [3–4 second pause] . . . I just don't think that you will not do this again . . . cause I think you will.

O   Yeah well you think wrong then, cause I'm . . .

V   [Interrupting] I'm not gonna sit here and argue with you Sam I'm telling you my opinion, I've been asked to come here today, to give my opinion.

O   Well you can't give an opinion of me cause you don't know me! [Defiant and upset]

V   I'm not saying I know you, I'm telling you the facts, that you were in my shop . . . on Saturday.

O   . . . yeah well I don't wanna hear your facts . . . [the offender's face has reddened as tears are fought back]

V   . . . You were in my shop on Saturday, and you've been, I mean we had a, a heroin addict sitting in the other day, who was banned as well, and she was sitting there in tears cause she was so ashamed. And you're not like that, I don't believe you're a bad person. I really don't believe that, but the cheek just to come back in even if you want just to buy a drink, I just don't understand it. [V is modifying and moderating his stance now that he has reduced O to tears] . . . I just hope that it, it, comes to a stop, I believe it will. Cause you're obviously quite upset by it now . . . but please don't come back into our shop.

O   [indignantly] Don't want to!

V   Thank you. Alright I'm finished.

For this offender, the 'restorative' conference was simply an extension of the humiliation undergone at the hands of the security staff and police on the day of the offence. There was no hint of empathy between victim and offender and the conference became a vehicle to reinforce the store's ban and to warn that any further trespass would result in a ban from the entire shopping centre. The case-study stands as a stark reminder that the restorative justice model can, in the wrong hands, turn into a highly stigmatising exclusionary encounter. It should not be assumed that only *commercial* corporations will act in this way. In case 303 (1999) the representative of a church told us that he had sought a conference outcome that would 'humiliate' the offender, on the basis that this was the best way to teach a much-needed moral lesson.

Not all corporate victims will pose such difficulties. Mainstream religious institutions might be expected to espouse inclusionary policies (notwithstanding the counter-example just provided), and those running public libraries have been found reluctant to employ security personnel for fear of destroying 'the convivial and user-friendly atmosphere of their institution'.[116] Nonetheless, exclusionary-minded corporate victims clearly pose particular difficulties for restorative justice.

The Tension between Corporate Policies and the Achievement of Empathetic Reintegrative Exchanges

Corporations are not alone in seeking security through risk management. Individual victims too may have internalised much of the 'exclusionary logics' inherent in the recent emphasis on community safety. But the corporate nature of some

---

[116] J Burrows and D Cooper, *Theft and Loss from UK Libraries: A National Survey*, Crime Prevention Unit Paper 37 (Home Office, London, 1992) 33.

victims may lend a distinctive rigidity to what takes place in a restorative process. This is because corporate victims, when taking part in a restorative justice conference, necessarily must do so through designated representatives. Unlike individual victims, these representatives are likely to be bound by the policies of the corporation on such issues as whether to demand material reparation or whether to insist that the offender be banned from corporate property. The content of that policy will in large part determine the scope for empathetic dialogue between offender and victim, as well as for meaningful reintegration.[117]

It is clear that some corporate victims have entered restorative conferences with rigid expectations. In the Bethlehem experiment, for example, two large retail stores regularly asked for 40 hours of community service while some retailers

> were constrained by their company policy to seek compliance with the civil claim and did not have the authority to alter that condition.[118]

These stores insisted that offenders paid a standard $150 (US) 'civil demand'.[119] Although the impact of such demands on the exchanges between victims and offenders is not discussed, it is difficult to believe that they will have helped to produce mutual understanding and victim empathy. Nor does it seem likely that offenders in these cases will have found the experience to be a fair and respectful one, particularly where the outcome can be regarded as disproportionate to the crime committed (as in the case of a 13 year old girl reported to have received 40 hours community service for the theft of one candy bar).[120] These findings seem consistent with a more general emphasis within the United States on responding to shop-theft by seeking what amounts to a punitive sum of compensation from any detected offenders. Virtually all states have approved the practice of retail businesses demanding enhanced monetary compensation from shop-thieves in the form of a 'civil demand'.[121] This has sharpened processes of social exclusion; research has found that advantaged offenders tend to buy their way out of trouble, resulting in an over-representation of poorer shop-thieves in the formal criminal justice system, and the perpetuation of the public image of crime as something committed by lower class individuals.[122] In some places, restorative conferences may simply be adding to this problem by providing an efficient mechanism through which stores can extract their pound of compensatory flesh from the poor, whether in the form of money or work.

Such problems are unlikely to manifest themselves in the same way across all types of jurisdiction. Marshall and Merry note that American mediation and

---

[117] On the importance of such exchanges see the chapter by Hoyle in this volume.
[118] P McCold and B Wachtel, *Restorative Policing Experiment: The Bethlehem Pennsylvania Police Family Group Conferencing Project* (Community Service Foundation, Pipersville Penn, 1998) 37.
[119] *Ibid*, 92.
[120] *Ibid*, 95.
[121] Bamfield, *Making Shoplifters Pay*, n 111 above, 23.
[122] M Davis, R Lundman and R Martinez Jr, 'Private Corporate Justice: Store Police, Shoplifters and Civil Recovery' (1991) 38 *Social Problems* 395, 406–07.

reparation schemes have generally placed a much greater emphasis on monetary compensation than their UK counterparts. They identify two contributing factors: first, the politicisation of the 'victim movement' in North America in the sense that victims' interests have been invoked in the demand for harsher treatment of offenders and greater rights for victims, and, second, the lack of alternative ways in which victims can receive compensation.[123] In the UK the mainstream victims' movement has a welfarist orientation (emphasising support services for victims but steering clear of debates on the appropriate levels of punishment for offenders) and alternative compensatory mechanisms are more developed; in Canberra, Australia, the victims' movement has sought to advance victims' rights *and* victims' support services within a restorative justice paradigm.[124] Clearly, then, it is important to consider the challenges that corporate victims pose to restorative justice in specific jurisdictional settings and contexts.

In the Thames Valley restorative sessions we saw no evidence of corporate victims attempting to use the process in the manner of a small claims court. If compensation was offered, it was accepted, but more often compensation was neither offered nor demanded. The usual pattern was for the conference to focus on reforming or deterring the offender with the issue of material reparation apparently seen as irrelevant to such attempts. Sometimes the corporate victim combined a policy of exclusion with reintegrative gestures, as in the following case-study 5013 (2000). The victim, a large supermarket, had been unable to send a representative to the conference for practical reasons. Instead, senior staff provided the facilitator (F) with a statement of their views which was relayed to the offender (O) in the restorative session:

F   I asked them what they'd like to see coming out of the conference, and they said, I mean, as you could expect, they didn't kind of want you in their stores. . .

O   Yeah.

F   . . . again, and I think you might expect that you are banned from all their stores. . .

O   Yeah.

F   . . . but on the positive, they said that they don't want the money back or anything, that's neither here nor there, and what they mainly wanted is that you get the help that you need to get out of it. So they were quite good, you know, they said, yeah, you've done what you've done, um, they didn't think court was the right place, they're happy that this process was going on, they only hope that they could be here today, and you could have heard it from them, but, yes, you did take something from them, but they want to see that you kind of get on the right road and move on from there.

---

[123] Marshall and Merry, *Crime and Accountability*, n 4 above, 116 and 174. The second explanatory factor is questionable given the relatively few UK victims who receive adequate compensation through the courts or criminal injuries compensation schemes. See Davis, *Making Amends*, n 4 above, 169.
[124] H Strang, 'The Crime Victim Movement as a Force in Civil Society' in H Strang and J Braithwaite (eds), *Restorative Justice and Civil Society* (Cambridge University Press, Cambridge, 2001).

Corporate victims, just like individual victims, differ greatly amongst themselves, both in their experiences of crime, and in their attitudes concerning appropriate criminal justice responses. It is this very diversity that concerns some commentators, who see victim involvement in quasi-sentencing processes as a recipe for unequal treatment and disproportionate outcomes.[125] These differences in view, however, suggest that it is not a foregone conclusion that corporate victims will reject reintegrative strategies, as is highlighted by the next sub-section.

Including and Reintegrating the Offender

A key feature in the first case-study[126] was that the facilitator shared many of the store detective's stigmatic and exclusionary feelings. Facilitators with a better understanding of the tenets of restorative justice may work more constructively with corporate victims and even cause them to re-assess their established methods for dealing with anti-social or criminal behaviour. The then Chief Constable, Sir Charles Pollard, gives an example from the High Wycombe area of the Thames Valley Police. He reports that a group of Asian youths were banned from using a privately owned shopping mall as a meeting place after behaving uncivilly towards shoppers. They saw this as grossly unfair, especially as there was no right of appeal, and their resentment led to conflict with the police on a nearby public street. Pollard suggests that the normal strategy of arrest and prosecution would have only made matters worse:

> The attitudes of those involved would have hardened even further into mutual cynicism and suspicion. Race relations in the town would be the poorer, the mall and its hinterland would have acquired a reputation as a 'crime hot spot' and shoppers, fearful of crime, would stay away with consequences for local economic prosperity.[127]

Instead, a police inspector convened a conference between retailers, police and youths to decide what should be done about the situation. Pollard writes:

---

[125] See especially A Ashworth, 'Victims' Rights, Defendants' Rights and Criminal Procedure' in A Crawford and J Goodey (eds), *Integrating a Victim Perspective within Criminal Justice* (Ashgate, Aldershot, 2000) and by the same author, 'Responsibilities, Rights and Restorative Justice' in M Maguire, R Morgan and R Reiner (eds), *The Oxford Handbook of Criminology*, 3rd edn (Clarendon Press, Oxford, forthcoming 2002) 586. This concern applies as much to individual as to corporate victims and therefore falls outside the scope of this chapter, although it is arguable that the diversity of responses to crime is greatest amongst corporate victims. Consider, for example, the radically different prosecution policies of the Inland Revenue and the Department of Social Security: D Cook, *Rich Law, Poor Law* (Open University Press, Milton Keynes, 1989).

[126] See p 157 above.

[127] Sir C Pollard, 'If Your Only Tool is a Hammer, All Your Problems Will Look Like Nails' in H Strang and J Braithwaite (eds), *Restorative Justice and Civil Society* (Cambridge University Press, Cambridge, 2001) 167–68.

The retailers voiced their fears that trouble would drive local shoppers away; after listening to them, the youths conceded that they should change some of their behaviour and language. They also agreed that when on the premises they should behave as asked by the security staff; in return, the security staff agreed to make sure the youths were aware of the mall's rules, and to consider an appeals system for use when people were banned from the centre. The police in their turn agreed to look into some of the incidents about which the youths complained, and to visit their youth club.[128]

The two quoted passages sum up quite well the difference between an exclusion-ary and inclusionary way of responding to corporate fears about the use of their premises by young people. White reports other attempts to incorporate young people into discussions over the use of semi-public space and notes how some shopping centres

now employ part-time youth workers and provide youth-specific services and activities as a means to encourage less conflictual relations with young people. . . [these attempts] represent a shift in thinking away from the use of coercive and authoritarian measures towards more inclusive and developmental measures.[129]

The importance of these lines of argument is that they suggest that corporations can be persuaded that an inclusionary approach to managing problematic behaviour may be in their own long-term best interests.

Sometimes, corporate victims need little persuading of the value of social inclu-sion. This may be either because they have a public service ethos in any case (as was noted of libraries above) or because exclusion seems potentially counter-productive to the aim of maximising turnover and profits. Whether exclusion will be perceived in this way may turn on how likely the victim thinks it is that the offender will re-victimise them if allowed back into corporate space. The next case-study (3001–2000) illustrates the contribution that corporate victims can make to reintegration.

On a single day, two girls had stolen items valued in total at £200 from numer-ous small shops and a library. A number of the shop managers attended the restorative conference, as did a representative from the local library services department. The victims spoke more in sorrow than in anger about the effects of the offence and the offenders' parents spoke of their surprise and disapproval of what the girls had done. The girls themselves were subdued and said relatively lit-tle, but were contrite. The victims were asked what they wanted from the conference. The representative of the library replied:

It's quite a difficult one. Because I think when you first spoke about this, invited me, I've been thinking about this for a while. I had a chat with some of my work colleagues and things. Um, and I probably want to [pauses for 3 seconds to find the right words] put

---

[128] *Ibid*, 168.
[129] R White, 'Hassle-Free Policing and the Creation of Community Space' (1998) 9 *Current Issues in Criminal Justice* 312, 319. See also R White, 'Social Justice, Community Building and Restorative Strategies' (2000) 3 *Contemporary Justice Review* 53.

out an olive branch and say, what I would like would be for you to come and join the library. I don't know if you are members or not, . . .not sure, come and borrow our books, come and sit and use the Internet in the library. Stuff like that. Maybe tell your friends that. . . . tell them what you think about the library, maybe you think it's a good place, not as boring as some people think they are. That's what I'd like.

Likewise, a shop manager said:

Me personally, I think they've done enough, in basically coming here in confronting us. . . as well as everything else. I think that's enough. And I hope that everyone in the room will still come in the shop and basically not feel embarrassed. I mean, the event's happened and now it's past and hopefully they will learn by their mistakes. . . . I think they've done enough in basically coming here . . . It's a voluntary thing, you didn't have to come, same with us.

One of the parents expressed her appreciation to the victims for giving her daughter 'a second chance'. Another parent (OS) then made a remark which prompted a series of responses which illustrate nicely the concerns that some corporate victims have about social exclusion.

OS Hopefully, that they've learnt their lesson, and hopefully in time I may be able to trust her. It might take a while. I hope that I can go into these shops again and not feel embarrassed.

V4 That would be a double blow for everybody as well. . .

V6 Quite.

V4 . . . the fact that the misdemeanours of the child affected the parents, so that they couldn't go in the shops, and then the shopkeepers would also lose the custom for ever more. Which in a small community is not a very good idea for us either. If that alone is avoided we would have done something. . .

V2 Could they, I think I was the only one out of all of you who didn't extend an invitation to the girls and their families, um, I mean, do come into the [shop] to see us. Only you and I will know what's happened here this evening. Um, come and make yourself known, come and see me. Um, and, I think that's quite an important step because you two are going to hopefully be customers in the future. Um, I'd like you to come in and feel that you are welcome. I think that's, that's one of the other steps of the process of all the healing's that going to be taking place. So do please come and see us.

The contrast with the first case-study[130] could scarcely be more stark. It is true that in this example the corporations involved are either small businesses or have a public service ethos whereas in the first example the corporation was a large chain store. But on occasion we observed representatives of large shops behaving in an inclusionary manner,[131] which suggests that it is possible for big commercial

[130] See p 157 above.
[131] See case study 5013 (2000) at p 161 above, for example.

corporations to take the view that reintegrating the offender is in their own best interests.[132]

Repeat Players and Routinised Victim Impact Lectures

The fact that corporate victims must act through representatives, combined with the intensity with which some corporations (such as large shops) are victimised, entails that some of those attending restorative processes may become 'repeat players'. For example, a supermarket may designate a particular store-detective as its representative for all conferences arising out of the shop-theft it experiences. This may be seen as advantageous by a restorative justice scheme's workers in that it would seem to reduce the need for preparation of the victim representative in each individual case while at the same time creating the prospect of a steady stream of victim–offender encounters or exchanges.[133] The downside of 'repeat player' victims is that the designated representative will soon become familiar with the methods and aims of a conference (or the expectations of a particular conference facilitator)[134] and accordingly enter the process with a distinct advantage over other participants. This will tend to exacerbate the power imbalance already likely to exist between offenders and corporate victims, particularly when the victim is a large commercial enterprise. Furthermore, in police-led schemes, there may be too great a degree of identification between the police officer facilitating the process and repeat corporate representatives, particularly where the latter are security staff (as is suggested by the first case-study above[135]). Here, the co-operation that characterises most interactions and relationships between public and private police[136] makes it less likely that facilitators will play an even-handed role as between offender and victim.

There is also a danger that a repeat victim's contributions to conferences will become increasingly formulaic and routinised, thus making the proceedings more court-like and less likely to produce empathetic dialogue between the participants. This danger will be especially pronounced where the repeat victim representative has no direct knowledge of the individual offence being dealt with in the

---

[132] A suggestion that might be made to such corporations is that a life-time ban will be difficult to enforce and possibly even counter-productive, whereas lifting or reducing a ban may be an appropriate way to respond to an offender who expresses contrition or makes reparation. One example is the HMV store which lifted a year long ban on a shoplifter after the latter gave the store a piece of artwork which expressed the emotions she had felt on being caught: Oxfordshire Youth Offending Team (2001) *Amends: Reparation Newsletter* Iss 2.

[133] For illustrations of the perceived value of repeat victim business see Davis, *Making Amends*, n 4 above, 119 and 173.

[134] Mediators in practice often seek to indicate to victims, when preparing them for a face-to-face encounter, the 'performance' required from them. See, for example, the case-study in Davis, *Making Amends*, n 4 above, 50–55 and the discussion at 168–69 of some of my own unpublished research.

[135] See p 157 above.

[136] See, for example, Wakefield, n 110 above, 138–43.

restorative process, or has experienced so many offences that they cannot be distinguished from one another. Routinisation is particularly likely to occur in schemes that ask victims of a particular type of crime to meet with a series of offenders who have committed that type of crime.[137] The Milton Keynes Shop Theft Initiative is one well known example.[138] Here, a rota operates under which each week a designated store manager will meet with all of those receiving a caution for shop-theft regardless of which local store was the actual victim. It is difficult to see how this store manager could do anything but talk about the effects of shop-theft in an abstract fashion in much the same way as a magistrate might. Indeed, routinisation may be encouraged by the staff of such a scheme in the hope of making the encounter with offenders as educative (or punitive, as the case may be) as possible. Thus, the police running the Milton Keynes initiative produced an 'aide-memoir[e] for store managers' which set out the 'points . . . to be covered during your interview with the offender.' The points the store managers are asked to cover include letting offenders know the consequences of their criminal activity on the store and its management, employees, customers and suppliers, and the likely short, medium and long term effects on society such as the price of goods, the effects on employment of local people and the possibility of the shop closing. Store managers are also encouraged to point out that some shops ban people who steal from their stores, and are primed to 'try to obtain an apology from the offender.' In 1997 I observed one such encounter and noted the lack of emotional engagement between offender and store manager, with the latter clearly trying to play out the role required of him by the initiative.[139]

The issue of routinised contributions by repeat victims was raised obliquely by the first case-study presented above. In that conference, the store detective referred to what he would 'normally' say about the effects of theft on 'his' shop. Sometimes we were able to observe a victim representative in more than one case. For example in cases 501 and 503 (1999) the same store detective gave essentially the same performance when asked to explain the harm caused by the offender's action (in both cases an item of small value). The main themes covered by the store detective included the cost of installing and maintaining security measures, the anxieties of shop staff when they observed a theft taking place, the fears of store detectives in apprehending thieves, the increase in the price of goods attributable to shop-theft, and the righteous anger the detective felt in relation to people who

---

[137] A similar problem seems to have arisen in the RISE drink-driving experiment where someone from a pool of around 20 community representatives participated in each conference. This appears to have led to a degree of uniformity: the representatives regularly sought, and obtained, the outcome of a blood donation by the offender. Young, 'Integrating a Multi-Victim Perspective', n 10 above, 216.

[138] The initiative has been the subject of two evaluations, although both of these focussed narrowly on the scheme's apparent impact on re-offending: H McCulloch, *Shop Theft: Improving the Police Response*, Crime Detection and Prevention Series Paper 76 (Home Office Police Research Group, London, 1996); R Willcock, *Retail Theft Initiative: Does it Really Work?* (K2 Management Development Ltd, 1999).

[139] Fieldnotes: Milton Keynes Police Station, 23 April 1997.

steal. In interview it was evident that this victim had great difficulty in distinguishing between these two cases. The many cases in which this representative had met offenders had become blurred in his mind. This representative was not particularly interested in meeting 'the offender', in exchanging stories, hearing an explanation, or receiving an apology, but rather was seeking to deter shop-theft more generally through exposing a succession of offenders to a lengthy moral lecture. Repeat victimisation was responded to by repeat performances of essentially the same monologue.

Who Represents the Victim?

While problems in identifying victims arise in many contexts,[140] the difficulties are particularly acute in the case of crimes committed against major corporations such as supermarkets. This can only add to the administrative burdens on the staff of restorative justice schemes. Not only may it take much time and effort to discover who would be the most suitable representative but there may then be further difficulties in locating the person able to authorise that representative's attendance at a restorative meeting.[141] Where the offender has committed robbery, those against whom force was used or threatened will be obvious victims in their own right and may well be the appropriate representatives for the corporation as a whole.[142] But the most common crime against corporations, shop-theft, may be committed without personal interaction with any individual within the corporation. Possible candidates to represent the corporation in a restorative process in response to such an offence include a store-detective, a cashier, a departmental manager, an assistant manager with responsibility for security, the store manager, the area manager, someone from headquarters with responsibility for security, or a company director.

A related issue is whether a nominated corporate representative will be regarded by an offender as a legitimate 'stakeholder' in the offence to be discussed within a restorative session. In some cases studied it was clear that the choice of corporate victim representative mattered deeply to offenders. Sending someone regarded as 'too junior' was taken as a signal that the corporation did not really care about the offence. It also might seem to offenders that they were not being given the opportunity to apologise to the 'right person' thus lessening the perceived value of the conference. Both of these points are illustrated by case 511 (1997) in which a teenager receiving a caution for shop-theft met a young

---

[140] Young, 'Integrating a Multi-Victim Perspective', n 10 above.

[141] A Wilcox with C Hoyle, *Final Report to the Youth Justice Board on the National Evaluation of Restorative Justice Projects* (Unpublished Draft Report, April 2002) 30.

[142] Although problems may arise where their views on reparation run counter to those of the corporation. See further M Wasik, 'Reparation: Sentencing and the Victim' [1999] *Criminal Law Review* 470.

departmental manager of a major store. After the conference the offender (O) spoke to the interviewer (I) as follows:

I   What were your feelings about meeting the victim, the guy from [the store]?

O   Well, he wasn't even the manager. I think that they were a bit wrong sending a young chap who hasn't even worked there long, because I've lived in [this town] most of my life, and I know the manager of [the store]. . . . At the end of the day, yeah, the person who was directly harmed is the manager, and I think if they're going to have the guts to send someone, they should send the manager, not one of his little people who could have only been working there for three months, saying 'oh you've stolen from my shop'. Like I said to him, it's not his shop at the end of the day. He doesn't look much older than me, you know what I mean? I mean, he's not even as old as my Dad. At the end of the day my Dad could tell me exactly the same, and I'd just say the same. Really, the manager was there when we got arrested, so therefore he should be here. He should be the one here. Not some little representative.

I   Did you have any contact with the manager at all?

O   All that happened is, I walked in and he goes 'why did you steal the [goods]?' and I said why and he said 'right, I'm ringing the police' and I said 'fine, go on then'. I mean he didn't even ask me to apologise or anything, and really, I don't. . . apologising to that guy in there, yeah I apologised but it's not really the same as saying to the manager himself. . . . It's not the actual guy is it.

I   Would you have been happier if the manager had turned up then?

O   Yeah, a lot happier.

I   Do you think you would have felt happier about the apology as well?

O   Yeah, because it would have been saying sorry to the right person, not to his little underdog or whatever he is. Because at the end of the day it's no good sending his Benson [servant] out to me. [laughs] No he wasn't, he was just, I mean I personally looked on him as basically just like a cashier. . . [laughs] just the average geezer off the street type thing.

Offenders (and their supporters) sometimes took umbrage at being asked to treat an offence against a corporate victim as a serious matter when the latter had decided not to attend the conference at all. To their way of thinking, if the matter was as serious as the facilitator was making out then surely victim representatives would have attended to speak for themselves. The clearest-cut example of this was case 3002 (2000) in which two male youths had entered a school one evening through an unlocked door and taken some items 'for a prank' from a cupboard. They were disturbed and ran away. The items were recovered. The school head-master declined to attend the cautioning session (for the offence of burglary) on the basis that the youths were not pupils of the school. Instead he provided the facilitator with a victim impact statement. In this he stressed the inconvenience and distress caused to school staff and their fears for their pupils' artwork (although there was no evidence to suggest that the latter was ever at any risk). It was clear that the two youths receiving the caution, and some of their supporters, were of the view that the incident was too minor to warrant formal police action, and this view was reinforced in their minds by the absence of any representatives from the school. Nonetheless, the facilitator cajoled the youths into agreeing to send a letter of apology to the school. Subsequently, when the facilitator asked the participants to comment on what they wanted out of the process, one of the supporters took the opportunity to express forceful criticisms of the absent victim.

> S4 The way I just see this is that school don't deserve any apologies when they can't send a representative, the headmaster preferably. But I don't know why they think that they deserve anything back. . . . It's like the school don't care isn't it?

It is not surprising that participants in some restorative sessions saw the process as making a mountain out of a molehill. Offences that result in a caution range from trivial 'pranks' to assaults serious enough to require medical treatment over many months. For those at the trivial end of the range, the lengthy series of questions and answers required by the restorative script can seem somewhat ridiculous, as indeed can a facilitator's (or store detective's) lengthy list of the possible consequences of relatively minor offending. The sense that facilitators are exaggerating the harm in order to make the offence fit the process is likely to become overwhelming when the victim in question is corporate and absent. In such circumstances many facilitators appeared to take the view that offenders would have difficulty in appreciating the impact of an offence on a corporate victim. These facilitators sometimes took it upon themselves to become a kind of representative or advocate for the victim and, in doing so, went beyond simply conveying the victim's views. In case 5011 (2000), for example, the facilitator allowed herself to become riled by what she took to be the offender's lack of concern about an offence of commercial burglary. The facilitator's tone became increasingly judgemental, provoking the offender into an increasingly defiant stance. By the time the process had reached the point at which the victim's views were meant to be summarised by the facilitator, the atmosphere was tense and strained. The facilitator then went through in great detail all the actual and possible ramifications of the offence, including the inconvenience caused to the store's key-holders and the alarm engineer, the increase in prices caused by 'shoplifting and burglary', the anxieties of staff, the general mistrust felt towards all future customers because 'when people come in the store they don't know whether they are going to steal or not', and the loss of staff bonuses because of general stock shrinkage 'out of which they could have bought their families Christmas presents.'

This laboured attempt to produce victim empathy predictably backfired, with the offender merely acquiescing sullenly when repeatedly directed by the facilitator to respond to this succession of points. While challenging stereotypes and techniques of neutralisation is a legitimate part of restorative processes, exaggerating or labouring the harm to victims is both unethical and potentially counter-productive. As the offender (O) put it when interviewed by a researcher (I) afterwards:

O   And, they read a letter out, well, read a conversation thing that the Police had had with the people in [the store] out.

I   So, how did you feel when you were listening to that?

O   Well, I wasn't really thinking about anything. I just thought, 'well, what's the point in telling me now, because I've already done it.' It's just like, some of the things they say, are just a bit stupid, because they're telling me all the people had to come out to get the alarm, and I don't really care about people who had to get an alarm. They're telling me stuff but they try and pick at every little thing. And they're, like, 'the people from [the store] care, and their families' and all this and they just try to make you feel guilty.

I   Is that what you think they were trying to, did you think they were a bit too picky?

O   Yeah. With the way it affected people.

I   Was there anything that you didn't know already about that?

O   No, I thought it was pathetic, though, the way they were all saying how all the families of people who worked in [the store] had been affected.

One response to the above points would be to argue that victims are entitled to convey to offenders the effects of the offence in whatever form they choose. But this ignores the crucial role that facilitators can play in shaping the victim's contribution, both when they signal to victims what they can or should say in the pre-conference preparation stage and in how they choose to facilitate the victim's contribution (whether or not the victim attends).[143] For example, we discovered that in one case a victim had told the facilitator to pass on the fact that he felt guilty for having left his property where it was bound to tempt someone to steal it. The facilitator remarked during interview, 'obviously I wasn't going to do that.' In another case the victim asked the facilitator to thank the offender for destroying a particular piece of property as that act had enabled the victim to get a brand new replacement at no cost to himself. Again, the facilitator did not pass on these sentiments. In a third case a corporate victim met with the offender and conveyed, in a restrained manner, the effect of the offence. The facilitator intervened to say 'weren't you going to say something about the effect it has on prices?' In short, there was a tendency on the part of some facilitators towards 'playing up' the impact of crime and particularly so in cases of corporate victimisation where it was assumed, usually wrongly, that only in this way would offenders come to feel remorse for what they had done.

---

[143] For further discussion of the problem of exaggeration by facilitators see Young and Goold, 'Restorative Police Cautioning in Aylesbury' n 105 above. For best practice see the chapter by Hoyle in this collection.

CONCLUSION

In the early 1970s, Dynes and Quarantelli observed that: 'Very few studies have taken specific aspects of organizations into account in understanding the victim–offender relationship.'[144] Little has changed since then. In part, this is because attempts to understand that relationship became unfashionable following criticisms that they amounted to 'victim-blaming',[145] but the turning of a blind eye to corporate victimisation (other than from the crime prevention perspective) is also a major factor. The centrality of the victim–offender relationship within the restorative justice paradigm, combined with the high proportion of cases involving corporate victimisation dealt with by the criminal justice system, makes such myopia untenable.

While this chapter has covered a range of issues, much more could be said about the attitudes of, and towards, corporate victims as manifested within restorative processes.[146] The more limited objective of this chapter was to establish that corporate victims pose some distinctive challenges to restorative justice values. Those discussed in some depth were the exclusionary nature of much corporate crime-control activity; the rigidity of corporate responses to victimisation inherent in policies laid down by management; the routinised nature of corporate contributions to restorative processes brought about by the repeat nature of much corporate victimisation and the use of 'repeat' representatives; and, the difficulties in determining who should represent the corporation. There is the space here to give only the most cursory consideration to how these challenges might be met. Some of them, such as the question of who can legitimately represent the corporation in a restorative justice conference, may be relatively easily addressed through more thorough and sensitive preparation and better training for facilitators. Others are more deep-rooted and require more complex solutions. In particular, the exclusionary mode of governance that many corporate victims employ is clearly in conflict with aims of reintegration and inclusion. Whether a restorative criminal justice system is workable in the absence of a more general acceptance of restorative values and processes must be somewhat doubtful. As Wachtel and McCold observe: 'You can't just have a few people running conferences and everybody else doing business as usual.'[147] In England and Wales, the existing criminal

---

[144] R Dynes and E Quarantelli, 'Organizations as Victims in Mass Civil Disturbances' reprinted in I Drapkin and E Viano (eds), *Victimology* (Lexington Books, London, 1974) 68.

[145] For discussion, see the chapter by Rock in this volume.

[146] For example, I have not touched on the issue of the extent to which participants in restorative sessions seek to ascribe a degree of responsibility to corporate victims for the offence that has brought them together, nor whether such 'victim-blaming' might be desirable in some circumstances. See further RV Clarke, 'Situational Prevention, Criminology, and Social Values' in A von Hirsch, D Garland and A Wakefield (eds), *Ethical and Social Perspectives on Situational Crime Prevention* (Hart Publishing, Oxford, 2000) 97–112, 107.

[147] T Wachtel and P McCold, 'Restorative Justice in Everyday Life' in H Strang and J Braithwaite (eds), *Restorative Justice and Civil Society* (Cambridge University Press, Cambridge, 2001) 129.

justice system itself encompasses many exclusionary elements and practices and, while this remains the case, it is unrealistic to expect restorative justice to work as intended.[148] If the Government is serious in its ambition to create a more inclusionary society, then it will need not only to reduce to a minimum exclusionary criminal justice processes, but also to get corporate victims to rethink their policies regarding the management of crime.[149] The latter will not be easy to achieve given that corporate nodes of governance,

> have far greater autonomy from state direction than do 'civil society' nodes that have developed under the impact of programs designed to responsibilise local citizens and organisations.[150]

Previous efforts by the state to encourage businesses to take an active role in crime prevention have met with only limited success. As Crawford notes:

> In large part, this is because it has been difficult to persuade businesses that it is in their economic best interests to do so, particularly as their primary concern remains the maximisation of profits.[151]

There are real conflicts of interest and value here which cannot simply be wished away or glossed over. Under current social arrangements it is arguable that there are structural limits, created by the nature of capitalism itself, to the scope for restorative justice processes to operate as intended. Yet, as this chapter has also shown, many corporate victims are willing to participate in restorative processes and, once within these processes, they do not necessarily behave in an exclusionary fashion. There is nothing that follows inevitably from the 'logic of capitalism'; social structures can be reconfigured through human agency. Similarly, the limits to restorative justice that appear to inhere within the nature of private enterprise and the pursuit of profit can be tested and transcended through the right combination of political leadership and a broad-based social commitment to bringing about a more inclusive society.

---

[148] See further R Young and C Hoyle, 'New, Improved, Police-Led Restorative Justice? Action-Research and the Thames Valley Police Initiative' in A von Hirsch, A Bottoms, J Roberts, K Roach and M Schiff (eds), *Restorative Justice and Criminal Justice: Competing or Reconcilable Paradigms?* (Hart Publishing, Oxford, 2002).

[149] An idea explored in a different context by D Bayley, 'Security and Justice for All' in H Strang and J Braithwaite (eds), *Restorative Justice and Civil Society* (Cambridge University Press, Cambridge, 2001) at 217. An analogy may be drawn here with the way in which local authorities can insist that a given proportion of a housing development is devoted to (less profitable) social housing. Could the state impose responsibilities on business corporations to devote a proportion of their profits (perhaps in return for tax relief) to reintegrative social practices such as attending restorative processes with a view to helping in the search for constructive ways of preventing, managing, and resolving crime?

[150] C Shearing, 'Transforming Security: A South African Experiment' in H Strang and J Braithwaite (eds), *Restorative Justice and Civil Society* (Cambridge University Press, Cambridge, 2001) 18.

[151] A Crawford, *Crime Prevention and Community Safety*, n 109 above, 187.

7

The Trial of Rose West: Contesting Notions of Victimhood

JO WINTER*

INTRODUCTION

IN 1995, FOLLOWING a highly publicised police investigation, Rose West was tried for the murders of ten young females. There was little direct evidence linking her to their deaths. The bodies were found in houses that had been occupied by Rose West and her husband, Fred West, but all the evidence of Rose's involvement in and knowledge of the killings was circumstantial.[1] Furthermore, there was neither forensic evidence nor eye-witness testimony that she had even met three of the victims. The prosecution's difficulty in proving her guilty of murder was compounded when Fred West accepted sole responsibility for all of these murders, as well as two others that took place before he met Rose, then committed suicide prior to the trial. Thus, there was a real possibility that Rose would be acquitted.[2] She was, however, found guilty and is now serving ten life sentences.

This chapter draws on a study designed to identify the subjectivities[3] created in the trial of Rose West. It employs the ideas that texts (in this case the transcripts of the trial) provide insights into dominant, gendered norms and identities, and that legal texts in particular play a role not only in reflecting such norms and subjectivities, but in creating them.[4] These ideas are of specific relevance when considering trials because the opposing narratives presented can be sociologically regarded as mere versions of the events under scrutiny in which highly selective

* I would like to thank Keele University Gender, Sexuality and Law Research Group for their comments on an early version of this chapter, and Carolyn Hoyle, Andrew Sanders and Richard Young for their invaluable advice on later drafts.
1 The prosecution conceded that the case against Rose West was wholly circumstantial (trial transcript, 3 October 1995, 38).

2 See B Masters, *She Must Have Known: The Trial of Rosemary West* (Doubleday, London, 1996).

3 The meaning of 'subjectivities' in this context draws on the work of Foucault. It refers to the construction of identities through knowledge and discourse (in this context, for example, the construction of feminine identity and victim identity). See M Foucault, *The History of Sexuality: Vol 1, An Introduction* (Allen Lane, London, 1979).

4 D Smith, *Texts, Facts and Femininity: Exploring the Relations of the Ruling* (Routledge, London, 1990) 3.

evidence[5] is imparted so as to be accessible to a jury.[6] This study investigated the ways in which these constructions of events exploited, and may have reinforced, pervasive societal norms of ideal victimhood and femininity.

Trials themselves are, statistically, a relatively rare feature of the criminal justice system; those involving charges of serial murder are very much rarer, and cases in which a woman is charged with such crimes are close-to unique. The unique nature of the trial of Rose West illustrates, within one case study, the diverse use of gendered norms in the construction (and reconstruction) of victims, offenders and events which takes place during the trial process. In this case such norms were of particular importance: on the one hand, the case was evidentially weak, but on the other, the huge media attention on the appalling fate of the murder victims meant that it was important to the credibility of the Crown Prosecution Service (CPS) to secure a conviction. It is arguable that a high profile case, such as this one, does not merely draw on societal expectations of gender and of victims but also directly reinforces them. The techniques of adversarial legal combat seen in the trial of Rose West, therefore, may have been more refined and deliberate than in less prominent cases. Examining the use of identities in this extreme form, I would argue, alerts us to their existence and their use in other cases, where they may be expressed more subtly, yet no less effectively.

A thematic analysis of the trial transcript[7] provided evidence of gender norms, identified by previous feminist work, such as domesticity, sexual passivity and maternity,[8] as well as themes relating to the construction of victim status, such as vulnerability and inscrutability. These themes, as will be seen later in this chapter, were interconnected. The latter proved to be relevant to a feminist perspective as well as being significant in their own right. The themes identified were explored by lexical analysis—the process of examining the form of language used—considering the use of stereotypes, of gendered language or terminology (such as 'woman' or 'girl') and the descriptions of individuals and events.[9] Also explored was the trial's treatment of symbolic places or objects; those which, in a feminist analysis, are socially understood to have particular meaning.[10] The emphasis and direction of the attention focused on norms of gender and victimhood were

---

[5] A Sanders 'Constructing a Case for the Prosecution' (1987) 14 *Journal of Law and Society* 229.

[6] WL Bennett and M Feldman, *Reconstructing Reality in the Courtroom* (Tavistock, London, 1981).

[7] The use of thematic analysis as a research methodology is discussed by O Holsti, *Content Analysis for the Social Sciences* (Addison-Wesley, London, 1969). Since the present study was a feminist analysis of the trial, particular attention was paid to themes relevant to such an approach.

[8] See for example C Smart 'Law's Power, the Sexed Body and Feminist Discourse' (1990) 17 *Journal of Law and Society* 194; C Smart and B Smart (eds), *Women, Sexuality and Social Control* (Routledge, London, 1978); C Smart 'The Legal and Moral Ordering of Child Custody' (1991) 18 *Journal of Law and Society* 485; D Nicolson, 'Telling Tales: Gender Discrimination, Gender Construction and Battered Women Who Kill' (1995) 3 *Feminist Legal Studies* 185; A Diduck, 'Legislating Ideologies of Motherhood' (1993) 2 *Social and Legal Studies* 461.

[9] See, for example, C Miller, *Words and Women* (Anchor Press, Garden City NY, 1976).

[10] Examples of this are the home, traditionally regarded as feminine, in contrast with pubs, which are masculine.

analysed, considering whether these subjectivities were used in a way that was constructive or destructive to the credibility of the participants in the trial.[11] The power of notions of victimisation, and consequently also of victim testimony within a contested trial, will be explored generally in the next section before it is considered in relation to the West trial in the second half of this chapter.

THE IMPORTANCE OF THE VICTIM TO THE TRIAL

From the earliest point of criminal justice intervention, the existence of a victim is important. The identification of the victim plays an important role in establishing, technically and evidentially, that a crime has taken place. On a technical level, acts which are not of themselves criminal may be rendered so by the non-consent of a victim. As an example, if a person consents to a minor assault there is said to be neither a criminal offence nor a victim.[12] Moreover, on an evidential level, the criminal charge of assault occasioning grievous bodily harm is unlikely to succeed in the absence of evidence from a victim who has suffered that harm. This chapter does not examine the technical, evidential importance of the victim within the West murder trial, but instead considers the emotive power of the concepts of victimhood that were employed.

It is argued that the way in which victims were presented (by both prosecution and defence lawyers) during the trial of Rose West relied on societal conceptions of femininity and of deviance from gender norms. The dependence on ideals of female and victim behaviour was arguably heightened in this particular trial because direct, forensic evidence was lacking. In a general context, Sarat argues that the nature of the trial itself, which is focused around the reconstruction of the victim's injury, means that 'victimisation' plays a central role in that process. The victim is often a crucial witness in the construction of the prosecution case. While in theory the trial is conducted by agents of the State in furtherance of the 'public interest', the victim has an importance in the process above and beyond that of an ordinary witness.

This view does not sit easily with the numerous claims that, at various stages of the criminal justice process, including that of the trial, the interests of victims are marginalised.[13] One way of reconciling these perspectives is to consider that while actual victims are still infrequently given an opportunity officially to voice their

---

[11] It should be noted however that my conclusions are drawn from analysis of the transcript content only, consequently the use of the techniques which it is suggested were adopted in the trial have not been confirmed by the barristers in question.

[12] *Wilson* (1996) 2 Cr App R 241.

[13] For example, J Shapland, J Willmore, P Duff, *Victims in the Criminal Justice System* (Gower, Aldershot, 1985); E Erez 'Who's Afraid of the Big Bad Victim? Victim Impact Statements as Victim Empowerment and Enhancement of Justice' [1999] *Criminal Law Review* 545; D McBarnet 'Victim in the Witness Box—Confronting Victimology's Stereotype' (1983) 7 *Contemporary Crises* 293.

opinions,[14] preconceived notions of victims' characteristics and needs are important to the operation of the criminal justice process and prevalent in criminal justice discourse.[15]

Our concepts of what constitutes 'victimisation' feed into our perceptions of the nature and severity of crime. Crimes without visible and identifiable 'victims' are often regarded as less serious than other crimes.[16] Indeed, it is a traditional argument that victimless crimes should not be regarded as crimes at all.[17] Conversely, and perhaps as result of that traditional argument, the seriousness of apparently-victimless crimes can be 'talked up' by identifying the 'hidden victims'. (Those who argue, for example, for the continued criminalisation of drug-use can transform this apparently victimless crime into a more serious one by identifying, as victims, the families of users or those burgled to fund users' habits.[18]) The existence and status of the 'victim', then, shapes conceptions of crime generally, and of the harm caused by individual offenders more specifically.[19] In this chapter it is argued that it was this search for consistent, dualistic identification of both victim and offender, and the desire to link the acts of the alleged offender to victimisation, that led to the contested nature of victimisation being an important aspect of the West trial process.

In a contested trial, the victim-witness is a source of evidence as to what happened. As such, credibility and character of the witness are open to attack from the defence, both when the defendant denies performing the act in question and when it is only the criminality of the act which is denied (for example, by asserting the 'victim's' consent to what would otherwise constitute a sexual assault).[20] Questioning the criminality of the act is an attack on the alleged 'victim' status of the

---

[14] See L Henderson 'The Wrongs of Victims' Rights' in E Fattah (ed), *Towards a Critical Victimology* (MacMillan, London, 1992) 111 and S Bandes 'Empathy, Narrative and Victim Impact Statements' (1996) 63 *University of Chicago Law Review* 361.

[15] For example, the preconceived notion that victims desire vengeance is used to support tougher sentencing regimes: D Garland, *The Culture of Control* (Oxford University Press, Oxford, 2001) 143.

[16] For example, crimes against institutions are frequently regarded as victimless and as less serious than those where a wronged individual can be identified, and thus are frequently overlooked by literature examining victimisation. See the chapter by Richard Young in this volume.

[17] For a discussion of this see D Miers, 'Taking the Law into their Own Hands' in A Crawford and J Goodey (eds), *Integrating a Victim Perspective within Criminal Justice* (Aldershot, Ashgate, 2000) 78.

[18] The Thames Valley Police initiative in restorative cautioning encourages this type of transformation. Its facilitators are trained to ask questions which will uncover hidden forms of 'victimisation'. For example, in one case a mother described the impact of her son's cannabis use on her in terms of sleeplessness, worry and shock. See R Young, 'Integrating a Multi-Victim Perspective into Criminal Justice Through Restorative Justice' in A Crawford and J Goodey *Integrating a Victim Perspective within Criminal Justice* (Ashgate, Aldershot, 2000) 243.

[19] Individuals who fail to fit contemporary stereotypes of victimhood can become 'invisible' even to the extent that no crime is perceived to have taken place. For example, victims of marital rape were legally denied victim status until relatively recently *R* (1992) 1 AC 598. Indeed, if sentence lengths are a reliable guide, they are still perceived as less deserving of victim status even after the criminalisation of marital rape: *M* (1994) 16 Cr App R (S) 770; *R. v Pearson (Kirk Paul)* [1996] 1 Cr App R (S) 309.

[20] D Brereton, 'How Different Are Rape Trials? A Comparison of the Cross-Examination of Complainants in Rape and Assault Trials' (1997) 37 *British Journal of Criminology* 242.

complainant. The corollary is that reinforcing victim status fortifies the court's perceptions of a defendant as an offender.

The trial of Rose West embodied these phenomena. The weak evidential link between her and the murder victims was obscured as the prosecution sought to emphasise characteristics of vulnerability and sexual passivity of the dead victims and the diametrically opposite characteristics—dominance and sexual aggression—of Rose. Moreover, a number of witnesses were introduced to give similar-fact evidence pertaining to Rose's violent sexuality and thus imply her involvement in sexual murder. The prosecution presented these women, not as mere witnesses, but as further victims of Rose West (surviving victims[21]). They provided a link between Rose and the dead victims which could not be established by forensic means. But in order to evidence such a link, it was essential that their testimony cast Rose in the role of offender in a series of crimes for which she was not on trial. Rose and her defence team challenged this evidence, arguing variously that the witnesses had consented to sexual activity or that they were lying. The defence thereby resisted the construction of these witnesses as victims and the construction of Rose as offender. Moving further from this construction of offender, the defence used traditional conceptions of femininity to present Rose herself as a vulnerable victim of a dominant husband.

The Emotive Power of the Victim

The power of a victim's testimony relating to their experience of suffering and victimisation has been explored by prolific research on the use and effect of victim impact statements. Some of this work has examined the presence and effect of emotion and empathy in the decision-making process and supports the more contextual approach to decision-making which results. Henderson justifies this support in the following terms:

> Empathy enables the decision maker to have an appreciation of the human meanings of a given legal situation. Empathy both aids the processes of discovery—the processes by which a judge or other legal decision maker reaches a conclusion—and the processes of justification—the procedure used by a judge or other decision maker to justify the conclusion —in a way that disembodied reason simply cannot.[22]

While Henderson considers that understanding victims improves juridical decision-making, critics of victim impact statements argue that the use of empathy in

---

[21] During the process of writing this paper a number of different ways of describing this group of witnesses/victims were considered. One possibility was 'survivors' (as now frequently used in relation to victims of rape and sexual abuse to deny the passivity implied by the term 'victim'. See P Rock 'Murderers, Victims and Survivors' (1998) 38 *British Journal of Criminology* 185, 187) however, this approach was at odds with the construction of their victimhood and passivity throughout the trial and so the term 'surviving victims' was coined.

[22] L Henderson 'Legality and Empathy' (1987) 85 *Michigan Law Review* 1574, 1575.

this context is intended to evoke anger and to empassion the listener against the defendant. As a consequence, statements can lead to an unbalanced empathetic response as they 'block the jury's ability to hear the defendant's story' and preclude the defendant from a similar empathetic understanding.[23] This unbalanced response is in part created, so the argument goes, because assumed victim reactions—vengeance and hatred—are portrayed by law not as emotional but as *rational* responses and as such take the form of legitimate legal discourse. They can then be distinguished from any potential emotional discourses directed at the defendant, such as compassion and empathy, which may otherwise compromise the authoritative, rational image of the legal system.[24]

One of the means by which empathetic responses are provoked during the course of a trial is through the use of rhetoric. Rhetoric is emotive discourse which draws on deeply embedded notions of right or wrong and asks the listener to respond.[25] Used effectively, it persuades and motivates the listener to act in response to the argument, and in the case of the jury, to convict or acquit. Within the context of the courtroom, Sarat argues that the effect of victim impact statements, for example, is to 'provide a narrative which moves the jury from strangeness to familiarity, overcomes distance and establishes identification'.[26] In creating a 'relationship' between the victim and jury the prosecution seek to mobilise the jury to exact vengeance on behalf of the victim. This argument may seem to conflict with research findings that legal professionals usually ignore victim impact statements.[27] However, Sarat's findings are important because they were based on the use of *oral* statements given in the context of *adversarial jury trial*, not, as in other studies, on the use of written statements during sentencing.[28]

The adversarial nature of the trial allows the use of methods beyond the bland and unimaginative presentation of evidence. Cases are constructed with a view to winning, and techniques are adopted to facilitate that process in the full knowledge that the adversarial techniques best suited for juries differ from those which may influence judges or other legal professionals.[29]

---

[23] S Bandes 'Empathy, Narrative and Victim Impact Statements' (1996) 63 *University of Chicago Law Review* 361, 370.

[24] *Ibid*, 369.

[25] P Goodrich, '*Jani Anglorum*: Signs, Symptoms, Slips and Interpretation in Law' in C Douzinas, P Goodrich, Y Hachamaritch (eds), *Politics, Postmodernity and Critical Legal Studies: The Legality of the Contingent* (Routledge, London, 1994) 111.

[26] A Sarat, 'Vengeance, Victims and the Identities of Law' (1997) 6 *Social and Legal Studies* 163, 177.

[27] For example, E Erez and L Rogers, 'Victim Impact Statements and Sentencing Outcomes and Processes' (1999) 39 *British Journal of Criminology* 216; A Sanders, C Hoyle, R Morgan and E Cape, 'Victim Impact Statements—Can't Work Won't Work' [2001] *Criminal Law Review* 447.

[28] *Ibid*.

[29] See Sebba's discussion of oral testimony by a dead victim's family to a jury which then had to decide whether or not to award a capital penalty: L Sebba, *Third Parties* (Ohio State University Press, Columbus Ohio, 1996). Generally on the construction and use of adversarial techniques see Bennett and Feldman, *Reconstructing Reality in the Courtroom*, n 6 above.

Thus, the identification of a victim not only aids in the legal construction of criminality, but may incite the jury to convict or acquit against the weight of the 'objective' evidence.[30] The emotive power associated with victim status and the benefits associated with identifying a victim, combined with the fact that victimhood is a flexible or constructed category, means that, on occasions, victim status may be actively sought or created by counsel in order to strengthen the effect of testimony. The way in which this occurred in the trial of Rose West is considered in later sections of this chapter.

The Ideal Victim

Whilst it is important for the prosecution to present both a victim and an offender to the court, it does not automatically follow that those who are technically victims of crime will be socially recognised as such. Indeed, the very concept of victimhood can be viewed as an identity or status developed through a process of publicly validated construction. According to Miers:

> An important dimension of this process is the negotiation of the suffering with professional observers and participants in formal settings such as courtrooms . . . so that it conforms with the stereotype projected by their available conventional responses.[31]

In order to conform to the stereotype of victimhood, it is necessary for victims' suffering to be presented 'in terms that comply with others' definitions of victimising events'.[32] The ideal victim, McBarnet observes, 'is the blameless white side of the black and white adversary dispute.'[33] Similarly, Christie identifies two key attributes associated with the stereotypical ideal victim: he or she must be both vulnerable and not to blame for his or her victimisation. To complete this image of the victim, therefore, the ideal offender will be portrayed as 'big and bad', and a stranger to the victim. Christie argues that 'ideal victims need—and create—ideal offenders. The two are interdependent.'[34] It is unsurprising therefore that within an adversarial system the prosecution should present the victim to the court in ideal terms, innocent and blameless for his or her fate. Harnessing this stereotype feeds the corresponding construction of the criminality of the offender.

The female victim as an ideal type has been explored through a large body of work examining rape trials. This is the point at which work on gender construction and that on victims have traditionally merged, revealing that female victimisation

---

[30] The principle of 'jury equity' is discussed in A Sanders and R Young, *Criminal Justice*, 2nd edn (Butterworths, London, 2000) 560.

[31] Miers, 'Taking the Law into their Own Hands', n 17 above, 80.

[32] *Ibid*, 79.

[33] D McBarnet, 'Victim in the Witness Box', n 13 above, 296.

[34] N Christie, 'The Ideal Victim' in E Fattah (ed), *From Crime Policy to Victim Policy* (Macmillan, Basingstoke, 1986) 25.

is frequently discussed in terms of sexual passivity and vulnerability and that claims of passivity and victimisation are countered in the courtroom by evidence of sexual aggression and promiscuity. Thus it is evident that the ideal-victim type conflates with the ideal-female type, being concerned with sexual conservatism and passivity.[35] The different uses of ideal-female-victim (and correlative ideal-female-offender) types within the West trial are discussed in the remaining parts of this chapter.

THE PROSECUTION'S CONSTRUCTION OF VICTIMS

The Dead Victims

As is usual in the adversarial system, there was considerable recourse to rhetoric in the trial of Rose West. The need for both the prosecution and defence to convince the jury of the truth of their particular versions of events leads to the selection of the evidence presented and the 'clothing'[36] of that evidence in persuasive argument.[37] One aspect of the traditional norm of femininity is that women do not commit violent crimes,[38] so a crucial aspect of the prosecution's work in this case was to persuade the jury of Rose West's dearth of femininity and thus of her capacity to have offended in this manner.

During the trial the prosecution's use of emotive language was most evident in opening and closing speeches. This is perhaps unsurprising, as these speeches do not constitute evidence and so counsel are permitted a considerable latitude in their monologues. They were able to 'speak on behalf' of the dead victims who were not present to testify to their own suffering. In the opening stages of the trial, it was important for the prosecution not merely to report that the murders had taken place, but also to introduce the jury to the full horror of the nature of the acts suffered by the victims. Although she had not been the first to die, the introduction began with an account of what had happened to Heather, the oldest natural child of both Fred and Rose West and perhaps, therefore, the victim likely to incite the most intense outrage and disgust:

> The skull had been hacked from the spine and the bones had been chopped to reduce the area into which the bones could be forced.[39]

---

[35] For example, see Smart and Smart (eds), *Women, Sexuality and Social Control*, and Smart 'Law's Power', both n 8 above.

[36] J Morrison and P Leith, *The Barrister's World* (Open University Press, Buckingham, 1992) 5.

[37] The use of rhetoric is likely to be strongest when the evidence is weak, see C Perelman, *The Idea of Justice and the Problem of Argument* (Richard Clay, Bungay,1963) 157.

[38] RE Dobash, RP Dobash and L Noaks, *Women and Crime* (University of Wales Press, Cardiff, 1995) ch 3.

[39] Trial transcript of 6 October 1995, 2.

This, together with the more general descriptions of the discovery of other bodily remains conveyed the cruelty of the acts surrounding the deaths while additional comments humanised the absent victims:

> . . . heads had been decapitated and in every set of remains bones were missing. Each was dumped without dignity or respect.[40]

> Their last moments on earth were as objects of the sexual depravity of this woman and her husband.[41]

Following these general assertions, each of the victims was considered independently, in chronological order of their deaths. Their lives before they met the Wests were described and this was followed by an account of their suffering, death and burials. Such a process of contextualisation has been regarded as important to the generation of empathetic responses, which I have argued above to be central to the trial process. Angier writes:

> One [must] be able to run a narrative through one's mind about what happened to the sufferer to bring the individual to his or her current state, and what might be done to help. To empathise is to understand beginnings, middles and possible ends.[42]

Each victim was first 'contextualised' and thus humanised as their family background and some of their characteristics were outlined. The jury were provided with a rounded image of the lives that had been ended, as the 'ghosts' were resurrected through description and the presentation of photographs.

The descriptions in the opening speech were continued and reinforced by the testimonies of relatives and friends of the dead.[43] Charmaine, for example, was referred to as 'a lovely little girl, happy little girl'.[44] The testimonies performed the same function as victim impact statements; they allowed the court to hear expressions of grief at the loss of the murder victims and to understand the loss of the victims, as people, to the individuals testifying and to society more generally. Testimony has been argued to be the most powerful form of dialogue in the courtroom and so these accounts may have been more important than the prosecution's rhetorical presentation of similar material.[45]

---

[40] *Ibid.*

[41] *Ibid.*

[42] N Angier, 'Scientists Mull Role of Empathy in Man and Beast', *New York Times*, 9 May 1995.

[43] In testifying about the loss of their relatives and friends, these witnesses may also have provoked an emotive response. The Victim's Charter recognises such close relatives of dead victims as 'official victims' and there have recently been moves by groups representing the friends and relatives of crime victims that those affected in this way should be recognised as victims in their own right. They are sometimes referred to as 'secondary victims'. See further, Rock, 'Murderers, Victims and Survivors', n 21 above, 188.

[44] Trial transcript, of 9 October 1995, 57.

[45] P Rock, *The Social World of an English Crown Court* (Clarendon Press, Oxford, 1993) 108.

The process of resurrecting and reifying the victims could have been problematic however as, excluding the West's own children,[46] they fell into two categories; those who were 'good', whose background and personality and characteristics were 'wholesome', and those who may have provoked the disapproval of the jury and thus less sympathetic and empathetic responses. In short, victims might have been classified in accordance with ideal and non-ideal types. As discussed above, it is more difficult to evince sympathy for those who do not fit with common understandings of social norms. Non-ideal victims may be regarded as undeserving of the same levels of empathy or as not demanding equal levels of retribution as ideal types, especially if their behaviour, or presence in perilous situations, is seen to be a contributory factor in the crime. To 'blame' the victim in this way is a tactic frequently employed by defence counsel in contested trials, especially (although not exclusively) those concerning sexual assaults.[47] Although, in the West trial, attacking the dead victims in this way could have been seriously detrimental to the defence's case,[48] the strategy was employed in relation to the prosecution witnesses, as discussed below.

The prosecution acknowledged evidence that some of the dead victims were less than 'ideal' in the early stages of the trial. Yet in so doing, behaviour deviating from norms of feminine and victim passivity was minimised using nebulous phrases such as 'difficult', rebellious', 'disruptive' and 'self-willed'. Nevertheless, evidence about the unconventional lives of some of the victims[49] seeped into the courtroom. The intense media interest in the case meant that much of the information about the victims was already in the public realm. Furthermore, evidence was heard during the course of the trial that it was the unconventional lifestyles of these victims that had brought them into contact with the Wests.

The prosecution adopted a means of talking about these victims which constructed them as 'vulnerable'. The difficulties of their childhoods and backgrounds (for example, surviving family break-up and spending periods in local authority care)[50] were explicit in the prosecution evidence. This contextualisation may have served to moderate the otherwise 'unfeminine' behaviour of these victims. For example, it was clear to the court that some of the victims were sexually active;

---

[46] One of the ten victims was the daughter of both Fred and Rose West, a second was the daughter of Fred.

[47] For example, women who move outside their allotted private space are regarded as running the risk of attack: see F Heidensohn, *Women and Crime* (MacMillan, London, 1985) 181.

[48] First, to seek to attack the dead victims could have been perceived as unreasonable given the evidence of the extent of the harm suffered: M Stone discusses the need to present a balanced and reasoned case in *Proof of Fact in Criminal Trials* (W Green and Son Ltd, Edinburgh, 1984) ch 17. Secondly, to do so would be offensive to the memory of the dead victims. It has been suggested that personal attacks on a witness may ally the jury with the witness and turn them against counsel: see D Napley, *The Technique of Persuasion* (Sweet & Maxwell, London, 1983) 77, 100. It should be noted that this did not prevent the strategy being employed with the surviving victims.

[49] For example, Lynda Gough, Carol Cooper, Shirley Hubbard, Juanita Mott, Shirley Robinson and Alison Chambers.

[50] For example Carol Cooper's difficult early life was described by her father, who placed her in local authority care after the break-up of his second marriage (trial transcript, 12 October 1995, 71).

Lynda Gough was even having sexual relationships with some of the lodgers at Cromwell Street. Constructing her as 'vulnerable' redeemed her from the potential disapproval that has been observed in relation to active sexuality in women.[51]

The most susceptible to the emotional response that 'inappropriate' behaviour 'contributed' to her death was Shirley Robinson. Shirley had participated in sexual relationships with both Fred and Rose West and eventually became pregnant by Fred. Descriptions of her childhood and her relationships with the Wests mitigated what might otherwise have been regarded as actively consensual, promiscuous behaviour. The prosecution explained that Shirley had been taken into local authority care and had lost touch with her family. The construction of Shirley was of a young girl seeking sanctuary in a family environment, and finding it only within the West's deviant household. This portrayal of her vulnerability may not only have diminished the impact of her apparently consensual sexual relationship but may have commanded *additional* sympathy from the jury.

If the victims were vulnerable, without the material or emotional resources to make choices about their own lives, active participation in a relationship with the Wests could be presented in terms of the ideal victim-as-stranger type. Rather than being complicit in the West's behaviour such victims were enticed to Cromwell Street as part of a pattern of conduct in which the couple frequently targeted susceptible persons. The importance of the establishment of a pattern of behaviour is discussed further below.

By contrast, Lucy Partington and Therese Siegenthaler, were unproblematic victims for the prosecution in that they were in every way 'blameless' for their fate. They accorded with feminine gender norms of sexual conservatism and, the prosecution argued, had not been involved in relationships with either of the Wests. Each was immersed in her studies with no time for boyfriends. Lucy was described as 'a serious minded but gentle girl' whose interests included art and music.[52] Therese was 'quiet and confident' she 'looked young and wore no make-up'.[53] Moreover, they accorded with the ideal-victim type in that they were strangers to their killers (both girls were kidnapped shortly prior to their murders) so it was undeniable that these victims played no initiating role in the events leading to their deaths. It is evident from the transcripts of the trial that both Lucy and Therese were the subject of much greater contextualisation than the other victims, perhaps because they were both exemplary characters and victims.

The chronological descriptions of the dead victims, however, provided more than contextualisation of each life and death; their cumulative power was that they constructed a pattern of the Wests' behaviour. Establishing this pattern was important in order to create evidential links both between the dead victims and between them and the surviving victims testifying during the trial. With regard

[51] S Lees, *Ruling Passions: Sexual Violence, Reputation and the Law* (Open University Press, Buckingham, 1997).
[52] Trial transcript of 6 October 1995, 54, 55.
[53] Trial transcript of 6 October 1995, 60.

to the dead victims, this pattern was expressed through the methodical, repetitive description of what had happened to each murder victim, with particular emphasis on similar facts, for example, the use of gags on the victims:

> other objects—now all too familiar—found with the body which are all to do with the gagging and restraining of this unfortunate young university undergraduate.[54]

> An object which has now become extremely familiar to you . . . It is a knotted cloth loop.[55]

As the summaries of the deaths and burials progressed through the opening speech so did the graphic nature of the language used to describe the suffering of the victims and disposal of their bodies. An escalation of the horror of the murders was therefore evident. The first description focused very little on the mechanics of the torture, death and burial. This contrasts with later examples:

> Tape with hair on it probably binding Lucy's mouth shut and ropes binding her limbs could only have been required to keep her alive but helpless . . . the only reason to keep her alive at all to further sexual pleasure.[56]

> . . . a mask made of consecutive winding of brown adhesive tape passing around the skull from below the chin to above eye level. Inserted in the front of this mask was a narrow plastic tube in the nostril position . . . its purpose can only have been to keep her wholly under control, unable to see, unable to cry out, just able to breathe. She had you may think, no chance at all . . . precisely when what you may think became the blessing of death came to her we cannot say.[57]

A number of features of the pattern of description are worth noting. First, the methodical repetition of the profiles of the victims appears to have mimicked and emphasised the methodical and serial nature of the murders. Secondly, the escalation of detail, horror and the use of emotive language created a understanding of the deaths as part of a process, a pattern, which culminated (as did the descriptions) in the murder of Heather, the West's own daughter:

> . . . she would have been an infant, a toddler, a very young child when first Charmaine[58] and then the others were killed one by one . . . At the time of Alison Chambers' death Heather West was just short of nine years old. Nearly eight years passed. Then she joined them . . . Heather did not leave home. She was murdered and she was buried naked in the garden.'[59]

The repetition of certain key facts in the submission and discussion of evidence of the murders was vital in order for the prosecution to introduce witnesses whose

[54] Trial transcript of 6 October 1995, 52.
[55] Trial transcript of 6 October 1995, 62.
[56] Trial transcript of 6 October 1995, 59–60.
[57] Trial transcript of 6 October 1995, 69–70.
[58] Note, however, that Charmaine was not the first victim, for Fred West had murdered at least twice before he met Rose.
[59] Quotations are taken from the trial transcript of 6 October 1995, 92, 95.

'similar-fact' testimony would otherwise have been irrelevant and inadmissible. The way in which these witnesses were presented, as surviving victims of Rose West, is discussed in the next section.

The Surviving Victims

The 'surviving victims' who testified at the trial were Caroline Owens, Miss A, Miss X, Anne Marie Davis and Kathryn Halliday. These witnesses were introduced to provide evidence that Rose participated in the types of activities—violent sexual and non-sexual attacks—which, in the case of the murder victims, had resulted in the deaths. Caroline Owens testified about a sexual assault made on her by the Wests in 1972. Both Miss X and Miss A came forward during the murder investigation recounting their abuse as teenagers by the couple. Anne Marie Davis, Fred West's daughter and Rose's stepdaughter, was abused by her father and stepmother throughout her childhood. Kathryn Halliday was Rose West's consenting sexual partner for a number of months. The prosecution's request to include their 'similar fact' evidence in the trial was opposed by the defence on the grounds that its 'probative value is of such low order that it does not outweigh the prejudicial value'.[60] The prosecution's submission was, however, successful and thereafter the similar fact evidence dominated the prosecution case.

By demonstrating Rose's involvement in rape and abuse the prosecution sought to prove that she must also have been involved in the murders.[61] As a result, the proceedings, in large part, became a (rape) trial within a (murder) trial. The witnesses were thereby transformed into an additional class of victims, linked to the dead women by their common experience, different because they were the surviving victims of Rose and Fred West's sexual offences. Moreover, in this 'rape trial', unusually, the defendant was a woman and so what emerged was the construction and counter construction of the femininity of both the surviving victims and the defendant.

The evidence given by these witnesses was understandably emotive. Their victim status was confirmed by their own perceptions of vulnerability and of the harm that they suffered:

> Sir I think that at the time I was very, very low. I was very, very vulnerable and the scenario would be like a moth to a flame.[62]

> I was screaming and crying . . . It hurt so much I just wished I was dead.[63]

---

[60] Trial transcript of 3 October 1995, 94. Within trials there exists a presumption that similar fact evidence is excluded. Such evidence can only be presented if it can be shown that its probative value out-weighs its prejudicial effect: *DPP v P* (1990) 90 Cr App R 325.

[61] Femininity was used in this way in a number of trials examined by A Ballinger in *Dead Woman Walking: Executed Women in England and Wales 1900–1955* (Ashgate, Aldershot, 2000).

[62] Trial transcript of 17 October 1995, 123.

[63] Trial transcript of 18 October 1995, 96.

Emphasising the characteristics which had already been stressed in relation to the murder victims, these surviving victims provided, for the prosecution, what is inevitably missing in murder trials, the power of the victims' testimonies. They conveyed what the dead victims could not.

The prosecution constructed its case by the type of questions asked and the mode of questioning. Case construction through carefully worded questions which control the portrayal of events described by witnesses is a normal court-room technique.[64] The question is, what is the objective of that construction? In this case, the objective was to amplify Rose's active role.

The testimonies described the attacks on the surviving victims in such a way that Fred's role appeared to be secondary, despite his admission of sole responsi-bility for the multiple rape and murder of these victims. This concentration on Rose's actions was legitimate, as it was Rose who was on trial. The effect, however, was to render Fred almost passive in the events that took place. His sole confes-sion was neutralised by references to Rose's dominant and initiating role. Caroline Owens was asked, 'who was the first person to lay a hand on you?', to which she answered, 'Rose'.[65] During Miss A's testimony it became clear that not only was it Rose, rather than Fred, who Miss A had visited in a friendly capacity prior to the attack, but it was Rose who led her into the bedroom where the attack took place, and then undressed her. Prosecution questioning reiterated these points:

You say that Rose led you into this room . . .?[66]

You said Rose started undressing you?[67]

The testimonies of the surviving victims showed the women not merely to be victims, but to be victims of Rose. It was the process of linking her, as an offender, to their victim status which allowed her similarly to be constructed as a murderer in relation to the bodies found. Rose's involvement in joint attacks was key to the prosecution's reliance on similar-fact evidence and as such, her role was heavily scrutinised:

What about Mrs West?[68]

What was Mrs West doing at that stage?[69]

What was Mrs West doing when he struck you?[70]

[64] W O'Barr, *Linguistic Evidence: Language, Power and Strategy in the Courtroom* (Academic Press, New York NY, 1982) ch 2; J Jackson 'Law's Truth, Lay Truth and Lawyer's Truth: The Representation of Evidence in Adversary Trials' (1992) *Law and Critique* 29.
[65] Trial transcript of 11 October 1995, 116.
[66] Trial transcript of 16 October 1995, 39.
[67] Trial transcript of 16 October1995, 40.
[68] Trial transcript of 10 October 1995, 131.
[69] Trial transcript of 10 October 1995, 133.
[70] Trial transcript of 10 October 1995, 134.

Another way in which Rose's role was emphasised as being of essential importance in the attacks was to reveal that Rose West's aggression and violence transgressed feminine norms of maternity and conservative, passive sexuality. Despite
the fact that the majority of the attacks on the surviving victims were joint enter-
prises, the particular harm caused by Rose was evidenced by examples of her
deviation from stereotypes of femininity. For example, Anne Marie (Rose's step-
daughter) who was repeatedly raped by Fred during her childhood, described him
as a symbol of safety whilst recalling a time when she was alone with Rose by saying, 'I felt frightened because my Dad was not there'.[71] Caroline Owens, who it
seemed was raped two or three times by Fred, described Rose's unusual behaviour
as shocking:

> . . . what Mrs West did was something that I had not come across before and it shocked
> me and upset me, and when Fred raped me it was all over in a couple of seconds . . . he
> started crying and he said he was sorry.[72]

It was Rose who assaulted Miss A with a vibrator[73] and, during the same attack,
made sexual remarks to Fred.[74] By contrast, Fred's presence and role were only
highlighted by the prosecution when peripheral and passive and thus in contrast
with Rose's dominance:

What was Fred doing at this time?

He was just stood there at the side of the bed.[75]

Where was Fred?

He was on the side of the bed.[76]

The testimony of Kathryn Halliday was used to provide similar evidence not of
Rose's offending (her sexual relationship with Halliday had been consensual) but
of her dominant sexuality. In a reversal of traditional gender roles, Rose West was
described as sexually aggressive while Fred West was a passive onlooker. In answer
to the question, 'how much of a role did Mr West play in the evening visits?'
Katherine Halliday answered:

> *Not as much as she did sir. I mean he was there. He was sometimes down with the children
> and he would occasionally come up and see if anybody wanted a drink.*[77]

She had earlier related 'we normally had sex but Fred would watch rather than
take part'.[78] While Rose was depicted in masculine terms—'She was a big woman

---

[71] Trial transcript of 18 October 1995, 100.
[72] Trial transcript of 10 October 1995, 151 and of 11 October 1995, 42.
[73] Trial transcript of 16 October 1995, 45.
[74] Trial transcript of 16 October 1995, 47.
[75] Trial transcript of 16 October 1995, 40.
[76] Trial transcript of 16 October 1995, 46.
[77] Trial transcript of 17 October 1995, 124.
[78] Trial transcript of 17 October 1995, 121.

and very very strong, physically strong, and would hold me down'[79]—Fred was feminised even to the extent that he was performing traditionally feminine tasks.

Anne Marie Davies' testimony may have disrupted this pattern of evidence since it was clear that Fred played a major role in her abuse. Her evidence, however, gave particular credence to the idea that Rose had deviated from norms of feminine sexuality and maternity. Rose was described as raping Anne Marie, her step-daughter, 'like a man'.[80] Anne Marie's testimony also deflected blame from Fred and was crucial in the construction of Rose's aggressive and deviant femininity. As with the previous testimonies concerning the joint attacks, the prosecution ensured that Rose's actions formed the focus of the testimony. The first incident described by Anne Marie was her first experience of abuse:

> While all of this was happening did your stepmother do anything other than sit on you?
>
> *She was laughing and smirking and joining in . . . my stepmother rubbed my breasts and was scratching them until they were bleeding.*[81]

Demonstrating Rose's central role in these attacks also significantly diminished her own recourse to claims of passivity and victim status, which are discussed further below.

However, it was important not merely to show that Rose was involved in sexual abuse but that she actively participated in those which shared some of the features of the murders of which she stood accused. Building on the evidence of the gagging of the dead victims, Rose's role in taping up and gagging the surviving victims became a subject of focus. It was made clear that it was Rose who produced the tape which restrained the girl.[82] The description of her taping of Miss A constitutes three pages of transcript, in comparison with the one page devoted to Fred's binding of the other female present. While the description of Fred's role focused on his actions—the position of the girl and how she was tied—Rose's role related to the actor:

> How was Rose doing this? Was she saying anything or how was she behaving when she was wrapping your wrists with the tape? Was she friendly?[83]

The example of the taping up of the victims illustrates how Rose's actions were constructed as central in the attack merely through the mode or technique of questioning adopted by the prosecution. As in the attack on Caroline Owens, Fred raped both girls. As with his role in the taping, the significance of the rapes was minimised. This discussion is not intended to question the validity of the prosecution strategy. However, that strategy was chosen from a variety of possibilities.

---

[79] Trial transcript of 17 October 1995, 125.
[80] Rose raped Anne Marie with a strapped-on vibrator.
[81] Trial transcript of 17 October 1995, 97.
[82] Trial transcript of 16 October 1995, 41.
[83] Trial transcript of 16 October 1995, 55.

Its effect appears to be intended to reduce the possibility of Rose being perceived as passive and thus also a victim (of Fred).

The testimony which best illustrates that the categories of victim and offender can be constructed through advocacy is that of Kathryn Halliday. Kathryn Halliday had been involved in a consensual sexual relationship with Rose West lasting several months. Yet her testimony embodied the same features as the other surviving victims: it portrayed their sexual relationship as non-consensual. Unlike the other victims, Kathryn Halliday did not suggest that she was, in legal terms, non-consenting, but she constructed the same sexually aggressive character portrait of Rose West that they did. This character portrait was at odds with the impression provided by her admissions during her cross-examination.[84] For example, she admitted that she was a willing visitor to Cromwell Street and that her story was printed in a newspaper under the headline 'My Kinky Sex In House Of Horror'.[85] During her testimony this 'kinky sex' is described in such a way that it appears non-consensual:

> She just came in, sat beside me, got undressed very, very quickly, almost too quickly. There were no niceties, no formalities . . . and I must admit I was very taken aback . . . I was then dragged up the stairs . . . It was very quick, very forceful.[86]

The inclusion and nature of the testimonies of the surviving victims helped shape the trial. Rose West was on trial for murder, yet through the similar fact evidence it appeared that either she was on trial for rape, or that the surviving victims' victimhood was elevated so that they gave voice to the dead victims experiences. The lengthy and emotive descriptions of their experiences enabled the prosecution to employ gender stereotyping which identified Rose as having transgressed important norms of female/feminine behaviour.

THE DEFENCE'S CONSTRUCTION OF VICTIMS

Undermining the Surviving Victims' Testimonies

The methods employed by the defence in response to the testimonies of the surviving victims were intended to undermine their status. Because they were victims of sexual abuse and rape, the techniques adopted by the defence mirrored those adopted by defence counsel in rape trials. Thus, the surviving victims' cross examinations created yet another 'trial within a trial'. These techniques include attacks on character, victim-blaming and rejoinder gender stereotyping. As Brereton shows, many defence techniques used in rape trials, such as attacks on character

---

[84] Trial transcript of 18 October 1995.
[85] Once again, it is not my intention here to challenge the truth of claims made in the trial, only to illustrate that testimonies and the statuses which they construct are always partial and contestable.
[86] Kathryn Halliday, trial transcript of 17 October 1995, 108–09.

and victim blaming, are also used in other trials involving interpersonal violence.[87] However, the particular characteristics of different offences provide the defence with different, as well as similar, weapons with which to attack alleged victims. The sexual nature of rape provides opportunities for undermining based on sexual stereotyping which, in turn, draw upon conventionally gendered norms, such as promiscuity and unreliability as a source of information about sexual history. For example, in the West trial:

What you say happened in Cromwell Street is a complete figment of your imagination.[88]

You have exaggerated that activity and have tried to portray yourself as a victim?[89]

Because of what happened to you on the previous occasion ... did that not act as a warning bell to you?[90]

At the age of thirteen you were virtually uncontrollable ... Did you used to keep the company of young soldiers?[91]

In December 1976 you had to attend the clinic in Cheltenham. Is that right ... For gonorrhoea?[92]

By adducing evidence of the victim's sexual history the defence not only sought to argue that the victims consented to the sexual intercourse, or that their sexual history led the defendant to believe that they had consented, but also used this evidence to discredit the victim. By attacking the victim's sexual behaviour and thus character, it was no doubt intended by the defence that the victims would appear less credible to the jury.[93] In accusing the women of lying, and of exaggerating, and contributing to, their victimisation, an attempt was made to undermine their victim status. In short, the defence drew on the now well-documented discourse of female pathology,[94] in an attempt to construct them as unreliable witnesses.

In addition to the challenge to the characters and veracity of the surviving victims, which in turn was intended to undermine their evidence of Rose West's sexual aggression, the defence sought to present their own victims to the court.

---

[87] Brereton 'How Different Are Rape Trials?', n 20 above.
[88] Trial transcript of 16 October 1995, 110.
[89] Trial transcript of 18 October 1995, 10.
[90] Trial transcript of 16 October 1995, 91.
[91] Trial transcript of 20 October 1995, 49.
[92] Trial transcript of 16 October 1995, 109.
[93] For examples of work exploring these techniques in rape trials see: J Temkin 'Sexual History Evidence—The Ravishment of s2' [1993] *Criminal Law Review* 3; J Temkin 'Prosecuting and Defending Rape: Perspectives from the Bar' (2000) 27 *Journal of Law and Society* 219; Lees, *Ruling Passions*, n 51 above, ch 3.
[94] Lees, *Ruling Passions*, n 51 above.

Rose West the Victim

The construction of the surviving victims by the prosecution as 'ideal' served an important purpose in the trial; it provided evidence of Rose West's deviant femininity. 'Femininity' can play an important role in trials of female offenders. Those who conform to norms of feminine behaviour fare better than those whose behaviour is perceived to be 'unfeminine'.[95] Understandings of femininity in the legal sphere have been imbued with notions of maternity and conservative sexuality. In relation to maternity, women are associated with caring, both for children and other dependants. Analyses of family law decisions, for example, have revealed that different standards of parenting are required of men and women; whilst women are required to care *for* their children (that is by providing practical day to day care), men are required only to care *about* them.[96]

With regard to sexuality, during rape trials the sexual histories of complainants are frequently used to suggest that the victim consented, or appeared to consent, to the alleged rape because, for example, she was not a virgin, had had several previous sexual partners, or had been in a sexual relationship with the defendant in the past.[97] The disapproval of active or aggressive sexuality, which is also evident in the social construction of female sexuality,[98] has been exploited in other areas to elicit prejudice against female witnesses, victims and offenders. For example, during the trial of Sara Thornton[99] several questions were put to the defendant implying her sexual promiscuity,[100] an issue which was superfluous to the case. A similar disapproval of her sexuality was evident in the appeal judgment.[101] Women who depart from the ideals of femininity may fare worse than those who conform.

We have seen that the victim-related evidence in Rose West's trial illustrated that she lacked maternal instinct and possessed an aggressive and violent sexuality. In particular, the evidence may have obliterated any attempt by Rose to present herself as feminine or as a victim.

---

[95] For example, see A Worrall, *Offending Women* (Routledge, London, 1990) chs 4 and 5.

[96] Smart, 'The Legal and Moral Ordering of Child Custody', n 8 above; for work exploring the construction of fatherhood see R Collier 'Waiting 'Til Father Gets Home: the Reconstruction of Fatherhood in Family Law' (1995) 4 *Social and Legal Studies* 15.

[97] Temkin, 'Sexual History Evidence', n 93 above.

[98] Socially, as well as legally, so-called promiscuous behaviour is subject to judgement and criticism. This is evident in the 'sheer number of words which define woman as sexually promiscuous (there are comparatively few for men)': J Mills, *Womanwords: A Vocabulary of Culture and Patriarchal Society* (Virago, London, 1991) xiii, see also Heidensohn, *Women and Crime*, n 47 above, 181.

[99] Sara Thornton was tried and found guilty of murdering her husband who she alleged had routinely physically abused her. Her conviction was later reduced to manslaughter. The case is reported at [1996] 2 All ER 1023 (CA).

[100] For example, the prosecution questioned her about whether she was in the habit of not wearing knickers, see J Nadel, *Sara Thornton: The Story of a Woman Who Killed* (Victor Gorlancz, London, 1995).

[101] Nicolson, 'Telling Tales' n 8 above.

Nevertheless, a key theme which was woven through the defence case was the presentation of Rose herself as a victim. This portrayal of Rose could have served a number of different purposes. First and foremost, it seems that it was intended to deny her status as offender, as the binary opposition of offender and victim makes it difficult for a victim to be seen as an offender and vice-versa. In addition, the portrayal of Rose as a victim embodied a construction of her as passive, which countered the prosecution portrayal of her aggression. Integral in this was the construction of passive sexuality. Finally, the portrayal of Rose as a victim was designed to explain her relationship with Fred and her claims of ignorance about his activities. These constructions were presented within the framework of 'female victimisation',[102] an established discourse that would have been familiar to the jury. The victimisation framework has the additional benefit of evoking emotion, empathy and sympathy in observers.

One problem which the defence had to surmount was the undeniable fact of Rose's aggressive sexuality. Since this could not be denied, it had to be portrayed as an aberration precipitated by her victimisation. For this to be at all possible the defence had to attempt to establish her prior sexual conservatism at the very beginning of her testimony. She demonstrated this sexual conservatism through a use of language which conveyed innocence:

> I resisted his [Fred's] advances.[103]

And when asked about her reaction to being asked out by Fred, she replied:

> Shock horror at first.[104]

The apparently conservative family she came from supported this portrayal. Rose described their 'shock horror' at her relationship with Fred and the extreme measures they took to stop it.[105]

However this approach was problematic as at the time discussed Rose was not sexually inexperienced. This obstacle to the construction of her sexual conservatism was dealt with through the simultaneous construction of her as a sexual victim. During her testimony Rose described how her sexual victimisation began when at fourteen she was deserted by her family and forced to live with her sister during which time she slept with her sister's thirty year old friend. She then went on to describe how the police later tried to intervene and take her back to her parents. Although it was not explicitly said, it was implicit in this evidence that Rose was exploited. Rose went on to explain how this exploitation and victimisation were compounded when she was raped by strangers on two separate occasions

---

[102] For example, notions of female victimisation draw on 'domestic violence' discourses which have been used to explain female offending (eg *Thornton* [1996] 2 All ER 1023 (CA), *Ahluwalia* [1992] 4 All ER 889). More generally portrayals of women as duped by their male partners have been used to explain female offending, see N Naffine, *Female Crime* (Allen and Unwin, Sydney, 1987) 49.
[103] Trial transcript of 30 October 1995, 38.
[104] Trial transcript of 30 October 1995, 40.
[105] For example, placing her in care.

during her teens and her account stressed her conventional female characteristic of physical weakness.[106]

This discourse of victimisation was used later to explain her susceptibility to Fred's 'persuasion' and thus her promiscuity and lesbianism.

> I am afraid I was nursing old wounds from past history in my family, particularly when my mum left me at my sister's . . . Because I thought my mum had left me and my dad had abused my mum, and I just wanted someone to love me . . . He promised me everything and because I was so young I suppose I fell for his lies . . . He promised to love me and to care for me and I fell for it.[107]

> I remember Fred saying to me about getting involved with Caroline Owens as a lesbian relationship, which would have been my first experience with a woman. I am afraid with his very persuasive manner, he did persuade me that Caroline Owens was willing to try it out.[108]

Exploitation was also evident in Rose's description of how Fred made her go out at night to clubs and bars:

> . . . to pick up other men really. That was what Fred intended me to do. He made it clear that this is what I was out there to do.[109]

During her testimony Rose explained that her victimisation by Fred continued throughout the marriage, which the defence and Rose sought to portray as unequal from the very beginning. Rose's description of Fred as 'dominating and controlling' served two further purposes. First it implicitly constructed her as passive:

> If I kept resisting he would use emotional blackmail and he would use anything. He could be very, very persuasive, pushy . . . he would say things like: 'You are not doing enough for the marriage' or 'I am the breadwinner . . . I bring home the money, you have got to play your part in the marriage somehow'. . . he would never let up.[110]

Her lack of agency also enabled her to explain her involvement in the attack on Caroline Owens:

> I was a young girl, I was about, I believe, nineteen at the time and he had a lot of influence over me . . . I believe I was as much as a victim as Caroline was.[111]

Thus, the criminal actions that were proven, Rose's attack on Caroline Owens, were explained by Fred's control of her.

The defence continued this construction in their examination of other witnesses in the trial (both prosecution and defence witnesses). Rather than

---

[106] Trial transcript of 30 October 1995, 39.
[107] Trial transcript of 30 October 1995, 46 and 45.
[108] Trial transcript of 30 October 1995, 98.
[109] Trial transcript of 30 October 1995, 89.
[110] Trial transcript of 30 October 1995, 80.
[111] Trial transcript of 30 October 1995, 102 and of 30 October 1995, 100.

appearing as the dominant party, as portrayed by the prosecution, Rose was portrayed as controlled and abused by Fred.

> Can you remember him coming in and saying something along these lines to Rose: That if she did not come back with him within ten minutes, that she would find that her place in his bed would be occupied by another woman?[112]

> . . . in fact you and Fred West were in your bedroom in your flat during the time that you thought that Mrs West was safely tucked up in hospital having given birth to her baby?[113]

> Did you ever see any signs that Mr West had actually physically ill-treated his wife?

> *Yes, I saw once when Rose came downstairs and her glasses had been broken and she had a black eye.*[114]

Fred West's Victims

Like the prosecution, the defence sought to bring evidence of 'surviving victims'. These were women who were the subject of lone attacks by Fred. By including evidence of these attacks the defence showed that Fred did murder, rape and abuse without Rose's involvement. They sought to show that it was possible that he had committed, alone and without Rose's knowledge, the murders with which Rose was charged, and that she was not the dominating party in their joint attack on Caroline Owens (the only sexual offence to which Rose admitted).

The strongest evidence to this effect was the murders of Rena West and Anne McFall, Fred's first wife and nanny/girlfriend respectively.[115] These women were killed before Rose and Fred met. However, the medical evidence relating to their deaths was presented in the trial by the prosecution pathologist who supervised all the excavations. Consequently, the evidence, which was dealt with briefly, was subsumed by the mass of medical evidence presented at the trial as part of the prosecution's case and did not stand out as significant to the defence case. Therefore the evidence of their deaths did not hold the emotive power associated with the deaths and abuse of the other victims.

The defence, however, also led evidence from a number of victims who testified that they were attacked by Fred alone, both before and after he met Rose. Half of these victims were however silenced by the judge. They were not given the opportunity to testify in person; their brief statements were read to the court by defence counsel. Likewise those with evidence relating to the deaths of Rena West and Anne McFall were sidelined in this way. As such, their victim status was undermined and they were marginalised by the court. Their statements were short and

---

[112] Trial transcript of 9 October 1995, 74.
[113] Trial transcript of 10 October 1995, 87.
[114] Trial transcript of 17 October 1995 87.
[115] Anne McFall lived with Anne Marie, Charmaine, Fred and Rena as a nanny. She later became pregnant by Fred.

factual and did not hold the emotive power evident in the testimonies of the defence victims. As we saw in relation to victim impact statements, discussed above, in not allowing the victims to testify the defence was disadvantaged as the power of live testimony allows the jury to assess the witnesses and affects their emotive response.[116] The muting of the defence witnesses denied them status equal to the prosecution witnesses.

As a consequence of the apparent success of the prosecution case in undermining Rose West's femininity through the evidence of the surviving victims, the defence failed to establish victim status for Rose. In particular, the sheer volume of testimony from the prosecution surviving victims and its emotive power overshadowed any attempt by the defence to present Rose as Fred's victim.

CONCLUSION

Studies in victimology have revealed the secondary victimisation suffered by victims who testify.[117] It is now accepted that the adversarial nature of the trial subjects victims who can be portrayed as less than ideal to degrading treatment which compounds their victimisation. But recourse to concepts of ideal and non-ideal victims can also be damaging in a more general way. In Rose West's case, the prosecution strategy of idealising the dead victims implicitly perpetuated the ideology of victim-blaming and the notion that only ideal victims deserve the jury's sympathy. This strategy ignored that fact that these victims (like all others) did not need to be portrayed as 'blameless' for their fate; their lifestyles were irrelevant.

Within individual adversarial trials there are direct benefits for the prosecution in a victim achieving 'ideal' status. Victim testimony, when credible, has emotive power. Equally, a credible victim is a good source of evidence as to the defendant's guilt. However, because victim status is itself a constructed identity, it can often be contested, in particular by undermining 'ideal' aspects of the stereotype. The flexibility of victim status may also mean, as in the present case, that the concept is employed in ways which stretch it beyond the complainant to encompass others in the trial. This may either shore up the claims of the 'original' victim, as did the surviving victims in the present case, or be used to undermine those claims by, for example, constructing the offender as a victim. In the context of female victims, or female potential victims, stereotypical notions of femininity may be exploited either to portray women in terms of ideal victims, or to attack that status.

We have seen how the construction and use of 'ideal' victim status can be affected by the nature of the evidence used in the trial. In the case study used above, the structure of the trial and consequent allocation of victim status were shaped in an important way by a judicial decision concerning admissibility of

---

[116] See generally Rock, *The Social World of an English Crown Court*, n 45 above, 108.
[117] For example, see work on the victims of rape: Lees, *Ruling Passions*, n 51 above.

evidence. Four groups of victim were constructed through the prosecution and defence cases that were presented to the court in Rose West's trial: those murdered by the Wests (the dead victims), a number of women who gave evidence for the prosecution under the similar fact rules (surviving victims), Rose West herself and the victims of Fred West's lone attacks. For the prosecution the inclusion of similar fact evidence enabled them to create an entire pool of new 'victims' to testify to the court. For the defence, the judge's decision to minimise the defence victims' evidence denied them an equivalent pool.

In Rose West's trial the nature and power of the testimonies of the surviving victims helped the prosecution to establish Rose as an offender by undermining her femininity and therefore the victim status which she sought. Whether or not Rose would have been convicted had different victim constructions been presented, we cannot know. What is certain is that the prosecution's job would have been considerably more difficult.

The present study demonstrates that the notion of 'victim' is not a discrete, predetermined category, but is a category that can be created through judicial decisions and through advocacy. Consequently, the status of 'victim' is contingent and constructed in the same way that the concept and identity of crime and criminals are.[118] If the move toward victims' rights continues on its present path[119] the polarisation of victims and offenders will continue.[120] This will undoubtedly have knock-on effects in court and the patterns identified in this case study may well become more exaggerated. Ultimately, claims of innocence from offenders may be unjustifiably undermined in cases with ideal victims and allegations of guilt unjustifiably undermined where victims do not live up to the ideal type.

---

[118] As established by criminological work beginning in the 1950s, eg H Becker, *Outsiders* (Free Press of Glencoe, London, 1963)

[119] H Reeves, 'The New Status of Victims in the UK: Opportunities and Threats' in A Crawford and J Goodey (eds), *Integrating a Victim Perspective within Criminal Justice* (Ashgate, Aldershot, 2000).

[120] On this polarisation, see Garland, *The Culture of Control*, n 15 above, and the chapter by Andrew Sanders in this volume.

8

Victim Participation in an Exclusionary Criminal Justice System

ANDREW SANDERS

INTRODUCTION

F OR MUCH OF the last two decades of the twentieth century there was an uncanny (and uncharacteristic) consensus among criminologists, policy makers and practitioners. It was that the criminal justice system neglected victims and, in many respects, treated them badly. By the end of the century things were changing, as indicated by the Home Secretary in 1999:

> For too long victims of crime have not been given the proper support and protection they deserve. This must change. I am determined to ensure that their needs are placed at the very heart of the criminal justice system.[1]

Over the last few years, numerous new initiatives providing services and specific roles for victims have been introduced and more are on the way. For example, Victim Support now receives substantial government funding to support victims of crime. A Witness Service supports witnesses (mostly victims) due to give evidence. Special assistance is given to children and other vulnerable and intimidated witnesses. Victims are kept informed about the progress of their cases if they so wish. Victims may make 'impact' statements and are consulted about aspects of their cases. But is concern for victims of crime the real motivation behind these initiatives? And even if it is, how successful are they in alleviating the problems victims face? And, perhaps most fundamentally, what kinds of rights and roles should victims have? In order to answer these questions, this chapter will examine victim participation in the context of the criminal justice system as a whole—a system which, I shall argue, is exclusionary. In a short text like this one has to be selective. Consequently I will not discuss the reporting of crime by victims, nor the many measures taken to encourage victims to give evidence in court, except insofar as these are necessary to advance the general argument.

---

[1] J Straw, 'Partners against crime' (1999) 71 (summer) *Victim Support Magazine* 8.

VICTIM PARTICIPATION AND THE ADVERSARIAL SYSTEM

Who are the Victims?

Analytically, it is convenient to separate 'victims' from 'offenders'. This enables analysts and policy-makers to formulate 'victim policy' with little or no regard for other criminal justice policy. Indeed one may argue that the re-invention of 'victimology' as a discipline in its own right encouraged and legitimated this division.[2] But separation is not so easy in the messy real world of criminal justice. As several of the chapters in this collection show,[3] 'offender' and 'victim' status can be contested. Good and bad fortune will sometimes determine which label one is left with.

Further, even though in particular cases 'offenders' and 'victims' can be clearly separated, this is not possible on a society-wide basis. Offenders are disproportionately represented among the most frequently victimised sections of society (young males at the poorest and most socially marginalised end of the social scale). The overlap between the 'victim' population and the 'offender' population is, in other words, huge. Moreover, most offenders are not primarily offenders in terms of their ways of life, just as few victims occupy a primarily victim role in their everyday lives. Most victims and offenders have more in common with each other (and with that dwindling number of people who fall into neither group) than they have with the small number of 'heavy-end' offenders who—we are told—present a disproportionate challenge to the forces of law and order. That said, the greatest similarity between victims and non-professional offenders is that both groups are extremely heterogeneous. Like most offenders, there is little to unite most victims apart from their victimisation, and this is rarely sufficiently life-changing to create a unity of standpoint or demand from victims as a (non)-group. Indeed, as Rock points out, apart from the victims of the most traumatic crimes, 'victims' as a group do not exist in the sense of being a pressure group, and most victim initiatives are a result of pressure for them, rather than by them.[4]

---

[2]   Victimology has a long history as a study of the aetiology of victims, paralleling positivist criminology's obsession with the aetiology of crime. The decline of positivist criminology in the 1960s and 1970s was therefore accompanied by the near-death of victimology. Victimology was revived in the 1980s primarily through an interest in the effects of crime on victims and victim involvement in criminal justice.

[3]   See especially the chapters by Heather Hamill and Jo Winter in this volume and see further, R Young, 'Integrating a Multi-Victim Perspective in Criminal Justice Through Restorative Justice Conferences' in A Crawford and J Goodey (eds), *Integrating a Victim Perspective within Criminal Justice* (Ashgate, Aldershot, 2000).

[4]   P Rock, 'Victims' Rights in England and Wales at the Beginning of the 21st Century' in J Ermisch, D Gallie and A Heath (eds), *Social Challenges and Sociological Puzzles* (Oxford University Press, Oxford, 2002). On victims of fraud, see M Levi and A Pithouse, 'The Victims of Fraud', in D Downes (ed), *Unravelling Criminal Justice* (Macmillan, London, 1992); B Spalek, 'Regulation, White Collar Crime, and the Bank of Credit and Commerce International' (2001) 40 *Howard Journal of Criminal Justice* 166.

Finally, there are crimes without obvious victims—drugs, public disorder, pollution, factory offences and so forth. As Winter argues in this volume, in the world of public rhetoric 'real' crimes require 'real' victims, and so crimes without victims are not real crimes at all. This kind of binary relationship reflects the binary nature of the adversarial system in England and Wales, in which complex patterns of events and relationships are generally cast in terms of one side against another. The remarkable effort and money put into the policing of drugs and public order offences are often justified, therefore, at least partially by reference to the unidentified victims—those assumed to have been terrorised by 'anti-social' youths, or to have been burgled by junkies seeking the means to feed their habits.

Conversely, victims of 'regulatory' offences (such as fraud, pollution and health and safety infractions) are rarely identified as such. This is despite these crimes usually producing more easily identifiable victims than do drugs and most public order offences, and despite the greater harm often suffered by victims of these 'regulatory' offences than by victims of burglary and public disorder. In the list of offences to which the Victims' Charter (discussed further below) applies, 'regulatory' offences are absent. The Charter applies instead to theft, burglary, criminal damage, arson, assault, domestic violence, racial harassment, sexual crimes and homicide. Indeed, the police and Crown Prosecution Service (which prosecutes solely police-enforced crimes) are the only law enforcement agencies mentioned in the Charter. Rock critically comments on the selectivity of victim status, observing that the Home Office's Victims Steering Group has no representatives who can speak for victims of road accidents and school bullying, but even he does not mention accidents at work and so forth.[5] As we shall see, the invisibility of non-police-enforced offences at the levels of the media and policy-making has led directly to their exclusion from the schemes and initiatives mentioned in the introduction to this chapter.

Victims Lost . . .

The adversarial criminal justice system means that, in formal terms, there are two sides to the (legal) story: prosecution and defence. Before the introduction of professional police forces, investigation and prosecution (its instigation and conduct) was, in most cases, the responsibility of the victim. This meant that prosecutions were rare because they were virtually impossible to sustain, except where the victim was wealthy or a member of a prosecution society. It was no 'golden age' for victims, but at least these arrangements—where the prosecutor and the victim

---

[5] Rock, 'Victims' Rights', n 4 above. Note that the Home Office's *Review of the Victim's Charter* (Home Office, London, 2001) invites views on whether the Charter should encompass victims or their bereaved relatives in road traffic accidents leading to death or serious injury. See section entitled ' . . . and re-discovered' below.

were more or less synonymous—ensured that victims were in control of, and knew what was happening in, their cases.[6]

After their introduction in the mid-nineteenth century, the professional police forces gradually took over investigation and prosecution. Victims may have kept in close touch with 'their' cases 100 years ago, as the early police forces were small and locally based, but by the 1970s amalgamations meant that each police force covered the area of at least one county. Police forces, the smallest of which comprised nearly 1,000 officers, had become bureaucracies positioned between victims and the courts and, therefore, when there was a prosecution, between victims and 'their' cases. In the mid-1980s a further bureaucracy was introduced between victims and the courts in the shape of the Crown Prosecution Service, which is now responsible for prosecuting all police cases.

Although much of the account given here is also true of Continental 'inquisitorial' systems, at least their non-adversarial nature allows, in principle, for three or more 'sides'. In the Anglo-American system there is only one side in which victims can participate, if they are to do so at all—that of the prosecution. This is notwithstanding that the interests of the prosecution are not always synonymous with those of victims. For example, the prosecution may wish to save time and money, and ensure conviction, by accepting a guilty plea to a less serious charge than that which the victim alleged (e.g. theft instead of robbery; indecent assault instead of rape).[7]

For many years victims were the forgotten actors in the criminal justice system. Neither the police nor the prosecution had any great interest in ascertaining the views or interests of, or facts about, the victim except in relation to information that could form legal 'evidence'—that is, evidence admissible in court. This frequently excluded much of what was relevant to lay people. It also meant that other useful, albeit not admissible, information was frequently not collected. Such information includes that which might be relevant in deciding whether to accept guilty pleas to lesser charges, that might affect sentence, or which indicates vulnerability or intimidation (factors which are now especially relevant for pre-trial and trial processes in the light of *Speaking Up for Justice*[8] and the Youth Justice and Criminal Evidence Act 1999).[9] Communication from victims to courts, and from courts to victims, was obstructed, leaving victims ignorant about what was happening in 'their' cases.

Explaining why this situation came about is beyond the scope of this chapter. But a word is needed on how it came to be allowed in legal terms. Under the common law 'expediency' approach (as distinguished from the Civil Law 'legality'

---

[6]   See generally, D Hay and F Snyder (eds), *Policing and Prosecution in Britain, 1750–1850* (Oxford University Press, Oxford, 1989).

[7]   H Fenwick, 'Charge Bargaining and Sentence Discount: The Victim's Perspective' (1997) 5 *International Review of Victimology* 23.

[8]   Home Office, *Report of the Interdepartmental Working Group on the Treatment of Vulnerable and Intimidated Witnesses in the Criminal Justice System* (Home Office, London, 1998).

[9]   Discussed in L Ellison, 'The Mosaic Art?' (2001) 21 *Legal Studies* 353.

approach common in Europe)[10] no crimes *need* to be investigated or prosecuted but anyone may investigate or prosecute. Victims can still take out private prosecutions if they wish (and if they can afford it) and occasionally they do. In theory, the police and victims are in the same legal position—they may prosecute, but need not, and have no particular prosecution powers (although the police do of course have extensive investigative powers denied to ordinary citizens which greatly facilitate prosecution).

Thus the police and Crown Prosecution Service do not prosecute 'for' the victim, but rather prosecute for the State. Offences are, again in theory, offences against society (not against the victim) and the consequence of conviction is punishment, not compensation (although again the situation in reality is not this straightforward). There is no legal requirement that the prosecution take any particular heed of the wishes or interests of victims, receive information from victims, or provide information to victims. Victims are simply citizens who may or may not be used as witnesses, which is again a matter wholly for the prosecution.

. . . and Re-Discovered

We might date the re-discovery of the victim to the rise of the new victimology which, in the 1970s, revealed that most crime known to the police was made known to them by victims. Indeed, much of the evidence on which arrest and prosecution rests comes directly from victims. An apparent paradox emerged: some criminologists argued that the 'expediency' system gave the police so much discretion on how to enforce the law that criminal justice processes were primarily driven by policing ideologies.[11] But victimologist-criminologists argued that policing was mainly shaped *by the public*[12] because the police are so dependent on victim-witness information.

In reality there is no paradox, because police discretion enables the police to use the information they choose in the ways they choose. Information from the public, in other words, is often a crucial starting point but it is a limited influence on the eventual shape and content of the 'official' offender population.[13] Nonetheless, at least one crucial insight from the 'policing by the public' school remains valid. That is, without co-operation from the public, and a willingness to be involved in criminal justice processes, much information would be denied the police and many witnesses would not be forthcoming. An unhappy public, and unhappy victims in particular, would seriously reduce the effectiveness of the criminal justice system. This, as we shall see, is a powerful motivating factor behind victim initiatives.

---

[10] Discussed in more detail in A Sanders and R Young, *Criminal Justice*, 2nd edn (Butterworths, London, 2000) ch 6.

[11] Eg S Box, *Deviance, Reality and Society* (Holt, Rinehart &Winston, London, 1971) ch 6.

[12] The title of a book by J Shapland and J Vagg, *Policing by the Public* (Routledge, London,1988)

[13] M McConville, A Sanders and R Leng, *The Case for the Prosecution* (Routledge, London, 1991) ch 2.

In the 1980s at least three developments created pressure on governments to establish accessible ways in which victims could be heard and could secure information about 'their' cases. First there was research of the kind referred to above. Second, the many victim initiatives being developed in America were becoming known about outside America.[14] Third, in 1985 both the UN and the Council of Europe published standards for the treatment of victims, although these are vague and minimal.[15] They have now been built upon by the publication in 1999 by the UN of a 'Handbook on Justice for Victims' and, in 2001, by an EU Framework Decision that is binding on all EU members.[16] This explicitly does not require that victims be treated as parties to prosecutions. However it does require, among other things, that legal systems treat victims with respect for their dignity (Article 2), privacy and safety (Articles 8 and 15), that they 'safeguard the possibility for victims to be heard during proceedings and to supply evidence' (Article 3) and provide information concerning their case, protection, support and so forth (Article 4), and that they:

> minimise as far as possible communication difficulties as regards their understanding of, or involvement in, the relevant steps of the criminal proceedings in question. (Article 5)

It also specifically mentions special treatment to 'level the playing field' for vulnerable victims (Articles 3 and 8 (4)).

Over the last decade or so, the victims' rights movement has grown in influence and visibility in England and Wales and internationally. This was reflected in the defendant-oriented pressure group JUSTICE writing a report supportive of all the developments in victim policy of the 1990s,[17] and in successive versions of the Victims' Charter. The first edition of this was in 1990, the second was in 1996 and at the time of writing (October 2001) a third is in preparation. The formal position of victims remains unchanged, in that they are not parties to proceedings and have no enforceable rights in relation to prosecution and subsequent decisions.[18]

---

[14] For a good survey of US initiatives, see L Sebba, *Third Parties: Victims and the Criminal Justice System* (Ohio State University Press, Columbus Ohio, 1996). For a British discussion of one type of initiative see A Ashworth, 'Victim Impact Statements and Sentencing' [1993] *Criminal Law Review* 498.

[15] United Nations, *Declaration of Basic Principles of Justice for Victims of Crime and Abuse of Power* (United Nations, Geneva, 1985) available from <http://www.unhchr.ch/>; Council of Europe, European Committee on Crime Problems, *The Position of the Victim in the Framework of Criminal Law and Procedure* (Office for Official Publications of the European Communities, Luxembourg, 1985) available from <http://cm.coe.int/ta/rec/1985/85r11.htm>. These declarations are briefly assessed in A Sanders, *Taking Account of Victims in the Criminal Justice System: A Review of the Literature* (Scottish Office, Edinburgh, 1999).

[16] EU Council of Justice and Home Affairs Ministers, *Standing of Victims in Criminal Proceedings* (Office for Official Publications of the European Communities, Luxembourg, March 2001). The EU's PHARE project requires 'candidate' countries to satisfy many criteria before entry is granted, one of which is compliance with the Framework Decision.

[17] JUSTICE, *Victims in Criminal Justice* (JUSTICE, London, 1998).

[18] H Fenwick, 'Procedural "Rights" of Victims of Crime' (1997) 60 *Modern Law Review* 317. Despite this, victims have been increasingly successful in judicial reviews of prosecution decisions. Technically this is not because their rights as victims have been violated (as they have none) but because

But the administrative response of the criminal justice system to victims has changed greatly.[19]

The Charters set out the 'responsibilities' of criminal justice agencies and what victims, correspondingly, are entitled to expect. Naturally, this is now giving rise to court challenges when these expectations have not been met. So far, the courts have resisted the plea to make Charter 'responsibilities' and 'expectations' legally enforceable.[20] In a Review of the Charter the Home Office raises the question of whether victims should have enforceable rights. It suggests a compromise: that 'guiding principles' (similar to those of the EU Framework decision listed earlier) be put on a legislative basis, thus creating 'headline rights for victims'; but that, 'Because of the evolving nature of the services provided' there should be no specific legislative rights.[21] Victims would still have to rely on complaints procedures, together with a newly created Victims' Ombudsman. The document seeks comments on these proposals but, at the time of writing, no concrete plans have been published.

AN INTEGRATED APPROACH TO CRIMINAL JUSTICE

Due Process and Crime Control

We have seen that until the 1970s it was easy for criminologists not only to ignore victims but to argue that this is precisely what criminologists and criminal justice systems ought to be doing. The investigation, prosecution, adjudication and sentencing of alleged offenders were matters for officials alone. The main lines of argument and conflict in criminal justice could be seen, therefore, schematically, as between the accused and the State. The analytical issue, as famously encapsulated by Packer in 1968, was whether the system was loaded primarily in favour of the accused, in which case it operated according to 'due process' norms; or whether it was loaded primarily in favour of the State, in which case it operated according to 'crime control' norms.[22] The normative issue was which way it *ought* to be loaded. The question of whether it was, or ought to be, loaded primarily in favour of *victims* did not arise at that time. When, later, it did arise, it was generally assumed that crime control systems favoured victims, although as I indicated earlier, this assumption would often be wrong.

---

prosecution policies have not been applied correctly or consistently. But the *effect* of these decisions is increasingly to force prosecutors to take account of victims.

[19] For discussion see H Reeves, 'The New Status of Victims in the UK: Opportunities and Threats' in A Crawford and J Goodey (eds), *Integrating a Victim Perspective Within Criminal Justice* (Ashgate, Aldershot, 2000); Sanders, *Taking Account of Victims*, n 15 above.

[20] Eg, *R v DPP ex p C*, discussed at text accompanying n 73 below, and in A Sanders and R Young, 'Discontinuances, The Rights of Victims and the Remedy of Freedom', *New Law Journal*, 19 January 2001.

[21] Home Office, *Review of the Victim's Charter*, n 5 above, 8.

[22] H Packer, *Limits of the Criminal Sanction* (Stanford University Press, Stanford Cal, 1968).

There are victim-oriented initiatives (which Ashworth would see as fulfilling 'service rights'[23]) that are compatible with both crime control and due process systems, such as victim support outside court, witness service support within court, and special measures for vulnerable and intimidated witnesses. Giving victims information about their cases is another example, to be discussed later. But initiatives that give victims a role in decision-making ('procedural rights') are largely incompatible with both due process and crime control approaches. For if victims wish, for example, not to prosecute where the evidence is strong or to impose little punishment for serious offences, crime control norms are undermined; conversely, if victims wish, for example, to prosecute where the evidence is weak or to impose harsh punishments when the crimes are minor or the mitigation is powerful, due process norms are undermined. If victims have a role in decision-making it is to enable their individual experiences to influence outcomes. However, the result of this is that similarly situated offenders, committing similar crimes, are not treated alike, which in itself offends due process norms. Thus, because he adopts a human rights perspective (basically a normative defence of the due process approach), Ashworth opposes procedural rights for victims, arguing that service rights can provide victims with all they legitimately require from the system.[24]

Ashworth's *normative* case against procedural rights and in favour of service rights has proved influential in academic debates, although it has recently been challenged by myself and colleagues, primarily because the service/procedural rights distinction does not hold up in practice.[25] But the crime control and due process models (and, therefore, Ashworth's human rights-based approach) are certainly no longer adequate *analytically*. For the fact is that in England and Wales, as in other common law jurisdictions and parts of the UK, victims do now have procedural rights (to be discussed in the next section), and these are likely to increase rather than to decrease. These developments must be understood, and not dismissed as superficial inconveniences that have no impact on, and are not integral to, the fundamental process.[26]

[23] Ashworth, 'Victim Impact Statements and Sentencing', n 14 above.

[24] A Ashworth, *The Criminal Process*, 2nd edn (Oxford University Press, Oxford, 1998) 33–37. Also see his 'Victims' Rights, Defendants' Rights and Criminal Procedure' in A Crawford and J Goodey (eds), *Integrating a Victim Perspective Within Criminal Justice* (Ashgate, Aldershot, 2000). For the argument that Ashworth's normative perspective is due process-based see Sanders and Young, *Criminal Justice*, n 10 above, ch 1.

[25] A Sanders, C Hoyle, R Morgan and E Cape, 'Victim Impact Statements: Don't Work, Can't Work' [2001] *Criminal Law Review* 447.

[26] For a sociological argument that the new victim policies are at the centre of late-modern penal policy, see D Garland, *The Culture of Control* (Oxford University Press, Oxford, 2001) ch 1. For a similar view, see K Roach, *Due Process and Victim's Rights* (University of Toronto Press, Toronto, 1999) ch 1.

The Victim-Rights Approach

If the crime control and due process models no longer encapsulate reality, what about a victim-rights approach? Using the purest form of this approach, victims would determine all decisions. Vengeful (and falsely accusing) victims would be able to insist on prosecution when there was *no* evidence, and would be able to insist on wildly disproportionate sentences. A human rights back-stop would be required if only to comply with our international obligations, but a backstop would, by definition, provide only minimal protection. Disparity—and consequent discrimination and unfairness—would be rife. Not only does this pure form fail to correspond with reality, but I am not aware of anyone who advocates it.

When victim-rights approaches are advocated, it is always in combination with other approaches. Cavadino and Dignan, for example, advocate this approach only within the context of a (yet-to-be-created) restorative justice-based system. Even then, they advocate giving the State the right of veto over prosecution decisions and the right to set desert-based maxima and minima for punishment.[27] They clearly lack confidence in a system where victims would have a profound influence. This is because defendants have human rights too, and giving victims free rein would jeopardise those rights. In similar vein, Roach advocates a 'non-punitive model of victims' rights' that would be based around principles of restorative justice and crime prevention. Rather than specify a safety net along the lines of that proposed by Cavadino and Dignan, Roach simply expresses the belief that due process rights for defendants would be respected in a non-punitive system.[28]

In another example, the approach taken by Beloof is less sophisticated than that of Cavadino and Dignan, but he does try to deal with the problem as presented in the system that currently operates.[29] His victim-rights approach (or, to use his term, victim participation model) is designed 'to ensure that the interest of the individual victim in the case is promoted'.[30] But, as he also acknowledges, 'A core interest of the victim is that the truth be revealed and an appropriate disposition reached'.[31] He recognises that the interests or desires of victims, if acted upon, can undermine due process values of truth and fairness, crime control values of efficiency, and the state's interest in many cases in prosecuting (or not prosecuting) regardless of the victim's wish. He therefore advocates a 'three

---

[27] M Cavadino and J Dignan, 'Reparation, Retribution and Rights' (1997) 4 *International Review of Victimology* 233. Interestingly, they do not discuss what rights victims should have in the non-restorative justice system that currently predominates in England and Wales and is likely to continue to do so for the foreseeable future.

[28] Roach, *Due Process and Victim's Rights*, n 26 above, ch 1.

[29] D Beloof, 'The Third Model of Criminal Process: The Victim Participation Model' (1999) 2 *Utah Law Review* 289.

[30] *Ibid*, 296.

[31] *Ibid*.

model' approach to understanding criminal justice, as compared with Packer's 'two model' approach.

Just as Packer's approach presents irreconcilable conflicts between crime control norms that favour conviction at the expense of the rights of suspects, and defendants and due process norms that favour the rights of suspects and defendants at the expense of convictions, so does Beloof's. But Beloof's approach presents, in addition, conflicts between the rights of victims and those of suspects and defendants on the one hand, and between the rights of victims and the demands of crime control on the other. What Beloof gives us is, essentially, a list of features of the criminal justice system—actual and desirable. When some of those features conflict with others he gives us no basis on which to understand how some are prioritised over others, nor how prioritisation *should* take place. Beloof takes an analytical model that sets out to illuminate irreconcilable value conflicts and adds to it a further set of irreconcilable elements.

We can see that the victim-rights approach, whether used alone or in combination with other approaches, is normatively unsatisfactory. Although Beloof's 'three model' approach appears to be descriptively accurate, it is analytically untidy. The problem at this level is two-fold. First, it is so hopelessly vague, because of all the irreconcilable conflicts already referred to, that it could hardly fail to be accurate. In other words, in any given system where victims are, for example, consulted over whether to prosecute, the 'three model' approach fails to specify whose views predominate when victims and prosecutors disagree. Different systems which give different priorities to the views of victims on this point would reach different results yet still be examples of the 'three model' approach. Second, this approach accepts official rhetoric at face value. If, as we shall see, most victim-based measures actually do little to meet the wishes or interests of victims, is it realistic to state that these measures are genuinely intended to meet these explicit purposes? What we need is an approach with more explanatory power, one that can better explain *why* the criminal justice system has developed a range of apparently victim-based measures which complement existing features of the system yet which largely fail to achieve their stated purposes.

Victim Policy at the Centre of Social Exclusion

Let us look at this topic from a different starting point. We drew attention earlier to some commonplaces of modern criminology, that 'victims' and offenders' cannot and should not be sharply differentiated, and that neither 'master status' is applicable to the majority of people, who sometimes offend or who sometimes are victims. But no-one listening to mainstream politicians or reading the popular media would think this. Both criminals and victims can therefore be seen as *social* categories. Foucault argues that power and knowledge are intimately related. Specifically, in this context, the increasing knowledge about crime produced by criminologists   facilitated the transformation of 'popular illegalities' in the eighteenth and nineteenth centuries into what we now think of as 'crime'.[32]

The reasons for this transformation are too complex to discuss here, but Foucault's main argument is that the objective was not so much to control 'criminals' better as to *differentiate* them from 'normal' people and to *exclude* them from normal society. The prison, which only came to be used as a regular punishment in the early to mid nineteenth century, was originally the main mechanism for this segregation, but in recent years forms of community punishment have been devised which continue to exclude and differentiate, examples of which are the use of electronic tagging, curfews and so forth. By these processes the majority of the working classes came to disapprove of what were once 'normal' (or quasi-normal or acceptable) activities and thus be less inclined to engage in these activities.[33] These processes also facilitate the distinction between 'real' crime and 'regulatory' offences (and other offences that are conventionally regarded as not serious) to which I drew attention earlier; there being therefore, no attempt to discourage the commission of these 'regulatory' offences. We need fear 'real' crime but not 'regulatory' crime because only 'real' crime is committed by 'real' criminals. A penal policy is created, in tandem with a legitimising criminology which Garland terms a 'criminology of the other'; 'of the threatening outcast, the fearsome stranger, the excluded and the embittered.'[34]

This helps to explain why the less effective—in the conventional rehabilitational or (individual) deterrent sense—prison and community penalties are, the more they are used.[35] Rehabilitation and deterrence may well have been among the original objectives of proponents of these measures and, to a small extent, are still. But if these had remained the primary objectives of punishment, something different would have been devised long ago, as high reconviction rates alone indicate how poorly most penal measures 'work' in the conventional senses of that term. At the risk of veering into functionalism, we could even say that high reconviction rates demonstrate (in an excluding society) the need for, and righteousness of, harsh penalties, erosion of civil liberties for presumed-offenders, differentiation and exclusion.

Garland argues that in late-modern society (that is, America and the UK from the late 1970s) the legitimacy of penal-welfarism became fatally undermined because of a combination of socio-economic and political change, the evident failure of the criminal justice system to control crime, and academic assaults from several directions. The result is a set of penal policies that focus on the

---

[32] M Foucault, *Discipline and Punish* (Penguin, London, 1977); E Thompson, *Whigs and Hunters* (Penguin, London, 1975).
[33] D Melossi, 'Changing Representations of the Criminal' in D Garland and R Sparks (eds), *Criminology and Social Theory* (Oxford University Press, Oxford, 2000).
[34] D Garland, 'The Limits of the Sovereign State' (1996) 36 *British Journal of Criminology* 445, 462.
[35] This is an over-simplification. For a speculative attempt to 'map' oscillations in the use of such measures, see Melossi, 'Changing Representations of the Criminal', n 33 above.

consequences of crime rather than its social causes. These policies conflict and converge as the State seeks to both adapt to its failure (by, for example, seeking crime prevention partnerships and by doing little about less serious offences) and deny it. Denial includes what Garland calls policies of 'punitive segregation' for more serious offences, such as 'three strikes and you're out' and the British equivalents.[36] This gives 'public opinion' the impression that 'something is being done'.[37] Garland argues that the new victim policy is central to 'punitive segregation', for at 'the centre of contemporary penal discourse is (a political projection of) the individual victim'.[38] Because the State can do little about crime, it turns its attention to the consequences of crime—victims in particular. It seeks to show that 'something is being done' for victims by arguing that this is a major objective of punitive segregation, so that even if punitive segregation fails in crime-reduction terms it can be claimed as a success in giving victims what they want (that is, what political projections of them are said to want).[39]

And so we have to acknowledge that official rhetoric and deep, underlying purposes diverge to a greater or lesser extent. Referring to the eighteenth century penal reforms that ushered in the era of retributive punishment, Foucault argued that,

> What was emerging no doubt was not so much a new respect for the humanity of the condemned . . . as a tendency towards a more finely tuned justice, towards a closer penal mapping of the social body.[40]

In other words, lying underneath the then-new eighteenth century penality was a redistribution of punitive power. By analogy, it may be that, lying underneath the even newer victims-rights agenda of 'punitive segregation' is another redistribution of punitive power. Why need we adopt such a cynical explanation for victims' rights when it may simply be that the role of victims' rights is to recognise the dignity, and reduce the secondary victimisation, of victims? The latter explanation, again, is doubtless partially true and may originally have been the main motivation of reformers. But we know from the US's experience how such movements can be hi-jacked.[41] Further we shall see that the plain fact is that victims' rights do not work *for victims*. If that were their objective they would have been radically reformulated along the lines, for example, set out in the final part of this section. At the least, adequate resources would have been provided; currently, probation

---

[36] See the Crime (Sentences) Act 1997. Measures adopted by the Labour government from this Conservative legislation include the automatic life sentence for second offences of severe violence, and minimum sentences for repeated drugs and domestic burglary offences.

[37] Garland, *The Culture of Control*, n 26 above, 135.

[38] *Ibid*, 144.

[39] Thus, for example, at a victims conference in 1997 a Home Office official listed a wide range of measures which, he claimed, were victim-based. These included the Crime (Sentences) Act, none of the measures in which had been sought by victims' groups.

[40] M Foucault, *Discipline and Punish*, n 32 above, 78.

[41] R Elias, *Victims Still: The Political Manipulation of Crime Victims* (Sage, Newbury Park Cal, 1993).

services, for example, have to rob Peter the offender to pay for services for Paul the victim.[42]

Why do I call this approach 'exclusionary'? At the most general level, the 'criminology of the other' requires policies of 'punitive segregation' to separate 'us' from 'them' ('criminals'). Policies that parade victims as the embodiments of 'us' cast 'them' out even further. Moreover, as Garland observes, as part of the 'something is being done about crime' approach, offenders' rights are eroded: 'A zero-sum policy game is assumed wherein the offender's gain is the victim's loss, and being "for" victims automatically means being tough on offenders'.[43] This is crime control ideology in the guise of Beloof's victim-participation model. Or, as Roach puts it, drawing on the similar Canadian experience, 'Victim's rights became the new rights-bearing face of crime control.'[44] But exclusionary policies do not only cast out criminals, both literally and in the sense of no longer 'deserving' human rights, they also exclude *victims*. For as Garland notes, though he does not pursue the point, it is not the interests and voices of individual victims or even victims' groups that are sought in these new policies, but those of a political projection of victims. It is for this reason that, in the UK, Victim Support has been careful not to join in the zero-sum game, and has not sought participatory rights of a decision-making kind. None of this has prevented the government announcing ever-more punitive policies in the name of victims.

A Socially Inclusive Approach to Victim Policy

Socially inclusive approaches rest normatively on a 'criminology of the self', which sees 'criminals' as both like the rest of 'us' and like offenders who are not usually classed as criminals. This is in contrast to the exclusionary 'criminology of the other'. Inclusive approaches reject the zero-sum game, which penal-welfarism also played by focusing on criminals at the expense of victims, and argue that the interests of victims and offenders can and should be pursued together. Rather than the idealised interests and views of victims being used to legitimate punitive segregation, the *actual* interests and views of individual victims would be used to assist in reintegration—of both victims and offenders—to the extent that is possible and necessary.

This does not describe any system in the present or past of which I am aware. Shapland, for example, who argues for 'criminal justice as a public service' in terms similar to those used above, argues that neither victims nor offenders are

---

[42] B Williams, 'The Victim's Charter: Citizens as Consumers of Criminal Justice Services' (1999) 38 *Howard Journal of Criminal Justice* 384.
[43] Garland, *The Culture of Control*, n 26 above, 11. Examples of such rights are those of silence, bail and jury trial—see, for instance, the Criminal Justice and Public Order Act 1994.
[44] Roach, *Due Process and Victim's Rights*, n 26 above, 32.

central to the concerns of criminal justice.[45] Some restorative justice approaches, however, are based on these principles and now occupy a space (albeit usually marginal) in most modern penal systems. The main problem with restorative justice is that it tends to assume that the opinions, rights and interests of victims and offenders are always reconcilable. This is as untenable as the view that one need always be traded off against the other. In many cases restorative justice schemes trample, to a greater or lesser extent, on the interests of both victims and offenders.[46] As Young argues, restorative justice advocates must recognise that restorative justice cannot always 'deliver' what victims want, and that inclusivity requires that restoration be prioritised.[47]

None of the other approaches that I have examined so far in this section provide a way of solving these conflicts of interest. Richard Young and I attempt to do so in our 'freedom model'. We argue that the essence of due process is to protect the freedom of suspects and offenders, and the essence of crime control (and, we could add victim-participation models) is to protect the freedom of victims, past and future. Given the earlier argument that 'victims' and 'suspects/offenders' are not discrete groups and that they overlap, one group should not be prioritised over the other.[48]

Thus criminal justice policy at every level should aim to maximise the totality of freedom. Giving effect to the *opinion* of a victim about, say, the severity of punishment does not increase the freedom of the victim as much as it reduces that of the offender; thus such opinions should not be sought by the criminal justice system. Informing victims of prosecution decisions and the reasons for them, on the other hand, does reduce secondary victimisation and thus increases the freedom of victims without reducing the freedom of suspects. Therefore, this type of victim-right should be provided. Insofar as restorative justice helps victims to 'buy in' to non-punitive constructive dispositions, both secondary victimisation and punitiveness can be reduced, increasing the freedom of both victim and offender.[49] The aim of victim participation within an inclusionary approach is to give effect to the views of victims where this increases the overall effectiveness of

---

[45] J Shapland, 'Victims in Criminal Justice: Creating Responsible Criminal Justice Agencies' in A Crawford and J Goodey (eds), *Integrating a Victim Perspective Within Criminal Justice* (Ashgate, Aldershot, 2000). Note that she expresses great surprise at what she sees, and does not use the terms 'inclusionary' or 'exclusionary'.

[46] For examples drawn from the burgeoning critical literature on restorative justice, see the chapters by Richard Young, Lode Walgrave, and Allison Morris and Gabrielle Maxwell in A Crawford and J Goodey (eds), *Integrating a Victim Perspective Within Criminal Justice* (Ashgate, Aldershot, 2000). More fundamental critiques are offered by R Delgado, 'Goodbye to Hammurabi: Analysing the Atavistic Appeal of Restorative Justice' (2000) 52 *Stanford Law Review* 751 and K Daly, 'Restorative Justice in Diverse and Unequal Societies' (1999) 17 *Law in Context* 167.

[47] R Young, 'Just Cops Doing "Shameful" Business?: Police-Led Restorative Justice and the Lessons of Research' in A Morris and G Maxwell, *Restorative Justice for Juveniles: Conferencing, Mediation and Circles* (Hart Publishing, Oxford, 2001) 198.

[48] Sanders and Young, *Criminal Justice*, n 10 above, chs 1and 12.

[49] Research indicates relatively high victim satisfaction levels in restorative justice schemes. See, for example, T Marshall, *Restorative Justice: An Overview* (Home Office, London, 1999).

criminal justice. Also, where applicable, it would aim to help victims to understand why their views are not given effect. This would be in order to reduce secondary victimisation by increasing victim satisfaction with the system and to reduce the exclusionary 'us' and 'them' gap. As we shall see in the final section, this approach need not be confined to restorative justice but can be seen in inquisitorial systems too.

THE 'RIGHTS' OF VICTIMS IN RELATION TO 'THEIR' CASES

Initial Law Enforcement Decisions

Victims have, for many years, been involved in initial law enforcement decisions, but in disparate ways in different contexts. Many offences only come to the attention of law enforcement agencies because members of the public (usually victims) report the crime. These decisions are reached by victims independently of law enforcement policies and practices only in a formal sense. In reality, decisions whether or not to report are influenced by what victims think will happen next. Thus, for many years, victims of sexual and domestic violence, for example, under-reported to a greater extent than did victims of other serious crime because many believed (with good cause) that the police would take little or no action. Over the last ten years the policies and practices of the police and Crown Prosecution Service have greatly changed. There is now a 'pro-charge' policy for domestic violence[50] and although, in this respect as in many others, practice has failed fully to keep up with policy change, domestic violence policy shifts in the early 1990s did bring about some change.[51] There is therefore good reason to think that there is now less under-reporting of sexual and domestic violence than there was ten years ago.

In relation to most police-enforced offences, anyone may, and no-one must, invoke the criminal process. So if the police do not wish to investigate, arrest and/or prosecute, then, in principle, the victim may do so. In reality, the police have far greater powers of investigation and arrest than do other people, and investigation and prosecution is very costly. Citizens' arrests and private prosecutions are therefore very rare.[52] As the *Stephen Lawrence* case illustrates, if the police do not prosecute, a private prosecution will nearly always fail. This is not just

---

[50] *Domestic Violence: Revised Circular to the Police*, Home Office Circular 19/2000.
[51] C Hoyle, *Negotiating Domestic Violence* (Clarendon Press, Oxford, 1998). In a follow up study of one police force the pro-arrest, pro-charge policy was not being fully implemented by officers. Indeed the arrest rate had not changed over the period from 1993 to 1996, although the charge rate was higher than it was previously. C Hoyle and A Sanders (Unpublished Report to the Nuffield Foundation, 1998).
[52] In the late 1970s private prosecutions constituted about 4% of all non-police prosecutions—ie considerably less than 1% of all prosecutions: K Lidstone, R Hogg and F Sutcliffe, *Prosecutions by Private Individuals and Non-Police Agencies* (HMSO, London, 1981). An informed guess suggests that the situation remains similar (private communication with Gary Slapper, October 2001).

because the police and Crown Prosecution Service are right in their judgements, but also because there is little that private individuals can do that State agencies will not have already considered and the initial investigation usually 'contaminates' anything that follows.[53] In relation to offences enforced by most other agencies, arrest is not possible (proceedings are usually by way of summons) and prosecution powers are vested exclusively in the agency concerned.

Since victims of all crimes are almost entirely reliant on law enforcement agencies in relation to initial decisions, agencies have developed their own policies in relation to different types of crime. Agencies take no formal action in relation to many more suspected offences than those where they investigate and/or arrest, let alone prosecute. Their decisions are based in part on strength of evidence and in part on 'public interest' considerations. For the last 25 years or so the latter have been set out in various government policy documents that are periodically revised to change the emphasis but not the fundamental elements.[54] Without exception, public interest considerations include: seriousness of offence (that is, is it worth prosecuting?); seriousness of offender (serious or persistent offenders are worth prosecuting even if the offence in question is trivial, and offenders with otherwise good characters or whose circumstances are particularly mitigating might be treated generously even if the offence is serious); and the interests and views of the victim.

The interests and views of victims are sought by the police through consultation and by a usually cursory assessment made by the investigating officer. If a victim expresses a clear view that a suspect should be prosecuted, the police have to balance this view against, first, what is thought to be best for the victim; and second, offence- and offender-seriousness. This is why so many domestic and sexual violence allegations used not to be investigated or result in arrest or prosecution. In addition to doubts about evidential sufficiency, these offences and/or the offenders were often thought to be non-serious. Now that views of seriousness have changed, even when victims express *anti*-prosecution views, and even when prosecution may *not* be in the interests of the victims of domestic violence, prosecution is supposed to take place anyway.[55]

Regarding crimes handled by agencies other than the police (non-police crimes), it seems that victims are rarely consulted. And, if they are, their views rarely, if ever, outweigh assessments of offence and offender seriousness by the enforcement agencies.[56] The result is that, whereas the police *usually* prosecute where they have arrested and have sufficient evidence (probably usually in accord

[53] W Macpherson, *The Stephen Lawrence Inquiry* Cm 4262–I (The Stationery Office, London, 1999).
[54] They include the Home Office's caution guidelines and the Code for Crown Prosecutors. Formally, they apply only to prosecution decisions, but they equally apply, loosely, to earlier decisions.
[55] Home Office Circular 19/2000, n 50 above. For discussion of this policy prior to the issue of the Circular, see C Hoyle and A Sanders, 'Police Response to Domestic Violence: From Victim Choice to Victim Empowerment' (2000) 40 *British Journal of Criminology* 14.
[56] On unlawful eviction, for example, see D Cowan and A Marsh, 'There's Regulatory Crime and then there's Landlord Crime: from "Rachmanites" to "Partners"' (2001) 64 *Modern Law Review* 831.

with the views of victims, although this is speculative), other agencies *rarely* prosecute, even in the minority of crimes where they investigate and secure sufficient evidence (probably not in accord with the views of victims, although this is even more speculative). In the Piper Alpha North Sea oil disaster in the 1980s, for example, 167 people died through negligence and error (which amount to offences under the Health and Safety Act 1974), yet no prosecutions ensued.[57] Fraud is rather more complicated, and cannot be dealt with in this short chapter. But the example of the BCCI bank fraud of the early 1990s illustrates that, again, victim interests are rarely considered and are never allowed to override more powerful interests (in that case, those of creditors).[58] Police and non-police agencies all have their own different enforcement policies, of which prosecution policies are a part. Clashes between the interests of crime control, those of victims, and those of other parties are therefore plain to see, illustrating the problem with Beloof's descriptive approach.

Much has been written as to why the different types of agency differ so greatly. Crudely, and with significant exceptions, non-police agencies adopt a 'compliance' approach that seeks to encourage law-adherence through education and persuasion. This is 'inclusionary' in the sense that offenders are drawn into the process of their own law enforcement, and retributive/deterrent prosecution processes are used only as last resorts for the most recalcitrant and serious offenders. Although prosecution, as usually practised by the police, is not necessarily exclusionary, it will tend to be more so than the compliance approach. Although the 'compliance' approach is defended on the grounds of efficiency and effectiveness, it is by no means clear that it is either, and there is no reason why, insofar as it does work, it should not work equally well for police-enforced crime.[59] Thus the policies of the two types of agency are largely inconsistent with each other for no good reason: non-police crimes are treated in a partially inclusionary way (it is partial because it excludes victims from the decision making process) and police crimes are treated in ways that have less potential for inclusionary practices.

Communication of Decisions to Victims

As noted earlier, the provision of information is a 'service' right and therefore unobjectionable in principle. This does not prevent it being problematic in practice. The Victims' Charter states that eligible victims—which does not include

---

[57] For general discussion see G Slapper, *Blood in the Bank* (Ashgate, Aldershot, 1999).
[58] Spalek, 'Regulation, White Collar Crime', n 4 above.
[59] G Slapper and S Tombs, *Corporate Crime* (Longman, Harlow, 1999). Arguably the 'compliance' approach is not intended to 'work', for it can be viewed more as about accommodating crime than about educating offenders out of it. Regulatory agencies that deal with poor people behave far more like the police. For discussion see Sanders and Young, *Criminal Justice*, n 10 above, ch 6. However, this argument need not be resolved for the purposes of this paper.

victims of offences prosecuted by non-police agencies—should be told when (if) suspects are caught and then whether the suspects are to be prosecuted. If they are to be, victims should be asked if they want further information on the case, namely the date of trial, final result, and any decisions to drop or substantially reduce charges (when there is plea bargaining, in lay terms). In early pilot projects this information was provided in letters sent by the police who acted as a 'One Stop Shop' (OSS). When violent or sexual offenders are sentenced to long periods of imprisonment (in practice, four years or more), the probation service offers to provide information about release dates. Comparison of these two information-provision services is instructive.

OSS was evaluated, by myself and my colleagues,when it was piloted in 1997. Nearly half of all eligible victims said that they did want to be kept informed in 'their' cases, but many of these expressed dissatisfaction after their cases had finished, and around 20 per cent found the information they had been given not useful at all. This was largely because they had not been told enough and had not been given the opportunity to discuss the decision that had been made. This is an endemic problem in a scheme where one agency (the police) informs victims of decisions that have been made by other agencies (the Crown Prosecution Service and the courts) and where the police are usually unaware of the reasons for those decisions. For some victims expectations had been raised, whether realistically or not, probably leaving them more dissatisfied than they would have been had they been given no information at all.[60] This is not surprising in the light of research (and common sense) showing that the receipt of 'bad news' is worse for many people than no news at all, unless that bad news is explained.[61]

In 2000–2001, a new initiative was piloted that aimed to address some of the problems of OSS. For the first time, the Crown Prosecution Service Code stated that 'It is important that a victim is told' about significant decisions.[62] Under the 'Direct Communication with Victims' initiative, prosecution lawyers inform victims of major developments in 'their' cases, such as discontinuance or substantial reduction of charges. Further, new guidelines issued in December 2000 state that in such cases the prosecutor should 'speak with the victim or the victim's family so that the position can be explained'.[63] It was originally envisaged that victims be informed by way of a formulaic letter referring to the 'evidential' and 'public interest' tests, but it was soon recognised that this would baffle most readers, dash their expectations of being better informed and, as with OSS, anger many of them.

---

[60] C Hoyle, E Cape, R Morgan and A Sanders, *Evaluation of the 'One Stop Shop' and Victim Statement Pilot Projects* (Home Office, London, 1998) summarised in C Hoyle, R Morgan and A Sanders, *The Victim's Charter: An Evaluation of Pilot Projects*, Home Office Research Findings No 107 (Home Office, London, 1999) and in Sanders *et al*, 'Victim Impact Statements', n 25 above.

[61] See discussion in H Fenwick 'Rights of Victims in the Criminal Justice System' [1995] *Criminal Law Review* 843 and in MacPherson, *The Stephen Lawrence Inquiry*, n 53 above.

[62] Code for Crown Prosecutors (2000) para 6.8.

[63] Both the CPS initiative and the new guidelines are discussed further in the section on 'Later Prosecution Decisions' below.

Consequently more detailed letters, which explain decisions by reference to the particular facts of the case, are now being piloted. Telephone conversations and meetings that would allow questions to be answered, processes clarified, and decisions to be discussed are also envisaged when victims request such interactions after reading the letter (subject to resource constraints and the training of prosecution staff). In the 2001–2002 fiscal year significant resources were made available to the Crown Prosecution Service specifically to advance this initiative.

Information on prisoners serving substantial prison sentences was provided in the form of one or more face-to-face meetings where parole and life licence processes are discussed and attempts are made to answer the questions of victims. Many of these questions range more widely than the mechanics of release decisions (they include, for example, the nature of the courses taken by prisoners, security classification in prison and so forth). Crawford and Enterkin found that, where victims expressed dissatisfaction, it was either because expectations about what they would find out had been wrongly raised (such as where the offender was being held) and/or because, in their particular cases, no satisfactory answers were given to their questions.[64] The service is variable in quality partly because it is provided by semi-professional mediators and volunteer Victim Support workers, supervised by probation officers. Some are better trained and more competent than others.[65] The elements of explanation and discussion in this initiative make it similar to the Crown Prosecution Service Direct Communication initiative. These are the elements which, when provided, are most appreciated by victims, both in the UK and in other jurisdictions.[66] Thus the new Crown Prosecution Service initiative is likely to be considerably more successful than was OSS.

The communication of information to victims is clearly improving in the sense that victims are increasingly being advised not only of decisions, but also of the reasons for those decisions. In other words, victims are helped to *understand* what is happening in their cases. This approach is consistent with the victims' rights model without infringing the principles of due process. While embodying elements of an inclusive approach, however, these developments are also exclusive in many ways. Information about prisoners is provided contemporaneously, but information about ongoing cases is usually provided after they reach a final disposal. This excludes victims, some of whom have further information to offer that could change the decision. Moreover, only prosecutors' decisions will be explained to victims. Court decisions, notably bail, verdict and sentence will still be the subject of OSS-style bald information.

---

[64] A Crawford and J Enterkin, *Victim Contact Work and the Probation Service* (CCJS Press, Leeds, 1999) ch 7.
[65] Different probation services have different service delivery models: H Nettleton, S Walklate and B Williams, *Probation Training with the Victim in Mind* (Keele University Press, Keele, 1997); Crawford and Enterkin, n 64 above, ch 4.
[66] For discussion of information-provision schemes in the Netherlands, see J Wemmers, 'Victims in the Dutch Criminal Justice System: The Effects of Treatment on Victims' Attitudes and Compliance' (1995) 3 *International Review of Victimology* 323.

More fundamentally, there is a limit to how much can be explained by letter or phone, or even in person, to someone who has not experienced the process in question. In other words, victims who do not participate in some way in decision making (and what I mean by this will be elaborated in further sections) are less likely than those who do participate to fully understand what happened and why. The lack of understanding that many victims have of the process, together with the (literal) exclusion of the victim from that process, exaggerates the distance between victims and offenders. During a review of the parole system in 2000–2001 the possibility of victims attending parole hearings was considered, but ultimately rejected.[67] Yet attendance (along with in-hearing explanation) would give victims insights that distanced explanations rarely provide. This is what happens in restorative justice-based conferences and some continental jurisdictions. The exclusion of victims, though less marked than was normal until recently, maintains the distance between victim and offender, and also maintains the 'us' and 'them' syndrome that is the hallmark of socially excluding practices. We will return to this in the concluding section of this chapter.

Later Prosecution Decisions

The freedom that law enforcement agencies have in deciding whether to prosecute is maintained in the later stages of prosecutions. Indeed, traditionally victims were not consulted about reductions in the number or seriousness of charges or even the complete termination of cases. This has changed in recent years.

Since 1986 the Crown Prosecution Service has prosecuted all police cases. The Code for Crown Prosecutors in 1992 explicitly required Crown Prosecutors to take account of the 'interests of the victim' (para 8) and: 'In some cases . . . to have regard' to the wishes of victims who decide that they do not want prosecutions to continue (para 8 (vii)). Consultation with victims who maintained a pro-prosecution view, or in cases where plea bargaining was contemplated, was neither encouraged nor envisaged. Yet consultation with the police, especially when discontinuance on public interest grounds was contemplated, was expected as a matter of routine practice (para 10). The version of the Code published in 2000 refers not only to the interests of victims, but also to 'any views expressed by the victim or the victim's family' (para 6.7), though the mechanism for securing these views is not specified. Although not stated directly, this part of the Code really applies to initial review decisions at the start of the prosecution, when the victims' interests and views are provided by the police and/or in victims' evidential statements.

During 2000 and 2001, the CPS began to pilot the 'Direct Communication with Victims' initiative discussed above, whereby prosecution lawyers were asked to inform victims of significant developments in 'their' cases. It was originally

---

[67] Home Office, *Review of Parole* (Unpublished, 2001).

envisaged that this would take the form of one-way communication only.[68] Neither the views of victims, nor the effects on them of the developments envisaged, were to be sought. At the time of writing this initiative has still not been fully implemented but it will have to take account of the *Attorney-General's Guidelines on the Acceptance of Pleas,* issued in December 2000.[69] They state that the prosecution should:

> speak with the victim or the victim's family so that the position can be explained and their views and interests can be taken into account as part of the decision making process. (para 5)

This brings decision-making in the latter stages of a case into line with initial decision-making by recommending that victims are 'not excluded from the decision making process', although the word 'consultation' is never used.[70]

The position of the victim in relation to plea bargaining and other major prosecution decisions has undoubtedly changed from what Fenwick rightly characterised only four years ago as a largely crime control position[71] to one more consistent with Beloof's victim rights model. Nevertheless, several problems remain. First, the new guidelines supplement the Code for Crown Prosecutors only in serious (that is, Crown Court) cases.[72] They do not apply, therefore, to non-police prosecutions or to cases tried in the Magistrates' courts. Victims in these instances remain as un-enfranchised at the end of the case as they are at the beginning.

Furthermore, what happens if a victim is not consulted? In *R v DPP ex parte C*[73] a teenage girl complained to the police that she had been sexually assaulted. Prosecutions were initiated but then (12 months after the original allegations) discontinued on evidential grounds. The victim was neither consulted nor informed about this, and sought judicial review of the decision to discontinue proceedings. This was refused because there was no duty to consult and no enforceable duty to inform her of the discontinuance. Although the Court of Appeal stressed that their decision related to the law in 1998 (when the alleged incidents occurred) there is no reason to think that the case would be decided differently now that the new Guidelines do require consultation.

If victims' 'rights' to consultation (and indeed information) were to become enforceable (a possibility which the unpredictability of the courts makes impossible to discount) what would be the consequences? We would move from the

---

[68] This statement was made in direct response to a question asked by the writer at a 'Direct Communication with Victims' inter-agency steering group meeting in July 2000.

[69] Available at <http://www.lslo.gov.uk>.

[70] Attorney-General's Press Release, 7 December 2000, accompanying the new Guidelines. The situation is now similar to that of most North American States. See Sebba, *Third Parties,* n 14 above, 195.

[71] H Fenwick, 'Charge Bargaining and Sentence Discount: The Victim's Perspective' (1997) 5 *International Review of Victimology* 23.

[72] Attorney-General's Press Release, 7 December 2000, accompanying the new Guidelines.

[73] Divisional Court, 10 March 2000 (Crown Office List): CO/1450/99.

current hollow 'rights' of victims to the blunt instrument of enforcement in court. This could result in victims being handed rights to make decisions. But victims making decisions, when their only role is that of 'aggrieved party', would fuel the 'us' and 'them' non-relationship and therefore social exclusion. An inclusive policy would seek to involve victims in the process, if they wished this (as Victim Support insists,[74] victims should not be burdened with decision-making responsibility as this could increase secondary victimisation). The aim would be to listen to victims' information and their views, but decision-making would be based on clear objective criteria derived from inclusive approaches such as the 'freedom' perspective.

Victim Impact Statements (VIS)

The 1996 Victims' Charter announced that victim impact statements (VIS) would be experimentally piloted for 'Charter cases' as they progressed through court, and permanently introduced for sexual offences and offences of serious violence after long-term imprisonment. There were two evaluations of the pilot projects. The first gauged the satisfaction of victims at the start of their cases and at the end. Most of the participants (77 per cent) were pleased that they participated at the start (only two per cent being displeased, the rest being neutral or not having a clear view), but only 57 per cent were pleased by the end (20 per cent were displeased).[75] Some victims did not say all that they had wanted to say, and for others the situation had changed after making their statements. The main reason for dissatisfaction was that many victims thought that their statements had been ignored.

The second evaluation examined the use of VIS by prosecutors and courts. Although it seems that few had actually been ignored, equally few had made any difference to prosecution decisions or to sentence. Some victims expected their VIS to make a conviction more likely. The lack of realism of some of these expectations is obvious to anyone who understands the system, but that is precisely the point: many victims do not understand the system, and the process of eliciting VIS does nothing to rectify this. Even where VIS could, in theory, make a difference (largely in sentencing), in reality they almost never did. This was because of a double bind in which, when victims told judges what they expected to hear they told judges nothing new, and when unexpected things were mentioned they had to be 'taken with a pinch of salt' in the absence of supporting evidence.[76] Neither victim dissatisfaction, nor its causes, are peculiar to the UK, or a result of the

---

[74] Reeves, 'The New Status of Victims in the UK', n 19 above.
[75] Hoyle *et al*, *Evaluation of the 'One Stop Shop'*, n 60 above.
[76] R Morgan and A Sanders, *The Uses of Victim Statements* (Home Office, London, 1999). This research, together with the first evaluation, is summarised in Home Office Research Findings No 107 (Home Office, London, 1999) and in Sanders *et al*, 'Victim Impact Statements' n 25 above.

experimental nature of VIS, as similar results have been found in, for example, America and Australia.[77]

The evaluation of VIS in relation to long-term prisoners by Crawford and Enterkin showed similarly raised, but unfulfilled, expectations. Sixty per cent of participating victims found receiving information to be more valuable, and more empowering, than VIS. Again, much of what victims say, or want to say, is deemed irrelevant. As one victim-liaison officer put it,

> When I come back [from interviewing a victim] I have a barrel full of concerns which are then sifted through and it becomes a thimble.[78]

Victims were upset that the reports appeared to be ignored and about the absence of feedback. Although Crawford and Enterkin found higher levels of satisfaction than did Hoyle *et al*, they still found 15 per cent to be dissatisfied. This is a significant minority, and it aggregates victims who were provided with information with those making VIS, the latter generally being more dissatisfied. Crawford and Enterkin also aggregate victim responses at all stages of their cases; one would expect, in the light of Hoyle *et al*'s findings, that dissatisfaction grew over the lifetime of the case.

For many victims, being asked to contribute, but then having their contribution ignored , is insulting. In the landmark case of *Thompson and Venables* (the murder of the toddler, James Bulger) the Lord Chief Justice had to decide whether a murder tariff should be the eight years set by the trial judge or the 15 years set by the Home Secretary. The Lord Chief Justice stated: 'I have found it of real value to have information as to the impact of the death on the family'.[79] He went on to summarise the traumatic effects of James Bulger's death. However, it is hard to see what value this information could have had, as the Lord Chief Justice deliberately set the prisoners' tariffs as low as possible, thus enabling their cases to be considered for release by the Parole Board immediately. The court's response to this point, provoked by the victim's father in his challenge to that decision, was that the victim's family had not been asked for its views on the tariff,[80] begging the question of what the point was of seeking the impact information. This is alluded to by the mother of James Bulger when, in another unprecedented decision, the victims' views *on risk* were sought by the Parole Board. She said:

> When I was told I could make a submission as to risk I thought at last someone was prepared to give proper weight to the concerns and the information that the family of the victim have . . . I hope you do not turn it into an empty gesture.

Like most VIS, that is exactly what it was, as the boys were ordered to be released immediately. Bitterness and resentment about the crime appears in such cases to

---

[77] Sebba, *Third Parties*, n 14 above; Sanders, *Taking Account of Victims*, n 15 above, ch 5.
[78] Crawford and Enterkin, n 64 above, 32.
[79] Divisional Court, 26 October 2000.
[80] Court of Appeal (Criminal Division) 16 February 2001.

be intensified as the process to which victims seek access denies them influence. It gives them a voice but not the dignity that attaches to being heard.

Morgan and Sanders commented that if VIS are to be continued, the Victims' Charter should be amended to make it clear that information from victims will *not* normally be taken into account by decision-makers. This was not entirely face-tious. After all, if the main aim of VIS is catharsis, why not be open about its lack of instrumental value? In reality, the objectives of VIS are muddled.[81] But even this recognition is to miss the point, which is well made in Paul Rock's recollec-tion of Canadian policy officials saying in the early 1980s that 'politically, you can't be too nice to victims.'[82] This is equally applicable to the UK in the new millen-nium. But 'being nice' and actually helping are not necessarily the same things. In 2000 the Government decided to introduce a modified VIS, a 'Personal Statement Scheme'.[83] Confronted with the findings of Hoyle *et al*, the responsible govern-ment Minister repeated the mantra that 'this is what victims want', deliberately ignoring the point that many wanted VIS only before they were made and then ignored.

VIS and its variants are probably more popular with people who have never used them than with those who have. They are good for idealised victims, rather than real victims. Even supporters of VIS, such as Erez, acknowledge raised expec-tations and, given the inevitably limited impact of VIS on decision-making, result-ing dissatisfaction (although they do not let this obstruct their advocacy of such schemes).[84] VIS provides solace for people who feel they could be the next victim. As potential victims outnumber real victims, VIS is a good vote-winner, even if dissatisfaction with the schemes results in their users expressing criticisms of the officials who design and implement them. It is likely, though, that the dissatisfac-tion more often amplifies the anger and hurt already felt towards the offender, thus increasing the victim–offender gap and doing nothing to reduce the exclu-sion of victims or offenders from 'normal' society. VIS is the most striking mani-festation of Garland's argument that victim policy facilitates differentiation (of the 'bad' from the 'unfortunate') and the 'criminology of the other' that justifies punitive segregation and intensifies the exclusionary tendencies of late-modern society. For in the non-Charter crimes there are no VIS, even though it is precisely these crimes where 'impact' cannot usually be imagined by criminal justice officials and where the victims' voices add a missing dimension.[85]

---

[81] I Edwards, 'Victim Participation in Sentencing: The Problems of Incoherence' (2001) 40 *Howard Journal of Criminal Justice* 39.

[82] Rock, 'Victims' Rights', n 4 above.

[83] Home Office Press Notice 147/2000, 26 May 2000.

[84] For a leading example, see E Erez, 'Integrating a Victim Perspective in Criminal Justice Through Victim Impact Statements' in A Crawford and J Goodey (eds), *Integrating a Victim Perspective Within Criminal Justice* (Ashgate, Aldershot, 2000).

[85] Excellent examples are provided in Spalek, 'Regulation, White Collar Crime', n 4 above.

CONCLUSION: SOCIAL EXCLUSION V SOCIAL INCLUSION

This chapter has discussed Garland's argument that victim policy in Britain and America is an integral part of the generally exclusionary penal policy of late-modernity. Most (although not all) of the four types of British initiative examined here provide empirical support for his argument.[86] Victims are used, as Ashworth puts it, 'in the service of severity' and also 'in the service of system efficiency'.[87] Should we, like Ashworth, argue against the most exclusionary rights—namely, participatory rights, VIS in particular? The answer is a qualified 'no', as his position makes sense only from a due process and human rights-based position. Sociologically, we need to recognise that this type of policy is central, not peripheral, to modern criminal justice policy. The question is how to meet the legitimate concerns of both Ashworth and many victims.[88] The answer is through a victim policy that is both participative and inclusionary.[89] This requires the 'victims' category to be broadened to include other crimes, and indeed other social harms (thus circumventing arguments about whether, for example, road accidents are crimes or not).[90]

Now let us place the specific initiatives discussed in this chapter into the framework set out earlier. We saw that consulting victims about prosecution decisions was not necessarily exclusionary, but at present it is done without input from suspects/offenders. Victims are asked to comment on people they often do not know. Such offenders are therefore more likely to be seen in terms of Garland's political projection of the typical offender (the 'Other') than as a real flesh-and-blood individual. The same is true of later prosecution decisions and the other decisions on which VIS supposedly impact.

This is one way in which restorative justice, for all its problems, is such an advance over conventional justice processes—all victims have the opportunity to meet, and discuss the offences with, offenders. Many take up this opportunity and many derive a benefit as a result.[91] Restorative justice also solves the problem of communication with victims, in that victims are present while decisions are being

---

[86] Roach, in *Due Process and Victim's Rights*, n 26 above, reaches similar conclusions with regard to Canada. Although he does not use the term, he promotes an 'inclusive' victims' policy for similar reasons to those argued here.

[87] A Ashworth, 'Victims' Rights, Defendants' Rights and Criminal Procedure' in A Crawford and J Goodey (eds), *Integrating a Victim Perspective Within Criminal Justice* (Ashgate, Aldershot, 2000); Crawford and Enterkin, *Victim Contact Work*, n 64 above, 14.

[88] A Sanders *et al*, 'Victim Impact Statements' n 25 above.

[89] See for example, L Sebba, 'The Individualization of the Victim: From Positivism to Postmodernism' in A Crawford and J Goodey (eds), *Integrating a Victim Perspective Within Criminal Justice* (Ashgate, Aldershot, 2000); Roach, *Due Process and Victim's Rights*, n 26 above.

[90] This type of argument was deployed during a Home Office meeting to discuss the draft Victims' Charter Consultation Document.

[91] C Hoyle, R Young and R Hill, *Proceed with Caution: An Evaluation of the Thames Valley Initiative in Restorative Cautioning* (Joseph Rowntree Foundation, York, 2002).

made, if they wish to be.[92] Their presence also enables the main excluding elements of communication to be reduced, in that victims can seek (and hopefully receive) explanations for policies, processes, actions and decisions. In other words, there can be dialogue between offenders, victims and criminal justice officials.

But restorative justice is not the only way of achieving these objectives—which is just as well, as 'punitive segregation' is likely to overshadow restorative justice for some time to come in actual penal practice. Inquisitorial systems, for example, allow far more participation on the part of victims than do adversarial systems.[93] In Hungary, Latvia and many other former USSR-dominated States, for example, victims are entitled to see major parts of the police file when the investigation is completed, and the prosecution file when (if) there is a prosecution. In Germany the victim can be an 'auxiliary prosecutor': victims are entitled to ask judges to put questions to the accused, may give a full oral account of the impact of the crime on them, and may express their views. While it is not generally believed that victim participation often affects decisions significantly, understanding is increased through participation, dialogue and sight of the material on the basis of which decisions are made.[94] What little research there is suggests that victim satisfaction is, as a result, relatively high in inquisitorial systems with direct participation.[95] What a contrast with the English *Bulger* case, where the victim's mother employed an expert to argue that the killers of her son should not be released on the grounds that they were risks, but did so without sight of the psychiatric and other reports on which risk assessments were based.

Tyler has argued that when offenders understand the process and see it as legitimate they are more ready to accept outcomes that they regard as unjust.[96] This should apply equally to victims. Thus, whether through restorative justice or inquisitorial-style victim participation, increased dialogue and understanding should reduce secondary victimisation and thus increase 'freedom' in the sense it was used earlier. So far, government has resisted developing victim policy on these lines, for reasons that are not clear. If it continues to do so, we may justifiably conclude that victims are being used in the service of exclusion.

---

[92] Where victims do not wish to meet with their offender but nonetheless seek involvement in the criminal process many of the benefits of victim-offender meetings can be achieved through sensitive forms of indirect mediation. See further the chapter by Hoyle in this volume.

[93] Sanders, *Taking Account of Victims*, n 15 above.

[94] This is based on my discussions with prosecutors and non-governmental organisation (NGO) workers in Hungary and Latvia. One domestic violence case was discussed, however, in which the police were persuaded to re-investigate and, consequently, alter their original decision not to prosecute.

[95] See, especially, E Erez and E Bienkowska, 'Victim Participation in Proceedings and Satisfaction with Justice in Continental Systems: The Case of Poland' (1993) 21 *Journal of Criminal Justice* 47.

[96] T Tyler, *Why People Obey the Law* (Yale University Press, New Haven Conn, 1990).

Bibliography

ADLER, Z, *Rape on Trial* (Routledge & Kegan Paul, London, 1987)

AGAR, M, *Professional Stranger* (Academic Press, New York NY, 1980)

AINSWORTH, PB, and PEASE, K, *Police Work* (British Psychological Society, Leicester, 1987)

ALTMAN, D, *Homosexual: Oppression and Liberation* (New York University Press, New York NY, 1993)

AMIR, M, *Patterns in Forcible Rape* (University of Chicago Press, Chicago Ill, 1971)

ANDERSON, E, *Streetwise* (University of Chicago Press, Chicago Ill, 1990)

ANGIER, N, 'Scientists Mull Role of Empathy in Man and Beast', *New York Times*, 9 May 1995

ANTILLA, I, *Victimology—A New Territory in Criminology*, Scandinavian Studies in Criminology, Vol 5 (Martin Robertson, London, 1974)

APPELFELD, A, *The Retreat* (Quartet Books, London, 1984)

ARCHER, J, 'Sex Differences in Aggression Between Heterosexual Partners: A Meta-analytic Review' (2000) 126 *Psychological Bulletin* 651

ASHWORTH, A, 'Victim Impact Statements and Sentencing' [1993] *Criminal Law Review* 498

——, *The Criminal Process*, 2nd edn (Oxford University Press, Oxford, 1998)

——, 'Victims' Rights, Defendants' Rights and Criminal Procedure' in A Crawford and J Goodey (eds), *Integrating a Victim Perspective within Criminal Justice* (Ashgate, Aldershot, 2000)

——, 'Responsibilities, Rights and Restorative Justice' in M Maguire, R Morgan and R Reiner (eds), *The Oxford Handbook of Criminology*, 3rd edn (Clarendon Press, Oxford, forthcoming 2002)

ATHENS, L, *Violent Criminal Acts and Actors Revisited* (University of Illinois Press, Urbana Ill, 1997)

AUSTIN, C, *The Prevention of Robbery at Building Society Branches*, Crime Prevention Unit Paper 14 (Home Office, London, 1988)

BALLINGER, A, *Dead Woman Walking: Executed Women in England and Wales 1900–1955* (Ashgate, Aldershot, 2000).

BAMFIELD, J, *Making Shoplifters Pay: Retail Civil Recovery* (Social Market Foundation, London, 1997)

BANDES, S, 'Empathy, Narrative and Victim Impact Statements' (1996) 63 *University of Chicago Law Review* 361

BART, PB, and MORAN, EG, (eds), *Violence Against Women: The Bloody Footprints* (Sage, Thousand Oaks Cal, 1993)

BAUMEISTER, RF, STILLWELL, A and WOTMAN, SR, 'Victim and Perpetrator Accounts of Interpersonal Violence' (1990) 59(5) *Journal of Personality and Social Psychology* 994

BAYLEY, D, 'Security and Justice for All' in H Strang and J Braithwaite (eds), *Restorative Justice and Civil Society* (Cambridge University Press, Cambridge, 2001)

BAZEMORE, G, and WALGRAVE, L, 'Restorative Juvenile Justice: In Search of Fundamentals and an Outline for Systemic Reform' in G Bazemore and L Walgrave (eds), *Restorative Juvenile Justice* (Criminal Justice Press, Monsey NY, 1999)

BECKER, C, *Criminal Theories of Causation and Victims* (Unpublished PhD dissertation, University of Cambridge, 1981)

BECKER, H, *Outsiders* (Free Press of Glencoe, London, 1963)

——, 'Whose Side Are We On?' (1967) 14 *Social Problems* 239

BELL, C, 'Alternative Justice in Ireland' in N Dawson, D Greer and P Ingram (eds), *One Hundred and Fifty Years of Irish Law* (SLS Publications, Belfast, 1996)

BELOOF, D, 'The Third Model of Criminal Process: The Victim Participation Model' (1999) 2 *Utah Law Review* 289

BENNETT, WL, and FELDMAN, M, *Reconstructing Reality in the Courtroom* (Tavistock, London, 1981)

BIDERMAN, A, and REISS, A, 'On Explaining the "Dark Figure" of Crime' (1967) 374 *Annals of the American Academy of Politics and Social Science* 1

BINNEY, V, HARKELL, G, and NIXON, J, *Leaving Violent Men: A Study of Refuges and Housing for Battered Women* (Women's Aid Federation, England, 1981)

BITTNER, E, *The Functions of the Police in Modern Society* (National Institute of Mental Health, Chevy Chase MD, 1970)

BLAGG, H, 'Reparation and Justice for Juveniles: The Corby Experience' (1985) 25 *British Journal of Criminology* 267

BLY, R, *Iron John: A Book About Men* (Addison-Wesley, New York NY, 1990)

BOGRAD, M, 'Feminist Perspectives on Wife Abuse: An Introduction', in K Yllö and M Bograd (eds), *Feminist Perspectives on Wife Abuse* (Sage, London, 1990)

BOURLET, A, *Police Intervention in Marital Violence* (Open University Press, Milton Keynes, 1990)

BOWLING, B, *Violent Racism Victimization, Policing and Social Context.* Clarendon Press, Oxford, 1998)

BOX, S, *Deviance, Reality and Society* (Holt, Rinehart &Winston, London, 1971)

BRAITHWAITE, J, *Crime, Shame and Reintegration* (Cambridge University Press, Cambridge, 1989)

——, *Restorative Justice and Responsive Regulation* (Oxford University Press, Oxford, 2002)

BRAITHWAITE, J, and MUGFORD, S, 'Conditions of Successful Reintegration Ceremonies: Dealing with Juvenile Offenders' (1994) 34 *British Journal of Criminology* 139

BRAND, S, and PRICE, R, *The Economic and Social Costs of Crime*, Home Office Research Study 217 (Home Office, London, 2000)

BRANNEN, J, 'The Study of Sensitive Subjects' (1988) 36 *Sociological Review* 552–63

BRERETON, D, 'How Different Are Rape Trials? A Comparison of the Cross-Examination of Complainants in Rape and Assault Trials' (1997) 37 *British Journal of Criminology* 242

BROWNE, K, and HERBERT, M, *Preventing Family Violence* (John Wiley & Sons, Chichester, 1997)

BROWNMILLER, S, *Against Our Will: Men, Women and Rape* (Penguin, London, 1975)

BUCHBINDER, D, *Performance Anxieties: Re-producing Masculinity* (Allen and Unwin, Sydney, 1988)

BUDD, T, *Violence at Work: New Findings from the 2000 British Crime Survey*, Occasional Paper (Home Office, London, 2001)

BUNT, P, and MAWBY, R, 'Quality of Policing' (1994) 2(3) *Public Policy Review* 58

BURGESS, AW, and HOLSTROM, LL, 'Rape Trauma Syndrome' (1979) 131 *American Journal of Psychiatry* 981

BURGESS-JACKSON, K, *Rape: A Most Detestable Crime: New Philosophical Essays on Rape* (Oxford University Press, Oxford, 1999)

Burrows, J, and Cooper, D, *Theft and Loss from UK Libraries: A National Survey*, Crime Prevention Unit Paper 37 (Home Office, London, 1992)

Buruma, I, 'The Joys and Perils of Victimhood' in A Lightman and R Atwan (eds), *The Best American Essays 2000* (Houghton Mifflin, Boston Mass, 2000)

Canadian Federal–Provincial Task Force on Justice for Victims of Crime, *Report* (Ministry of Supply and Services Canada, Ottawa, 1983)

Cannavale, F, and Falcon, W, *Improving Witness Cooperation* (Government Printing Office, Washington DC, 1976)

Carlen, P, *Jigsaw* (Open University Press, Buckingham, 1996)

Cavadino, M, and Dignan, J, 'Reparation, Retribution and Rights' (1997) 4 *International Review of Victimology* 233

Chan, J, 'Changing Police Culture' (1996) 36 *British Journal of Criminology* 109

Christie, N, 'The Ideal Victim' in EA Fattah (ed), *From Crime Policy to Victim Policy: Reorientating the Justice System* (Macmillan, London, 1986)

Clark, L, and Lewis, D, *Rape: The Price of Coercive Sexuality* (Women's Press, Toronto, 1977)

Clarke, RV, 'Situational Crime Prevention' in M Tonry and D Farrington (eds), *Building a Safer Society: Strategic Approaches to Crime Prevention*, Crime and Justice: A Review of Research (University of Chicago Press, Chicago Ill, 1995) Vol 19

——, 'Situational Prevention, Criminology, and Social Values' in A von Hirsch, D Garland and A Wakefield (eds), *Ethical and Social Perspectives on Situational Crime Prevention* (Hart Publishing, Oxford, 2000)

Clarke, RV, Ekblom, P, Hough, M and Mayhew, P, 'Elderly Victims of Crime and Exposure to Risk' (1985) 24(1) *The Howard Journal of Criminal Justice* 1

Cohen, S, *Folk Devils and Moral Panics* (Paladin, London, 1973)

——, *States of Denial* (Polity Press, Cambridge, 2001)

Collier, R, 'Waiting 'Til Father Gets Home: the Reconstruction of Fatherhood in Family Law' (1995) 4 *Social and Legal Studies* 15

Connell, RW, *Gender and Power* (Stanford University Press, Stanford Cal, 1987)

Conroy, J, *War as a Way of Life: A Belfast Diary* (Heinemann, London, 1987) 90

Conway, P, *Development of a Service-based Response to Those Under Threat from Paramilitaries in Northern Ireland* (Unpublished MSc (Social Work) Dissertation, Faculty of Economics and Social Sciences, Queens University Belfast, 1994)

Cook, D, *Rich Law, Poor Law* (Open University Press, Milton Keynes, 1989).

Council of Europe, European Committee on Crime Problems, *The Position of the Victim in the Framework of Criminal Law and Procedure* (Office for Official Publications of the European Communities, Luxembourg, 1985) available from <http://cm.coe.int/ta/rec/1985/85r11.htm>

Cowan, D, and Marsh, A, 'There's Regulatory Crime and then there's Landlord Crime: from "Rachmanites" to "Partners"' (2001) 64 *Modern Law Review* 831

Crawford, A, *The Local Governance of Crime* (Clarendon Press, Oxford, 1997)

——, *Crime Prevention and Community Safety* (Longman, London, 1998)

Crawford, A, and Enterkin, J, *Victim Contact Work and the Probation Service* (CCJS Press, Leeds, 1999)

Cretney, A, and Davis, D, *Punishing Violence* (Routledge, London, 1995)

DALTON, C, 'Where We Stand: Observations on the Situation of Feminist Legal Thought' (1987–88) 3 *Berkeley Women's Law Journal* 1

DALY, K, 'Restorative Justice in Diverse and Unequal Societies' (1999) 17 *Law in Context* 167

——, 'Restorative Justice: The Real Story' (paper presented at the Scottish Criminology Conference, Edinburgh, 21–22 September 2000)

——, 'Conferencing in Australia and New Zealand: Variations, Research Findings and Prospects' in A Morris and G Maxwell (eds), *Restorative Justice for Juveniles: Conferencing, Mediation and Circles* (Hart Publishing, Oxford, 2001)

——, 'Mind the Gap: Restorative Justice in Theory and Practice' in A von Hirsch, J Roberts, AE Bottoms, K Roach and M Schiff (eds), *Restorative Justice and Criminal Justice: Competing or Reconcilable Paradigms?* (Hart Publishing, Oxford, forthcoming 2002)

DAVIS, F, 'Deviance Disavowal' in H Becker (ed), *The Other Side* (Free Press, New York NY, 1964)

DAVIS, G, *Making Amends: Mediation and Reparation in Criminal Justice* (Routledge, London, 1992)

DAVIS, G, BOUCHERAT, J, and WATSON, D, 'Reparation in the Service of Diversion: The Subordination of a Good Idea' (1988) 27 *Howard Journal of Penal Reform* 127

DAVIS, M, LUNDMAN, R, and MARTINEZ, R Jr, 'Private Corporate Justice: Store Police, Shoplifters and Civil Recovery' (1991) 38 *Social Problems* 395

DAVIS, R, LURIGIO, A, and SKOGAN, W, *Victims of Crime* (Sage, London, 1997)

DELGADO, R, 'Goodbye to Hammurabi: Analysing the Atavistic Appeal of Restorative Justice' (2000) 52 *Stanford Law Review* 751

DENZIN, N, *The Research Act* (Aldine de Gruyter, Chicago Ill, 1970)

Department of Health and Social Services Registrar General Northern Ireland, *Belfast Urban Area Report* (HMSO, Belfast, 1992).

DIDUCK, A, 'Legislating Ideologies of Motherhood' (1993) 2 *Social and Legal Studies* 461

DIGNAN, J, 'Repairing the Damage: Can Reparative Work in the Service of Diversion?' (1992) 32 *British Journal of Criminology* 453.

——, 'Reintegration Through Reparation: A Way Forward for Restorative Justice?' in A Duff, S Marshall and R E Dobash (eds), *Penal Theory and Practice: Tradition and Innovation in Criminal Justice* (Manchester University Press, Manchester, 1994)

DOBASH, RE, and DOBASH, RP, *Rethinking Violence Against Women* (Sage, London, 1998)

DOBASH, RE, DOBASH, RP, and NOAKS, L, *Women and Crime* (University of Wales Press, Cardiff, 1995)

DOEZEMA, J, 'Loose Women or Lost Women? The Re-emergence of the Myth of "White Slavery" in Contemporary Discourses of "Trafficking in Women"' (Paper presented at the ISA Convention, Washington DC, February 1999)

DOUGLAS, M, (ed), *Witchcraft Confessions and Accusations* (Tavistock, London, 1970)

DYNES, R, and QUARANTELLI, E, 'Organizations as Victims in Mass Civil Disturbances' reprinted in I Drapkin and E Viano (eds), *Victimology* (Lexington Books, London, 1974)

EAMES, MH, KNEAFSEY, B, and GORDON, D, 'A Fractured Peace: A Changing Pattern of Violence' (1997) 50 *British Journal of Plastic Surgery* 416

EDGAR, K, and O'DONNELL, I, 'Assault in Prison' (1998) 38 *British Journal of Criminology* 635

EDLEY, N, and WETHERELL, M, 'Masculinity, Power and Identity', in Mairtin Mac an Ghaill (ed), *Understanding Masculinities: Social Relations and Cultural Arenas* (Open University Press, Buckingham, 1996)

EDWARDS, I, 'Victim Participation in Sentencing: The Problems of Incoherence' (2001) 40 *The Howard Journal of Criminal Justice* 39

EDWARDS, SM, *Female Sexuality and the Law* (M Robertson, Oxford, 1981)

——, *Policing Domestic Violence: Women the Law and the State* (Sage, London, 1989)

EINSTADTER, W, 'The Social Organization of Armed Robbery' (1969) 17(1) *Social Problems* 64

EKBLOM, P, and SIMON, F, with BIRDI, S, *Crime and Racial Harassment in Asian-run Small Shops: The Scope for Prevention*, Crime Prevention Unit Paper 15 (Home Office, London, 1988)

ELIAS, R, *Victims Still: The Political Manipulation of Crime Victims* (Sage, Newbury Park Cal, 1993)

ELLISON, L, 'The Mosaic Art?' (2001) 21 *Legal Studies* 353

EREZ, E, 'Who's Afraid of the Big Bad Victim? Victim Impact Statements as Victim Empowerment and Enhancement of Justice' [1999] *Criminal Law Review* 545

——, 'Integrating a Victim Perspective in Criminal Justice Through Victim Impact Statements' in A Crawford and J Goodey (eds), *Integrating a Victim Perspective Within Criminal Justice* (Ashgate, Aldershot, 2000)

EREZ, E, and BIENKOWSKA, E, 'Victim Participation in Proceedings and Satisfaction with Justice in Continental Systems: The Case of Poland' (1993) 21 *Journal of Criminal Justice* 47

EREZ, E, ROEGER, L, and MORGAN, F, 'Victim Harm, Impact Statements and Victim Satisfaction with Justice: An Australian Experience' (1997) 5 *International Review of Victimology* 37

EREZ, E, and ROGERS, L, 'Victim Impact Statements and Sentencing Outcomes and Processes' (1999) 39 *British Journal of Criminology* 216

ERICSON, R, *Making Crime* (Butterworth, Toronto, 1981)

ERICSON, R, and HAGGERTY, K, *Policing the Risk Society* (Clarendon Press, Oxford, 1997)

ETHERINGTON, K, *Adult Male Survivors of Childhood Sexual Abuse* (Pennant, Brighton, 1995)

EU COUNCIL OF JUSTICE AND HOME AFFAIRS MINISTERS, *Standing of Victims in Criminal Proceedings* (Office for Official Publications of the European Communities, Luxembourg, March 2001)

FAGAN, J, 'Social Processes of Delinquency and Drug Use Among Urban Gangs' in CR Huff, *Gangs in America* (Sage Publications, London, 1990)

FARRINGTON, DP, 'Human Development and Criminal Careers' in M Maguire, R Morgan and R Reiner (eds), *The Oxford Handbook of Criminology*, 2nd edn (Clarendon Press, Oxford, 1997).

FEELEY, M, and SIMON, J, 'Actuarial Justice: the Emerging New Criminal Law' in D Nelken (ed), *The Futures of Criminology* (Sage, London, 1994)

FENWICK, H, 'Rights of Victims in the Criminal Justice System: Rhetoric or Reality?' [1995] *Criminal Law Review* 845

——, 'Charge Bargaining and Sentence Discount: The Victim's Perspective' (1997) 5 *International Review of Victimology* 23

——, 'Procedural "Rights" of Victims of Crime' (1997) 60 *Modern Law Review* 317

FLATEN, C, 'Victim Offender Mediation: Application with Serious Offences Committed by Juveniles' in B Galaway and J Hudson (eds), *Restorative Justice: International Perspectives* (Criminal Justice Press, Monsey NY, 1996)

FOSTER, J, *Villains* (Routledge, London, 1990)

FOUCAULT, M, *The History of Sexuality: Vol 1, An Introduction* (Allen Lane, London, 1979)

——, *Discipline and Punish*, AM Sheridan-Smith (trans) (Penguin, London, 1979)

——, 'Two Lectures', in C Gordon (ed), *Power/Knowledge: Selected Writings 1972–1977* (Harvester Press, Brighton, 1980)

FRISCH, M, *The Fire Raisers* (Methuen, London, 1962)

GAQUIN, DA, 'Spouse Abuse: Data from the National Crime Survey' (1978) 2 *Victimology* 632

GARLAND, D, 'The Limits of the Sovereign State: Strategies of Crime Control in Contemporary Society' (1996) 36(4) *British Journal of Criminology* 445

——, *The Culture of Control* (Oxford University Press, Oxford, 2001)

GARLAND, D, and SPARKS, R, 'Criminology, Social Theory, and the Challenge of our Times' in D Garland and R Sparks (eds), *Criminology and Social Theory* (Clarendon Press, Oxford, 2000)

GARTON, A, *Preliminary Report on the Leeds Reparation Scheme* (Unpublished research paper, 1986)

GEERTZ, C, *The Interpretation of Culture: Selected Essays* (Basic Books, New York NY, 1973)

GEHM, J, 'Mediated Victim–Offender Restitution Agreements: An Exploratory Analysis of Factors Related to Victim Participation' in B Galaway and J Hudson (eds) *Criminal Justice, Restitution, and Reconciliation* (Criminal Justice Press, Monsey NY, 1990)

GENN, H, 'Multiple Victimization' in M Maguire and J Pointing (eds), *Victims of Crime: A New Deal?* (Open University Press, Milton Keynes, 1988)

GEORGE, M, 'Riding the Donkey Backwards: Men as the Unacceptable Victims of Marital Violence' (1994) 3 *The Journal of Men's Studies* 137

——, *Beyond All Help?* (Dewar Research, London, 1998)

GIDDENS, A, *Modernity and Self Identity* (Polity Press, Cambridge, 1991)

GIRLING, E, LOADER, I, and SPARKS, R, *Crime and Social Change in Middle England* (Routledge, London, 2000)

GLIDEWELL, I, *The Review of the Crown Prosecution Service: A Report*, Cmnd 3960 (HMSO, London, 1998)

GOFFMAN, E, 'On Cooling the Mark Out' (1952) 15(4) *Psychiatry* 451

——, *Asylums* (Anchor Books, New York NY, 1961)

GOODRICH, P, '*Jani Anglorum*: Signs, Symptoms, Slips and Interpretation in Law' in C Douzinas, P Goodrich, Y Hachamaritch (eds), *Politics, Postmodernity and Critical Legal Studies: The Legality of the Contingent* (Routledge, London, 1994)

GOYER, PF, and EDDLEMAN, HC, 'Same Sex Rape of Non-incarcerated Men' (1984) 141(4) *American Journal of Psychiatry* 578

GRACE, S, *Policing Domestic Violence in the 1990s* (HMSO, London, 1995)

GRIFFIN, S, 'Rape: The All-American Crime' (1971) 10 *Ramparts* 26

GRIFFITHS, C, 'The Victims of Crime and Restorative Justice: The Canadian Experience' (1999) 6 *International Review of Victimology* 279

GRIFFITHS, D, and MOYNIHAN, F, 'Multiple Epiphysical Injuries in Babies ("Battered Baby Syndrome")' (1963) 11 *British Medical Journal* 1558

GROTH, N, and BURGESS, W, 'Male Rape: Offenders and Victims' (1980) 137 *American Journal of Psychiatry* 576

GUSFIELD, J, *Symbolic Crusade* (University of Illinois Press, Urbana Ill, 1963)

HACKING, I, *Rewriting the Soul: Multiple Personality and the Sciences of Memory* (Princeton University Press, Princeton NJ, 1995)

HAGAN, J, and MCCARTHY, B, *Mean Streets* (Cambridge University Press, Cambridge, 1998)

HALL, C, *White, Male and Middle Class: Explorations in Feminism and History* (Polity Press, Cambridge, 1992)

HALL, S, *Drifting into a Law and Order Society* (Cobden Trust, London, 1980)

HALL, S, Critcher, C, Jefferson, T, Clarke, J and Roberts, B, *Policing the Crisis* (Macmillan, London, 1978)

HAMILL, H, *Hoods and Provos: Crime and Punishment in West Belfast* (Unpublished DPhil Thesis, Department of Sociology, University of Oxford, 2002)

HAMMERSLEY, M, and Atkinson, P, *Ethnography: Principles in Practice* (Routledge, London, 1995)

HANMER, J, and GRIFFITHS, S, 'Domestic Violence and Repeat Victimisation' (Briefing note, Police Research Group, Home Office, London, undated)

HARDING, J, *Victims and Offenders: Needs and Responsibilities* (Bedford Square Press, London, 1982)

HARRIS, IM, *Messages Men Hear: Constructing Masculinities* (Taylor & Francis, London, 1995)

HARVEY, M, *An Ecological View of Psychological Trauma and Recovery from Trauma* (Harvard University Press, Cambridge Mass, 1990)

HAY, D, and SNYDER, F, (eds), *Policing and Prosecution in Britain, 1750–1850* (Oxford University Press, Oxford, 1989)

HEIDENSOHN, F, *Women and Crime* (MacMillan, London, 1985)

HENDERSON, L, 'Legality and Empathy' (1987) 85 *Michigan Law Review* 1574

——, 'The Wrongs of Victims' Rights' in E Fattah (ed), *Towards a Critical Victimology* (MacMillan, London, 1992)

HICKSON, FCI, DAVIES, PM, HUNT, AJ, WEATHERBURN, P, MCMANUS, TJ, and COXON, APM, 'Gay Men as Victims of Non-consensual Sex' (1994) 23 *Archives of Sexual Behaviour* 281–94

HICKSON, FCI, HENDERSON, L, and DAVIES, P, *Patterns of Sexual Violence Among Men* (Unpublished summary research report, 1997)

HILLMAN, RJ, O'MARA, N, TAYLOR-ROBINSON, D, and HARRIS, JRW, 'Medical and Social Aspects of Sexual Assault of Males: A Survey of 100 Victims' (1990) 40 *British Journal of General Practice* 502

HILLYARD, P, 'Popular Justice in Northern Ireland: Communities and Change' in S Spitzer (ed), *Research in Law, Deviance and Social Control,* Vol 7 (JAI Press, London and Greenwich Conn, 1984)

HOLSTEIN, J, and MILLER, G, 'Rethinking Victimization: An Interactional Approach to Victimology' (1990) 13(1) *Symbolic Interaction* 103

HOLSTI, O, *Content Analysis for the Social Sciences* (Addison-Wesley, London, 1969)

HOME OFFICE, *Report of the Interdepartmental Working Group on the Treatment of Vulnerable and Intimidated Witnesses in the Criminal Justice System* (Home Office, London, 1998)

HOME OFFICE, 'Home Secretary Announces National Victim Statements', Home Office Press Release 147/2000 (Home Office, London, 2000)

——, *The 2000 British Crime Survey England and Wales*, Home Office Statistical Bulletin No 18 (Home Office, London, 2000)

——, Lord Chancellor's Department and The Attorney-General, *A Review of the Victims' Charter* (Home Office, London, 2001)

——, *Review of Parole* (Unpublished, 2001)

——, *Review of the Victim's Charter* (Home Office, London, 2001)

HOOD, R, and JOYCE, K, 'Three Generations: Oral Testimonies on Crime and Social Change in London's East End' (1999) 39 *British Journal of Criminology* 136

HOUGH, M, and MAYHEW, P, *The British Crime Survey: First Report* (HMSO, London, 1983)

——, and ——, *Taking Account of Crime: Key Findings from the Second British Crime Survey* (HMSO, London, 1985)

HOWARD LEAGUE FOR PENAL REFORM, *Annual Report 1952–1953* (Howard League for Penal Reform, London, 1953)

HOWARTH, G, and ROCK, P, 'Aftermath and the Construction of Victimisation: "The Other Victims of Crime"' (2000) 39(1) *Howard Journal of Criminal Justice* 58

HOWARTH, K, *Oral History: A Handbook* (Sutton Publishing, Stroud, 1998)

HOYLE, C, *Negotiating Domestic Violence: Police, Criminal Justice and Victims* (Clarendon Press, Oxford, 1998)

HOYLE, C, CAPE, E, MORGAN, R, and SANDERS, A, *Evaluation of the 'One Stop Shop' and Victim Statement Pilot Projects* (Home Office, London, 1998)

HOYLE, C, MORGAN, R, and SANDERS, A, *The Victim's Charter: An Evaluation of Pilot Projects*, Home Office Research Findings No 107 (Home Office, London, 1999)

HOYLE, C, and SANDERS, A, (Unpublished Report to the Nuffield Foundation, 1998)

——, and ——, 'Police Response to Domestic Violence: From Victim Choice to Victim Empowerment?' (2000) 40 *British Journal of Criminology* 14

HOYLE, C, and YOUNG, R, 'Restorative Justice: Assessing the Prospects and Pitfalls' in M McConville and G Wilson (eds), *The Handbook of the Criminal Justice Process* (Oxford University Press, Oxford, forthcoming 2002)

HOYLE, C, YOUNG, R, and HILL, R, *Proceed with Caution: An Evaluation of the Thames Valley Police Initiative in Restorative Cautioning* (Joseph Rowntree Foundation, York, 2002)

HUCKLE, PL, 'Male Victims of Rape Referred to a Forensic Psychiatric Service' (1995) 35(3) *Medicine, Science and the Law* 187

HUDSON, J, and GALAWAY, B, (eds), *Restitution in Criminal Justice* (Lexington Books, Lexington Mass, 1977)

HUMAN RIGHTS WATCH, *To Serve Without Favour: Policing, Human Rights and Accountability in Northern Ireland* (Human Rights Watch, New York and London, 1997)

HUMPHREYS, L, *Tearoom Trade: A Study of Homosexual Encounters in Public Places* (Gerard Duckworth, London, 1970)

IMMARIGEON, R, 'Restorative Justice, Juvenile Offenders and Crime Victims: A Review of the Literature' in G Bazemore and L Walgrave (eds), *Restorative Juvenile Justice: Repairing the Harm of Youth Crime* (Criminal Justice Press, Monsey NY, 1999)

JACKSON, J, 'Law's Truth, Lay Truth and Lawyer's Truth: The Representation of Evidence in Adversary Trials' (1992) *Law and Critique* 29

JANKOWSKI, J, *Islands in the Street: Gangs and American Urban Society* (University of California Press, Berkeley Cal, 1991)

JAYARATNE, TE, and STEWART, AJ, 'Quantitative and Qualitative Methods in the Social Sciences: Feminist Issues and Practical Strategies' in J Holland and M Blair (eds), *Debates and Issues in Feminist Research and Pedagogy* (Open University Press, Clevedon, 1995)

JOHNSON, K, and colleagues, *Cautions, Court Proceedings and Sentencing: England and Wales, 2000*, Home Office Statistical Bulletin 20/01 (Home Office, London, 2000)

JOHNSTON, V, LEITNER, M, SHAPLAND, J, and WILES, P, *Crime on Industrial Estates*, Police Research Group Crime Prevention Unit Series Paper No 54 (Home Office Police Department, London, 1994)

JOHNSTONE, G, *Restorative Justice: Ideas, Values and Debates* (Willan Publishing, Cullompton, 2002)

JONES, T, MACLEAN, B, and YOUNG, J, *The Islington Crime Survey* (Gower, Aldershot, 1986)

JUSTICE, *Victims in Criminal Justice* (JUSTICE, London, 1998)

KANTOR, G, 'Victim-Blaming and Victim-Precipitation, Concept of' in N Rafter (ed), *Encyclopedia of Women and Crime* (Oryx Press, Phoenix Ariz, 2000)

KATZ, BL, 'The Psychological Impact of Stranger Versus Non-stranger Rape on Victims' Recovery' in A Parrot and L Bechhofter (eds), *Acquaintance Rape: The Hidden Crime* (Wiley, New York NY, 1991)

KATZ, J, *Seductions of Crime* (Basic Books, New York NY, 1988)

KELLY, L, *Surviving Sexual Violence* (Polity Press, Cambridge, 1988)

KELLY, L, BURTON, S, and REGAN, L, 'Researching Women's Lives or Studying Women's Oppression?' in M Maynard and J Purvis (eds), *Researching Women's Lives from a Feminist Perspective* (Taylor & Francis, London, 1994)

KEMP, C, NORRIS, C, and FIELDING, N, 'Legal Manoeuvres in Police Handling of Disputes' in D Farrington and S Walklate (eds), *Offenders and Victims: Theory and Policy* (British Society of Criminology, London, 1992)

KEMPE, C, SILVERMAN, FM, STEELE, BF, DROEGEMUELLER, W and SILVER, HK, 'The Battered Child Syndrome' [1962] 181 *Journal of the American Medical Association* 17

KENNEDY, L, 'Nightmares Within Nightmares: Paramilitary Repression in Working-Class Communities' in L Kennedy (ed), *Crime and Punishment in West Belfast* (The Summer School, West Belfast, 1995)

KENNEDY-BERGEN, R, *Wife Rape—Understanding the Response of Victims and Service Providers* (Sage, Thousand Oaks Cal, 1996)

KERSHAW, C, BUDD, T, KINSHOTT, G, MATTINSON, J, MAYHEW, P, and MYHILL, A, *The 2000 British Crime Survey: England and Wales*, Home Office Statistical Bulletin No 18 (Home Office, London, 2000)

KERSHAW, C, CHIVITE-MATTHEWS, N, THOMAS, C, and AUST, R, *The 2001 British Crime Survey: England and Wales* (Home Office Statistical Bulletin 18 January 2001)

KITSUSE, J, and CICOUREL, A, 'A Note on the Uses of Official Statistics' (1963) 11 *Social Problems* 131

KLAPP, O, *Heroes, Villains and Fools: The Changing American Character* (Prentice-Hall, Englewood Cliffs NJ, 1962)

KLEMPERER, V, *To the Bitter End* (Weidenfeld and Nicolson, London, 1999)

KNOX, C, 'The "Deserving" Victims of Political Violence: "Punishment" Attacks in Northern Ireland' (2001) 1 *Criminal Justice* 181

KNUDTEN, RD, 'Will Anyone be Left to Testify?' in E Flynn and J Conrad (eds), *New and Old Criminology* (LEAA, US Department of Justice, Washington DC, 1978)

KNUDTEN, RD, MEADE, AC, KNUDTEN, MS and DOERNER, WG, *Victims and Witnesses: Their Experiences with Crime and the Criminal Justice System* (LEAA, US Department of Justice, Washington DC, 1977)

KRULEWITZ, J, and PAYNE, E, 'Attributions about Rape: Effects of Rapist Force, Observer, and Sex Role Attitudes' (1978) 8(4) *Journal of Applied Social Psychology* 291

KURKI, L, 'Restorative and Community Justice in the United States' in M Tonry (ed), *Crime and Justice: A Review of Research* (University of Chicago Press, Chicago, 2000) Vol 27

LACEY, HB, and ROBERTS, R, 'Sexual Assault on Men' (1991) 2(4) *International Journal of STD and AIDS* 258–60

LACEY, N, 'Modern Feminist Theory' (1989) 9 *Oxford Journal of Legal Studies* 383

LAFREE, GD, 'The Effect of Sexual Stratification by Race on Official Reactions to Rape' (1980) 45 *American Sociological Review* 842

LAMB, S, *The Trouble with Blame: Victims, Perpetrators and Responsibility* (Harvard University Press, Cambridge Mass, 1996)

LANDSHEER, J, HART, HT, and KOX, W, 'Delinquent Values and Victim Damage: Exploring the Limits of Neutralization Theory' (1994) 34 *British Journal of Criminology* 44

LAUNAY, G, 'Bringing Offenders and Victims Together: A Comparison of Two Models' (1985) 24 *Howard Journal of Criminal Justice* 200

LEA, J, and YOUNG, J, *What is to be Done about Law and Order?* (Penguin, London, 1984)

LEE, C, *Talking Tough: The Fight for Masculinity* (Arrow, London, 1993)

LEE, RM, *Doing Research on Sensitive Topics* (Sage Publications, London, 1993)

LEES, S, *Ruling Passions: Sexual Violence, Reputation and the Law* (Open University Press, Buckingham, 1997)

LEIBLING, A, *Suicides in Prison* (Routledge, London, 1992)

LERNER, M, *The Belief in a Just World* (Plenum Press, New York, 1980)

LEVI, M, 'White-Collar Crime Victimization' in N Shover and and JP Wright (eds), *Crimes Of Privilege: Readings in White-Collar Crime* (Oxford University Press, Oxford, 2001)

LEVI, M, and PITHOUSE, A, 'The Victims of Fraud', in D Downes (ed), *Unravelling Criminal Justice* (Macmillan, London, 1992)

LIDSTONE, K, HOGG, R, and SUTCLIFFE, F, *Prosecutions by Private Individuals and Non-Police Agencies* (HMSO, London, 1981)

LIPSKY, M, and OLSON, D, *Commission Politics: The Processing of Racial Crisis in America* (Transaction, New Brunswick, 1977)

LOCKTON, D, and WARD, R, *Domestic Violence* (Cavendish, London, 1997)

LOEBER, R, DELAMATRE, M, TITA, G, COHEN, J, STOUTHAMER-LOEBER, M, and FARRINGTON, DP, 'Gun Injury and Mortality: The Delinquent Backgrounds of Juvenile Victims' (1999) 14 *Violence and Victims* 339

LOFLAND, J, *Deviance and Identity* (Prentice-Hall, Englewood Cliffs NJ, 1969)

LOWMAN, J, and MACLEAN, B, 'Introduction' in *Realist Criminology: Crime Control and Policing in the 1990s* (University of Toronto Press, Toronto, 1992)

MacKinnon, CA, *Toward a Feminist Theory of the State* (Harvard University Press, London, 1989)

MacPherson, W, and Yantzi, M, *Victim–Offender Reconciliation Program* (Kitchener, Ontario, 1979)

MacPherson, W, *The Stephen Lawrence Inquiry* Cm 4262–I (The Stationery Office, London, 1999)

Maguire, M, 'The Impact of Burglary on Victims' (1980) 20(3) *British Journal of Criminology* 261

——, *Burglary in a Dwelling* (Heinemann, London, 1982)

——, 'Crime Statistics, Patterns, and Trends: Changing Perceptions and their Implications' in M Maguire, R Morgan and R Reiner (eds), *The Oxford Handbook of Criminology*, 2nd edn (Clarendon Press, Oxford, 1997)

Mann, C, 'Getting Even? Women Who Kill in Domestic Encounters' (1988) 5 *Justice Quarterly* 33

Marshall, T, 'The Evolution of Restorative Justice in Britain' (1996) 4 *European Journal on Criminal Policy and Research* 21

——, *Restorative Justice: An Overview* (Home Office, London, 1999)

Marshall, T, and Merry, S, *Crime and Accountability: Victim/Offender Mediation in Practice* (HMSO, London, 1990)

Marshall, T, and Walpole, M, *Bringing People Together: Mediation and Reparation Projects in Great Britain* (Home Office, London, 1985)

Masters, B, *She Must Have Known: The Trial of Rosemary West* (Doubleday, London, 1996)

Matravers, A, *Justifying the Unjustifiable: Stories of Women Sex Offenders* (Unpublished PhD thesis, University of Cambridge, 2000)

Mattinson, J, and Mirrlees-Black, C, *Attitudes to Crime and Criminal Justice: Findings from the 1998 British Crime Survey*, Home Office Research Study 200 (Home Office, London, 2000)

Matza, M, *Delinquency and Drift* (Wiley, New York NY, 1964)

Mawby, R, *Burglary* (Willan Publishing, Cullompton, 2001)

Maxfield, M, *Fear of Crime in England and Wales* (HMSO, London, 1984)

Mayhew, P, Elliott, D and Dowds, L, *The 1988 British Crime Survey* (HMSO, London, 1989)

Maynard, M, and Purvis, J, *Researching Women's Lives from a Feminist Perspective* (Taylor & Francis, London, 1994)

McBarnet, D, 'Victim in the Witness Box—Confronting Victimology's Stereotype' (1983) 7 *Contemporary Crises* 293

McCold, P, *Restorative Justice: An Annotated Bibliography* (Criminal Justice Press, Monsey NY, 1997)

——, 'Restorative Justice—Variations on a Theme' in L Walgrave (ed), *Restorative Justice for Juveniles: Potentialities, Risks and Problems* (Leuven University Press, Leuven, 1998)

——, 'Primary Restorative Justice Practices' in A Morris and G Maxwell (eds), *Restorative Justice for Juveniles* (Hart Publishing, Oxford, 2001)

McCold, P, and Wachtel, B, *Restorative Policing Experiment: The Bethlehem Pennsylvania Police Family Group Conferencing Project* (Community Service Foundation, Pipersville Penn, 1998)

McConville, M, 'Justice in the Dock' *The Times Higher Education Supplement,* 8 February 1990

McConville, M, Sanders, A, and Leng, R, *The Case for the Prosecution: Police Suspects and the Construction of Criminality* (Routledge, London, 1991)

McCracken, G, *The Long Interview* (Sage Publications, Newbury Park CA, 1988)

McCulloch, H, *Shop Theft: Improving the Police Response*, Crime Detection and Prevention Series Paper 76 (Home Office Police Research Group, London, 1996)

McGarrell, E, Olivares, K, Crawford, K, and Kroovand, N, *Returning Justice to the Community: The Indianapolis Juvenile Restorative Justice Experiment* (Hudson Institute Crime Control Policy Center, Indianapolis Ind, 2000)

McLeod, M, 'Women Against Men: An Examination of Domestic Violence Based on an Analysis of Official Data and National Victimisation Data' (1984) Victimology 171

McQuoid, J, 'The Self-Reported Delinquency Study in Belfast, Northern Ireland' in J Junger-Tas, G-T Terlaun and MW Klein (eds), *Delinquent Behavior Among Young People in the Western World: First Results of the International Self-Report Delinquency Study* (Kugler Publications, Amsterdam and New York NY, 1994)

Melossi, D, 'Changing Representations of the Criminal' in D Garland and R Sparks (eds), *Criminology and Social Theory* (Clarendon Press, Oxford, 2000)

Mendelsohn, B, 'Une nouvelle branche de la science bio-psycho-sociale' (1956) 11(2) *Revue internationale de la police technique* 95

——, 'The Origins of the Doctrine of Victimology', reprinted in I Drapkin and E Viano (eds), *Victimology* (DC Heath and Company, Lexington Mass, 1974)

Merry, S, *Urban Danger* (Temple University Press, Philadelphia Penn, 1981)

Mezey, GC, and King, MB, 'The Effects of Sexual Assault on Men: A Survey of 22 Victims' (1989) 19 *Psychological Medicine* 205

Miers, D, 'Taking the Law into their Own Hands: Victims as Offenders' in A Crawford and J Goodey (eds), *Integrating a Victim Perspective within Criminal Justice* (Ashgate, Aldershot, 2000)

Miers, D, Maguire, M, Goldie, S, Sharpe, K, Hale, C, Netten, A, Uglow, S, Doolin, K, Hallam, A, Enterkin, J, and Newburn, T, *An Exploratory Evaluation of Restorative Justice Schemes*, Crime Reduction Research Series Paper 9 (Home Office, London, 2001)

Miles, MB, and Huberman, AM, *Qualitative Data Analysis: An Expanded Sourcebook* (Sage Publications, London, 1994)

Miller, C, *Words and Women* (Anchor Press, Garden City NY, 1976)

Mills, J, *Womanwords: A Vocabulary of Culture and Patriarchal Society* (Virago, London, 1991)

Mirrlees-Black, C, *Domestic Violence: Findings from a New British Crime Survey Self-completion Questionnaire*, Home Office Research Study 191 (Home Office, London, 1999)

Mirrlees-Black, C, and Ross, A, *Crime Against Retail and Manufacturing Premises: Findings from the 1994 Commercial Victimisation Survey*, Home Office Research Study 146 (Home Office, London, 1995)

Mooney, J, *The Hidden Figure: Domestic Violence in North London*, Report by Centre for Ciminology, Middlesex University (Islington Council, London, 1993)

Moore, D, Forsythe, L, and O'Connell, T, *A New Approach to Juvenile Justice: An Evaluation of Family Conferencing in Wagga Wagga* (Charles Stuart University, Wagga Wagga, 1995)

Moore, E, and Mills, M, 'The Neglected Victims and Unexamined Costs of White-Collar Crime' (1990) 36(3) *Crime & Delinquency* 408

MORGAN, D, *Discovering Men* (Routledge, London, 1992)

MORGAN, J, and ZEDNER, L, *Child Victims: Crime, Impact, and Criminal Justice* (Clarendon Press, Oxford, 1992)

MORGAN, R, and SANDERS, A, *The Uses of Victim Statements* (Home Office, London, 1999)

MORRIS, A, and GELSTHORPE, L, 'Something Old, Something Borrowed, Something Blue, but Something New? A Comment on the Prospects for Restorative Justice under the Crime and Disorder Act 1998' (2000) *Criminal Law Review* 18

MORRIS, A, and MAXWELL, G, 'The Practice of Family Group Conferences in New Zealand' in A Crawford and J Goodey, *Integrating a Victim Perspective Within Criminal Justice* (Ashgate, Aldershot, 2000)

——, and ——, (eds), *Restorative Justice for Juveniles: Conferencing Mediation and Circles* (Hart Publishing, Oxford, 2001)

MORRIS, T, 'British Criminology: 1935–1948' (1988) 28 *British Journal of Criminology* 164

MORRISON, J, and LEITH, P, *The Barrister's World* (Open University Press, Buckingham, 1992)

MUNCK, R, 'The Lads and the Hoods: Alternative Justice in an Irish Context' in M Thomlinson, T Varley and C McCullough (eds), *Whose Law and Order? Aspects of Crime and Social Control in Irish Society* (Sociological Association, Dublin, 1988)

MYERS, MF, 'Men Sexually Assaulted as Adults and Sexually Abused as Boys' (1989) 18 *Archives of Sexual Behaviour* 203

NACRO, *Victim Policy: Guidance for Piloting YOTs* (NACRO, London, 2000)

NADEL, J, *Sara Thornton: The Story of a Woman Who Killed* (Victor Gorlancz, London, 1995)

NAFFINE, N, *Female Crime* (Allen and Unwin, Sydney, 1987)

NAPLEY, D, *The Technique of Persuasion* (Sweet & Maxwell, London, 1983)

NETTLETON, H, WALKLATE, S and WILLIAMS, B, *Probation Training with the Victim in Mind* (Keele University Press, Keele, 1997)

NEWBURN, T, and MERRY, S, *Keeping in Touch: Police-Victim Communication in Two Areas* (HMSO, London, 1990)

NEWBURN, T, and STANKO, EA, 'When Men are Victims: The Failure of Victimology' in T Newburn and EA Stanko (eds), *Just Boys Doing Business?* (Routledge, London, 1994)

NEWBURN, T, CRAWFORD, A, EARLE, R, GOLDIE, S, HALE, C, MASTERS, G, NETTEN, A, SAUNDERS, R, HALLAM, A, SHARPE, K and UGLOW, S, *The Introduction of Referral Orders into the Youth Justice System: Second Interim Report*, RDS Occasional Paper No 73 (Home Office Research, Development and Statistics Directorate, London, 2001)

——, ——, ——, ——, ——, ——, ——, ——, ——, —— and ——, *The Introduction of Referral Orders into the Youth Justice System: Final Report*, Home Office Research Study 242 (Home Office Research, Development and Statistics Directorate, London, 2002)

NICOLSON, D, 'Telling Tales: Gender Discrimination, Gender Construction and Battered Women Who Kill' (1995) 3 *Feminist Legal Studies* 185

NOLAN, PC, McPHEARSON, J, and McKEOWN, R, 'The Price of Peace—The Personal and Financial Cost of Paramilitary Punishments in Northern Ireland' (2000) 31(Jan) *Injury* 41

O'BARR, W, *Linguistic Evidence: Language, Power and Strategy in the Courtroom* (Academic Press, New York NY, 1982)

OAKLEY, A, 'Interviewing Women: A Contradiction in Terms' in H Roberts (ed), *Doing Feminist Research* (Routledge & Kegan Paul, London, 1981)

OFSHE, R, and WATTERS, E, *Making Monsters: False Memories, Psychotherapy, and Sexual Hysteria* (André Deutsch, London, 1995)

OROS, C, LEONARD, K, and KOSS, M, 'Factors Related to a Self-attribution of Rape by Victims' (1980) 6(2) *Personality and Social Psychology Bulletin* 193

ORTNER, SB, 'Is Female to Male as Nature is to Culture?' in MZ Rosaldo and L Lamphere (eds), *Woman, Crime and Society* (Stanford University Press, Stanford Cal, 1974)

OXFORDSHIRE YOUTH OFFENDING TEAM (2001) *Amends: Reparation Newsletter* Issue 2

PACKER, H, *Limits of the Criminal Sanction* (Stanford University Press, Stanford Cal, 1968)

PAGELOW, MD, ' "The Battered Husband Syndrome" Social Problem or Much Ado about Little?' in N Johnson (ed), *Marital Violence* (Routledge & Kegan Paul, London, 1985)

PAHL, J, *A Refuge for Battered Women: A Study of the Role of a Women's Centre* (HMSO, London, 1978)

——, 'Refuges for Battered Women: Social Provision or Social Movement?' (1979) 8 *Journal of Voluntary Action Research* 25

PAINTER, K, *Wife Rape, Marriage and the Law* (University of Manchester Press, Manchester, 1991)

PARKER, T, *The Courage of His Convictions* (Hutchinson, London, 1962)

PAWSON, R, and TILLEY, N, *Realistic Evaluation* (Sage, London, 1997)

PEARCE, F, *Crimes of the Powerful* (Pluto Press, London, 1976).

PEARSON, G, *Hooligan* (Macmillan, London, 1983)

PEASE, K, 'Repeat Victimisation: Taking Stock' (Briefing note, Police Research Group, Home Office, London, undated)

PEDERSEN, W, 'Adolescent Victims of Violence in a Welfare State' (2001) 41(1) *British Journal of Criminology* 1

PERELMAN, C, *The Idea of Justice and the Problem of Argument* (Richard Clay, Bungay, 1963)

PICKUP, F, WILLIAMS, S, and SWEETMAN, C, *Ending Violence Against Women: A Challenge for Development and Humanitarian Work* (Oxfam Publications, Oxford, 2001)

PINEAU, L, 'Date Rape: A Feminist Analysis' in L Francis (ed), *Date Rape: Feminism, Philosophy and the Law* (Pennsylvania State University Press, University Park Penn, 1996) 1–26

PITCH, T, 'From Oppressed to Victims: Collective Actors and the Symbolic Use of the Criminal Justice System' (1990) 10 *Studies in Law, Politics, and Society* 103

PLATT, A, 'Prospects for a Radical Criminology in the USA' in I Taylor, P Walton and J Young (eds), *Critical Criminology* (Routledge, London, 1975)

——, ' "Street Crime"—A View from the Left' (1978) 9 *Crime and Social Justice* 29

PLECK, E, Pleck, J, H, Grossman, M, and Bart, P, B, 'The Battered Data Syndrome' (1978) 2 *Victimology* 680-84

PLUMMER, K, *Telling Sexual Stories* (Routledge, London, 1995)

POLAND, T, *A Report on the Logistics of Crime and Young People in West Belfast* (Unpublished report commissioned by PBNI and presented at a meeting of the West Belfast Partnership Board, January 2000)

POLLARD, C (Sir), 'If Your Only Tool is a Hammer, All Your Problems Will Look Like Nails' in H Strang and J Braithwaite (eds), *Restorative Justice and Civil Society* (Cambridge University Press, Cambridge, 2001)

Povey, D, and colleagues, *Recorded Crime: England and Wales, 12 Months to March 2001,* Home Office Statistical Bulletin 12/01 (Home Office, London, 2001)

President's Task Force on Victims of Crime, *Final Report* (Government Printing Office, Washington DC, 1982)

Radzinowicz, L, and King, J, *The Growth of Crime* (Penguin, Harmondsworth, 1979)

Redshaw, J, and Mawby, R, 'Commercial Burglary: Victims' Views of the Crime and the Police Response' (1996) 1 *International Journal of Risk, Security and Crime Prevention* 185

Reeves, H, 'The New Status of Victims in the UK: Opportunities and Threats' in A Crawford and J Goodey (eds), *Integrating a Victim Perspective Within Criminal Justice* (Ashgate, Aldershot, 2000)

Reeves, H, and Mulley, K, 'The New Status of Victims in the UK: Opportunities and Threats' in A Crawford and J Goodey, *Integrating a Victim Perspective within Criminal Justice* (Ashgate, Aldershot, 2000)

Reiner, R, 'The Mystery of the Missing Crimes' (1994) 1 (2) *Policing Today* 16

——, *The Politics of the Police* (Oxford University Press, Oxford, 2000)

Reinholtz, RK, Muehlenhard, CL, Phelps, JL, and Satterfield, AT, 'Sexual Discourse and Sexual Intercourse: How the Way we Communicate Affects the Way we Think about Sexual Coercion' in PJ Kalbfleisch and MJ Cody (eds), *Gender, Power and Communication in Human Relationships* (Lawrence Erlbaum Associates, Mahwah NJ, 1995)

Reiss, A, *The Police and the Public* (Yale University Press, New Haven Conn, 1970)

Renzetti, C, 'Violence and Abuse in Lesbian Relationships: Theoretical and Empirical Issues' in RK Bergen (ed), *Issues in Intimate Violence* (Sage, London, 1998)

Reswick, PA, 'The Trauma of Rape and the Criminal Justice System' (1984) 9(1) *The Justice System Journal* 52

Reynolds, T, 'Restorative Justice—A New Way Forward for Victims of Crime?' (2000) 18(2) *Howard League Magazine* 8

Rhode, D, *Justice and Gender: Sex Discrimination and the Law* (Harvard University Press, London, 1989)

Richardson, D, and May, H, 'Deserving Victims? Sexual Status and the Social Construction of Violence' (1999) 47 *Sociological Review* 308

Roach, K, *Due Process and Victim's Rights* (University of Toronto Press, Toronto, 1999)

Rock, P, *The Social World of an English Crown Court* (Clarendon Press, Oxford, 1993)

——, 'Murderers, Victims and Survivors' (1998) 38 *British Journal of Criminology* 185

——, *After Homicide: Practical and Political Responses to Bereavement* (Clarendon Press, Oxford, 1998)

——, 'Victims' Rights in England and Wales at the Beginning of the 21st Century' in J Ermisch, D Gallie and A Heath (eds), *Social Challenges and Sociological Puzzles* (Oxford University Press, Oxford, 2002)

Rolph, CH, 'Wild Justice' *New Statesman,* 18 January 1958

Sampson, R, 'Personal Violence by Strangers' (1987) 78 *Journal of Criminal Law and Criminology* 327

Sanday, PR, 'The Socio-Cultural Context of Rape: A Cross Cultural Study' (1981) 37 *Journal of Social Issues* 5

Sanders, A, 'Constructing a Case for the Prosecution' (1987) 14 *Journal of Law and Society* 229

SANDERS, A, *Taking Account of Victims in the Criminal Justice System: A Review of the Literature* (Scottish Office, Edinburgh, 1999)

SANDERS, A, HOYLE, C, MORGAN, R, and CAPE, E, 'Victim Impact Statements: Don't Work, Can't Work' [2001] *Criminal Law Review* 447

SANDERS, A, and YOUNG, R, *Criminal Justice*, 2nd edn (Butterworths, London, 2000)

——, and ——, 'Discontinuances, The Rights of Victims and the Remedy of Freedom', *New Law Journal*, 19 January 2001

SARAT, A, 'Vengeance, Victims and the Identities of Law' (1997) 6 *Social and Legal Studies* 163

SASSON, T, *Crime Talk: How Citizens Construct a Social Problem* (Aldine de Gruyter, New York NY, 1995)

SAUNDERS, DG, 'Wife Abuse, Husband Abuse or Mutual Combat? A Feminist Perspective on the Empirical Findings' in K Yllö and M Bograd (eds) *Feminist Perspectives on Wife Abuse* (Sage, London, 1990)

SCALES, AC, 'The Emergence of Feminist Jurisprudence: An Essay' (1986) 95 *Yale Law Journal* 1373

SCHAFER, S, *The Victim and His Criminal* (Random House, New York NY, 1968)

SCHUR, E, *Crimes Without Victims* (Prentice-Hall, Englewood Cliffs NJ, 1965)

SCHWENDINGER, H, and SCHWENDINGER, J, 'Defenders of Order or Guardians of Human Rights' in I Taylor, P Walton and J Young (eds), *Critical Criminology* (Routledge, London, 1975)

SCOTT, M, and LYMAN, S, 'Accounts, Deviance and Social Order' in J Douglas (ed), *Deviance and Respectability* (Basic Books, New York NY, 1970)

SEBBA, L, *Third Parties: Victims and the Criminal Justice System* (Ohio State University Press, Columbus Ohio, 1996)

——, 'The Individualization of the Victim: From Positivism to Postmodernism' in A Crawford and J Goodey (eds), *Integrating a Victim Perspective Within Criminal Justice* (Ashgate, Aldershot, 2000)

——, 'On the Relationship between Criminological Research and Policy' (2001) 1(1) *Criminal Justice* 27

SEGRAVE, K, *Shoplifting: A Social History* (McFarland & Company, London, 2001)

SEIDLER, VJ, *Rediscovering Masculinity: Reason, Language and Sexuality* (Routledge, New York NY, 1989)

——, *Man Enough: Embodying Masculinities* (Sage, London, 1997)

SHANLEY, ML, *Feminism, Marriage and the Law in Victorian England* (Princeton University Press, Princeton NJ, 1989)

SHAPLAND, J, 'Preventing Retail-Sector Crime' in M Tonry and D Farrington (eds), *Building a Safer Society: Strategic Approaches to Crime Prevention* (University of Chicago Press, Chicago Ill, 1995)

——, 'Creating Responsible Criminal Justice Agencies' in A Crawford and J Goodey, *Integrating a Victim Perspective within Criminal Justice* (Ashgate, Aldershot, 2000)

——, 'Victims in Criminal Justice: Creating Responsible Criminal Justice Agencies' in A Crawford and J Goodey (eds), *Integrating a Victim Perspective Within Criminal Justice* (Ashgate, Aldershot, 2000)

SHAPLAND, J, and VAGG, J, *Policing by the Public* (Routledge, London,1988)

SHAPLAND, J, WILLMORE, J, and DUFF, P, *Victims in the Criminal Justice System* (Gower Publishing, Aldershot, 1985) 16

SHEARING, C, 'Transforming Security: A South African Experiment' in H Strang and
J Braithwaite (eds), *Restorative Justice and Civil Society* (Cambridge University Press,
Cambridge, 2001)

SHEARING, C, and STENNING, P, 'Modern Private Security: Its Growth and Implications' in
Crime and Justice: An Annual Review of Research (Chicago University Press, Chicago Ill,
1983) Vol 3

SHEPHERD, J, 'Violent Crime in Bristol: An Accident and Emergency Department Perspective' (1990) 30(3) *British Journal of Criminology* 289

SHEPTYCKI, JWE, *Innovations in Policing Domestic Violence* (Avebury, Aldershot, 1993)

SHERMAN, L, 'Hot Spots of Predatory Crime' (1989) 27 *Criminology* 27

SHERMAN, L, STRANG, H, BARNES, G, BRAITHWAITE, J, INKPEN, N, and TEH, M, *A Progress Report
on the Canberra Reintegrative Shaming Experiments (RISE)* (June 1998), available at
<http://www.aic.gov.au/rjustice/rise/progress/1998.html>

SHERMAN, L, STRANG, H, and WOODS, D, 'Recidivism Patterns in the Canberra Reintegra-
tive Shaming Experiments (RISE)' (Center for Restorative Justice, Research School of
Social Sciences, Institute of Advanced Studies, Australian National University,
Canberra, 2000)

SHORT, J, *Poverty, Ethnicity and Violent Crime* (Westview Press, Boulder Col, 1997)

SKOGAN, W, *The Police and the Public in England and Wales: A British Crime Survey Report*
(HMSO, London, 1990)

SKOLNICK, JH, *Justice Without Trial* (John Wiley & Sons, London, 1966)

SLAPPER, G, *Blood in the Bank* (Ashgate, Aldershot, 1999)

SLAPPER, G, and Tombs, S, *Corporate Crime* (Longman, Harlow, 1999)

SMART, C, *Women, Crime and Criminology* (Routledge & Kegan Paul, London, 1977)

——, 'Law's Power, the Sexed Body and Feminist Discourse' (1990) 17 *Journal of Law and
Society* 194

——, 'The Legal and Moral Ordering of Child Custody' (1991) 18 *Journal of Law and
Society* 485

SMART, C, and SMART, B, (eds), *Women, Sexuality and Social Control* (Routledge, London,
1978)

SMIGEL, E 'Public Attitudes Towards Stealing as Related to the Size of the Victim Organization' (1955) 21 *American Sociological Review* 320

SMITH, DE, *Texts, Facts and Femininity: Exploring the Relations of the Ruling* (Routledge,
London, 1990)

SMITH, DJ, *Police and People in London* (Policy Studies Institute, London, 1983) Vol 1

SMITH, LJF, *Concerns about Rape* (HMSO, London, 1989)

——, *Domestic Violence: An Overview of the Literature* (HMSO, London, 1989)

SOFSKY, W, *The Order of Terror* (Princeton University Press, Princeton NJ, 1997)

SOUTH, N, 'Drugs: Use, Crime and Control' in M Maguire, R Morgan and R Reiner (eds),
The Oxford Handbook of Criminology, 2nd edn (Clarendon Press, Oxford, 1997)

SPALEK, B, 'Regulation, White Collar Crime, and the Bank of Credit and Commerce International' (2001) 40 *Howard Journal of Criminal Justice* 166

SPARKS, R, 'Reason and Unreason in Left Realism: Some Problems in the Constitution of the
Fear of Crime' in R Matthews and J Young (eds), *Issues in Realist Criminology* (Sage,
London, 1992)

——, *Television and the Drama of Crime: Moral Tales and the Place of Crime in Public Life*
(Open University Press, Buckingham, 1992)

STANKO, E, *Intimate Intrusions* (Routledge & Kegan Paul, London, 1985)

——, 'The Day to Count: Reflections on a Methodology to Raise Awareness about the Impact of Domestic Violence in the UK' (2001) 1 *Criminal Justice* 215

STANKO, E, and HOBDELL, K, 'Assault on Men: Masculinity and Male Victimisation' (1993) 33 *British Journal of Criminology* 400

STANLEY, L, and WISE, S, *Breaking Out: Feminist Consciousness and Feminist Research* (Routledge & Kegan Paul, London, 1983)

STONE, M, *Proof of Fact in Criminal Trials* (W Green and Son Ltd, Edinburgh, 1984)

STRANG, H, 'Justice for Victims of Young Offenders' in A Morris and G Maxwell (eds), *Restorative Justice for Juveniles: Conferencing, Mediation and Circles* (Hart Publishing, Oxford, 2001)

——, 'The Crime Victim Movement as a Force in Civil Society' in H Strang and J Braithwaite (eds), *Restorative Justice and Civil Society* (Cambridge University Press, Cambridge, 2001).

STRANG, H, BARNES, G, BRAITHWAITE, J, and SHERMAN, L, *A Progress Report on the Canberra Reintegrative Shaming Experiments (RISE)* (July 1999)

——, ——, —— and ——, *Experiments in Restorative Policing: A Progress Report on the Canberra Reintegrative Shaming Experiments (RISE)* (Australian Federal Police and Australian National University, Canberra, 1999) also available at <http://www.aic.gov.au/rjustice/rise/progress>

STRAUS, MA, 'Measuring Intrafamily Conflict and Violence: The Conflict Tactics (CT) Scale' (1979) 41 *Journal of Marriage and Family* 75

STRAUS, MA, and GELLES, RJ, *Physical Violence in American Families* (Transaction Publishers, London, 1990)

STRAUS, MA, GELLES, RJ, STEINMETZ, SK, *Behind Closed Doors: Violence in the American Family* (Anchor Books, Garden City NY 1981)

STRAUSS, A, *Mirrors and Masks* (Free Press, Glencoe Ill, 1959)

STRAW, J, 'Partners against crime' (1999) 71 (summer) *Victim Support Magazine* 8

SUTHERLAND, E, and CRESSEY, D, *Principles of Criminology*, 5th edn (JB Lippincott Co, Chicago Ill, 1955)

SYKES, C, *A Nation of Victims: The Decay of the American Character* (St Martin's Press, New York NY, 1992)

SYKES, G, and MATZA, D, 'Techniques of Neutralization: A Theory of Delinquency' (1957) 22 *American Sociological Review* 664

TAYLOR, I, *The New Criminology* (Routledge & Kegan Paul, London, 1973)

TAYLOR, I, Walton, P, and Young, J, (eds), *Critical Criminology* (Routledge & Kegan Paul, London, 1975)

TEMKIN, J, 'Sexual History Evidence—The Ravishment of s2' [1993] *Criminal Law Review* 3

——, 'Prosecuting and Defending Rape: Perspectives from the Bar' (2000) 27 *Journal of Law and Society* 219

THOMPSON, E, *Whigs and Hunters* (Penguin, London, 1975)

THOMPSON, W, and MULHOLLAND, B, 'Paramilitary Punishments and Young People in West Belfast: Psychological Effects and the Implications for Education' in L Kennedy (ed), *Crime and Punishment in West Belfast* (The Summer School, West Belfast, 1995)

TONTODONATO, P, and EREZ, E, 'Crime, Punishment and Victim Distress' (1994) 3 *International Review of Victimology* 33

TYLER, T, *Why People Obey the Law* (Yale University Press, New Haven Conn, 1990)

UMBREIT, M, and BRADSHAW, W, 'Victim Experience of Mediating Adult vs. Juvenile Offenders: A Cross-National Comparison' (1997) 61(4) *Federal Probation* 33

UMBREIT, M, COATES, R, and VOS, B, 'Victim Impact of Meeting with Young Offenders: Two Decades of Offender Mediation Practice and Research' in A Morris and G Maxwell (eds), *Restorative Justice for Juveniles* (Hart Publishing, Oxford, 2001)

UNITED NATIONS, *Declaration of Basic Principles of Justice for Victims of Crime and Abuse of Power* (United Nations, Geneva, 1985) available from <http://www.unhchr.ch/>

——, *Draft Declaration on Basic Principles on the Use of Restorative Justice Programmes in Criminal Matters* (United Nations, New York NY, 1999)

US DEPARTMENT OF JUSTICE OFFICE OF JUSTICE PROGRAMS, *Survey of State Prison Inmate—1991: Women in Prison*, Bureau of Justice Statistics Special Report NCJ–145321 (GPO, Washington, DC, March 1994), cited in PW Cook, *Abused Men: The Hidden Side of Domestic Violence* (Praegar, London, 1997)

VAN DIJK, J, and TERLOUW, G, 'An International Perspective of the Business Community as Victims of Fraud and Crime' (1996) 7 *Security Journal* 157

VARESE, F, *The Emergence of the Russian Mafia: Dispute Settlement and Protection in a New Market Economy* (Unpublished DPhil Thesis, Faculty of Social Studies, University of Oxford, 1996)

VIANO, E (ed), *Victims and Society* (Visage Press, Washington DC, 1976)

VON HENTIG, H, *The Criminal and his Victim* (Yale University Press, New Haven Conn, 1948)

VON HIRSCH, A, GARLAND, D, and WAKEFIELD, A, (eds), *Ethical and Social Perspectives on Situational Crime Prevention* (Hart Publishing, Oxford, 2000)

WACHS, E, *Crime-Victim Stories: New York City's Urban Folklore* (Indiana University Press, Bloomington Ind, 1988)

WACHTEL, T, and McCOLD, P, 'Restorative Justice in Everyday Life' in H Strang and J Braithwaite (eds), *Restorative Justice and Civil Society* (Cambridge University Press, Cambridge, 2001)

WADDINGTON, PAJ, 'Police (Canteen) Sub-culture' (1999) 39 *British Journal of Criminology* 287

WAKEFIELD, A, 'Situational Crime Prevention in Mass Private Property' in A von Hirsch, D Garland and A Wakefield (eds), *Ethical and Social Perspectives on Situational Crime Prevention* (Hart Publishing, Oxford, 2000)

WALGRAVE, L, 'Extending the Victim Perspective Towards A Systemic Restorative Justice Alternative' in A Crawford and J Goodey (eds), *Integrating a Victim Perspective within Criminal Justice* (Ashgate, Aldershot, 2000)

WALKER, J, and McNicol, L, *Policing Domestic Violence: Protection, Prevention or Prudence?* (Relate Centre for Family Studies, Newcastle, 1994)

WALKER, LE, *The Battered Woman Syndrome* (Springer, New York NY, 1984)

WALLER, I, and OKIHIRO, N, *Burglary: The Victim and the Public* (University of Toronto Press, Toronto, 1974)

WARSHAW, R, *I Never Called it Rape: The Ms Report on Recognising, Fighting and Surviving Date and Acquaintance Rape* (Harper and Row, New York NY, 1988)

WASIK, M, 'Reparation: Sentencing and the Victim' [1999] *Criminal Law Review* 470.

WASSERMAN, M, 'Rape: Breaking the Silence', *The Progressive*, November 1973

WEED, F, *Certainty of Justice: Reform in the Crime Victim Movement* (Aldine de Gruyter, New York NY, 1995)

WEIS, K, and BORGES, SS, 'Victimology and Rape: The Case of the Legitimate Victim' (1973) 8 *Issues in Criminology* 71

WEITEKAMP, E, 'Research on Victim–Offender Mediation: Findings and Needs for the Future' in European Forum for Victim–Offender Mediation and Restorative Justice (ed), *Victim–Offender Mediation in Europe* (Leuven University Press, Leuven, 2000)

WEMMERS, J, 'Victims in the Dutch Criminal Justice System: The Effects of Treatment on Victims' Attitudes and Compliance' (1995) 3 *International Review of Victimology* 323

WESTERVELT, S, *Shifting the Blame: How Victimization Became a Criminal Defense* (Rutgers University Press, New Brunswick NJ, 1998)

WHITE, R, 'Hassle-Free Policing and the Creation of Community Space' (1998) 9 *Current Issues in Criminal Justice* 312

——, 'Social Justice, Community Building and Restorative Strategies' (2000) 3 *Contemporary Justice Review* 53

WHYTE, WF, *Street Corner Society* (Chicago University Press, Chicago Ill 1955)

WIERSMA, E, 'Commercial Burglars in the Netherlands: Reasoning Decision-makers?' (1996) 1 *International Journal of Risk, Security and Crime Prevention* 217

WILCOX, A, with HOYLE, C, *Final Report to the Youth Justice Board on the National Evaluation of Restorative Justice Projects* (Unpublished Draft Report, April 2002)

WILKINS, L, *Delinquent Generations* (HMSO, London, 1960)

——, *Social Deviance* (Tavistock, London, 1964)

WILLCOCK, R, *Retail Theft Initiative: Does it Really Work?* (K2 Management Development Ltd, 1999).

WILLIAMS, B, 'The Victim's Charter: Citizens as Consumers of Criminal Justice Services' (1999) 38 *Howard Journal of Criminal Justice* 384

WOLFGANG, M, *Patterns in Criminal Homicide* (University of Pennsylvania Press, Philadelphia Penn, 1959)

WORRALL, A, *Offending Women* (Routledge, London, 1990)

WRIGHT, RT, and DECKER, SH, *Burglars on the Job: Streetlife and Residential Break-ins* (Northeastern University Press, Boston Mass, 1994)

——, and ——, *Armed Robbers in Action* (Northeastern University Press, Boston, 1997)

WUNDERSITZ, J, and HETZEL, S, 'Family Conferencing for Young Offenders: The South Australian Experience' in J Hudson, A Morris, G Maxwell and B Galaway (eds), *Family Group Conferences* (The Federation Press, Annadale NSW, 1996)

WYRICK, A, and COSTANZO, M, 'Predictors of Client Participation in Victim–Offender Mediation' (1999) 16 *Mediation Quarterly* 243

YLLÖ, K, 'Political and Methodological Debates in Wife Abuse Research' in K Yllö and M Bograd (eds), *Feminist Perspectives on Wife Abuse* (Sage, London, 1990)

YOUNG, J, *The Exclusive Society* (Sage, London, 1999)

YOUNG, R, *Research Report on the Wolverhampton Reparation Scheme* (Institute of Judicial Administration, University of Birmingham, Birmingham, 1987)

——, 'Reparation as Mitigation' [1989] *Criminal Law Review* 463

——, 'Integrating a Multi-Victim Perspective in Criminal Justice Through Restorative Justice Conferences' in A Crawford and J Goodey (eds), *Integrating a Victim Perspective within Criminal Justice* (Ashgate, Aldershot, 2000)

——, 'Just Cops Doing "Shameful" Business?: Police-Led Restorative Justice and the Lessons of Research' in A Morris and G Maxwell, *Restorative Justice for Juveniles: Conferencing, Mediation and Circles* (Hart Publishing, Oxford, 2001)

YOUNG, R, and GOOLD, B, 'Restorative Police Cautioning in Aylesbury—From Degrading to Reintegrative Shaming Ceremonies?' [1999] *Criminal Law Review* 126

YOUNG, R, and HOYLE, C, *Restorative Cautioning: Strengthening Communities in the Thames Valley* (confidential interim study) (Centre for Criminological Research, University of Oxford, Oxford, 1999)

——, and ——, 'New, Improved, Police-Led Restorative Justice? Action-Research and the Thames Valley Police Initiative' in A von Hirsch, A Bottoms, J Roberts, K Roach and M Schiff (eds), *Restorative Justice and Criminal Justice: Competing or Reconcilable Paradigms?* (Hart Publishing, Oxford, 2002)

ZEDNER, L, 'Victims' in M Maguire, R Morgan and R Reiner (eds), *The Oxford Handbook of Criminology*, 3rd edn (Clarendon Press, Oxford, forthcoming 2002); 2nd edn (Clarendon Press, Oxford, 1997)

ZEHR, H, 'Reparation: Where from Here?' in *Repairing the Damage: Proceedings of the First National Symposium on Mediation and Criminal Justice* (FIRM, Beaconsfield, 1989)

——, *Changing Lenses: A New Focus for Crime and Justice* (Herald Press, Scottsdale Penn, 1990)